WAR OVER THE STEPPES

OSPREY
PUBLISHING

WAR OVER THE
STEPPES

The air campaigns on the Eastern Front 1941–45

E. R. HOOTON

First published in Great Britain in 2016 by Osprey Publishing,
PO Box 883, Oxford, OX1 9PL, UK,
1385 Broadway, 5th Floor, New York, NY 10018, USA.
E-mail: info@ospreypublishing.com

Osprey Publishing, part of Bloomsbury Publishing Plc

A CIP catalogue record for this book is available from the British Library

E.R. Hooton has asserted his right under the Copyright, Designs and Patents Act, 1988, to be
identified as the Author of this Work.

ISBN: 978 1 4728 1562 0
PDF ISBN: 978 1 4728 1563 7
ePub ISBN: 978 1 4728 1564 4

Index by Rob Munro
Typeset in Bembo
Originated by PDQ Media, Bungay, UK
Printed in China through World Print Ltd.

16 17 18 19 20   10 9 8 7 6 5 4 3 2 1

Top cover image: 6 GIAP-ChF Yak-9Ds fly in close formation for the camera in the summer of 1944.
(*via G F Petrov*)
Bottom cover image/title page image: A Junkers Ju 87D Stuka from II./StG 1 sets off on another
mission. (*via John Weal*)

Osprey Publishing supports the Woodland Trust, the UK's leading woodland conservation
charity. Between 2014 and 2018 our donations will be spent on their Centenary Woods project in
the UK.

www.ospreypublishing.com

CONTENTS

FOREWORD

The Eastern Front was the decisive theatre of the European element of World War II. In a conflict known to the Russians as the Great Patriotic War (*Velikoi Otechestvennoi Voine*), the Soviet Union steadily eroded the foundation of Nazi Germany's power, its ground forces, and eased the way for its Western allies in Western and Southern Europe.

In the post-Stalinist era the inside study of this struggle gradually became apparent through the efforts of Russian historians whose efforts reached a wider Western audience through the work of historians such as John Erickson, Albert Seaton and David M. Glantz. The work was expanded by both Russian and Western historians in the post-Cold War world to provide a detailed picture of the ground war in this titanic struggle.

The history of the air war, however, remains clouded. In part this is because few Western historians appear to have researched the subject, possibly on the grounds that it was merely an extension of the ground war. There is also the problem that the various archives are scattered across the former Soviet Union. For a long time, therefore, the subject has seen accounts of German and of Russian operations considered largely in isolation.

To use a cooking analogy, it is like preparing a feast with fresh ingredients and pre-cooked food. Historians of the German side not only possess a wealth of published material in the shape of formation accounts and aircraft histories, but they also have access to the material in the Bundesarchiv, some of which is duplicated in the US and UK National Archives, including post-war studies conducted by the USAF and RAF. However, they unconsciously tend to reflect Josef Goebbels' propaganda about heroes of civilisation fighting the barbaric hordes with little knowledge of the 'other side of the hill'. Also some published accounts do not always accurately reflect sources, notably Hermann Plocher's account of *Zitadelle*, which should be compared with Stephen H. Newton's volume, *Kursk – The German View*.

In Russian there is a huge quantity of published material in memoirs, service studies on matters such as air defence and long range bombing, as well as formation and unit histories. The drawback with these sources is that it is often difficult to analyse operations because the writers reflect the Soviet tendency to 'shock and awe' readers with impressive-looking statistics. There is also a distinct reluctance to consider enemy documentation, which leads to frequent, grandiose claims for enemy strength and for damage inflicted.

Yet a mass of material is now available online, including Russian websites with detailed information on Soviet air formations, numerous books and even German casualties in the East from 1941 to 1943 taken from 6 *Abteilung* records. The new generation of Russian historians, such as Dmitri Khazanov and Vitali Gorbach, are willing to combine Soviet and German archive material to produce excellent works on air operations in 1941, over Stalingrad and over Kursk, some of which have been translated into English. Yet few Western aviation historians have studied the Eastern Front air war in depth, with the notable exception of Swedish aviation historian Christer Bergström.

It is by combining a wide range of material published in the West with Western archive and Russian online material that I have tried to produce the first detailed account in English of German and Russian air force operations. I have focused upon what I describe as 'the main front', which lay between the Baltic and the Black Sea and then the Danube valley, for operations in northern Finland and northern Norway were very much a sideshow. I have attempted a comprehensive picture, but space constraints mean I have had to paint in very broad strokes and largely ignore acts of bravery.

At first sight what emerges does not contradict the long-established view that the air forces were largely committed to the direct and indirect support of the armies, with little interest in strategic bombing. Yet it is also clear that the subject had greater depth than previously realised – for example, the Luftwaffe's gradual rejection of Operational Level missions, which had helped spearhead the rise of Nazi Germany, in favour of Tactical Level missions; or, to put it another way, it went back to the future in a form of air warfare that by 1942 had been discredited.

By contrast, the Russians, while predominantly a Tactical Level force, retained and strengthened their Operational Level capability, with considerable Western aid, although Soviet air operations also grew more sophisticated as the war progressed. I hope this account will, for the first time in English, also explain the factors that inhibited Soviet air power even when its numerical superiority became overwhelming – notably limitations in production and training. What I did find surprising were the parallels between the problems and solutions of the Long Range Aviation (*Aviatsiya Dahl'nevo Deystiviya*, ADD) and RAF Bomber Command, and also the response of the Home Air Defence (*Protivovozdushnaya Oborona*, PVO) to the perceived threat from the V1.

I also hope I have described the growth of light night bombing that increased in importance on both sides. For the Russians it was initially a cheap form of offensive power that was then harnessed to expand the (Army) Air Force (*Voyenno-Vozdushnye Sily*, VVS), while for the Germans it became an arm that grew ever more important.

I have tried to introduce readers to the leading architects and exponents of each side's air power, but they will have to follow up other sources if more detailed personal information is required. I also make no excuse for the profusion of statistics designed less to 'shock and awe' the reader and more to indicate the scale of activity. I have also tried to introduce the reader to the personal lives of the airmen and airwomen on both sides, which I hope readers will find interesting.

In writing of operations I have had to examine numerous sources, many of which are contradictory. Any errors are mine and mine alone, but I hope that other writers will not follow my mistakes when producing further works on this subject.

FOREWORD

While the author's name is on the title, no book is their work alone. I would first of all like to thank Osprey's Publisher, Marcus Cowper, and its Managing Director, Richard Sullivan, but especially the ultra-efficient Samantha Downes for her liaison work. I have also received a tremendous amount of assistance from a number of people who provided valuable help in key areas. They are Ulf Balke, Nik Cornish, Nigel Eastaway, Dr Jennifer Hooton, Jörg Huthmann, Robert Forsyth, Eddie Nielinger, Martin Streetly and Paul Thompson. I would also like to pay tribute to two 'Old Eagles' who are no longer with us but were of the greatest help to me, Alex Vanags-Baginskis and Hans-Eberhard Kruger.

E. R. Hooton
March 2016

GLOSSARY

A-Tag	D-Day (*Angriffstag*)
AD/AK/AP	Aviation Division/Corps/Regiment (*Aviatsionnaya Diviziya/Aviatsionnyy Korpus/Polk*)
ADD	Long Range Aviation (*Aviatsiya Dahl'nevo Deystiviya*)
AON	Armies for Special Employment (*Armiya Osobogo Naznachiya*)
AP	Aviation Regiment (*Aviatsionnyy Polk*)
AufKlGr	Reconnaissance Group (*Aufklärungsgruppe*)
BAA	Bomber Army (*Bombardirovochnaya Aviatsionnaya Armiya*)
BAP/BAD/BAK	Bomber Regiment/Division/Corps (*Bombardirovochnaya Aviatsionnaya Polk/Diviziya/Korpus*)
DB	Long Range Bomber (*Dalniy Bombardirovschik*). Also known as DB-3 and later renamed Il-4.
DBA	Long Range Bomber Aviation (*Dahl'niy Bombardirovochnaya Aviatsiya*)
DBAP	Long Range Bomber Regiment (*Dahl'niy Bombardirovochnyy Aviatsionnyy Polk*)
DD	Long Range (*Dahl'nevo Deystiviya*)
FAGr	Long Range Reconnaissance Group (*Fernaufklärungsgruppe*)
FARR	Royal Romanian Air Force (*Forţele Aeriene Regale ale Romaniei*)
FEBA	Forward Edge of the Battle Area
Flak	Anti-aircraft Gun (*Fliegerabwehrkanone*)
Flivo	Air Force Liaison Officer (*Fliegerverbindungsoffizier*)
GAL	Romanian Combat Air Group (*Gruparea Aeriană de Luptă*)

GLOSSARY

GCI	Ground-Controlled Interception
GKO	State Defence Committee (*Gosudarstvennyi Komitet Oborony*)
GRU	Red Army Intelligence (*Glavnoe Razvedyvatelynie Upravlenie*)
Gv	Prefix for Guards (*Gvardeyskii*)
GVF	Civil Air Fleet (*Grazhdanskiy Vozdushnyy Flot*)
IAA	Fighter Army (*Istrebitelyenaya Aviatsionnaya Armii*)
IAP/IAD/IAK	Fighter Regiment/Division/Corps (*Istrebitelyenaya Aviatsionnaya Polk/Diviziya/Istrebitel'nyy Aviatsionnyy Korpus*)
IFF	Identification Friend or Foe
Jabo	Fighter-bomber (*Jagdbomber*)
Jafü	Fighter Commander (*Jagdfliegerführer*)
JG	Fighter Wing (*Jagdgeschwader*)
KG	Bomber Wing (*Kampfgeschwader*)
KG zbV	Transport Wing (*Kampfgeschwader zur besonderen Verwendung*)
Koluft	Army–Air Force Coordination Officer (*Kommandeur der Luftwaffe*)
LTF	Air Transport Commander (*Lufttransportführer*)
MTAP	Mine-Torpedo Regiment (*Minno-Torpednyy Aviatsionnyy Polk*)
NAGr	Short Range Reconnaissance Group (*Nahaufklärungsgruppe*)
NBAD/NBAP	Night Bomber Aviation Division/Regiment (*Nochnoy Bombardirovochnyy Aviatsionnaya Diviziya/Nochnoy Bombardirovochnyy Aviatsionnyy Polk*)
NII-VVS	Air Force Scientific Test Institute (*Naucho-issledovatelskii Institut-VVS*)
NJG	Nightfighter Wing (*Nachtjagdgeschwader*)
NKAP	People's Commissariat for the Aircraft Industry (*Narodnoi Komissariat Aviatsionny Promyshlennosti*)
NKVD	People's Commissariat for Internal Affairs (*Narodny Komissariat Venutrennikh Del*)
NSFK	National Socialist *Flieger Korps*
NSGr	Night Attack Group (*Nachtschlachtgruppe*)

11

OAG	Special Air Group (*Osobaya Aviagruppa*)
OAP	Independent Air Regiment (*Otedel'naya Aviapolk*)
OAP GVF	Independent Civil Air Fleet Regiment (*Otedel'naya Aviatsionnyy Polk GV Flot*)
ObdL	Air Force Commander-in-Chief (*Oberbefehlshaber der Luftwaffe*)
OKH	Army Supreme Command (*Oberkommando des Heeres*)
OKL	Air Force Supreme Command (*Oberkommando der Luftwaffe*)
OKW	Armed Forces Supreme Command (*Oberkommando des Wehrmacht*)
Osoaviakhim	Society of Friends of Defence and the Aviation-Chemical Construction Industry of the USSR (*Obshchestvo druzhei oborony i aviatsionno-khimicheskogo stroitelstva SSSR*)
PoW	Prisoner-of-War
PVO	Home Air Defence (*Protivovozdushnaya Oborona*)
RAF	Royal Air Force
RAG	Reserve Air Group (*Rezervnaya Aviatsionnaya Gruppa*)
RLM	German Air Ministry (*Reichsluftfahrtministerium*)
RUS	Radio Aircraft Detector (*Radio Ulavlivatel Samoletov*)
SAD/SAK/SAP	Mixed Air Division/Corps/Regiment (*Smeshannaya Aviatsionnaya Diviziya/ Smeshannyy Aviatsionnyy Korpus/ Polk*)
SAGr	Naval Reconnaissance Group (see *Aufklärungsgruppe*, AufKlGr)
SB	High Speed Bomber (*Skorostnoy Bombardirovochnyy*)
SBAP	High Speed Bomber Aviation Regiment (*Skorostnoy Bombardirovochnyy Aviatsionnaya Polk*)
SchG/SG	Attack Wing pre-October 1943/post-October 1943 (*Schlachtgeschwader*)
ShAD/ShAK/ShAP	Assault Division/Corps/Regiment (*Shturmovaya Aviatsionnaya Diviziya/ Shturmovaya Aviatsionnyy Korpus/ Polk*)
Smersh	NKVD counter-intelligence organisation, literally 'Death

GLOSSARY

	to Spies' (*Smert Shpionam*)
SON	Gun-Laying Station or anti-aircraft gun fire control radar (*Stancyia Orudiynoi Navodki*)
SPB	Combined Dive-Bomber (*Sostavnoi Pikiruyuschii Bombardirovschik*)
Stavka	Supreme General Staff and High Command (*Shtab Verkhovnogo Glavnovokommandovaniya*)
StG	Dive-Bomber Wing (*Stukageschwader*)
Stuka	Dive-Bomber (*Sturzkampfflugzeug*)
TAD/TAP	Transport Aviation Division/Regiment (*Trahnsportnyy Aviatsionnaya Diviziya/Polk*)
TB	Heavy Bomber (*Tyazholy Bombardirovschi*)
TBAP	Heavy Bomber Regiment (*Tyazhyoly Bombardirovchnyy Aviatsionnyy Polk*)
TFF	Transport Air Commander (*Transportfliegerführer*)
TrAD	Transport Division (*Trahnsportnyy Aviatsionnaya Diviziya*)
TsAGI	Aviation Industry Research Institute (*Tsentralnyy Aero-gidrodinamicheskiy Institut*)
UAG	Shock Air Group (*Udarnaya Aviatsionnaya Gruppa*)
USAAF	United States Army Air Force
VA	Air Army (*Vozdushnaya Armiya*)
VMF	Navy (*Voyenno-Morskoy Flot*)
VVS	(Army) Air Force (*Voyenno-Vozdushnye Sili*)
VVS-FA	Frontal Aviation Air Force (*Voyenno-Vozdushnye Sili-Frontovaya Aviatsiaya*)
VVS-KBF/VVS-ChF	Baltic, Black Sea Air Forces (*Voyenno-Vozdushnye Sily Baltiyskogo Flota/Chernomorskogo Flota*)
VVS-RKKA	Red Army of Workers and Peasants Air Force (*Voyenno-Vozdushnye Sili-Raboche-krest'yanski Krasnoi Armiyy*)
VVS-VMF	Naval Fleet Air Force (*Voyenno-Vozdushnye Sili-Voyenno-Morskoy Flot*)
ZG	Twin-engined Fighter Wing (*Zerstörergeschwader*)

COMPARATIVE RANKS

Russian	German	Translation
Leytenant	Leutnant	Lieutenant
Starshiy Leytenant	Oberleutnant	Senior Lieutenant
Kapitan	Hauptmann	Captain
Maior	Major	Major
Podpolkovnik	Oberstleutnant	Lieutenant Colonel
Polkovnik	Oberst	Colonel
General-maior	Generalmajor	Major General
General-leitenant	Generalleutnant	Lieutenant General
General	General	General
General-polkovnik	Generaloberst	Colonel General
Marshal	Generalfeldmarschall	Field Marshall

CHAPTER 1

FROM FRIENDS TO FOES
Russian and German Air Power 1924 to 1941

On 31 December 1940, hundreds of Russian airmen met at the Pilots' House on Gorki Street in Moscow with their wives and girlfriends to 'eat, drink and be merry' as they welcomed in the New Year.[1] In crowded rooms people chattered and toasted each other while couples waltzed and tangoed on the dance floor in celebration of the end of their three-year ordeal.

On 1 December 1934, the popular Leningrad Party boss Sergei Kirov was assassinated outside his own office. This triggered Soviet leader Josef Stalin's nascent paranoia and offered him an excuse to purge his rivals, or as Greta Garbo's Ninotchka observed, 'There are going to be fewer, but better, Russians.' The purge initially focused upon the Communist Party, but from May 1937 it swept through the armed forces with the arrest of the Red Army's leading commanders, including Marshal Mikhail Tukhachevskii. His radical ideas were based upon mechanised forces capable of driving deep into enemy territory, with air support clearing the way. But his failure to make it work, because Red Army command and control lacked radios, was used to push him into the execution chamber.

During the next two years the armed forces suffered a holocaust at the hands of the People's Commissariat for Internal Affairs (*Narodny Komissariat Venutrennikh Del*, NKVD), with thousands of officers arrested,

15

hundreds executed and many more cashiered on suspicion of disloyalty merely for seeking to modernise the forces. The impact upon Soviet air power was devastating, with the Red Army of Workers and Peasants Air Force (*Voyenno-Vozdushnye Sili-Raboche-krest'yanski Krasnoi Armiyy*, VVS-RKKA), usually referred to as the (Army) Air Force (*Voyenno-Vozdushnye Sili*, VVS), losing more than a third of its officers in 1937. A total of 4,773 personnel were dismissed, of whom 1,590 were arrested, including the commander-in-chief, two chiefs-of-staff, most district air commanders and the head of air training.

Those associated with air power also suffered, with aircraft designers Andrei Tupolev, Vladimir Myasishchev and Vladimir Petlyakov arrested, together with the entire staff of the Aviation Industry Research Institute (*Tsentralnyy Aero-gidrodinamicheskiy Institut*, TsAGI). An aircraft-design Gulag was established where Tupolev began work on his Tu-2 medium bomber, although it was not until 1940 that he was sentenced to 15 years in jail for being 'a French spy'. He would be released in July 1941 to 'conduct important defence work', but he was not formally 'rehabilitated' until 1955.

The new generation of military leaders lacked their predecessors' experience, while the climate of fear undermined their self-confidence. At any moment a disgruntled junior or a tortured acquaintance might denounce them and, to avoid displeasing their superiors, they rarely displayed any initiative. The result was the appalling failure of Soviet air power during the Winter War with Finland, whose 120 aircraft faced down nearly 3,900 Soviet aircraft almost to the end. The VVS commander, General-leitenant Yakov Smushkevich, who had led airmen with distinction in Spain and China, was 'kicked upstairs' as Deputy Defence Minister in March 1940, and five months later became General Inspector of the VVS. He was replaced by fighter ace General-leitenant Pavel Rychagov, who was credited with 20 victories in Spain while serving under Smushkevich. Rychagov had also distinguished himself in the summer of 1939 during future Marshal Georgii Zhukov's Khalkin-Gol campaign against the Japanese on the Mongolian border.

Prowling through the Pilots' House that December night in 1940 was a man who had suffered indirectly during the Purges, but would soon lead Stalin's long range bombers. Aleksandr Golovanov was Aeroflot's Chief Pilot and an instrument flying expert. He was also a former member of the secret police who turned to civilian aviation and honed his skills during a training course in France. When he returned to the Soviet Far East in 1937 he learned that his brother-in-law had been shot as 'an enemy of the people' and his local Communist Party had deemed him guilty by association, removing his Party membership card and banning him from flying.

Golovanov and his wife became pariahs, ignored by everyone and forced to sell almost everything to survive. Ironically, his NKVD friends saved him by arranging his transfer to Moscow, where he renewed his career and regained his Party membership card. Although a civilian, Golovanov is reported to have flown some of the NKVD's victims from the Far East to Moscow. During the Winter War he flew leaflet missions at night using the skills common among Civil Air Fleet (*Grazhdanskiy Vozdushnyy Flot*, GVF) pilots.

He was astonished to discover Russian bomber crews, including those in the long range force, were unable to emulate these feats, and he tried to persuade the VVS leadership to improve navigation and instrument flying training.[2] Leningrad Party boss Andrei Zhdanov showed some interest in the subject during the Winter War but Rychagov was dismissive, although he did create a navigation academy in March 1940. However, its instructors had little experience in instrument flying, so Golovanov now sought a meeting in more pleasant surroundings to put his case.

In the Pilots' House he encountered Smushkevich, who was with the Aviation Industry Minister (Commissar) Andrei Shakhurin. Smushkevich was interested, but felt he was under a cloud after the Winter War. He also lacked the technical expertise to make a presentation, so he suggested Golovanov write directly to Stalin, and offered to have a courier convey his letter to the Kremlin. Golovanov followed his advice, and after meeting Stalin he was transferred to the Long Range Bomber Aviation (*Dahl'niy Bombardirovochnaya Aviatsiya*, DBA) to form an operational training unit, 212th Independent Long Range Air Regiment (OAP, DD) in February 1941, with GVF pilots and two PS-84 'flying classrooms', while in March work began on a VVS electronic navigation aids system.

Rychagov was still not impressed, unlike DBA head General-leitenant Ivan Proskurov, who had been deputy commander of the Far Eastern VVS before his appointment in October 1940. Also formerly Head of the Red Army Intelligence (*Glavnoe Razvedyvatelynie Upravlenie*, GRU), Proskurov was an experienced bomber pilot who had also seen combat in Spain – indeed, he was responsible for the bombing of the German pocket-battleship *Deutschland* in 1937. Smushkevich was also pleased with the expansion of the DBA for he was all too aware that Russian air power was a giant with feet not of clay but of sand.

The VVS had blossomed in the 1930s, having especially benefited from the industrial cornucopia of the First and Second Five Year Plans (1928–32 and 1933–37). The new factories produced more than 20,000 aircraft and VVS strength rocketed – in 1924 it had 341 combat aircraft, which rose to 1,285 (including 48 TB-3 heavy bombers that could carry two tonnes of bombs 1,100 kilometres) by 1 January 1929. In 1933, at the beginning of the Second Five Year Plan, front-line strength was 3,156 (including 647 heavy bombers), and by 1937 it was 8,139, including 443 medium and heavy bombers. When Germany invaded Poland on 1 September 1939, the VVS had 7,321 aircraft, including 569 TB-3 four-engined heavy bombers organised into three Armies for Special Employment (*Armiya Osobogo Naznachiya*, AON), and by June 1941 the total had doubled to 15,599 combat aircraft and 3,934 trainers; but, as George Canning observed, 'Statistics can tell you everything you wish to know, except the truth.'

Until 1939, the quantitative expansion was matched by a qualitative one, as shown by Tupolev's bomber designs. In 1930 there was the maiden flight of a four-engined bomber based upon Junkers corrugated duralumin (aluminium) technology that became the TB-3, which served until 1945. Yet within four years Tupolev had produced a smoothed duralumin, stressed-skin design as the SB, with two M-100 engines –

deliveries began in 1936.[3] Industry was able to meet contemporary fighter requirements for both traditional, slow but 'agile' I-15/I-15bis biplane fighters with fixed undercarriages and 'fast' I-16 Donkey (Ishak) monoplane fighters with retractable undercarriages. Yet they suffered from industrial weakness for, with limited aluminium production, these Polikarpov fighters and the I-153 Seagull (Chaika) interceptor biplane with retractable undercarriage were largely of wooden construction, augmented by duralumin, steel and doped fabric. Like all the biplanes, the Chaika lacked the performance either to sustain attacks on enemy bomber formations or to inflict serious damage with their four rifle-calibre machine guns. Later Ishaks had heavy (12.7mm) machine guns or even 20mm cannon, which were more destructive, and all of these fighters, together with the SBs, proved effective over Spain and China. Nevertheless, experience showed the need for advanced replacements.

Their development and production proved prolonged as the Soviet aircraft industry expanded steadily from 1939 to 1941. In Shakhurin the Soviet Union had a dynamic and able administrator who was a graduate of the Moscow Engineering-Economics Institute and who had briefly served in the Red Army. From 1934 he had worked with, or in, the aviation industry, and would be a safe pair of hands throughout the war. Shakhurin headed the People's Commissariat for the Aircraft Industry (*Narodnoi Komissariat Aviatsionny Promyshlennosti*, NKAP or *Narkomaviaprom*), which was established in January 1939. In the next two years he supervised a steady expansion of the industry with the NKVD using Gulag labour to build new plants in Kuibyshev, in Siberia. He also took a leaf from the British in taking over civilian factories and facilities that could be used for aircraft production. Via these means he had significantly expanded production capacity by the time of the German invasion of Poland in September 1939, and had some 174,360 workers who switched to 24-hour production in March 1941.

Yet his ministry did not have supreme authority in the highly politicised field of aircraft development and manufacture. An exception was the Air Force Scientific Test Institute (*Naucho-issledovatelskii Institut*, NII-VVS), which conducted state acceptance trials and also monitored aircraft for technical problems for which it provided solutions. But the designers, notably Aleksandr Yakovlev, exploited contacts with senior Party officials, the Party regional organisations and ultimately Stalin himself. Stalin changed his mind four times about authorising production of the four-engined TB-7 bomber! This might also have been influenced by his ne'er-do-well son Vasilii, who was in the VVS and would play an undistinguished role in air operations.

Yet despite Shakhurin's efforts there were significant weaknesses, for the expansion was fuelled by drafting much unskilled labour into the factories which in turn resulted in half the components they made having to be rejected. This shortage of skilled workers made it difficult for the craft-based and under-capitalised industry to introduce sophisticated, all-metal, stressed-skin aircraft, which required more working hours to build than traditional designs. The weakness was illustrated when Moscow decided to build the famed DC-3 airliner at Factory 84, leading to production of the PS-84 transport (Li-2 from 9 September 1942). This was not a copy of the Douglas aircraft but a Russian version whose empty weight was more than one tonne less than the original, but whose two Russian engines developed only 2,000hp, compared with the 2,800hp of their American equivalents, thus making it up to 50km/h slower and reducing range from 2,575 kilometres to 2,330 kilometres.

Despite the problems, factories were expected to increase production, but the Purges had removed the best managers, leaving inexperienced men in fear of the NKVD. Their priority was to meet production targets with little regard for quality or adequate stocks of spares. Indeed, quality was regarded as a 'bourgeois' concept and therefore treasonous. Tupolev, for example, would always rush aircraft into production despite shortcomings, which he would later work to overcome. He failed, however, with the SB's forward defence, which remained a pair of machine guns that could move vertically but not laterally.

Production of modern aircraft was also handicapped by the Soviet economic system based upon extremely bureaucratic central planning on a 'top-down' model. The development and marketing of new technological products depends upon vision and the willingness to take risks – features rarely found among bureaucrats, with the result that the Soviet Union lagged behind Germany and its future Western allies in key elements of technology. Aluminium was the basis of modern aircraft production, yet the Soviet Union produced only 60,000 tonnes in 1939 compared with Germany's 194,000 tonnes, while the 100,000-tonne 1941 target compared badly with the 324,000 tonnes received by the Reich in 1941. The Russians tried to buy aluminium from Germany, but the first deliveries were due only in the summer of 1941. Throughout the war Moscow depended upon its allies to augment its own limited resources.

The Russian electronics industry also trailed behind its European competitors, and indeed continues to do so in the 21st century. Consequently, the VVS would be short of navigation aids throughout the war. Furthermore, while radio-telephone transmitter–receivers (transceivers) were in service with the Luftwaffe and the RAF in 1939, they did not become universal in Soviet-built combat aircraft until 1943. The need to have them in fighters was recognised by Russian pilots serving in Spain as early as 1937, but their reports were pigeonholed. This meant that until 1943, only formation leaders had transmitters while the remainder of the pilots had receivers, which hindered cooperation in air combat. Worse still, throughout the war the Russians had only high frequency (HF) radios, even in foreign aircraft, at a time when their allies and enemies had HF, VHF (very high frequency) and even UHF (ultra high frequency) sets. Reception on many of the radios installed in Russian aircraft was poor due to low quality and bad installation.[4] Russian radar was also hamstrung by the Purges when Pavel Oshchepkov, the man spearheading development, was arrested and not released until 1946. Even when its allies delivered some modern sensors, the Soviet Union lagged compared with the Germans.

The petrochemical industry also caused problems for the VVS. When exposed to sunlight the Perspex in aircraft canopies tended to degrade and become opaque – a problem which does not appear to have been overcome until later in the war. Because of this, even in the bitter Russian winter, pilots would fly with open canopies and often end up with blackened, frost-bitten cheeks. The oil refineries produced only 70–78 octane fuels (B-70, B-74 and B-78) that front-line units had to mix with additives to provide the fuel required for the high-performance engines installed in combat aircraft. B-70 was used for trainers and night bombers and B-89 was the equivalent of the Luftwaffe's 87-octane B4, used for bombers and transports. German fighters used C3 (94–100 octane) and Western fighters had 100–130 octane fuel. The Russians produced little of the essential ingredient – tetraethyl lead – in this high octane fuel, so all of their fighters, including Western ones, were restricted to B-95.[5] Additives created a crisis for General-polkovnik Sergei Rudenko's 16th Air Army (*Vozdushnaya Armiya*, VA) in the summer of 1944 on the verge of the great 'Bagration' offensive, for which it had the largest concentration of Soviet aircraft. Although he received thousands of tonnes of fuel, they lacked additives without which aircraft performance was degraded and engine running time reduced to 20–30 hours between overhauls. Yet Moscow's bureaucrats claimed they were unnecessary and refused to supply them. Rudenko passed concerns to his political officer or commissar, General Konstantin Telegin, and then they discovered that the octane labels were unreliable with different readings in nominally the same batch. Telegin raised the matter at the State Defence Committee (*Gosudarstvennyi Komitet Oborony*, GKO), which brought Stalin into the picture, and he ordered the distribution of additives that brought the fuel up to the correct octanes within two days.

In 1939 and 1940 the aircraft industry produced more than 10,000 aircraft per year, while a December 1940 plan called for 16,000 in 1941. During the first half of that year 3,900 aeroplanes rolled out of the plants, and this rose to 11,800 during the remaining six months of 1941. Total engine production that year was 28,700 units, although the Soviet aero-engine industry suffered the perennial problem of developing reliable, high-performance motors. Instead, they usually produced derivatives of imported designs, while the change to new engines meant that production output dropped from 22,686 in 1939 to 21,380 the following year, although it then recovered. However, the engines that powered the wartime generation of Russian-built VVS aircraft were often unreliable, leaked oil and were difficult to maintain.

The collective impact of these problems was severe. The Ilyushin DB-3 medium bomber with composite construction of a wooden fuselage and steel wings, and the improved DB-3F (Il-4 from March 1942), began to augment the TB-3 from 1939. However, the new heavy bomber, Petlyakov's four-engined TB-7 (Pe-8 from January 1942), proved more difficult to produce. Indeed, although its maiden flight took place in December 1936, only a handful were in service by 1941.

Spearheading the re-equipment programme from 1939 was a new generation of fighters – Yak-1, MiG-3 and LaGG-3, together with light bombers such as the twin-engined Yak-2/4 and single-engined Su-2, all of which began to trickle into the regiments from 1940. In their aircraft-design Gulag, Petlyakov and Myasishchev began work on a long range escort fighter, rather like the Bf 110, but in 1940 this was changed at the NKVD's behest to a long range dive-bomber as the Pe-2.

Many pilots distrusted the new aircraft, and with some reason. The MiG-3 was not only heavy but some had defective synchronisers that meant the nose-mounted machine guns shot off their propellers when fired, the hydraulics of the LaGG-3 were extremely unreliable, the Yak-1 engine proved troublesome and the canopy tended to stick when the aircraft dived.

One field where the VVS was ahead was in ground-attack, or 'assault' (*Shturmovaya*), aviation. Its assault trooper (*Shturmovik*) pilots provided the Red Army's spearheads with direct air support by strafing and bombing enemy concentrations. Most of these aircraft were armoured versions of the single-engined Polikarpov R-5 army cooperation biplane, the R-5Sh and R-Z, augmented by I-5 and I-15bis fighters. Experience in Spain had confirmed the need for the dedicated ground-attack aircraft, and Sergei Ilyushin began designing the Il-2, whose pilot and engine were in an armoured compartment with armoured glass windscreen. The aeroplane entered production in 1941, and it would be the backbone of VVS ground-attack units despite the fact it was never a very stable weapons platform.

Unfortunately for the VVS, the re-equipment programme was bungled, for rather than withdraw units to re-equip, the bureaucrats often despatched a quota of new aircraft to regiments. At the Baltic District's Kovno airfield, for example, two fighter regiments had 253 aircraft, including 128 MiG-3s, while a few bomber regiments on the airfield received the Su-2 and others small numbers of Pe-2s.

Many of the new generation of aircraft would receive affectionate nicknames often based upon their official designations. The Yakovlev fighters were called 'Yakovs' (Jacob/Jake/Jim) or 'Yakis' (Jakes), the Pe-2 was 'Peshka' (Pike) while the single-seat Il-2 would be called 'Gorbun' (Hunchback), although throughout the war the Il-2 was commonly called 'Ilyusha' and the units that flew them were known as 'Mudlarks' (Ilovs), based upon the word for mud (*il*). Not all the names were complimentary, and the lumbering, wooden LaGG-3 with its unreliable hydraulics was reportedly described as a Guaranteed Lacquered Coffin (*Lakirovannyi Garantirovannyi Grob*), although some have dismissed this claim, arguing that the Soviet authorities would have regarded it as 'defeatism'.[6] The new aircraft helped to fuel a further expansion of the VVS, and in February 1941 it was decided to create 106 regiments, including 15 (later 13) equipped with long range bombers. In 1939 regiments were organised into air brigades, but the Winter War showed the need to concentrate air power into larger formations. Each district was reorganised into a number of divisions, with two to five regiments of three to five squadrons, each with 12 aircraft, augmented by a few independent army cooperation squadrons with R-5s. Most divisions were mixed (*Smeshannaya*), with both fighter and strike (bomber or assault) regiments, and every army had at least one to support its operations. Dedicated fighter and bomber divisions tended to remain under district command, fragmenting VVS strength. Although each army headquarters was supposed to have a VVS commander, few did, and few of them would prove competent.

Their operations, together with those of reserve units, the DBA and PVO, were coordinated in peacetime by District VVS commanders who became Front VVS commanders in wartime. With the disbandment of the AON in the winter of 1939–40, the long range bombers were concentrated into the DBA and organised into bomber divisions (usually of three regiments) and then paired into corps from 5 November 1940. One or two corps were assigned to each Western military district, which, in the event of war, would become a Front (army group). To support the new divisions, work started on reorganising the rear services' infrastructure, although this was not scheduled for completion until August 1941.

For the Soviet Union, the prospects of war seemed to recede in August 1939 when the USSR and Nazi Germany signed a non-aggression pact that helped Hitler take Poland and allowed Stalin to regain territory lost to nationalists during the Russian Revolution. Stalin sought to buy time for a renaissance of his forces by bribing Germany with substantial quantities of food and raw materials, but he knew that sooner or later the Nazis and Communists would fight.

The pact allowed the Red Army to invade eastern Poland and the Baltic states and deploy up to 250 kilometres west of the original frontier, but this aggravated VVS problems. Each regiment was supposed to have its own airfield, but there were few in the occupied areas. The Russians hastily began an extensive construction programme, which was hampered by two severe winters and the NKVD, who were responsible for its execution. NKVD head Lavrenti Beria would criticise his subordinates on 22 May 1941, for trying to build large numbers of airfields rather than well-equipped air bases. This left most VVS squadrons on little more than cleared fields. Indeed, of 1,100 VVS airfields, only 200 – mostly DBA bases in the rear – had concrete runways, while there were too few satellite airfields to house dispersed regiments.

Within the Western District only 16 of 62 airfields had concrete runways, while none of the 23 scheduled for the Baltic District had been completed. Furthermore, some 30 'airfields' were actually airstrips designed as satellites to the main bases. On 10 April 1941, Moscow approved plans for another 251 airfields, mostly in the West, but work had not begun by the time the Germans attacked. With space at a premium, 14 airfields held two or three regiments. Most of the available airfields were too close to the German border. The situation was most acute north of the Pripet Marshes, where the Russians had advanced deeper into Poland but found fewer suitable airfield sites. In the Baltic Military District 39 per cent of the aircraft were concentrated in three airfields, while in the Western District 45 per cent were on six airfields. South of the Pripet Marshes the advance was shorter and sites more plentiful – only 25 per cent of the Kiev District's aircraft were on four airfields, including 206 at Lvov, while in the small Odessa District 17 per cent of the aircraft were in Odessa itself.

On 27 December 1940, Defence Minister (Commissar) Marshal Semon Timoshenko ordered all airfields within 500 kilometres of the border to be camouflaged by 1 July 1941. Progress was slow, and attempts within the Kiev District during the spring of that year to build revetments for aircraft, vehicles and supplies were hamstrung by labour shortages. Acute shortages also plagued the VVS. The lack of accommodation meant that in the Western District some pilots were billeted five kilometres from their bases, while few airfields had adequate stocks of fuel and ammunition. There were also severe shortages of trained radio operators for the district VVS headquarters, which were often at a third of establishment. This left commanders dependent upon landlines, with fatal consequences in the summer of 1941.

Rychagov faced tremendous challenges in trying to prepare the VVS for future combat – he needed to re-equip his regiments, ensure their crews were adequately trained, provide sufficient supplies for a prolonged campaign and organise an infrastructure that could move those supplies, repair damaged aircraft and bring in replacements. This required a mature individual with broad experience in all aspects of military aviation and the administrative skills to address the prime problems in detail. What Moscow got was a 30-year-old who had peaked in the Winter War as commander of a small air force on a minor Arctic front, who disliked 'flying a desk' and preferred to visit the regiments to enjoy the convivial company of fellow airmen. Smushkevich was also no administrator, and being crippled with leg injuries following a crash, he frequently had to work from his bed, which he moved into his office.

The only silver lining was that, unlike the mechanised forces, there were few disputes over doctrine. In a comprehensive review of the Red Army's Winter War shortcomings, Smushkevich noted, 'The need to divide the VVS into the Red Army's air arm to operate with the ground forces and an Operational Level air arm supporting large-scale operations has been proved beyond reasonable doubt.'

Soviet military aviation was divided into four elements – Frontal Aviation Air Force (*Voyenno-Vozdushnye Sili-Frontovaya Aviatsiaya*, VVS-FA), Naval Fleet Air Force (*Voyenno-Vozdushnye Sili-Voyenno-Morskoy Flot*, VVS-VMF), Long Range Bomber Aviation (*Dahl'niy Bombardirovochnaya Aviatsiya*, DBA) to March 1942 then Long Range Aviation (*Aviatsiya Dahl'nevo Deystiviya*, ADD) and Home Air Defence (*Protivovozdushnaya Oborona*, PVO). The VVS-FA and VVS-VMF provided support for the Red Army and the Red Navy at the Tactical/Operational Level (army and army group levels), with operational command delegated to army groups (Fronts) and armies, each with their own air commander. DBA was under the control of the Defence Ministry in peacetime and VVS headquarters in wartime, and was to conduct Operational/Strategic Level missions (army group and the rear) with formations assigned to front commands, as were many fighter regiments of the PVO.

While it recognised the value of defending, and attacking, industrial and administrative centres, the Red Army leadership had no truck with Italian General Giulio Douhet's claims that strategic bombing alone could win a war. Indeed, the Russians would use the term 'attacks upon administrative, political and military sites in the hinterland'.

The VVS's army support mission would be reflected throughout the Great Patriotic War against Germany and her allies. From the beginning to the end of this conflict, nearly two-thirds of VVS sorties (63.44 per cent) were at the Tactical Level either supporting the troops in the forward edge of the battle area (FEBA) or shielding them from air attack, while 5.52 per cent were spent striking Operational Level (operations for commands up to army group/front headquarters) targets. Another 14.62 per cent of sorties were escort missions, while 11.18 per cent were reconnaissance. DBA would also be diverted to Tactical Level air support, which accounted for 40.44 per cent of its sorties, while 45.80 per cent were Operational or Strategic Level attacks. Before the war VVS doctrine anticipated destroying enemy air power in the air and on the ground, while the PVO covered the assembly of reserves for a counter-offensive in which Soviet airmen would pound enemy communications to ease the way for the armoured formations.

The Red Army leadership could see for itself the potent power demonstrated by combining mechanised forces with air power, and during 1940 there was growing disquiet about the ability of the VVS. Confusion about organisation and the execution of operations became all too clear in December 1940, at the moment when Hitler published his directive for the invasion of the Soviet Union. During the summer of that year, following the successful German campaigns in the West, Timoshenko summoned senior officers to the Defence Ministry for a conference on the Red Army's status. Afterwards, five reports were presented looking at the latest ideas in warfare, including one by Rychagov on 'Combat aviation in the offensive and the struggle for air superiority.' This sparked a bitter argument over the best way to achieve air superiority. The Baltic and Kiev District VVS commanders, General-leitenantii Gregorii Kravchenko and Yevgenii Ptukhin, said their experience fighting the Japanese at Khalkin-Gol and the German–Italian forces in Spain showed this goal was best achieved in the air. Rychagov straddled the fence and advocated the destruction of the enemy both in the air and on the ground, but he produced no concrete plans to achieve this goal.

From 8 January 1941, watched intently by Leningrad Party boss Andrei Zhdanov as Stalin's representative, the senior commanders conducted war games involving German invasions, firstly in the Western (Belorussia and eastern Poland) District and then the Kiev District. The Red Army was judged to be successful in its defence of these areas, although the exercises had a considerable degree of unreality. Yet Zhdanov was sceptical, and when the war games concluded, Stalin summoned the participants to the Kremlin on 13 January to discuss the results. He was not pleased by the explanations and demanded realistic discussions among the commanders, which led the VVS officers to complain bitterly about their structure and training.

While these complaints were largely dismissed, the Communist Party's Central Committee decided on 25 February to introduce the aviation division instead of the smaller aviation brigade, and Rychagov apparently implemented this on 10 April. Of more immediate effect was Stalin's appointment of Georgii Zhukov as Army Chief-of-Staff on 14 January. Although he was an advocate of air power, having been a grateful customer at Khalkin-Gol, his pursuit of excellence began a process which, ironically, almost destroyed the VVS.

The war games confirmed the Soviet General Staff's belief that the main enemy thrust would be towards the Baltic states and Belorussia, but Stalin was convinced the Germans would go for the Ukraine's mineral and agricultural riches. Consequently, the defence plan was a compromise, with the largest concentration in the Kiev and Odessa Districts, while retaining substantial forces in the Baltic and Western Districts. Naturally, VVS dispositions in 1941 reflected this, although General-maior Aleksandr Novikov had some 1,000 aircraft, plus 227 PVO fighters, to shield Leningrad from the Finns (See Table I-1).

Kravchenko had been sent to the General Staff Academy and replaced in the Baltic District by General-maior Aleksei Ionov, who had another 1,200 aircraft, while in the Western District, General-maior Ivan Kopets had 1,500 aircraft.[7] The largest concentration – more than 1,900 aircraft, and 114 PVO fighters – was under Ptukhin, augmented by more than 800 aircraft plus 72 PVO fighters in the Odessa District under General-maior Fyodor Michugin.

These figures exclude some 180 reserve aircraft, but on 1 June 1941, only 1,597 (19.4 per cent) were new generation aircraft. Some 768 of these were in the southern districts, the latter also receiving most of the 600 modern aircraft delivered to the military districts in the following weeks. Nevertheless, by 22 June only 27 per cent of combat aircraft were modern, with 690 aircraft awaiting delivery from the factories. Most of the DBA's 1,300 aircraft were modern DB-3s but, with the

Table I-1: The VVS in the West – 1 June 1941

District	Fighter	Bomber	Assault	L. R. Reconn	Total
Leningrad	601/33	355/36	74/2	31/1	1,061/72
Baltic	668/95	441/45	85/5	6/–	1,200/145
Western	863/111	531/74	85/3	53/1	1,532/189
Kiev	1,195/134	506/73	135/7	64/2	1,900/216
Odessa	448/82	223/36	29/–	117/5	817/123
Total	3,775/455	2,056/264	408/17	271/9	6,510/745
DBA	–	1,333/318	–	–	1,333/318
Grand Total	3,775/455	3,389/582	408/17	271/9	7,843/1,063

Notes: Figures – Total/Unserviceable.

These figures exclude 380/99 Corps (tactical reconnaissance) aircraft.

In addition, there were 1,179 PVO fighters in the western USSR, of which 413 were attached to the Western Military Districts.

exception of nine TB-7s, the 212 heavy bombers were obsolete.[8] The VVS reconnaissance force was similar in size to the Luftwaffe's, but many of its 270 long range aircraft lacked cameras – an essential sensor found in all *Fernaufklärungstaffeln* aeroplanes.

Because Soviet industry (like its counterpart in Germany) was more interested in producing aircraft than spares, the number of serviceable aeroplanes declined. On 1 June 1941, 12.9 per cent of VVS and DBA aircraft in the West were officially unserviceable (that figure was nearly 24 per cent in the DBA). This total may in fact be an underestimate, although it compares favourably with the Luftwaffe, where the figure was 26 per cent. However, the Russian numbers may relate only to aircraft undergoing overhauls or major repairs, for it is worth noting that on 15 June, 29 per cent of all tanks were being overhauled while 44 per cent were unserviceable with lesser problems.

In addition to air forces supporting the armies, the Navy also had small forces supporting each fleet. The strongest naval air concentration was the Baltic Sea Air Force (*Voyenno-Vozdushnye Sily Baltiyskogo Flota*, VVS-KBF) with 656 aircraft (including 353 fighters and 172 bombers), closely followed by the Black Sea Air Force (*Voyenno-Vozdushnyye Sily Chernomorskogo Flota*, VVS-ChF) with 624 (including 346 fighters and 138 bombers). The NKVD also had a small air force in the West, with 12 squadrons (150 aircraft) of mostly reconnaissance aircraft, but with some SB bombers and two squadrons of MBR-2 flying boats.

THE ENEMY

Across the frontier, Germany's armed forces (Wehrmacht) were preparing to invade the Soviet Union in a dramatic conclusion to the dynamic relationship between the two air forces that ranged in the 1920s and 1930s from combat to close collaboration then to proxy war and finally uneasy collaboration. In the aftermath of World War I, German volunteer airmen helped to defend the newly created Baltic states and clashed with those of the new Bolshevik Russian state, who were fascinated by the Junkers all-metal aircraft they captured but whose ribbed duralumin structures they could not reproduce.

Then Weimar Germany and Soviet Russia, both orphans of the World War I storm and international pariahs in the post-war world, began to develop a rapprochement. They agreed in 1924 to clandestine German development of the latest military technology, to which the Soviet Union would gain access. One of the first fruits of this was the creation of an aircraft factory at Fili, near Moscow, that used Junkers technology, and which would soon be assigned to Tupolev. The secret development of aircraft and weapons, as well as air- and groundcrew training, was organised by Oberst Hermann von der Lieth-Thomsen, who had been head of the Army's Aviation Troops (*Fliegertruppen*) and later Chief-of-Staff of the Army Air Service (*Luftstreitkräfte*). This was carried out 440 kilometres southeast of Moscow on the river Voronezh at a military airfield near the town of Lipetsk, where the Luftwaffe's first generation of combat aircraft were developed.

The cooperation was extremely successful and mutually beneficial, so the Russians were dismayed when Berlin began to run down its activities in Lipetsk from 1931 in favour of development in Germany. On 14 July 1932, Berlin decided to create an air force, and the process of closing Lipetsk accelerated when the Nazis came to power six months later, so that in September 1933 the base became the exclusive property of the VVS.[9] The aircraft developed at Lipetsk clashed with the new generation of Russian warplanes in Iberian skies three years later as Berlin (with Rome) waged a proxy war with Moscow supporting opposite sides in the Spanish Civil War. The conflict cost the Luftwaffe 41 aircrew dead and 232 aircraft destroyed, while the Soviet Union lost 99 aircrew and all the combat aircraft (675 to 750) it sent to Spain, where some of those who faced each other would hold prominent positions on opposing sides in 1941. Relations between Moscow and Berlin returned to uneasy cooperation after their Molotov–Ribbentrop Non-Aggression Pact of August 1939 that allowed Germany a free hand in Poland, by which time the Luftwaffe had 3,609 combat aircraft.

Both sides recognised that the Pact was a marriage of convenience to buy time and exploit diplomatic options, but Stalin's opportunism helped to hasten the 'divorce'. When the Germans, aided by Russian food and mineral supplies, struck westward in May 1940, Stalin anticipated the Wehrmacht would become involved in a prolonged conflict with France and Britain leading to military stalemate, as in 1914. In June he annexed first the Baltic states and then the former Russian territory of Bessarabia from Romania, which brought the Soviet Union closer to Adolf Hitler's prime source of oil. Stalin was stunned when the Wehrmacht conquered almost all of Western Europe within six weeks, which allowed Hitler to consider his options. Following the seizure of Bessarabia, the Führer noted on 18 July that 'thoughtful preparations must be made' for the invasion of the USSR.

A fortnight later, during an Armed Forces Supreme Command (*Oberkommando des Wehrmacht*, OKW) conference, Hitler announced he would strike the Soviet Union the following spring, and a deployment plan, 'Eastern Construction' (*Aufbau Ost*), was drawn up. Furthermore, from the autumn of 1940 two *Heeresgruppen* and three *Armeeoberkommandos* were sent to East Prussia and Poland, together with their attached *Heeresflieger* – long-range and short-range reconnaissance squadrons (*Fern- und Nahaufklärungsstaffeln*) with 140 aircraft. The two regional air forces (*Luftflotten*) in the East, Generaloberst Alfred Keller's *Luftflotte* 1 in

East Prussia and Poland and Generaloberst Alexander Löhr's *Luftflotte* 4 in Austria and Slovakia, had only fighters and reconnaissance aircraft assigned at that time.

During the summer of 1940 Hitler's strategic objectives were the subjugation of Great Britain and possible intervention in the Mediterranean, with the invasion of Russia a fallback. In October, for want of other gainful employment, both OKW and Army Supreme Command (*Oberkommando des Heeres*, OKH) began outline planning for an offensive into Russia, although the decision to strike eastwards was only formally adopted on 18 December, when OKW published outline directive *Weisung Nr 21* for *Unternehmen* (Operation) *Barbarossa*. The objective was to destroy the Red Army in western Russia and pursue it to a point from which enemy bombers could not reach the Reich. Generalfeldmarschall Fedor von Bock's *Heeresgruppe Mitte* (Army Group Centre) would spearhead the assault from Poland and drive into Belorussia, then assist Generalfeldmarschall Wilhelm Ritter von Leeb's *Heeresgruppe Nord* (Army Group North) in its advance from East Prussia through the Baltic states to Leningrad. Meanwhile, Generalfeldmarschall Gerd von Rundstedt's *Heeresgruppe Süd* (Army Group South) would advance into the Ukraine from southern Poland and Eastern Europe to take Kiev. Once the initial objectives were achieved the Wehrmacht would then advance to a line from Archangel, in the Arctic Circle, to the river Volga. From airfields west of this line the Luftwaffe would pound the surviving Russian factories in the Urals.

Preparations continued throughout the winter of 1940–41, but all hopes of striking in the spring were dashed by events in the Balkans. The Germans were preparing to strike Great Britain's ally, Greece, from Bulgaria when an uprising in Yugoslavia in March 1941 brought the prospect of another Balkan front as in World War I. The Wehrmacht acted rapidly and ruthlessly to conquer both countries, then take the island of Crete to prevent it becoming a bomber base. This diversion not only delayed *Barbarossa* but also cost the Wehrmacht men and material, especially the Luftwaffe, which lost 302 combat aircraft and 121 transports as well as 730 aircrew, while its airborne force was decimated for the second time in a year. Worse, the Luftwaffe had to maintain a presence in the Mediterranean theatre that would act on the Eastern Front rather like the moon on Earth's tides, controlling the ebb and flow of aircraft over the next few years.

The Luftwaffe's role in the forthcoming campaign, as in the previous ones, was defined by its first, and greatest, chief-of-staff, Generalleutnant Walter Wever. This brilliant staff officer was gifted by the Army to the Luftwaffe in 1933, and learned about air power from scratch, including gaining his 'wings'. At that time it was a tenet of conservative military faith that the focus of air power should be at the Tactical Level, with spare capacity used at the Strategic Level. Douhet's heresy that Strategic Level air power alone could win a conflict by destroying the enemy's means of production and their will to fight, had gained root only in Great Britain's RAF and the US Army Air Corps.

Wever, who was killed in a flying accident in 1936, opted to square the circle by focusing air operations at the Operational Level, especially communications and troop concentrations. Once the Wehrmacht achieved a Tactical Level breakthrough, with some direct air support, the new doctrine would help exploit such a success by disrupting the enemy's attempts to weave a new defensive front. This proved part of the foundation to what was popularly called *Blitzkrieg*, but what the Germans called Breakthrough Tactics (*Schwerpunkttaktik*), smoothing the way for a rapid advance by mechanised forces that overran the enemy air forces' infrastructure to ease the Luftwaffe's task.

This was demonstrated during the campaign in May 1940, when the German Panzers' dash towards the Channel forced Allied air forces to abandon their airfields in its path, which in turn reduced the air threat to the spearheads and allowed the Luftwaffe to shield the exposed southern flank. Flexible task forces executing specific missions were a key element in Wehrmacht doctrine, and the Luftwaffe was no exception. *Luftflotten* controlled regional operations, with one to three Air Corps (*Fliegerkorps*) sometimes augmented by ad hoc task forces known as Air Commands (*Fliegerführer* or *Flfü*). The *Fliegerkorps* usually had single-role wings (*Geschwader*), with a headquarters flight (*Stabs Kette*) and up to three groups (*Gruppen*) each of three 12-aircraft squadrons (*Staffeln*). Reconnaissance squadrons (*Aufklärungsstaffeln*) were also organised into administrative *Gruppen* but were deployed individually.

The *Heeresflieger* were established to ease army fears that the Luftwaffe would fight a private war and neglect the senior service's interests. Liaison between the two services was the responsibility of the Luftwaffe General and the Army Commander-in-Chief (*General der Luftwaffe beim ObdH*) and Inspector of Reconnaissance Generalleutnant (General from 1 July 1941) Rudolf Bogatsch, who delegated operational command to Luftwaffe officers – *Kommandeur der Luftwaffe* (*Koluft*) at army group (*Heeresgruppe*) and army (*Armee Oberkommando*) level, or Group Aviation Staffs (*Gruppenfliegerstäbe*) at corps level.

These officers coordinated *Heeresflieger* operations and forwarded general requests for air support to the *Fliegerkorps*. The allocation of fighter and strike (bomber, dive-bomber, fighter-bomber) squadrons was the sole prerogative of the *Fliegerkorps* commander and his staff. However, from May 1941, he might create a temporary tactical air support command under a Close Air Support Leader (*Nahkampfführer*) – usually a Stuka (Ju 87) *Staffelkapitän* under the operational control of the Airforce Liaison Officer (*Fliegerverbindungsoffizier*, abbreviated to *Flivo*), whose motorised command post was close to spearhead corps or division command posts. Tactical air support for specific missions or larger areas might be assigned to another ad hoc command described as a Battle Formation (*Gefechtsverband*).

One Luftwaffe advantage was a substantial dedicated transport force with some 500 robust Ju 52/3ms, nicknamed 'Aunty Ju' (*Tante Ju*). Each of these aircraft was capable of carrying up to two tonnes of supplies loaded through wide doors on the starboard side. They not only helped the Luftwaffe to advance rapidly to forward airstrips, but also provided emergency supplies to forward army units. However, the Mediterranean theatre also had call on these resources, which prevented full deployment to the Russian Front. Indeed, as early as 23 June 1941, Luftflotte 1's He 111 bombers were being used in the transport role. By contrast, the Russians had to mobilise the GVF on 25 June, creating nine groups with 593 aircraft – most of which were single-engine light transports. The only dedicated transports were the PS-84 and the G-2, a civil version of the TB-3 bomber. The latter was effectively the *Tante Ju's* cousin, being capable of carrying four tonnes of equipment. Nevertheless, the DBA was soon forced to use its TB-3 as transports.

It was an article of faith within the Wehrmacht that Germany's defeat in World War I was largely due to fighting on two fronts, so news of *Weisung Nr 21* was received with unease, especially within the Luftwaffe. In a rare moment of confrontation, its commander, Reichsmarschall Herman Göring, quoted Hitler's own arguments from *Mein Kampf* to the author, who briefly wavered then retorted, 'Why don't you stop trying to persuade me to drop my plans for Russia? I've made up my mind.'

The Luftwaffe leadership was the weakest in the Wehrmacht, for while Göring – a former fighter pilot like Rychagov – was the nominal commander, most decisions were taken by Chief-of-Staff General Hans Jeschonnek, who, like many of the VVS leaders, had been promoted too high, too soon. Göring, who was lazy, ignorant of technological developments and had a short attention span, sought to grasp as much power as possible in his podgy fingers, including nominally running the Reich's economy, but he soon proved incapable of running anything efficiently. He liked to be called 'The Iron Man' (*Der Eiserne*), but his corpulence and drug addiction reflected his love of luxury and good living, so most members of the Wehrmacht referred to him as Fatty (*Der Dicke*), a nickname shared with Lieth-Thomsen. Göring's comment as head of the Luftwaffe that 'Everything that flies is mine' reflected his megalomania, yet he played little part in detailed decision-making for the Luftwaffe. Instead he preferred to make crook's tours of Europe, seizing art treasures, while during the later air campaigns over Britain he devoted more time to purloining naval air units, ostensibly withdrawing them for re-equipment then absorbing them in the Luftwaffe's order of battle, than to operations.

Göring had an excellent deputy in Generalfeldmarschall Eberhard Milch, a talented, hardworking administrator who understood the value of new technology. When Milch's enemies revealed he had a Jewish father, it was Göring who declared him a kosher Aryan, but the Reichsmarshall never trusted his deputy. He recognised that Milch's inveterate intriguing as much as his competence made him a serious potential rival so he sidelined him as General Inspector and ensured he was excluded from decision-making. This suited Jeschonnek, one of Milch's numerous enemies, who had played a key role in developing Luftwaffe tactics and doctrine, although his demand that the two latest bombers, the Ju 88 and the He 177, be capable of dive-bombing prolonged their development. Jeschonnek's lack of operational experience, personal sensitivity and abrasiveness isolated him from other senior commanders, and this was aggravated by his shared refusal with Göring to confront Hitler. The Reichsmarshall recognised Jeschonnek was no political threat, which allowed Göring to receive the plaudits while leaving his subordinate to do the hard work and be the whipping boy when things went wrong.

Jeschonnek's unwavering support for Hitler eventually broke his friendship with Operations chief Generalmajor Otto Hoffman von Waldau, who opposed *Barbarossa* because it would overstretch the Luftwaffe. The chief-of-staff merely parroted the Führer's prediction that the new campaign, as in the previous summer, would last only six weeks. Perhaps Waldau recalled his own rhetorical comment to Luftwaffe Quartermaster (*Generalquartiermeister*) Oberst Hans-Georg von Seidel as they crossed Berlin's equivalent of Paris Etoile, der Grosser Stern, west of the Brandenburg Gate, in the summer of 1939: 'Do you think we will live to see this called Red Army Square?'[10] Ultimately, Hitler could count upon Luftwaffe support because he bribed all the Wehrmacht's senior commanders, the amounts depending upon rank.

Göring's determination to ensure his leadership was unchallenged led to the disastrous appointment of Generaloberst Ernst Udet to direct German aircraft development as *Generalluftzeugmeister*. The German aircraft industry arose like the proverbial phoenix from the ashes and expanded rapidly, aided by generous state funding that translated into ultimate state control, although manfacturers were allowed a loose rein. The commercial companies running the state-owned factories had

1,725,000 workers by 1941 and made substantial profits. Furthermore, they easily out-produced their Western European rivals to build some 8,300 aircraft in 1939. But by the summer of 1940, with the Reich controlling the Channel coast, there was a belief that the war was over, which cut demand for aircraft and led companies to hoard materials.

Meanwhile, designers pursued private flights of fancy such as the Bv 141, Bv 222, Fw 191, Ju 288, Ju 290 and Me 321, which were of only peripheral value to the Reich's war effort and wasted large amounts of scarce resources. In 1940 the Reich produced 10,826 aircraft compared with 14,436 in Britain, which produced 18,825 in 1941 while German production rose to 11,776. Moreover, German manufacturers, like the Russians, focused upon completed aircraft to the detriment of spares production, which was why so many German aeroplanes were unserviceable in June 1941. Planning was also chaotic, with new production schedules replaced almost before the ink was dry.

The failure to increase German production was partly due to complacency within the leadership from Hitler and Göring downwards, but much of it was Udet's fault. He was the most successful surviving German fighter ace of World War I, a charming man, a raconteur, a caricaturist and a brilliant pilot. But he was no engineer, his single attempt to establish himself as a manufacturer ended in bankruptcy, and he possessed neither the administrative skills nor the determination to bring the companies into line. Worse he was the Lord of Misrule, who allowed his subordinate engineers and administrators to create a labyrinthine organisation in pursuit of their own agendas, leading to numerous aircraft sub-types for specialised roles.

Udet literally sought to rise above his trouble by escaping into the skies, but his close friendship with Deputy Führer Rudolf Hess, who 'defected' in May 1941, aroused the suspicions of Gestapo head Heinrich Himmler. These were strengthened by his telephone indiscretions, monitored by Göring from the basement of the Air Ministry (*Reichsluftsministerium*), and his contacts with German émigrés in Sweden. In August 1941 he was banned from flying, Göring fearing that Udet may also defect. While serving as *Generalluftzeugmeister*, Udet had failed to increase production significantly. Furthermore, the development of combat aircraft to replace the pre-war designs had been haphazard at best. Consequently, development continued of aircraft with lethal flight characteristics, such as the Me 209 single-seat and Me 210 two-seat fighters, long after these programmes should have been cancelled.

It was a telling comment on Udet's organisation that engine overheating problems in the new Fw 190 fighter were overcome through the initiative of a lowly *Jagdgeschwader* technical officer. During the summer of 1941 Milch was inserted into Udet's organisation to tackle the aircraft industry's worst excesses, and he used this excuse to extend his control of the organisation, causing tensions with Udet and his increasingly worried subordinates. Despite bureaucratic resistance, in August 1941 Milch introduced a new production concept with 13 aircraft and four aero-engine companies, directing a network of assembly and component factories that would bear fruit the following year.

The Luftwaffe was aware of planning for *Barbarossa*, but formal planning, in which *Luftflotte* 1 Chief-of-Staff Generalmajor Heinz-Hellmuth von Wühlisch was prominent, only began on 13 January 1941. Even Jeschonnek had to recognise the new campaign posed problems, and on 27 February he informed his Army opposite number, Generaloberst Franz Halder, that the low ratio of aircraft to space meant that only key areas could be guaranteed air support. OKH therefore warned field commanders that complete air superiority was unlikely, and that they should expect greater exposure to enemy air attacks than in previous campaigns. Interestingly, the fighter commanders (*Jagdfliegerführer* or *Jafü*) who had coordinated each *Luftflotte*'s fighter operations were now disbanded and their role devolved to the *Fliegerkorps*.

During March and April it was agreed Keller's *Luftflotte* 1 would support Leeb while *Luftflotte* 2's Generalfeldmarschall Albert Kesselring, at that time based in the Low Countries, would spearhead Bock's attack. The two *Luftflotten* wargamed the *Heeresgruppen* plans and also discussed details with *Panzergruppen* commanders. Löhr, on the other hand, was totally involved in the Balkans campaign to the point where

Luftflotte 4 was able to despatch only a small liaison staff to discuss Rundstedt's future operations.

At a joint-services conference chaired by Halder in early January, Seidel outlined his preparations, which were aided by the extensive network of airfields and installations established in Poland to support the Luftwaffe's training organisation. Keller's *Luftflotte* 1 shielded the Reich's eastern border with a handful of squadrons, but when the Germans bolstered their forces in the East in late 1940 the *Heeresflieger* had used existing facilities. However, *Barbarossa* called for new airfields (105 new ones in southern Poland alone, mostly for the *Heeresflieger*), while existing bases were expanded. In addition, Generalleutnant Wolfgang Martini, the head of the Signal Service, wove the web of telephone, teleprinter and radio networks that were at the core of the Luftwaffe's greatest asset – the command and control system that provided the *Luftflotten* with incredible command flexibility.

The Luftwaffe in the East would require 14,000 tonnes of supplies a day, and the assembly of stores began during the winter of 1940–41 and accelerated following the March thaw. Nevertheless, on the eve of *Barbarossa* there was a shortfall of 15,000–20,000 tonnes, while the Wehrmacht itself suffered a severe shortage of motor transport. To provide administrative support for the advance, including providing signal, maintenance and transport facilities, the Luftwaffe created Special Duty Air Districts (*Luftgaustäbe zbV*), with two assigned to each *Luftflotte*. Despite all the activity, security remained tight, and two chiefs-of-staff and old friends Oberst Hermann Plocher (*FliegerkorpsV*) and Kurt Zeitzler (1 *Panzergruppe*) spent a fortnight making excuses for their presence in the same Polish hotel before they learned they would be operating together!

Much depended upon an accurate assessment of enemy air strength, with photo-reconnaissance a prime source of information. Oberst Theo Rowehl's 'High-altitude Research Centre' (*Versuchstelle für Höhenflüge*), also known as Special Detachment (*Sonderkommando*) Rowehl, had been conducting clandestine photo-reconnaissance of Soviet territory intermittently from 1934 to 1939, when the emphasis switched to the West. Until 21 September 1940, Hitler banned photo-reconnaissance of

Russia for fear of alerting Stalin, but now, barely a week after the failure of the Luftwaffe's last attempt to seize control of the English skies, Air Force Commander-in-Chief (*Oberbefehlshaber der Luftwaffe*, ObdL) was authorised to conduct a systematic reconnaissance of the Soviet Union up to 300 kilometres beyond the frontier. This required some reorganisation, and it was not until October that ObdL's own reconnaissance formation, AufKlGr ObdL, began operations from East Prussia and Romania using He 111s, Do 215B-2s, Ju 86Ps and Ju 88Bs flying from Cracow and Budapest. These machines would eventually fly more than 500 sorties, 152 of them in 1941.

The photo-reconnaissance aeroplanes often flew at an altitude of 9,000–12,000 metres initially over the frontier area, but when no fighter opposition was encountered they ranged deeper, until restricted in February 1941 to the line Murmansk–Moscow–Rostov, with the emphasis on the Minsk–Kiev area.[11] Rowehl's aircraft not only flew deep-penetration reconnaissance but were also used for carrying in agents, with the loss of just a single Ju 86P that was forced down by bad weather near Vinnitsa on 15 April. It was blown up by the crew before they were captured. Russian troops recovered some of the film from the aeroplane, and reported to the General Staff that it showed airfields. However, fear of German reaction kept the crew safe, despite the evidence of espionage, and they would eventually be released by advancing German troops. They were extremely lucky, for the fate of Luftwaffe aircrew who fell into Russian hands was extremely uncertain from the start. On 22 June 1941, Oberleutnant Rudolf Naumann's crew failed to return from a bombing mission, and they were murdered by their captors five days later, while Hauptmann Willi Stemmler, who was also shot down that same day, escaped and survived with the help of Ukrainian peasants, reaching German lines during July.

There are reports of both sides shooting parachuting airmen in the air or even on the ground, while on 25 June a Russian pilot and two *Kampfgeschwader* (KG) 76 crewmen, who had all bailed out after the former rammed their bomber, exchanged shots before the Germans were taken prisoner. Their fate is unknown, but many Luftwaffe airmen were executed after interrogation, including two *Jagdgeschwader* (JG) 3 pilots shot down during the battle of Kursk in 1943 and officially described as 'Killed while trying to escape after being questioned.'[12] Some Russian airmen killed in revenge for lost family – a 519th Fighter Regiment (*Istrebitelyenaya Aviatsionnaya Polk*, IAP) pilot who downed a Bf 109 landed beside it and shot the German as he surrendered, while the regimental commander of 85th Guards Fighter Regiment (*Gvardeyskii Istrebitelyenaya Aviatsionnaya Polk*, GvIAP) allowed a Jewish pilot to take a captured German 'for a ride'.

The fate of Russian airmen was little better, with many of those captured in 1941 dying of neglect in woefully inadequate prison camps. Others perished in cruel experiments, one of which involved testing Arctic sea immersion suits for the Luftwaffe. Later they would be forced into labour gangs, and those who proved troublesome, such as the commander of 306th Assault Division (*Shturmovaya Aviatsionnaya Diviziya*, ShAD), Polkovnik Aleksandr Isupov, and those who tried to organise escapes, were executed in concentration camps. The problem of using Russian airmen as labour was illustrated by Starshii Leitenant Mikhail Devyataev of 104th GvIAP, shot down in 1944. In February 1945 he was working at an airfield near Swinemünde and managed to steal a He 111 and fly himself and ten fellow-prisoners across the lines. However, such were NKVD suspicions about returning prisoners-of-war (PoWs) that he was not awarded the title of Hero of the Soviet Union until 1957!

Indeed, communist authorities regarded with deep suspicion those Russian aircrew who were brought down behind enemy lines who then managed to return, often after great hardship. In late 1942 the NKVD created a Counter-Intelligence Department that, the following year, was given the name 'Death to Spies' (*Smert Shpionam*) or Smersh.[13] Escaped PoWs had little official sympathy and one pilot, rebuked for not shooting himself, pointed out his hands were burned and his pistol smashed. He would remain under a cloud of suspicion for the rest of his life. Another pilot never received back his medals. Kapitan Aleksandr Filatov of 30th GvIAP, who had 21 individual and four shared victories to his name, was never awarded the title of Hero of the Soviet Union or allowed a post-war career in the VVS because he was twice shot down and captured.

To escape an awful fate at the hands of the enemy, both sides' airmen would try to help their comrades escape. When Major Hubertus Hitschold, *Kommandeur* of I./StG 2, and his gunner crash-landed near Vilna on 23 June, their fellow Stuka *Experte* (ace) Oberleutnant Bruno Freitag, *Staffelkapitän* of 3./StG 2, landed nearby and rescued them. Hauptmann Hans-Ulrich Rudel rescued six aircrew, but his seventh attempt saw the Ju 87 bogged down and he had literally to run for his life. Russian airmen performed similar feats, usually with fighters or Il-2s, but one lucky pilot rescued a heavy bomber crew in a TB-3!

Photographic reconnaissance was augmented by Martini's communications intelligence (comint) network, which had been directed against the Soviet Union from 1936. The network of 'Weather Stations' was expanded along the Reich's eastern frontier from 1939 onwards, and then extended into Finland, Hungary and Romania. Although Russian headquarters preferred to communicate by landline so as to avoid eavesdropping by Germany's comint network, there was still enough information for the final report by Luftwaffe Intelligence chief Oberst Josef 'Boy' (Beppo) Schmid to provide a reasonably accurate forecast of the strength and disposition of Soviet air forces in western Russia.

This was calculated at 7,300 aircraft, compared with the actual figure of 8,223, but these numbers ignored the Western air defence and naval air forces, which had 1,179 and 1,445 aircraft respectively. Schmid estimated the Russians had another 5,000 aircraft (the actual figure was 5,203), but failed to determine enemy dispositions or the quality of the new generation of aircraft. Changes in Soviet air organisation meant that his estimate of enemy formations at 23 air divisions was considerably less than the 79 that the VVS actually had, of which 55 were in the West. Schmid also believed the enemy were still equipped with the obsolescent aircraft the Luftwaffe had encountered in Spain. In April 1941 the Russians, who bought 30 modern German aircraft in 1940, allowed a delegation led by the Moscow Air Attaché, Oberst Heinrich Aschenbrenner, to visit aircraft and aero-engine factories. The delegation was very impressed, but Schmid ignored its report, believing that, like the French before Munich, they had been deceived.

In May the *Luftflotten* began moving into their battle stations, Keller transferring his headquarters from Berlin to Norkitten, near Insterburg, East Prussia. On 22 May Kesselring's *Luftflotte* 2 departed Brussels and arrived in Warzaw-Bielany with hopes of repeating its success in May 1940 when it annihilated the Belgian Air Force on the ground. Löhr's headquarters moved from Vienna to Jasionsk, near Rzeszow, in June, and in the same month the *Fliegerkorps* headquarters – three from the West – were transferred like a well-oiled machine.

Keller was joined by General Helmut Förster's *Fliegerkorps* I, to which was added, on 21 April, Oberst Wolfgang von Wild's naval aviation *Flfü Ostsee*. Löhr received General Robert Ritter von Greim's *Fliegerkorps* V, which would support Generaloberst Ewald von Kleist's *Panzergruppe* 1, and Keller's old command, *Fliegerkorps* IV, now under Generalleutnant Curt Pflugbeil. The latter arrived in the Romanian town of Ramnicul-Sarat to exchange places with General Wolfram von Richthofen's *Fliegerkorps* VIII, although this still left Löhr with a third of the Luftwaffe strike force to support Rundstedt, with Pflugbeil's squadrons augmented by the Royal Romanian Air Force (*Forţele Aeriene Regale ale Romaniei*, FARR) with 572 aircraft (including 212 fighters and 125 bombers), of which 79 were unserviceable.

Richthofen joined Kesselring to support Generaloberst Hermann Hoth's 3 *Panzergruppe* and 9 *Armee*, but his forces took three weeks to complete a move to Ratsky, near Suwalki, where it arrived on 7 June. *Fliegerkorps* VIII's transport, however, barely arrived in time after a three-week journey from the Balkans. Richthofen would operate alongside General Bruno Loerzer's *Fliegerkorps* II, which moved to Otwock, near Warsaw, to support Generaloberst Heinz Guderian's 2 *Panzergruppe* and 4 *Armee*. Its arrival meant that Kesselring had more than half the Eastern Front strike force, including almost all the *Stuka-* and *Schlachtflieger*, and had the unique advantage of equal numbers to his foe. The transfer of aircraft posed a major security problem, which was partly overcome by delaying it until a month before the launch of *Barbarossa*. *Gruppen* and

TABLE I-2: THE LUFTWAFFE IN THE EAST, 22 JUNE 1941

Type	Luftflotte 1	Luftflotte 2	Luftflotte 4*	Total
Single-engined fighter	159/21	362/155	272/69	793/245
Twin-engined fighter	–	161/36	–	161/36
Bomber	241/48	300/115	356/131	897/294
Dive-bomber/ Attack	–	416/105	40/20	456/125
Long range reconn	92/22	113/30	97/28	302/80
Tactical recon	87/17	170/28	149/12	406/57
Seaplanes	27/5	–	–	27/5
Total	606/113	1,522/469	914/260	3,042/842

Notes: Total/unserviceable.
In addition there were 183/61 single-engined and 17/7 twin-engined fighters in the eastern home defence organisation.
* Includes Deutschen Luftwaffe Mission in Romania.

Staffeln began flying eastwards as nine flying schools were transferred westwards, thus helping to confuse Soviet intelligence. In all the Luftwaffe deployed some 2,500 aircraft, together with some 440 from the Army and Navy, while the eastern air districts *Luftgaue* had 200 fighters to shield the Reich from Russian retaliation (See Table I-2). It was a formidable force, but weaker than May 1940 when 4,174 aircraft were committed. Indeed, only 897 bombers were available compared with 1,657 (excluding Norway) in May 1940, although five *Kampfgruppen*, with about 100 bombers, in Western Europe were earmarked in June 1941 for deployment in the East as overall bomber strength dropped from 1,760 in May 1940 to 1,338 in June 1941.

The majority were modern designs with stressed-skin airframes and the inventory was similar to that which had conquered Northern and Western Europe the previous summer. With the exception of the Ju 88, these aircraft were familiar to the Russians, who had encountered them in Spain. The Bf 109E single-seat fighters were augmented by the Bf 109F, both being called 'Messers' by the Russians, but the *Zerstörergruppen* retained the Bf 110C/E long range, twin-engined fighters. The *Kampfgruppen* retained the He 111H bomber, but the Do 17Z was being phased out in favour of the Ju 88A. The dive-bomber units, best known by the German acronym Stuka, retained the Ju 87B, augmented by some long range Ju 87Rs, while the lone ground-attack (*Schlacht*) *Gruppe* had the Hs 123 biplane, known as the 'Ein, Zwei, Drei'.[14] The 'eyes' of the Luftwaffe and Army were vital, with the *Fernaufklärungsstaffeln* equipped with a mixture of Do 17Ps, Ju 88Ds and some Bf 110Fs. The newly formed Night Reconnaissance Squadrons (*Nachtaufklärungsstaffeln*) had the Do 17P, while the army's *Nahaufklärungsstaffeln* had the Hs 126A, whose braced wings earned it the Russian nickname 'Crutches' (*Kostii*).

The qualitative superiority of German aircraft helped compensate for the Russians' quantitative superiority. Luftwaffe airmen were not only better equipped but also better trained and more experienced – a situation that would certainly last until the summer of 1944. After ab initio training with the paramilitary National Socialist *Flieger Korps* (NSFK) they received up to 150 hours basic training at A/B *Fliegerschule* followed by 60 hours advanced training at C *Fliegerschule*, including instrument training. Up to 60 hours of further training followed at specialist schools, at which bomber crews were trained to use electronic navigation and bombing radio aids, so that by the time they joined the *Geschwader* Operational Training Groups (*Ergänzungsgruppe*) for aircraft familiarisation and further combat training they would have up to 300 hours in their log books. However, German training was handicapped by a lack of central direction and a shortage of resources, both personnel and material, which was ominous for the Luftwaffe's long-term prospects. The desire to make up casualties meant fewer hours were flown in schools and more in the *Ergänzungsgruppe*, although pilots still acquired some 250 hours training.

Smushkevich was well aware of serious VVS training problems. Until the flying training course was doubled in 1937 it lasted about a year and was based upon the paramilitary organisation *Osoaviakhim*, which had schools in almost every town and city to provide ab initio training. After four months with *Osoaviakhim*, student pilots went for a nine-month course at a military school for advanced and operational training, extended to two years in 1937, but the minimum objective was to give pilots at least 50 hours in their log books before they joined their squadrons, where they were lucky to fly 30 hours a month.

While Soviet education policies had raised overall educational levels, there were many non-Russian areas, especially east of the Urals, where people remained relatively illiterate and innumerate, leaving the VVS largely dependent upon Russians and European non-Russians. This limited manpower led to Timoshenko making a series of bizarre instructions. On 14 March 1940, an order was issued to accelerate training courses – despite there being a severe shortage of instructors, many of whom had been drafted into new regiments – and rush new aircrew into the squadrons. The pace of training accelerated again in February 1941 but nothing was done to increase the number of instructors, so to meet the new quotas schools simply focused upon training pilots to take off and land. There was little or no aerobatic training – indeed, the Russians had nothing like the Bü 133 Jungmann aerobatic trainer, while limited navigation training would create a perennial problem for the VVS.

More importantly, on 22 December 1940, Timoshenko abandoned the principle of volunteer airmen and ordered that conscripts deemed capable of becoming aircrew should be drafted into the flight schools, but when they arrived they were shocked by yet another of his bizarre directives. Officers and especially airmen officers had always had a high status in the Soviet Union, and in August 1938 Timoshenko's predecessor, Marshal Kliment Voroshilov, decided that a newly qualified pilot would be commissioned as a *leitenant*. Early in 1941 Timoshenko reversed this decision on the grounds that the new pilots lacked the experience to be officers and they now started as *serzhanti* (sergeants). Deprived of the officer's eagle insignia, which they called 'The Chicken', would-be officers found themselves commanded by sergeants while married men could not live off base with their wives and families. Many of the new airmen were so demoralised that in protest they refused to wear rank badges, and others went absent without leave while many took to drink, which some paid for by selling their bed linen.

Yet morale among Soviet airmen appears to have remained high during the war, although like any service it included those who, in the RAF term, 'lacked moral fibre'. Patriotism was extremely high even among those who had suffered at the hands of the Soviet state from the Purges and the great Ukrainian famine. Few would volunteer for the pro-German *Ostfliegerstaffeln* and many would join the Party as full members or Young Communists (*Komsomolsks*).

Patriotism also motivated the Luftwaffe veterans or 'Old Hares' (*Alte Hasen*), who were conservative and largely shared the feelings of racial superiority which, with anti-Semitism, were common in Western Europe and North America at that time. They had a profound dislike of the Left, which they believed was responsible for much of Germany's ills in the previous two decades and which was also wrapped in anti-Semitism. Yet among Catholic aircrew there was disquiet about the Nazis' treatment of the Church, and in protest ace Werner Mölders returned his medals.

From 1941 they were joined by 'New Hares' (*Neuses Hasen*) brought up in the Hitler *Jugend* for whom racial superiority was an article of faith. They believed implicitly that power belonged to those who could grab it and hold it, and they had a deep distrust of the forces of traditional conservatism such as the aristocracy and the Roman Catholic Church. In a British PoW camp one transport pilot was heard to boast about joining an SS friend hunting Jews and then sleeping with a Jewish girl who hoped, in vain, it would save her life.

Even in the latter part of the war few were willing to defect. One of the few was KG 51's Major Egbert von Frankenberg und Proschlitz, an aristocrat, who appears to have defected in May 1943 and would be a founding member of the Soviet-organised National Free Germany Committee (*Nationalkomitee Freies Deutschland*). In part this was due to the bonds of comradeship, for many 'Old Hares' had served in Poland, Western Europe and the Balkans, while some *Geschwaderkommodore* and *Gruppenkomandeuren* had fought the Russians over Spain.

Throughout the Russo–German struggle Luftwaffe aircrew seem to have flown far more sorties than those of the VVS, although neither side had the combat tour system used by the Americans and British. This withdrew aircrew from combat after a fixed number of missions or hours so as to reduce risks from combat fatigue by resting a cadre of veterans. They could be used for instruction, allowing student airmen to learn valuable operational lessons, or undertake staff duties to broaden their knowledge and also spread their combat experience. Once rested, aircrew could return for another tour.

By contrast, the Nazi and Communist systems expected their airmen to fly until they dropped, the only 'rest' they received being when their squadrons were withdrawn for re-equipment. Luftwaffe aircrew did receive home leave and, if their squadrons were withdrawn to Germany, they might stay at rest homes in picturesque southern Germany, where the presence of 'Spitfire widows' (women who had married airmen in the hope of collecting their pensions) was unsettling and unwelcome. By contrast, home leave was almost unknown in the Red Army, and one VVS veteran noted he received none until 1948! If a regiment was based near airmen's homes their commander might permit them to visit their families for a few days, but this was a rarity. However, lulls offered the opportunity to send pilots to rest homes to recuperate.

From 1942 onwards the Soviet Supreme General Staff and High Command (*Shtab Verkhovnogo Glavnovokommandovaniya*, Stavka), adopted a policy of resting units before major operations both to rebuild them and to improve operational training. An analysis of the records of 37 VVS Guards divisions indicates they were out of the line on average for just 59 days during the war.[15] Yet VVS aircrew still tended to fly fewer sorties during the war than their enemies, and were generally junior to them in rank. Indeed, all those who flew the largest numbers of sorties were *Leitenantii*. In the Soviet DBA, which was closer to the Luftwaffe's *Kampfgruppen*, the top pilots were Stepan Kretov and Vasilii Osipov with 400 sorties, Feodorsii Parashenko and Pavel Taran who flew 388 and 386, respectively, and Vasilii Smirnov who accumulated 278 to become the top four-engined bomber pilot in the East. VVS bomber pilots, usually flying the Pe-2, also accumulated high mission tallies led by Nikolai Kuznetsov with 360, followed by Pavel Plotnikov with 343 and Vasilii Efremov with 340.

Night bomber pilots, who would hop over the lines on short-range missions three or four times a night, outmatched the *Kampfflieger*. Indeed, eight pilots, mostly from the female 588th/46th Guards Night Bomber Aviation Regiment (*Gvardeyskii Nochnoy Bombardirovochnyy Aviatsionnyy Polk*, GvNBAP) or 'Night Witches' (*Shenskii*), accumulated more than 900 sorties, including 1,000 by Irina Sebrova, whose nearest rival, Konstantin Mihalenko, was close behind with 997. Many *Shturmoviks* began their careers in night bomber regiments that were converted to assault units, with Alexei Zaitsev being credited with 844 sorties and another seven pilots who followed a similar career path accumulating between 371 and 587 sorties. The leading pure 'Ilyusha' ace was Ivan Fonaryov who flew 346 sorties, followed by Talgat Begeldinov (305) and Mikhail Putilin (301), while Alexei Maruzenko had about 300.

These records may be contrasted with Knight's Cross Oak Leaf (*Ritterkreuz Eichenaub*) recipients, who largely served in the East. At least four bomber pilots had more than 400 sorties – 546 for Major Heinrich Höfer, 467 for Major Hermann Wittmann, 430 for Hauptmann Dieter Lukesch and 410 for Oberstleutnant Hans-Henning Freiherr von Beust, all of whom survived the war. Of some 50 *Stuka-* and *Schlachtflieger* pilots that received these decorations, at least a dozen flew more than 1,000 sorties, including 1,300 by Hauptmann Herbert Bauer and 1,200 each by Oberleutnanten Gustav Schubert and Hendrik Stahl, while Rudel flew 2,530 – probably a record for the Eastern Front.

The contrast is especially clear among fighter pilots (Tables I-3 and I-4). While Russian aces Major Sultan Amet-Khan (49 victories including 19 shared) and Major Vladimir Lavrinenkov (46 victories including 11 shared) had the unusual distinction of flying on the first and last days of the war, their totals were 'only' 603 and 448 sorties, respectively. Lavrinenkov was behind enemy lines between September and December 1943, initially as a prisoner and, following his escape, as a guerrilla or partisan.

Aces were excellent pilots with quick reactions and accurate shots, but it is interesting to compare the Luftwaffe's top ten Eastern Front aces (*Experten* or *Kanonen*), selected from a list of 75 who had achieved 100 victories, with their Russian equivalents.[16] Between them, the Germans scored 2,456 victories in the East alone and flew an average of 744 sorties, although some of these were on home defence duties. By contrast, the top ten VVS aces scored 550 victories and flew an average of 393 sorties, although ace Kapitan Grigoriy Rechkalov, with 43 victories (eight shared) recorded 821 sorties – the highest among the Soviet Union's top 50 Soviet aces.

Russian pilots received a bounty for victories – 1,000 roubles for a fighter and 1,500–2,000 roubles for a bomber/reconnaissance aircraft, although at the commissar's 'suggestion' most of this money was converted into war bonds. Many of the German victories were achieved in the golden days of the 1941 advance, including Gerhard Barkhorn's first kill on 2 July 1941. However, the world's ranking ace, Erich Hartmann, opened his account as late as 5 November 1942, and was transferred to the West in January 1945 in an eventful career that included 14 forced landings.

The Russian pilots lacked neither courage nor dedication, so the disparity in terms of activity and success had other causes apart from Stavka resting formations. In part it reflected the superior training of the Germans who, unlike the Russians, were able to operate in poor weather conditions. When the war swung in favour of the Red Army, the VVS would often outstrip its supply lines while supporting the Soviet advance, and this would also restrict operations. With fighter pilots, their success, or otherwise, in combat also reflected different organisation. Spain had taught the Luftwaffe that fighters could operate more effectively in a paired 'chain' (*Rotte*) rather than in trios (*Kette*) to provide more flexible formations, the *Rotten* being linked into Swarms (*Schwärme*). The Russians initially flew in triple elements (*zveno*), but losses compelled them to reduce the fighter *zveno* to two aircraft (*para*), commonly described by the very un-socialist term of 'Master' and 'Slave' (*vedushchiy i vedomyy*), although the pairing system would not be

TABLE I-3: TOP TEN LUFTWAFFE ACES IN THE EAST

Name	Eastern Front Victories	Sorties
Hauptmann Erich Hartmann	350	825
Major Gerhard Barkhorn	301	1,104
Major Günther Rall	271	800
Oberleutnant Otto Kittel	267	583
Major Walter Nowotny	255	442
Major Wilhelm Batz	234	445
Oberst Hermann Graf	202	800
Hauptmann Helmut Lipfert	200	700+
Major Heinrich Ehrler	198	400+
Oberleutnant Walter Schuck	189	500+

officially adopted until 1943.[17] There was also a sharp distinction between the two sides' fighter doctrine. The Luftwaffe maintained the World War I policy of encouraging pilots to build up large personal scores, even among those who did not have a 'sore throat' – a desire for the *Ritterkreuz*. Perhaps the Germans instinctively recognised what analysis later demonstrated – only five per cent of fighter pilots became aces (five or more victories), but they accounted for 40 per cent of all victories. To achieve these goals they had the best aircraft and were shielded by their wingman or 'watchdog' (*Rottenhund*), who became a bodyguard or 'bullet catcher'.

By contrast, the Soviet Union, while publicising the achievements of its aces, discouraged 'individualism'. Indeed, Rechkalov, who became a double Hero of the Soviet Union, clashed with Pokryshkin, the man regarded as the Father of Soviet Fighter Aviation and commander of 9th GvIAD. Pokryshkin criticised Rechkalov's pursuit of personal victories rather than focusing upon his duties as deputy commander of 16th GvIAP, and in May 1944 he persuaded 7th Fighter Corps (*Istrebitelyenaya Aviatsionnaya Korpus*, IAK) commander, General-maior Aleksandr Utin, that Major Boris Glinka, older brother of Dmitri Glinka and a 31-victory

TABLE I-4: TOP TEN VVS ACES

Name	Victories			Sorties
	Individual	Shared	Total	
Major Ivan Kozhedub*	62	–	62	330
Kapitan Grigoriy Rechkalov	56	5	61	415+
Polkovnik Aleksandr Pokryshkin	53	6	59	560
Kapitan Nikolai Gulayev	56	3	59	250
Kapitan Vitalii Popkov	41	17	58	475
Kapitan Kirill Yevstigneyev	53	3	56	283
Kapitan Nikolai Skomorokhov	46	8	54	605
Major Dmitri Glinka	50	–	50	About 300
Kapitan Alexandr Koldunov	46	1	47	412
Major Arsenii Vorozheikin	45	1	46	300

*Kozhedub was also credited with two USAAF P-51s shot down in error over Berlin. For obvious reasons they are not included in his official score.

ace (2 shared), would be a better regimental commander. It is also worth noting that most Soviet aces had shared kills, unlike the Germans.

The generally lower quality of Soviet airmen was exacerbated before the German invasion by the dilution of quality through the rapid expansion of the VVS via the formation of new regiments using experienced crews, whose place was then taken by raw recruits. Inexperienced regimental commanders, 91 per cent of whom had been in post for less than six months, also cut flying time to reduce accidental losses for fear they would be arrested by the NKVD as 'saboteurs' and 'wreckers'.

While the VVS objective was to provide each pilot and crew with six hours flying time and one hour of combat training per week, the severe winter weather with snow, ice and fog largely grounded the VVS. Then as the weather improved in April 1941 there were fuel shortages, so the average Baltic District pilot flew only 15.5 hours per month and the figures literally went south from there, with nine hours in the Western District and four in the Kiev District. Too often this involved little more than a quick circuit, with little attempt at formation, gunnery or bombing practice. In the Western Military Districts a return on 1 June showed there were some 10,078 pilots, of whom just over half (5,711) were officially rated as fully combat trained. Of 1,831 bomber pilots in these areas, barely a quarter were trained for night operations, while in the DBA, the figure was 223 – less than 13 per cent – out of 1,735. At the same time only 1,377 pilots were training on the new aircraft, with 399 officially rated combat worthy – 72 per cent of 'Peshka' pilots, 80 per cent of MiG-3 pilots and 32 per cent of LaGG-3 pilots were officially qualified on their new aircraft.

The air accident rate remained a cause for concern and, once Zhukov had settled in, Timoshenko revealed his disquiet at the VVS's lack of preparation and Rychagov's suitability as commander. They launched an investigation into training and presented a report to the Central Committee on 12 April 1941. This noted that poor aircrew flight discipline and maintenance meant the VVS suffered two or three fatal accidents every day, losing up to 900 aeroplanes a year. In the first quarter of the year there had been 156 crashes and 71 'breakdowns' that had led to the loss of 138 aircraft and 141 aircrew. It was possibly during this meeting that, when asked to comment by Stalin on the accident rate, Rychagov retorted, 'Of course we will continue to have many accidents as long as you keep making flying coffins.' Stalin ominously replied, 'You should not have said that.'

Timoshenko and Zhukov sought Rychagov's immediate removal, and also demanded some of his officers be court-martialled. Stalin not only approved but added to the list of those who would face judgement, including DBA head Proskurov who had been in command for less than six months. He sanctimoniously commented, 'That would be the honest and just thing to do.' Proskurov was replaced by Polkovnik Leonid Gorbatsevich, who promptly banned Golovanov's navigation training flights.

Yet the catalogue of accidents continued and, following the countrywide May Day parades, Shakhurin received a memo complaining about serious defects in the new aircraft issued to the Moscow and Kiev Districts. One of the first 'Peshka' regiments, 48th Bomber Regiment (*Bombardirovochnaya Aviatsionnaya Polk*, BAP), suffered numerous accidents due to airframe and engine failure, and a pilot who investigated an oil leak that caused an engine fire found a piece of rag in a fuel pipe! By the spring most of the 425 Pe-2s delivered to the VVS had suffered some form of serious defect that disrupted training to such an extent that only 100 of 1,682 aircrew were fully qualified to fly them.

This was no longer Rychagov's problem, however, for he had been transferred to the General Staff Academy and replaced by his deputy, General-leitenant Pavel Zhigarev. The latter had transferred from the cavalry to the VVS in 1927 to become an extremely experienced officer. Zhigarev had risen steadily through the ranks (although his appointments tended to last between six and 12 months) until he transferred to Moscow in December 1940, having previously headed a Far Eastern army's VVS. He had also led Soviet airmen in China, after which he had been head of operational training. Zhigarev was an excellent choice, and his partnership with chief-of-staff General-maior Pavel Volodin, another Far Eastern veteran, boded well. But just as the VVS finally received a competent command team, it was wrecked by an anonymous Lufthansa pilot.

For a month, until 21 March 1941, the PVO had been under the command of Ptukhin then General-polkovnik Grigorii Shtern, who had previously fought both in Spain and the Far East. The PVO was organised into corps, divisions and brigades, depending upon the importance of the area to be defended, and was largely gun-based. Its fighters were responsible for a 100–120 kilometre-deep band of territory either around key urban areas or from the border, with individual regiments or divisions attached to the districts. However, on 19 June it was decided to create 6th and 7th IAK PVO in Moscow and Leningrad, respectively.[18] A chain of observer posts detected and tracked numerous German reconnaissance aircraft, and Shtern realised this boded ill. He could also rely upon a chain of 30 radars west of the Urals. In 1933 Russian physicist Pavel Oshchepkov had suggested to Chief-of-Staff of the Red Army General Headquarters Marshal Mikhail Tukhachevskii that it might be possible to detect aircraft with radio waves. Following a meeting at the Academy of Sciences in January 1934, a design bureau was created in Leningrad to produce an experimental bi-static, radio-location system called *Bistro* (Rapid) which operated at 4.7m (64MHz), produced near 200W and was frequency-modulated by a 1kHz tone. This could detect aircraft at ranges of about three kilometres up to an altitude of 1,000 metres, and led Tukhachevskii to order another five for field trials, and to ask Kirov to facilitate production.

However, it was not proper radar, despite Russian claims to the contrary, for it could not measure range. Despite *Bistro's* performance being steadily improved, the measurement of range proved an insurmountable hurdle. Several organisations were looking at radar, but with Oshchepkov's arrest during the Great Purge in June 1937 the Red Army signal organisation took overall responsibility for development. In July 1938 *Bistro*, redesignated *Reveny* (Rhubarb) the following month, was improved into a 4m (75MHz) pulsed-transmission system, with a peak power of about 500W that made it capable of detecting aircraft flying at altitudes up to 7,500 metres some 95 kilometres away.

Reveny entered production as the mobile RUS-1 in the autumn of 1939 despite it still being unable to detect range. However, as its two antennae were some 40 kilometres apart, operators could compare the returns to triangulate the target's location on paper. An improved version with 50kW peak-power, a single antenna and 120-kilometre range was first tested in October 1939, and it could provide range, course, speed and even approximate numbers of targets detected. Designated RUS-2 *Redut* (Redoubt) in the mobile version and *Permatit* (Pegmatite) in static form, this became the foundation of wartime Soviet radar coverage. *Redut* was just entering service when war broke out, and at the same time the Russians were also working on a radar fire control sensor called *Zenit* (Zenith). Two RUS-1s covered the western approaches to Moscow while eight shielded the approaches to Leningrad, with others in the Caucasus. All sites had to report to the anti-aircraft corps, for their performance was inadequate to provide Ground-Controlled Interception (GCI) to fighter regiments.

Stalin banned fighters from shooting down the German reconnaissance aircraft in the spring of 1941, pilots being instructed to 'invite' the intruder to land. Most of the Luftwaffe's snoopers were flying too high for interception in any case. Indeed, when three MiG-3s took off to investigate an unidentified aircraft flying at high altitude over the Baltic states on 10 April 1941, two crashed after entering a spin at 11,000 metres due to pilot inexperience, one pilot being killed. There was no possibility of Russian aerial reconnaissance because the Soviet General Staff banned flights within ten kilometres of the frontier.

The official attitude and the acute awareness that something unpleasant was being prepared across the border left all Soviet military leaders in the Western Districts in an agony of indecision. For the VVS commanders who would soon be in the eye of the storm – Ionov, Kopets and Ptukhin – the strain was greater as signs grew that Soviet air power faced a new purge. In what proved a vain effort to save their lives, the commanders abandoned any thoughts of initiative in favour of total obedience to Moscow's orders. The exception was Kopets who ordered 43rd Fighter Division (*Istrebitelyenaya Aviatsionnaya Diviziya*, IAD) commander General-maior Georgii Zakharov to fly a reconnaissance mission along the border in a U-2, which produced abundant evidence of a build-up. Nevertheless, Moscow refused to allow the district to bring its forces to battle readiness. All the VVS commanders could do was to try to use what authority remained to ensure their men were ready for action. Ptukhin pressed his units to familiarise themselves with their new aircraft and expanded his infrastructure while Ionov emphasised training.

Meanwhile, a deadlier threat to the VVS was materialising as spring turned to summer, with Beria's NKVD sharks beginning to circle

Rychagov and Proskurov. Although the Purge tornado of 1937 had largely blown itself out by the summer of 1939, Beria's men still kept their hands in by maintaining files on almost everyone and routinely picking up some unfortunate who would be savagely beaten until they confessed, and gave the names of other 'plotters'. On 10 March 1941, they arrested Novikov's deputy, General-maior Aleksandr Levin, who had spent most of his career in training, and soon he was damning his colleagues, together with Smushkevich, Rychagov and General-polkovnik Aleksandr Loktionov, Smushkevich's predecessor. Also under investigation was Zhigarev's chief-of-staff, Volodin, who had been their 'guest' in 1939, as well as Ptukhin and the Baltic District's Ionov, who had been appointed on 10 May 1941, having been deputy commander since December 1940. He had flown with Imperial Air Corps in the Great War and, ominously, he had spent much of his career in the training organisation, apart from briefly commanding an air brigade.

Beria's bully boys were also looking at the PVO and were soon investigating Shtern for 'associating with known enemies of the people', while the head of the Moscow PVO, Spanish Civil War veteran General-leitenant Petr Pumpur, another former NKVD 'guest', was again in their sights. Just as Levin was being arrested Pumpur sent his deputy, Polkovnik Nikolai Sbytov, to inspect PVO bases, and he returned with alarming news of supply shortages. Pumpur argued that the supplies would be provided when necessary, following the Party line when he stated there was no immediate threat. Perhaps Sbytov was more astute than his superior for instead of going over his head to Shtern, he passed on his report to the Moscow Party leader, who called a meeting on 3 May 1941 in which he tongue-lashed the generals. As a matter of routine the minutes of the meeting were forwarded to Stalin, who ominously called for the court martial of 'the guilty parties'.

This investigation had just begun when, on 15 May, the regular Lufthansa flight from Warsaw landed at Moscow airport, where routine checking of documents revealed that the PVO had not cleared the flight! While one airfield realised this, telephone failure prevented it informing the local anti-aircraft forces.[19] Stalin was quickly informed and the NKVD arrested Pumpur on 31 May – just a day after Swiss-born General-leitenant Ernest Schacht, the Orel District air commander and former Moscow District aviation training chief, had also been detained by the NKVD. On 8 June Timoshenko received the investigation report, which revealed that the GVF had indeed notified the PVO of the flight. The PVO, however, had not become aware of the problem until 17 May. Although the report confined itself to comments and reprimands, the NKVD was now unleashed upon the VVS and the PVO.

On 8 June Shtern was arrested, followed six days later by Smushkevich – he was taken from his hospital bed by NKVD men in white hospital coats. On 17 June VVS Deputy Chief-of-Staff General-leitenant Pavel Yusupov was also arrested, and he was joined in the cells by Loktionov two days later, Rychagov on 24 June and Volodin on 27 June, the NKVD almost having to dodge bombs to grab their prey. Loktionov, Smushkevich, Shtern, Volodin and Rychagov (together with his wife) would be shot without trial outside Moscow on 28 October 1941, along with seven other generals in what appears to have been an act of NKVD 'house-cleaning'. Pumpur, Levin, Schacht and Yusupov lived on until 23 February 1942, when they all felt the fatal pistol against the back of their necks.

Other marked men were briefly saved including Ptukhin, who had previously been commander of the Leningrad District VVS. His successor, Novikov, was inspecting installations inside the Arctic Circle on 20 June when he was summoned to Moscow. He telephoned Timoshenko the following day to ask why, whereupon he was informed of his transfer to Kiev and replacement by General-maior Aleksandr Nekrasov. He received orders to be in Kiev by 0900hrs on 23 June, so bought a rail ticket then packed his suitcase, but the German invasion meant he remained in Leningrad. On 13 September Novikov would meet Zhukov, an old acquaintance, who observed, 'We tried twice to send you to Kiev but it didn't work.'

Stalin was more concerned with internal threats than the Nazis, and he seemed to sleepwalk through a cacophony of alarm bells from across the border. He even believed Hitler when the latter assured him that the military build-up in the East was to shelter the Army from British bombing! Stalin recognised that Soviet forces were not ready to meet the Germans, and he was desperate to avoid anything that would provoke war with his neighbour. He dismissed all intelligence reports itemising German preparations and intentions, even one from a network of anti-Nazi sympathisers that included members of Schmid's Luftwaffe Intelligence organisation, known to the Germans as Red Chapel (*Rote Kapelle*). When the NKVD passed on a report from 'a reliable Luftwaffe staff source' on 16 June Stalin read it, then said, 'Tell the "source" in the German Air Force General Staff to fuck his mother.'

Rote Kapelle continued to send high quality information for another year but the Gestapo then broke it up aided by GRU stupidity with the radio transmission in clear of the names and addresses of several members. Schmid was sent on 14 October 1942, to command forces in Africa, but he returned to hold important home defence positions to the end of the war. Like him, his successors at the head of Luftwaffe Intelligence were all relatively lowly *Oberste*.[20]

In his near-hysterical desire to avoid giving the Germans an excuse for invasion, Stalin banned the camouflage or dispersal of aircraft at their airfields and countermanded the order for a general blackout, including airfields, issued on his own initiative by Baltic District commander General-polkovnik Fedor Kuznetsov. When PVO units received orders confirming they were not to fire on German reconnaissance aircraft all personnel had to sign a receipt, and one officer whose battery disobeyed in June was lucky to escape execution. The order astonished former artillery chief General-polkovnik Nikolai Voronov, who replaced Shtern, especially as maps plotting the intruders' courses clearly showed German intentions.

All warnings met the same response: 'Don't panic, the Gaffer (*Vozhd*) knows all about it.' Yet even Stalin could not totally ignore the ominous signs in the West, and he reluctantly agreed to take some precautions. On 18 June PVO batteries were informed they were to go on alert in three days' time, and on 19 June Timoshenko authorised camouflage of the airfields. Finally, on the evening of 21 June, a Saturday, Stalin ordered Moscow's air defences on a higher state of alert. Yet the Western Districts' airfields remained exposed and alerts would be hamstrung by the fact that up to a third of the airmen were away from their units. Aircraft were lined up rather than dispersed in an effort to demonstrate to superiors that the units could immediately respond to orders, as well as making it easier to prepare aircraft. There was a shortage of auxiliary equipment such as starters and petrol bowsers and anti-aircraft defences were virtually non-existent, with only a few exposed airfields having multi-barrel rifle-calibre machine guns.

Just after midnight on 21/22 June, Timoshenko and Zhukov telephoned Stalin with new evidence of an imminent invasion, and they were summoned to the Kremlin for a discussion held during a thunderstorm. Stalin reluctantly accepted there would be an attack, but still refused to sanction the generals' demand to place the Western Districts on a war footing and confined the orders to a vague alert. This included a demand for the dispersal and camouflage of all aircraft by dawn on 22 June, but commanders were warned they were 'not to give way to provocative actions of any kind that might produce major complications'. The orders left them bemused, apart from the Odessa District's General-maior Matveii Zakharov, who had already ordered his squadrons to disperse. In most districts Timoshenko's order was not received because German agents and their supporters had cut wire communications. Indeed, in the Western District only 10th Mixed Air Division (*Smeshannaya Aviatsionnaya Diviziya*, SAD) received the order.

The order was more easily issued than executed for Sunday was a day of rest even in the atheist Soviet Union. Most officers and men in the West were enjoying a Saturday night out at the theatre, the cinema, in dance halls and bars, while married men spent what, for many, would prove to be the last time with their families. Meanwhile, troops on the frontier noted an ominous increase in air activity, some involving the dropping of Brandenburg Regiment commandos who joined nationalist sympathisers in cutting telephone wires to begin the disruption of Russian communications.

Across the border as D-Day (*Angriffstag*, A-Tag) approached, the Luftwaffe and the Wehrmacht argued about how the former would open the campaign. Jeschonnek and Waldau wished to strike airfields after the Army's artillery preparation began at dawn, but Halder feared that by then the alerted 'birds' would have flown. The Luftwaffe's argument carried the day with Hitler, who decreed that the air strikes would begin at dawn, although this meant taking off from airfields that often lacked runway lights. The airmen then faced a 40-minute flight through the night and pre-dawn gloom, but the wily *Luftflotten* overcame the problem by using three-aircraft *Ketten* of experienced crews to make the initial attacks upon fighter bases, crossing the border at high altitude then swooping down on their targets.

Meanwhile, the Germans completed their preparations, the *Luftflotte* and *Fliegerkorps* commanders visiting Berlin on 4 June to receive the latest intelligence from Schmid. Eleven days later these same commanders were summoned to Göring's home, Carinhall, for a last-minute pep talk on the same day that OKW informed its eastern armies and the *Luftflotten* that A-Tag would be 22 June at 0330hrs. By now the last bombs, together with boxes of food, ammunition and spares, had reached the supply depots. *Heeresgruppen* staff had also completed their preparations, with Bock providing Kesselring with a list of high priority targets, including the VVS signals centre at Minsk.

As they arrived in the East the bemused Luftwaffe aircrew concluded they were about to strike the Russians, but were unsure exactly when until they were roused around midnight for target briefings and the Führer's proclamation of an Eastern Front designed to pre-empt a Russian attack. By then petrol bowsers had fuelled their aircraft, armourers had cranked bombs into bomb-bays and onto wing racks as *Luftflotten* and army commands transmitted coded messages at 0100hrs to indicate they were ready to attack.

The crews smoked a final cigarette, urinated over tyres or tail fins, wished each other good luck by saying 'Break an arm and a leg' (*Hals und Beinbruchen*) then climbed aboard. Soon a stream of aircraft were taking off and heading towards the glow of dawn. Russian bomber crews were also in the air because on 20 June Zhigarev had ordered an intensive night training programme that saw the last aircraft landing on the morning of the 22nd to be lined up beside the runways. Crews then made their weary way to bed while mechanics conducted checks and prepared to refuel the aircraft, whose unpainted metal finish glittered in the early morning sun.

At 0315hrs (0415hrs Moscow time) there was a glow in the west as German guns began their preparation, while in the east Luftwaffe minelayers swooped low over the approaches to the Russian naval bases of Kronstadt and Sevastopol. As the Wehrmacht crossed the frontier 15 minutes later, the Luftwaffe swooped. Soon the telephones at the Soviet Defence Ministry were ringing incessantly, each with a report of devastating air attacks. The Russians faced the continent's largest and most battle-hardened air force at a time when their own had huge numbers of elderly aircraft lined up on overcrowded air bases. Furthermore, the VVS was hamstrung by poor communications and infrastructure, while simultaneously the NKVD had decimated the leadership cadre. It was the perfect storm!

CHAPTER 2

INVASION AND RETREAT
June 1941 to April 1942

From the morning of Sunday 22 June 1941, the Luftwaffe fell like the wrath of God upon the atheist Soviet Union and helped the Wehrmacht bound eastwards as if in Goethe's seven-league boots, every step bringing catastrophe to the Russians.

The battle for air supremacy opened with two waves striking airfields. The first, involving 47 per cent of the total strike force (637 aircraft), claimed the destruction of 800 aircraft, while the second claimed 700 victims, for a total loss of 35 German aircraft. Much of the damage was inflicted by 1.9kg SD 2 and 10kg SD 10 anti-personnel bomblets that detonated 50 centimetres above the ground with a 12-metre lethal zone, unexploded ordnance providing an instant minefield – although their supersensitive fuses blew up several bombers en route to targets during the day.[1] These missions were so successful that total Luftwaffe losses on the opening day of *Barbarossa* amounted to just 78 aircraft – 61 destroyed or badly damaged by enemy action and 17 in accidents, with a further 89 damaged, including 50 by enemy action.

On A-Tag the Luftwaffe was credited with destroying 1,489 aircraft on the ground and 322 in the air, while ObdL calculated that between 22 June and 5 July the Russians lost 4,990 aircraft, compared with 491 German aircraft destroyed and 316 damaged. These figures included trainers, transports and even aircraft of the former Baltic state air forces, but Russian casualties increased as they recovered from their surprise and began striking back like hornets.[2] The attacks stunned Soviet leaders such as General-maior Sergei Chernykh, commander of the Western District's 9th SAD at Bialystok. His division suffered only light losses to *Fliegerkorps* VIII's initial blow, but failed to disperse the survivors and lost 347 in follow-up attacks; 9th SAD was disbanded on 23 June and the NKVD arrested Chernykh on 9 July for 'criminal inaction' and shot him 18 days later.

A Soviet Defence Ministry report noted the loss of 1,260 aircraft in the West on 22 June, 732 to enemy action, including 528 on the ground, while another 736 either force-landed or suffered major damage in accidents, many directly, or indirectly, due to Luftwaffe action. The report concluded that by 17 July the VVS had lost 1,840 aircraft to enemy action, 767 on the ground, while 1,932 suffered major damage ostensibly not to enemy action. The figures are underestimates, for many units under-reported their losses due to the fear of an NKVD visit. For example, 64th IAD claimed 80 of its 239 fighters destroyed or damaged on 22 June, but the next day recorded its strength at 100. Indeed, on 31 July the VVS staff calculated that 5,240 aircraft were 'unaccounted losses'.

Russian strength returns for 22 and 24 June suggest losses at 3,922 aircraft, including some 2,000 on the first day, while force strength comparisons of 1 June and 24 June suggest the loss of 47 per cent or 3,085 aeroplanes. Kesselring's *Luftflotte* 2 repeated its success of 10 May 1940, by slashing Western District/Front strength by 66 per cent (1,020 aircraft) within two days, while the Luftwaffe noted that by 6 July 1,290 enemy aircraft were in German hands, of which 426 were damaged beyond repair. The Luftwaffe continued to seek out airfields that the Russians belatedly dispersed and camouflaged, aircraft also being daubed with camouflage paint.

Yet because most airmen were away from their bases on 22 June, few were casualties, although many were 'horseless' (*bezloshadnyy*). They drove, or flew, to rear bases to acquire new mounts, sometimes obsolete I-5 biplanes, and in the Baltic states and the Ukraine they sometimes ran the gauntlet of nationalist snipers. Many of those who returned to the fray quickly perished, as the Luftwaffe, during the next fortnight, turned the skies over the western Soviet Union into an aerial abattoir.

Moscow's instructions further delayed the airmen's response. Standing on a cratered airfield surrounded by blazing aircraft and buildings, the Baltic District's 148th IAP commander, Maior Georgii Zaitsev, received a Defence Ministry message ordering him not to respond to 'provocations' or to shoot down aircraft. He exploded, 'They've bombed us, covered us with blood and we aren't allowed to touch them!' Orders to attack the Germans arrived only four hours later.

The Soviet leadership received little information on the main axes of advance because landline communications were cut, while the handful of reconnaissance aircraft that took off were frequently intercepted. Soviet signallers were slow to restore landlines, while district staffs were reluctant to use radios because they were unfamiliar with them. Generals were left to guess where the 'Fascists' were advancing, selecting the most likely areas in a concept known as 'bombing off the map'. The surviving Frontal Aviation bombers, mostly SBs, with a sprinkling of 'Peshkas', began to take off from mid-morning, while the DBA, transferred to Zhigarev's operational control at 0644hrs Moscow time, spent much of the morning with patriotic rallies. It eventually received orders from about 1000hrs, with bombers rolling down the runways in the early afternoon.

Because there was no time to contact the fighter fields, even in the same division, the bombers usually flew unescorted. Few regiments had mastered formation flying, and the formidable German flak often broke up the flocks to expose the hapless crews to shark-like fighter attack. Opposite *Luftflotte* 2, the last 18 airworthy SBs of 39th SBAP were shot down in flames attacking the German spearheads because they lacked self-sealing fuel tanks. The loss of 64 bombers on the ground and in the air left 13th BAD with three operational aircraft by the end of the day, while in the DBA's 3rd AK, of 70 DBs dispatched by 96th AP DD, 22 were lost and another blew up on take-off. Many returning aircraft had wounded onboard, but the airfields did not have enough ambulances to take them all to hospital.

Russian generals who were unable to impose their will upon the battlefield made ever more strident demands for action, irrespective of its relevance. On 26 June Western District/Front commander General Dimitrii Pavlov demanded 1st Heavy Bomber Regiment (*Tyazhyoly Bombardirovchnyy Aviatsionnyy Polk*, TBAP) of 3rd AK bomb a river crossing in broad daylight from a cloudless sky. Regimental commander Polkovnik Ivan Filippov protested, 'This guarantees the death of the entire regiment. It will be a useless death which will be a gift to the fascists.' Pavlov retorted. 'You coward! The regiment will take off immediately and you will report on its performance!' Filippov took his time preparing his aircraft and successfully attacked at night, while another regimental commander who obeyed Pavlov's order lost all three TBs. Pavlov was justifiably desperate as his command disintegrated, and four days later he was arrested by the NKVD and shot on 22 July.

German fighter claims reflected the scale of the slaughter. On 6 July Major Johannes Trautloft's JG 54 (*Luftflotte* 1) was credited with 65 out of 73 bombers attacking a German bridgehead near Ostrov, while two days later Major Günther Lützow's JG 3 (*Luftflotte* 4) was caught on the ground by 27 bombers but took off and claimed them all. On 12 July, also in *Luftflotte* 4, Hauptmann Richard Leppla shot down JG 51's 500th victim of the campaign, while Oberstleutnant Werner 'Vatti' (Daddy) Mölders, *Kommodore* of JG 51, claimed his 100th and 101st victories within three days. On 19 July he was appointed *Inspekteur der Jagdflieger* and withdrawn from operations. The Soviet bomber force lashed out like blinded giants, but their blows were rarely effective and their routes marked by towering columns of black smoke or the descent of distinctive square parachutes. Fighters and assault aircraft roamed randomly along the front and some Russian fighter pilots were so desperate that they rammed the enemy when they ran out of ammunition in what would be called Taran attacks.[3] On the first day of the invasion Soviet airmen reportedly flew 6,000 sorties between the Arctic and the Black Sea, but many simply circled their airfields to shield them from attack in combat air patrols. Those that struck the invader brought back grossly optimistic reports of damage inflicted – 200 enemy aircraft destroyed by the end of the first day and 662 by the end of June were figures quoted in reports their superiors triumphantly sent back to Moscow.

Many of these superiors sought to appease Stalin as the Luftwaffe exploited its air superiority to support the mechanised spearheads. German plans for airborne forces to support their spearheads were doomed by May 1941's slaughter of airborne units in Crete, although on 25 June some 35 commandos of Regiment Brandenburg dropped to take bridges over the Dvina near Bogdanov ahead of Leeb. From 25 June the Luftwaffe concentrated upon 'vertical envelopment' (*vertikalen Umfassung*) through direct and indirect army support (*unmittelbare* and *mittelbare Heeresunterstützung*), dropping a monthly average of 23,270 tonnes of bombs to the end of November.

Crews flew intensively in the long, bright, summer days – five to eight daily sorties for fighter pilots, four to six for *Kampfgruppen* and seven or eight for *Stukagruppen*. Direct support involved attacks on obstacles to progress, while indirect support focused upon communication routes, specifically roads and railways, to prevent the enemy rallying. Within hours of the invasion Soviet troops found their storage depots laid waste, trains trapped in sidings or on exposed stretches of railway line, landline communications cut and every road movement attracting a rain of bombs. Their 7th Tank Division lost 63 of 368 tanks and all of its transport in a 14-hour march, but attacks upon rail marshalling yards, often at low level, proved less effective than expected. Instead, the Luftwaffe struck open stretches of line both to destroy rolling stock and to make several cuts in the line, which might take up to six hours to repair.

The Russians soon restricted daylight movement to small groups, and by entering brooding woods and forests whenever a reconnaissance aircraft appeared, saved themselves but prevented their commanders exercising effective control. The *Kampfgruppen* used one or two *Ketten* per *Gruppe* to fly armed reconnaissance missions, which attacked targets of opportunity, while Stukas and bombers disrupted counter-attacks before they could begin. The crude road system meant that the chokepoints were at river crossings, rather than towns or villages, troop concentrations being hit from 1,000–1,200 metres. To avoid 'friendly fire' incidents the ground

TABLE II-1: NEW RUSSIAN ORGANISATION JUNE 1941

District	Front
Leningrad	North
Baltic	Northwest
Western	West
Kiev	Southwest
Odessa	South

forces displayed signal panels, used pyrotechnics and carried the Reichsbanner on their vehicles, yet even this did not guarantee safety. Luftwaffe attacks enabled the mechanised forces to drive deep into enemy territory, envelop whole armies and force the VVS to abandon airfields, workshops and supply depots. This disrupted attempts to stop the advance, while in the chaos unserviceable aircraft were destroyed together with serviceable aircraft that lacked fuel or pilots.

Almost immediately the frontier military districts were redesignated Fronts (see Table II-1), and on 10 July Stavka created a VVS command for the Northwest, West and Southwest Directions, adding another layer of command to a force that was shrinking every day. By now the VVS on the main front had only 1,679 aircraft, the DBA had 688 bombers and the PVO in the West had 1,179 fighters.

From 15 July shortages saw regimental establishments halved to 30 aircraft, with Stavka using the surplus aeroplanes to form a reserve under its own control. From 21 July the VVS was ordered to create flexible task forces or Reserve Air Groups (*Rezervnaya Aviatsionnaya Gruppa*, RAG) each of several regiments and up to 100 aircraft, although the first, 2nd RAG, was not activated until 18 August. The shortage of long range reconnaissance aircraft meant the role was assigned on 3 July to Golovanov's 212th OAP DD, although its DBs had to receive extra armour and improved armament prior to performing this demanding mission.

Meanwhile, the crises multiplied in the West starting with the West Front, where Kopets faced Kesselring, Loerzer (*Fliegerkorps* II) and Richthofen (*Fliegerkorps* VIII). Kesselring was the perpetual optimist, hence his nickname of 'Smiling Albert', who concealed an unhappy marriage. Richthofen, a cousin of the famed 'Red Baron', was a minor air ace in his own right and an extremely able professional who had trained at Lipetsk. He played a major role developing the aircraft the Luftwaffe used in Russia, and his *Fliegerkorps*, with its Stukas, was nicknamed the *Nahkampffliegerkorps* (Close Air Support Corps), although he had opposed Ju 87 development. Loerzer was Göring's old comrade-in-arms and a major air ace in World War I, but his post-war life had been such an anti-climax that for a time he worked as a cigar salesman. Personally brave, he was no staff officer, and was criticised by the Army. He would eventually be kicked upstairs after involvement in corruption scandals.

Kesselring opened his campaign by striking 26 Western District airfields, while Loerzer systematically neutralised every fighter base within a 300-kilometre arc before he and Guderian reprised their previous year's success on the Meuse. But Guderian was soon grumbling as Loerzer's airfields were left behind by the rapidly advancing Panzers. Kesselring quickly transferred the tactical air support task to 'Old Eagle' (World War I airman) and former Lufthansa pilot Generalmajor Martin Fiebig, who became *Nahkampfführer* II, although he was handicapped by a shortage of radios. There was little strategic reconnaissance undertaken once *Barbarossa* began, and photographic interpretation was sometimes poor. Indeed, on 27 June horse-drawn vehicles were hammered near Orsha after being mistaken for tanks. The strain on everyone was considerable, and on 28 June Kesselring's signals chief, Generalmajor Gotthard Seidel, committed suicide.

Kopets had commanded fighters in Spain and been Deputy Commander of the Leningrad District VVS during the Winter War, but the scale of the Western District overwhelmed him for, like Udet, he disliked 'flying a desk' and preferred to supervise training on the new fighters. When the Germans attacked, his chief-of-staff was in a Moscow hospital and his replacement was a logistics specialist, leaving Kopets steering a rudderless ship. He quickly lost touch with his forward airfields, and although he ordered the bombers to smite the enemy, he had neither the means nor experience to coordinate attacks upon

Guderian. Losses were heavy as a result. On the first day his surviving aircraft reported flying 1,896 sorties, but 204 were lost in the air and four crashed or force-landed.

On 23 June Kopets flew over his wrecked fighter fields, returned to his headquarters and shot himself. He was replaced by his deputy, General-maior Andrei Taiurskii, who reported to Moscow the next day that eight of his 28 regiments had been wiped out and four were down to a single aircraft. West Front strength evaporated like the morning dew from 512 aeroplanes on 24 June to 465 on 30 June and 369 on 10 July. Taiurskii also suffered from the worst communications problems in the western VVS, and it was not until 25 June that they were restored, leaving squadrons to fight private wars in the meantime. The West Front's poor response to the crisis inevitably attracted punishment, and the Red Army's political chief, the loathed General-polkovnik Lev Mekhlis, demanded a purge that included Taiurskii. He was arrested on 2 July and executed shortly thereafter, being replaced by Polkovnik Nikolai Naumenko, the former commander of the Leningrad District's 2nd SAD.

Nothing could stop Bock's remorseless progress, despite 37 per cent of West Front's 9,067 sorties in July being bomber attacks upon mechanised spearheads in response to Stavka demands, the 1,206 tonnes of bombs dropped having little effect. It was difficult to find the FEBA because troops feared inviting enemy air attack and failed to mark out their front lines, while in-flight targeting by coded radio messages proved a failure. Losses were heavy, and some mortally wounded bombers deliberately, or accidentally, crashed into columns. Aircraft also tried to support Red Army mechanised counter-attacks directly and indirectly – for example, 70 TB-3s brought in 150 tonnes of fuel on 30 June for a push at Grodno.

To prevent Smolensk's isolation the West Front was reinforced on 10 July by 120 bombers of 3rd AK DD and 150 aircraft of the newly formed Reserve Front VVS under General-maior Boris Pogrebov, the former Ural District VVS commander. Naumenko was ordered to coordinate air operations in this area.[4] A Central Front VVS was created on 24 July under General-maior Grigorii Vorozheikin – another former

NKVD 'guest' – with 75 serviceable aircraft to bring total air strength around Smolensk to 300 aeroplanes, but by 1 August the West Front was down to 180 aircraft. Former South Front VVS commander General-maior Fyodor Michugin commanded it from 16 August, and during that month it flew 6,930 sorties and dropped 1,060 tonnes of bombs.

Operations around Smolensk from 10 to 31 July turned from relieving encircled troops to barricading the road to Moscow, the VVS flying 5,200 sorties supported by 220 DBA bombers. South of Smolensk, the Bryansk Front was created on 16 August under the command of General-maior Fedor Polynin. Although the former CO of 13th BAD had only 138 serviceable aircraft and a few bombers at his disposal, he repeatedly struck Guderian during the course of 4,816 sorties between 18 August and 24 September.

Richthofen provided effective support for the spearheads through the *Flivo*, with the shortest response time generally being two hours. *Fliegerkorps* VIII had almost all the Stukas, while Loerzer, who relied upon *Kampfgruppen* or *Zerstörerrgruppen* for close air support and battlefield interdiction, saw a steady stream of losses to ground fire. As the Germans drove eastwards they encountered vast amounts of equipment that seemed to confirm Hitler's claim that they had pre-empted a Russian attack. Yet frequent moves and the difficulty supplying units in the front line cut Luftwaffe sortie rates. *Luftflotte* 2 flew 2,272 sorties on A-Tag, 1,027 on 26 June, 862 the next day and 260 on 29 June, while the number of serviceable aircraft fell from 1,752 on 22 June to 960 a week later. This reflected a general decline in operational aircraft in the East from 2,272 on 22 June to 1,544 on 10 July and 1,654 on 10 August.

With the Luftwaffe's help, Bock's *Panzergruppen* enveloped the Soviet Belorussian armies at Minsk (27 June) and then at Smolensk (16 July), where Kesselring's strike force contained the enemy. It was also an 'equaliser' for the overstretched troops, although on one occasion Major Otto Weiss' II.(*Schl*)/LG 2 repeated its experience in Arras 13 months earlier and had to defend its own base. Overcrowded airstrips were sometimes threatened, and the German groundcrews or 'black men' (*Schwarzemänner*) had the extra burden of defending them.[5] This did not prevent Halder peevishly complaining after a meeting with Waldau on 1 July that ObdL's plans were 'in an absolute muddle'.

Before the Smolensk pocket was reduced, Richthofen was transferred northwards on 3 August to *Luftflotte* 1 with nine *Gruppen* (293 aircraft), leaving two *Stukagruppen* with Loerzer, who now had 19 *Gruppen* with 600 aircraft to support *Heeresgruppe Mitte*. The sudden decline of Luftwaffe strength, aggravated by bad weather, saw a brief renaissance of Russian air power, skilfully directed by Polynin, around the German salient of Yelna, east of Smolensk. Despite all of Kesselring's efforts the salient was abandoned early in September.

Richthofen's move reflected Hitler's strategic incoherence, for while OKH wished to continue the advance on Moscow, OKW *Weisung Nr 21* demanded that once the Russian forces in Belorussia were destroyed, Leeb's advance on Leningrad would have priority. *Weisung Nr 33* of 10 July confirmed this strategy, but also demanded Kesselring fly retaliatory attacks on Moscow – that day he received three of six *Kampfgruppen* (58 bombers) transferred from *Luftflotte* 3 in the West, the others going to Keller's *Fliegerkorps* I.

Unlike Kesselring, Keller's *Luftflotte* 1, with only Förster's *Fliegerkorps* I and Wild's *Fliegerführer Ostsee*, faced odds of two-to-one, but he was undaunted. His initial assault was successful, and helped Generaloberst Erich Hoepner's *Panzergruppe* 4 push into the former Baltic states, but fierce resistance and limited resources temporarily halted them until Richthofen's arrival.

The first attacks upon Ionov's squadrons left only 4th SAD unscathed at Tallinn, some 600 kilometres from the border, and the forward regiments licking their wounds. Ionov flew 2,000 sorties on the first day but lost 98 aircraft, many of them unescorted bombers. The DBA was also active, with 3rd AK DD's attacks on Hoepner's *Panzergruppe* 4 joined on 25 June by 1st AK DD, yet the Northwest Front's strength rapidly evaporated from 703 aircraft on 24 June to 181 aircraft (56 bombers) six days later, and 155 aeroplanes by 10 July.

On 25 June the NKVD arrested Ionov and most of the Northwest Front VVS staff, apart from his deputy General-maior Ivan Zhuravlev.

Ionov would be shot on 23 February 1942 for 'mismanagement, sabotage and links with the enemies of the people', yet the front commander and his staff were merely dismissed and demoted on 10 July. This may reflect the fact that the front had not disintegrated, yet the VVS remained a rudderless ship until 1 July, when General-maior Timofei Kutsevalov was brought in from the Far East to discover his command existed largely in name only.

As he approached Leningrad, Keller, a World War I bomber baron nicknamed 'Bombshelter' (*Bombenkeller*), faced a more formidable opponent in Novikov's North Front VVS. Novikov, the son of a peasant, had come into aviation accidentally when, as an infantry officer, he won a raffle for a short flight then switched to the VVS. He possessed a brisk efficiency and attention to detail that his superiors appreciated, and was fortunate that his opponents, the Finns, lacked the strength and will to destroy him on the ground, although he suffered no such inhibitions. Novikov's campaign from 25 June to 1 July succeeded, but his bomber force dropped from 428 to 223 by 10 July. Yet on that date he still had 837 aircraft, while the Leningrad PVO's 7th IAK under Polkovnik Stepan Danilov had 232 fighters. It was little wonder, therefore, that Zhukov, sent to supervise operations in the Ukraine during June, wanted Novikov to head the Southwest Front VVS. Only the intervention of Leningrad Party chief Zhdanov kept him in the north.

Novikov learned of Ionov's arrest from Zhuravlev, who assumed command of an air group covering the southwestern approaches to Leningrad as the PVO hastily removed RUS-1 radars. Their poor performance meant they were decommissioned by 17 August and replaced by four RUS-2s, whose prototype had made its combat debut as recently as 3 July. Novikov was stripped of forces to meet the new threat, but to combat the Finns he could rely on the cooperation of both General-maior Mikhail Samokhin, who would command the VVS-KBF throughout the war, and Danilov, who came under his formal operational control on 14 August.

When formed 7th IAK had 225 fighters but only 203 pilots, although it was quickly reinforced. During June it flew more than 1,900 sorties, which had risen to 7,286 by the end of July – 97 per cent were interceptions, including engaging the first bombing raid on 20 July. In late July the North Front had 759 aircraft, of which 592 were defending Leningrad, and it received only 34 replacements. During this time Starshii Leitenant Petr Pokryshev of 154th IAP was developing the 'master' and 'slave' fighter formation, although three-man formations remained the official norm. Novikov turned a blind eye to this disobedience.[6]

Soviet intelligence quickly learned of Richthofen's arrival and Novikov realised it heralded a new offensive. But while with *Weisung Nr 33* and the arrival of Richthofen all seemed set for an advance to Leningrad, *Fliegerkorps* VIII's orders were actually to support only Generaloberst Georg von Küchler's 18 *Armee* as it advanced along the coast until it isolated Leningrad by cutting the railway to Moscow. For some reason this was not communicated to the commander of OKH, Generalfeldmarschall Walther von Brauchitsch, Leeb or Keller.

The assault was renewed on 8 August in heavy rain, which restricted German air support on eight days and grounded it on three. Richthofen hammered the enemy, and the ferocity of his operations shocked Leeb, who described him as 'merciless'. Over 12 days *Fliegerkorps* VIII flew 5,042 sorties and dropped 3,351 tonnes of bombs, including 98 containers of incendiaries, to help 18 *Armee* reach Leningrad's suburbs at the price of 27 aircraft shot down and 143 damaged.[7] From 10 to 30 August Keller flew 17,591 sorties, including 11,108 strike, with five sorties a day being normal, at the cost of 81 aircraft. However, by mid-August half his aircraft were unserviceable.

On 10 August Novikov had 560 combat aircraft, of which 418 faced the Germans, and four days later he was reinforced by 126 naval aircraft. The naval airmen had been heavily involved, and by 21 August had lost 175 aircraft, including many lumbering MBR-2 flying boats. Meanwhile, from the first hour of the invasion, the Luftwaffe began to neutralise the Soviet naval presence – the largest in the Baltic – when Wild's aircraft laid mines outside Leningrad. Until the Baltic iced up in December Wild's airmen sank with bombs or mines six destroyers, 15 small warships and two auxiliaries, as well as 48 merchantmen (82,061grt).

Most were sunk when the Baltic Fleet abandoned its base in Tallinn between 27 and 29 August and ran the gauntlet of air attacks as it sailed to sanctuary in Leningrad's Kronstadt naval base. Of 27,800 passengers, many of them wounded, some 11,000 were lost, including 3,000 civilians (mostly Party officials and their families). The minelaying force was augmented in August by II./KG 4, but Wild's aircraft were also used to sweep naval minefields by bombing them. Wild also supported the capture of islands off Estonia during *Unternehmen Beowulf* I/II, which included a gliderborne assault by commandos who were supplied by four Me 321 Gigant (Giant) gliders. He was then confined to operations in the western Gulf of Finland, although allowed to attack the White Sea–Baltic Canal until his command was disbanded on 27 October. His staff was kept together, and early in the New Year moved to the Crimea as *Flfü Süd*.

To meet the threat to Leningrad the North Front was split in two on 23 August, and Novikov became air commander of the new Leningrad Front with 327 aircraft, as PVO air and artillery regiments engaged the Wehrmacht. Novikov fought off all Red Army efforts to fragment his forces and focused upon high-intensity ground attacks. He also created an area where a few of his exhausted pilots could take turns to rest – a foresight shared by few other Russian air leaders. The radar defences of the city were joined, and then replaced, by five RUS-2s. With a range of 140 kilometres and greatly increased reliability, this equipment allowed Danilov, who was replaced by Polkovnik Evgenii Erlykhin on 26 September, to reduce patrols and instead scramble fighters to meet radar-detected threats. This reduced the wear and tear inflicted upon 7th IAK fighters, thus extending their operational lives.

By the time the Wehrmacht was at Leningrad's doors in early September, the Leningrad Front had 381 aircraft, augmented by 152 naval aeroplanes, while Keller had 1,004 aircraft, 481 of which were serviceable. Both sides were reinforced in early September, the Germans with Ju 87Rs and the Russians with 139 assorted aircraft, which gave Novikov 424 serviceable aeroplanes, excluding Danilov's fighters. On 2 September Keller began his assault upon Leningrad, briefly rested two days later, then renewed the assault by flying 1,004 sorties (600 strike) on the 6th. Novikov, by contrast, flew only 339, including 36 bomber sorties.

That day Hitler announced a new change in strategic direction, with his priorities being the destruction of Soviet forces in the Ukraine and the securing of a front line along the River Dnieper. On Bock's right, Guderian had begun advancing southwards on 23 August, but, as a concession to Brauchitsch and Halder, an advance upon Moscow, *Unternehmen Taifun* (Typhoon), would follow. Keller and Leeb were stunned by an order to transfer half of Leeb's command, including Richthofen, to Kesselring by 15 September, and Leeb's last-ditch attempt to retain Richthofen on 12 September was rebuffed by OKH, which said *Taifun* had priority.

Keller had already secured a major success on 8 September when his bombers destroyed many of the warehouses holding Leningrad's food stocks, leaving it with only 45 days of supplies. Leningrad Party boss Zhdanov failed either to restock them or to evacuate civilians as the Germans began to isolate the city, and these factors contributed to the city's notorious winter famine. By 12 September the Germans were only 15 kilometres from the city centre as the VVS-KBF shielded a bridgehead to the west around Orianbaum.

As a sop Keller was allowed to retain Oberst Oskar Dinort's StG 2 to pick off the Baltic Fleet at Kronstadt, which was defended by 40 navy fighters that flew 680 sorties and a RUS-2 radar which appeared to have contributed little to the defence. A four-day campaign involving some 400 sorties began on 20 September, but the 250kg and 500kg bombs had little effect on the larger warships, forcing Richthofen to order one-tonne armour-piercing ordnance. These were used from the 21st day when Rudel split the battleship *Marat* in two, but the offensive ultimately proved disappointing. Two destroyers, two submarines and three smaller warships, along with three merchantmen (4,205grt), were sunk, while another battleship, two cruisers, four destroyers, three submarines and an auxiliary vessel were damaged at the cost of six aircraft, mostly to ground fire. The defending naval fighters were ineffective because they were committed in small formations at low and medium altitude to avoid anti-aircraft fire.

By then the remaining VVS squadrons had all but melted away through transfers and losses – by 14 September Novikov had only 268 aircraft. The pressure eased with Richthofen's departure, Keller flying only 4,801 sorties in October compared with 16,119 the previous month, and the effort would halve every month through to the end of the year.[8] From 16 October Keller helped the Wehrmacht creep towards Lake Ladoga, which was reached at Tikhvin, some 175 kilometres east of Leningrad, on November 8 to complete the city's isolation. To hold the town *Flfü Tikhvin* was established under Oberst Hans Raithal, *Kommodore* of KG 77, but his airfield was exposed. Indeed, a Soviet counter-attack retook the town on 9 December, in a month when Keller flew 1,986 sorties.

The loss of *Fliegerkorps* VIII began a slow decline for *Luftflotte* 1, which was left with some 250 aircraft. Keller tried to maintain pressure upon the city and its defenders through bombing but this ceased from 19 December and was not renewed until 4 April 1942. Fortunately for Keller, Novikov was also in dire straits as his command withered away, with serviceable strength dropping from 254 aircraft in late October to 216 by the end of November and 175 by the New Year.

The immediate crisis had passed but the starving people of Leningrad were dying in the streets as Moscow sought to overcome Zhdanov's terrible errors. A GVF fleet, which grew to 70 Li-2s and TB-3s, began flying up to six sorties a day from 20 September. When the Germans reached Lake Ladoga this was halved and, to compensate, aircraft were heavily overloaded, carrying up to three tonnes of supplies – twice their permitted load. German fighters proved a hazard, but fighter cover and escort were soon provided, the latter with auxiliary fuel tanks. By December the transports had brought in 5,042 tonnes of supplies and mail, together with 3,000 troops, and evacuated women and children.

With the arrival of winter the transports had to contend with strong winds and ice. Lake Ladoga froze over, and from the night of 22/23 November a road, the 'Road of Life' (*Doroga Zhizni*), was built across it and usually covered by naval fighters, including British-supplied Hurricanes, Tomahawks and Kittyhawks, to provide the city with a tenuous lifeline. The fighters had radar to provide GCI and in February 1942 a separate command was established under one of Novikov's deputies, General-maior Vasilii Zhdanov (no relation to the Party leader), to shield the lifeline until the thaw. Between November and April 1942 it brought in 339,500 tonnes of supplies, including 224,500 tonnes of food, covered by 5,000 of 7th IAK's 12,600 sorties in this period.

Novikov's dynamic defence contrasted positively with the performance of most other district commanders, and Zhdanov was especially impressed. On 1 February he summoned Novikov to his sick bed and informed him he had been urgently summoned to Moscow. Given the fate of his colleagues, the news probably sent a tingle of fear down Novikov's spine, but he departed in the front's only serviceable 'Peshka'. Bad weather delayed his arrival until 3 February, when he was officially informed he would be Zhigarev's First Deputy Commander, and be replaced by his chief-of-staff, General-maior Stepan Rybalchenko. Novikov met Stalin that evening and, after familiarising himself with the situation, began work on 5 February.

German progress in the Ukraine was slower than in the northern theatres because the initial assault of *Luftflotte* 4 under Löhr was less successful, while Russian resistance in the air and on the ground proved fiercer than elsewhere. Löhr, the turncoat one-time Austrian Air Force commander, and his Romanian allies opened their campaign by striking 23 Kiev and 11 Odessa District airfields. The Russians reported that the districts lost 277 and 23 aircraft, respectively, but some sources put Odessa's losses at 50. These attacks continued during the following days, and Southwest Front noted by the end of June it had lost 911 aircraft – 697 to enemy action, including 304 on the ground, and 276 damaged aircraft abandoned, while another 214 were lost in accidents. This left 568 aircraft, of which a third were unserviceable, and although Ptukhin's airmen flew some 600 sorties a day until the end of June, nearly half were to cover communications or in a vain effort to win air superiority.

Ptukhin was one of Southwest Front's most capable officers, having distinguished himself as the Winter War air commander. His preparations for the invasion of Bessarabia in 1940 impressed the demanding Zhukov, who recommended Ptukhin as PVO head in February 1941. Ptukhin was unhappy in this role and successfully requested a return to the Kiev District within a month, but the district's air defence was doomed by the decision to move his headquarters by rail on 22 June from Kiev to join General-polkovnik Mikhail Kirponos' Southwest Front headquarters at Tarnopol. Restoring command and control from there proved difficult because of slashed landlines and a reluctance to use radios, so coordination often depended upon couriers in U-2s. In the power vacuum created by the German invasion, division and corps commanders simply fought private wars that added to the butcher's bill, and it is likely that in the chaos an SB regiment accidentally bombed a Hungarian town to bring Budapest into the war on the German side. Then the NKVD drove a bulldozer into the train-wreck.

Ptukhin had barely arrived in Tarnopol when the NKVD demanded, on 23 June, the dismissal of his chief-of-staff, General-maior Nikolai Laskin. Then Ptukhin was summoned to NKVD headquarters on 3 July and arrested, followed by Laskin nine days later, with both facing charges of being part of a 'counter-revolutionary conspiracy', although they were not shot until 23 February 1942, possibly during another round of NKVD house-clearing. Ptukhin's replacement was General-leitenant Feodor Astakhov, the VVS Director of Equipment, who had commanded the Kiev District in 1937–39. He arrived to be met by his old driver, who informed him that he had just delivered Ptukhin to NKVD headquarters and been told not to wait!

The shambles deprived Southwestern Front of adequate air support, with no more than 400 sorties being flown a day, which caused the mechanised forces to be smashed when a counter-offensive against Rundstedt's left from 24 June was routed. Greim's *Fliegerkorps* V played a major role in thwarting this effort, flying 360 sorties on 26 June alone for the loss of 21 aircraft. Its aircraft interdicted roads, causing the Russians severe shortages of fuel and ammunition, then struck armoured concentrations. German bombers proved a major threat to enemy artillery, but with fighters committed to air superiority operations, there were few for escort missions. The *Kampfgruppen* suffered heavily, partly

Many Luftwaffe fighter pilots cut their operational teeth on Tupolev's twin-engined SB-2 and -3 bombers during the opening stages of the air war in the East. Among the hundreds brought down was this example being inspected by army troops on the central sector. *(via John Weal)*

An impressive line-up of 'Doras' of 3./StG 77. The bareheaded figure on the left of the group is Feldwebel Herbert Rabben, who was considered by many to be one of the best pilots ever to fly with StG 77. He would be awarded the Knight's Cross after the *Geschwader's* incorporation into the *Schlacht* arm. *(via John Weal)*

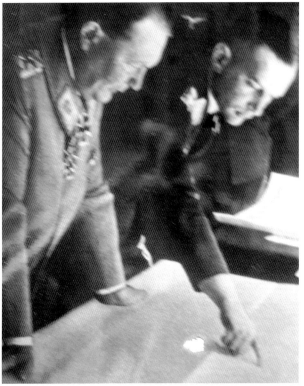

Reichsmarschall Hermann Göring and *General der Flieger* Hans Jeschonnek examine a map at ObdL headquarters. Chief-of-staff Jeschonnek was the executive commander of the Luftwaffe, which made him the whipping boy for the lazy Göring, who was always happy to take the plaudits. (*Der Adler*)

A German bomber strikes an airfield on 22 June 1941, when the Luftwaffe enjoyed its greatest success. Russian records indicate that by 17 July the Soviet Union had lost at least 4,500 aircraft, and it took two years for the VVS to recover. (*Der Adler*)

ABOVE • A *Nahaufklärungstaffeln* observer makes a last-minute check of his map while a *Schwarzermänner* runs the engine. The backbone of these *Staffeln* in 1941 was the Hs 126, nicknamed 'Crutches' (*Kostii*) by the Russians because of its metal wing braces. (*Der Adler*)

RIGHT • A Stuka tail gunner photographed the successful cutting of a Russian railway line as the aircraft pulls out of its dive. With few hard-topped roads in the Soviet Union, railways were vital to both sides for large-scale transport, especially during the spring and autumn thaws. (*Der Adler*)

The bombed rail bridge near Vitebsk in 1941. Bridges were the easiest way across Russia's great rivers, and their destruction could trap armies, as the Germans discovered in Belorussia in 1944. (*Der Adler*)

In the early days of *Barbarossa* the *Kampfgruppen* pounded Russian installations, including barracks. Here, a Ju 88 circles burning buildings as the crew assess their success. (*Der Adler*)

The losses suffered during the opening days and weeks of *Barbarossa* were not all one-sided. This A-5 of 8./KG 76 – note the jettisoned cabin canopy in foreground – was lucky to make it back to Schippenbeil for a belly landing after being hit by Soviet anti-aircraft fire. (*via John Weal*)

Given III./JG 3's somewhat dubious powers of aircraft recognition during the opening stages of *Barbarossa*, it would be interesting to speculate what this victorious pilot – returning to base southwest of Zhitomir, wings waggling to indicate a kill – is going to claim. In fact, on the date this photograph was taken, the *Gruppe* contented itself with a quartet of DB-3 bombers and a dozen assorted Polikarpov fighters. (*via John Weal*)

The thaws or *rasputitsa* had a devastating effect upon air operations by reducing grass-covered airfields to marshes. Here, an airman walks across duckboards during such a period at a Stuka base. Grass-covered airfields did have one advantage – they could be used whatever the wind direction. (*Der Adler*)

The Germans quickly learned that once the Russians had established a bridgehead across a river it was extremely difficult to drive them out. Such bridgeheads might be supplied by raft, rubber dinghies or pontoon bridges. Here, a *Panzerjäger* Ju 87G strafes a pontoon footbridge. (*Der Adler*)

A Stuka flies low over a German tank as smoke and dust from bombed defences rises over a Russian battlefield. Close air support became a major role for the Stukas, and General Wolfram von Richthofen once claimed his Ju 87s were operating within grenade-throwing range of the German infantry. (*Der Adler*)

The Il-2 ground-attack aircraft, usually called 'Ilyushas', were normally for close air support, striking defensive positions or hunting tanks with their 37mm cannon or PTAB hollow-charge bombs. (*Courtesy of the Central Museum of the Armed Forces, Moscow via Stavka*)

Low-level attacks took the 'Ilyushas' into intense ground fire and aircraft frequently required patching up like this one. The robust Il-2s were very popular with their crews, despite the very dangerous work they faced daily. (*Courtesy of the Central Museum of the Armed Forces, Moscow via Stavka*)

Before climbing into their 'Ilyusha', Assault Troopers (*Shturmoviks*) make a last-minute check of the map to determine the exact location of friendly troops and their targets to avoid 'friendly fire' incidents. (*Courtesy of the Central Museum of the Armed Forces, Moscow via Stavka*)

An Li-2 transport ready to receive passengers at a forward airfield. The Li-2 was not a licence-built DC-3 but rather a Russianised-version with inferior performance to the few C-47s received under Lend–Lease. (*From the files of the RGAKFD in Krasnogorsk via Stavka*)

Russian aircraft strafe Ju 88s at what appears to be a recently occupied airfield in central or north Russia, since it lacks revetments. Attacks on Luftwaffe airfields were always a gamble because they were strongly defended. (*Courtesy of the Central Museum of the Armed Forces, Moscow via Stavka*)

III./KG 51 joined II. *Gruppe* at Balti at the end of August 1941 fresh from its re-equipment in the Reich. The unit's new A-4s sport the bright yellow trim indicative of a III. *Gruppe*. In KG 51's case this was applied to the front edge of the engine nacelles and as a thin outline to the *Geschwader* badge. It is believed that the spinner colours identified the *Staffel* within the *Gruppe*. (*via John Weal*)

A pair of *Friedrichs* from III./JG 51 pictured on the central sector in the autumn of 1941. (*via John Weal*)

'Black men' (*Schwarzemänner*) push a Ju 52/3m free from the ice and snow so it can take off. The Russian winter proved a severe challenge for the Luftwaffe, especially in 1941–42 when engines froze and tools broke. (*Der Adler*)

Hero of the Soviet Union Snr Lt A A Lipilin of 41st IAP. By October 1941 he had flown 112 sorties and claimed eight and three shared victories, as well as numerous targets destroyed on the ground. Flying on the northwest front, Lipilin survived the war. (*Dmitriy Khazanov and Andrey Yurgenson*)

MiG-3 pilot Jr Lt Verkhovtsev of 72nd SAP, Northern Fleet Air Force. (*Dmitriy Khazanov and Andrey Yurgenson*)

Inverted and in flames, an Il-2 falls to earth. The original one-man 'Ilyushas' were nicknamed 'Hunchbacks' (*Gorbatii*), but the need for a rear-gunner soon became obvious. Regiments originally modified their aircraft in the field until the Il-2m3s began to roll off the production lines. (*Nik Cornish at www.Stavka.org.uk*)

A group of MiG-3s from 7th IAK fly in loose formation over central Leningrad. The high tower of the famous Peter and Paul Cathedral on the north bank of the Neva River can be seen below the fighters. (*Dmitriy Khazanov and Andrey Yurgenson*)

This 9th IAP MiG-3 hit trees while making a forced-landing following engine failure shortly after take-off. (*Dmitriy Khazanov and Andrey Yurgenson*)

Pilots of 124th IAP, which was involved in the defence of Moscow during the second half of 1941. These men are, from left to right, Dmitriy Zanin, Aleksander Pronin, Nikolay Tsisarenko and Grigoriy Ivanchenko. (*Dmitriy Khazanov and Andrey Yurgenson*)

Aircraft production chief Generaloberst Ernst Udet (left) and his fighter chief Major Werner 'Vatti' (Daddy) Mölders. The latter was summoned to Udet's funeral following his suicide on 17 November 1941, but perished in a flying accident en route. (*Der Adler*)

The Bf 110 *Zerstörer* (long range fighter) was increasingly used, like this ZG 1 aircraft in the winter of 1941–42, as a long range fighter-bomber. By late 1943 even this role was becoming impossible. (*Der Adler*)

A nurse supervises the loading of a stretcher into an S-2, the medical evacuation version of the U-2/Po-2. The ADD and GVF used Li-2s to take the wounded for long-term treatment in the interior. (*Courtesy of the Central Museum of the Armed Forces, Moscow via Stavka*)

The first winter of the war in Russia took a heavy toll on men and machines alike. Here, a seemingly endless line of railway flatbed wagons has been loaded with damaged Ju 88s for transportation to the rear for major repair work. (*via John Weal*)

During the winter of 1941–42 personnel manning the myriad aircraft workshops immediately behind the front line laboured around the clock to expeditiously repair and overhaul MiG fighters. (*Dmitriy Khazanov and Andrey Yurgenson*)

Stalingrad 1941–42. Troops unload supplies flown in to Pitomnik by Ju 52/3ms of *Blindflugschule* (Blind Flying School) 2. The transport crews made superhuman efforts to keep the beleaguered *6. Armee* supplied by air. (*via John Weal*)

Commander first of *Luftflotte* 4 then *Luftflotte* 3 and finally *Luftflotte* 6, Generaloberst Otto Dessloch was a Bavarian 'Old Eagle' who commanded bomber units during the 1930s then switched to flak regiments in October 1939. His return from the 'dark side' began early in 1942. (*Der Adler*)

Aleksandr Evgenevich Golovanov rose from Polkovnik to Marshal during the war as head of Soviet Long Range Aviation (ADD) then 18th VA. A civilian pilot, he had suffered under the Purges but was lucky to get a second chance, partly because he had once been a member of the Secret Police. (*Der Adler*)

A stick of bombs from an aircraft of III./KG 51 goes down on Tuapse harbour, narrowly missing a row of eight Soviet submarines. This photograph is believed to have been taken during the raid of 23 March 1942, which resulted in the sinking of the 2121-ton auxiliary minelayer *Nikolai Ostrovsky*, the tug *Veshilov*, a small survey vessel (the GS.13) and an unidentified cutter. Two submarines, the *D 5* and the *S 33*, were also damaged. (*via John Weal*)

because they were called upon to make low-level attacks on the battlefield, which helped to reduce KG 51's strength by the end of June from 92 to 37 Ju 88s. It was not until 29 June that Greim received Stukas, and the following day Stavka ordered Southwest Front to withdraw to the fortifications along the old border – the so-called Stalin Line – covered by the VVS, which continued to strike the spearheads.

Barbarossa was an unwelcome 49th birthday present for Greim, a Bavarian fighter ace who after World War I became a law student, a bank employee and a mercenary before joining the Luftwaffe, with whom he had commanded *Fliegerkorps* V since its formation in 1939. He supported Kleist's advance eastward as it enveloped Kirponos' centre around Uman from the north, the advance aided by attacks upon the rail network. By 9 July Soviet rail movement had ceased west of the Dnieper, with numerous abandoned trains and rolling stock. Indeed, Southwest Front's rail network had been cut 200 times by mid-August. Air transport was an inadequate substitute, although the Kiev GVF group, with 131 aircraft (110 single-engined), provided the trapped armies with 200 tonnes of supplies and drums of fuel, while TB-3 heavy bombers not only brought in supplies but also evacuated 3,620 wounded.[9] As the Germans completed their envelopment in heavy rain and thunderstorms on 2 August, TB-3s newly arrived from the Far East dropped 60 tonnes of supplies.

By 10 July the Wehrmacht had reached the Dnieper opposite Kiev, and Astakhov personally directed every available aircraft supporting a counter-attack to prevent an assault upon the city – this amounted to just 614 poorly coordinated sorties. Greim stopped this at the cost of 18 aircraft, then rain turned roads into marshes and every Ju 52/3m was assembled to fly supplies to forward airfields or isolated troops. Greim's efforts to destroy the six Dnieper bridges around Kiev were handicapped by poor airfields that restricted bomber loads. Although hit 42 times, the bridges all remained operable, while Greim was now down to some 220 aircraft.

Astakhov's situation was equally serious, with decimated regiments and spares shortages, while many 'horseless' aircrew sent to the rear for new 'mounts' discovered West Front had priority. The DBA played a major role trying to stop the Panzer columns, but during the first month of the war in this theatre alone it lost 216 bombers, including 145 DBs (one per 28.5 sorties), often flying low-level daylight missions without escort. The situation was so desperate that on 10 July a dozen TB–3s, which had been previously used to bring up paratroops, attacked east of Zhitomir, but fighters shot down seven.

By 13 July Astakhov reported he had lost 1,295 aircraft, despite 991 returning from repair depots, but had 202 serviceable DBA bombers. He had also lost 718 aircrew, including 303 pilots dead and missing, but had a surplus after sending wrecked regiments to the rear. The abandonment of supplies, support vehicles such as petrol bowsers and even tools made it difficult to keep the remaining aircraft in the air. Dispersal was difficult because there were only a few, poorly protected and overcrowded, air bases, and most of those being used in the defence of Kiev were simply fields that became marshes when it rained.

Inadequate reconnaissance was a major problem too, and of 14,130 sorties flown at the front between 22 June and 22 July, only 749 (5.3 per cent) were reconnaissance. The task was assigned to SB regiments, augmented by the new Yak-2/4, which were supposed to probe 250 kilometres behind the lines. However, by the end of June all the reconnaissance SBs had been lost, while the Yaks proved too slow, underarmed and mechanically unreliable. Astakhov was now limited to generating tactical reconnaissance missions only, these being undertaken by pairs of fighters that flew barely 20 kilometres behind enemy lines.

At the Uman pocket an unseemly dispute developed between Greim and Generalfeldmarschall Walther von Reichenau, whose 6 *Armee* held the pocket's northern side. The overstretched Greim rejected Reichenau's requests for support and, to avert a crisis of confidence, Rundstedt's and Löhr's staffs jointly allocated air support to thwart any relief attempt from Kiev, while JG 3 *Kommodore* Oberstleutnant Günther Lützow was appointed *Nahkampfführer Nord* with three *Gruppen*, one equipped with Stukas. On his own initiative, Greim despatched every aircraft despite low cloud, rain and high winds just as the defenders of the Uman pocket were about to be overwhelmed, and they pounded the enemy for three days in the south. It was largely through his efforts that the Red Army was stopped, and by 8 August the last Russians had been mopped up, bringing Astakhov's losses to 1,750 aircraft through enemy action and 510 to accidents.

The perils of day bombing meant that on 8 August Astakhov ordered airfields to be prepared for night operations, not only by a heavy bomber regiment but by two converted squadrons and a Night Bomber Aviation Regiment (*Nochnoy Bombardirovochnyy Aviatsionnyy Polk*, NBAP) equipped with R-5s and initially tasked with attacking airfields from 500–1,000 metres. Astakhov would later note, 'Night raids on enemy airfields are quite effective, even when using older aircraft types, with minor losses on our side.' The Southwest Front created its own NBAP on 25 September, and the idea proved so successful that from November dozens of NBAPs were created from bomber, reconnaissance and training units.

Kleist had now established a foothold over the Dnieper near Dnepropetrovsk that allowed him to threaten Kiev from the south, but the bridge supporting his forces was under constant air attack – 12 raids on 31 August alone. By 8 September it had been damaged and repaired 15 times (three times due to air attacks), and Rundstedt considered abandoning the bridgehead. However, he realised this would undermine attempts to envelop Kiev. The VVS, whose Southwest and South Fronts were down to 986 aircraft by the end of August, staged hornet-like attacks that did little damage but added to the overall sense of unease, while night raids became increasingly troublesome.

By now the great salient around Kiev was attracting German attention like iron to a magnet, and on 12 August a supplement to *Weisung Nr 34* ordered its envelopment. Löhr had moved his headquarters to Vinnitsa on 1 August, but the Luftwaffe was stretched to the limit with 1,005 serviceable aircraft, 626 strike, on 6 September. Löhr had 273 while Kesselring had only 251, with Keller still possessing the lion's share, although he soon lost Richthofen. Even before the *Weisung Nr 34* supplement was published, Guderian's 2 *Panzergruppe* (supported by Fiebig and Loerzer) had turned south with Generaloberst Maximilian

Freiherr von Weichs' 2 *Armee* to cross the river Desna. The timely arrival of four *Gruppen* from Richthofen enabled Loerzer to assemble seven *Kampf-,* three *Stuka-* and three *Jagdgruppen* and one *Jabogruppe* with some 500 aircraft for this thrust, with the close support *Staffeln* ready to operate from forward landing grounds at short notice.

Within a day VVS reconnaissance detected Guderian's move south, but could not discern his intentions. Polynin, with 360 aircraft, initially believed it was to avoid his bombing! He was reinforced with 1st RAG (450 aircraft) and 100 DBA bombers, and between 29 August and 4 September the VVS and DBA flew 4,000 and 2,860 sorties, respectively, but to little effect. The VVS did pick off vehicles, which were difficult to replace, as Guderian struggled down bog-like roads, thus increasing consumption of scarce petrol and oil. The advance was aided by Loerzer, and on 27 August alone his crews flew 180 Stuka and 40 Bf 110 sorties to support the spearhead. Nevertheless, progress was agonisingly slow, but occasionally boosted by the capture of Soviet supplies.

Astakhov could do little to stop the Germans, although during the last ten days of August his units daily flew 300 sorties, including 20 to 30 at night. By 1 September he was down to 163 serviceable aircraft, despite reinforcements from the Kharkov and North Caucasus Districts. It became increasingly obvious in Moscow that Kiev faced encirclement, yet Stalin refused to sanction a withdrawal. The situation quickly deteriorated, for on 12 September Kleist drove out of the Dnepropetrovsk bridgehead supported by Greim with three *Kampf-,* two *Stuka-* and four *Jagdgruppen.* The *Fliegerkorps* hammered the Red Army and the rail network, with Loerzer's men flying 80 to 100 sorties a day, while Greim's crews flew 1,422 sorties from 12 to 21 September to drop some 600 tonnes of bombs for the loss of 17 aircraft and 14 damaged. With the Luftwaffe's aid, the *Panzergruppen* met on the evening of 14 September just as bad weather grounded most aircraft.

Two days after the link-up Greim outran his supplies, leading to a two-day hiatus, while Löhr's own transport difficulties prevented relief. Fortunately there was little aerial opposition, with a daily average of just 300 Russian sorties. As Greim's bombers struck Kiev to prevent its use as a redoubt, the Luftwaffe helped to thwart many breakout attempts. By 26 September the last embers of resistance had cooled in a catastrophe that caused Stalin to secretly offer Hitler terms similar to those of Brest-Litovsk in 1918. The surviving squadrons departed the pocket, with the last aeroplane, from 36th IAD, flying out on 20 September together with U-2s each carrying up to four people.

Some 200 'horseless' airmen were trapped, however, together with half the groundcrews. Many of these men subsequently perished trying to escape. Kirponos and most of his staff were killed, but the VVS leaders managed to escape. Astakhov reached Soviet lines in early November, bearded and with a frayed jacket, torn trousers and boots held together with wire. To escape detection he had buried his Party card, and for this sin he was sidelined into civil aviation, although he was promoted to Marshal of Aviation in August 1944. His command lost more than 1,100 aircraft between 7 July and 26 September, with another 200 abandoned, while the DBA lost 100–150 aircraft.

With the collapse of the Kiev pocket, the Wehrmacht was poised to complete the destruction of the Soviet Union. But the balmy summer breezes were cooling and rain provided a shield for the Russians as the autumn *rasputitsa* (roadless time) turned the roads into marshes and reduced the flow of supplies to a trickle. It delayed Rundstedt's drive into the Donets Basin and the Crimea during October and November, supported by Greim and Pflugbeil, respectively. Opposing their progress was the reformed Southwest Front, now under the command of General-maior Fedor Falaleev, a former VVS Inspector General.

Greim's bombers disrupted enemy communications, especially railways (which became KG 55's speciality), to pave the way for the advance upon Rostov, but supply problems meant that for a month this was covered by only three single-engined *Gruppen* under Major Clemens Graf Schönborn-Wiesentheid as *Nahkampfführer Süd*. Until the multi-engined units could move forward to the former Russian airfield at Taganrog, Greim kept them closer to their supply depots, which severely reduced their bomb loads. He was steadily milked of units, with most of his *Jagdgruppen* going to *Luftflotte* 2. The last went to the Crimea on

22 October, although it soon returned. Kharkov fell two days later, and Kleist (whose command later became 1 *Panzerarmee*) advanced towards Rostov.

From Taganrog, despite numerous VVS attacks, Greim struck the rail network feeding reinforcements to the city. On 12 November, however, five of his six *Kampfgruppen* were sent westwards to rest and re-equip, leaving him with just nine serviceable bombers. There was some compensation with the arrival of KG 27, which helped Kleist take Rostov on 21 November, but a week later a Russian counter-offensive retook the city. Rundstedt was pushed behind the River Mius and replaced by Reichenau, who praised the *Nahkampfführer* for covering the retreat in low cloud and snow. At Rostov the Russians captured some 'Messers', which they put into service augmented by Yaks under the command of 590th IAP CO Maior Gennadi Telegin, and they served until March 1942, when the regiment joined South Front's 56th Army.[10]

Meanwhile, Pflugbeil took over the southern sector, where pressure from some 500 aircraft under Falaleev and General-maior Konstantin Vershinin (South Front air commander) prevented him supporting operations in the Crimea. Greim's *Fliegerkorps* V was withdrawn to Brussels on 30 November for minelaying around Great Britain, but part of it, under chief-of-staff Plocher, was transferred to Smolensk to support *Fliegerkorps* VIII. On 1 April 1942, it became *Luftwaffenkommando Ost*. Greim barely had time to unpack before a crisis in the Crimea required him to lead his staff to the peninsula, where they arrived on 2 January 1942, to become Special Staff, Crimea (*Sonderstab Krim*).

Pflugbeil had supported the right of his fellow Saxon Rundstedt, his attack being spearheaded by Generaloberst Eugen Ritter von Schobert's 11 *Armee*, which struck eastwards with the Romanians from 2 July. 'Old Eagle' Pflugbeil had served with escort and bomber formations during World War I, then joined the Weimar Army and the Luftwaffe, where he spent most of his career in administrative posts before assuming command of *Fliegerkorps* IV during the Battle of Britain. He and the FARR opened a ten-day campaign to eliminate enemy air power, but delayed reconnaissance meant many airfields were undetected.

Furthermore, on the eve of *Barbarossa* Michugin dispersed his aircraft.

Michugin was transferred north on 26 June and succeeded by General-maior Petr Shelukhin, the Moscow District VVS Deputy Commander whose defence faced a lacklustre FARR. The front lost only 204 aircraft between 1 July and 1 August, 113 to enemy action. Nevertheless, only 258 were left serviceable. When *Stukagruppen* were transferred from Loerzer the pace of the advance picked up, with the port of Odessa being invested on 19 August and Schobert marching east to the Dnieper Bend. Fierce resistance kept the Romanians out of the port until it was abandoned on the night of 16/17 October to strengthen the defence of Sevastopol. In shielding Odessa the Russians flew more than 8,000 sorties, 4,614 by General-maior Viktor Rusakov's VVS-ChF, and lost 86 aircraft. By the end of the siege the FARR had 267 aircraft in the East, having flown 10,704 sorties for the loss of 118 combat and 18 support aircraft.

Throughout this siege, and later that of Sevastopol, the Luftwaffe interdicted Soviet sea lanes. The cruiser *Chervona Ukraina*, two destroyers, five small warships and 32 merchantmen (93,745grt) had been lost to bombs or Luftwaffe-laid mines by the end of April 1942, with the pace accelerating when Wild's staff arrived to become *Flfü Süd* on 1 December under Pflugbeil. The torpedoing of SS *Armenia* (4,727grt) by KG 28 on 7 November 1941, was the worst disaster in Soviet merchant marine history as it was evacuating 5,000 patients and staff of Sevastopol's hospitals. Only eight were saved. The campaign also damaged numerous ships, including the cruisers *Krasny Kavkaz* and *Voroshilov*.

Events focused south of the Dnieper Bend, where Schobert was killed on 12 September when his Fi 156 Storch landed in a minefield. He was replaced by General Erich von Manstein. Within a week he and Pflugbeil struck towards the Crimean Peninsula opposed by the South Front that had been reinforced by 5th RAG and VVS-ChF, each with 200 aircraft. As Manstein approached the peninsula Rusakov ordered General-maior Vasilii Ermachenkov to defend it. On 26 September Vershinin replaced Shelukhin, who was sent to Siberia to run the district VVS, and he played no further role in operations against the Germans.

Rusakov was promoted deputy commander of the VVS-KBF on 21 October, and he was eventually killed in a flying accident on 30 June 1942. He was replaced by General-maior Nikolai Ostryakov, who, in turn, would be replaced by Ermachenkov following his death in combat on 24 April 1942.

From 26 October Manstein and Pflugbeil fought their way to Sevastopol and Kerch. Although the latter committed up to 13 *Gruppen*, heavy rain restricted air operations and delayed an assault on Sevastopol. Pflugbeil's fighters were directed by *Inspekteur der Jagdflieger* Mölders, who held a roving commission on the Eastern Front and unofficially kept his hand in, with his last victory coming on 8 November. Nine days later Udet, worn down by Milch's intrigues and his own declining health, shot himself. A state funeral was decreed at Berlin, for which the Luftwaffe's 'Great and Good' were summoned. Mölders answered this summons, but his He 111 crashed in fog on 22 November and he was killed.

To relieve pressure on Sevastopol the Russians landed upon the Kerch Peninsula from 26 December, undetected because of bad weather and Pflugbeil's shortage of reconnaissance aircraft. To contain the threat Manstein abandoned his assault on Sevastopol. *Sonderstab Krim*'s arrival and a build-up to six *Gruppen* helped to stabilise the situation, with Greim assuming operational control of Wild's *Fliegerführer Ostsee* on 15 January, but the deteriorating situation to the north sucked away *Staffeln* and his command was disbanded on 11 February. One week later Wild was made responsible for air operations in the Crimea, where there was stalemate. Meanwhile, the Rostov counter-offensive carried the Russians back to the Donets and created a huge salient around Izyum, south of Kharkov, before it was contained during the second half of January.

The problems of the Southern Front by the end of 1941 were nothing compared with the crisis in the north. Kiev cleared the way for *Taifun*, which OKH and ObdL were anxious to complete, the latter because Kesselring and Loerzer were earmarked for the Mediterranean. Certain of victory, ObdL also drew up plans to garrison the East, and there was an end-of-term atmosphere that led Jeschonnek to telephone

Richthofen and inform him that *Fliegerkorps* VIII would spend the New Year in Bavaria and Austria, although Richthofen was less optimistic.

Despite its successes the Luftwaffe was in serious trouble, yet its losses to enemy action, including air ambulances and liaison aircraft, steadily decreased from 451 destroyed in July to 86 in December to total 1,611. Between 22 June and 31 December the Luftwaffe lost 2,480 aircraft in the East, of which 2,209 were on operations. A further 1,911 were damaged, of which 1,260 were on operations. A third of the total losses (869) were due to accidents involving exhausted crews, and the accident rate increased as the campaign went on, accounting for 60 per cent of damaged aircraft – Milch's inspection tours noted airfields littered with them. The human cost was also high, with 6,300 casualties (including 3,100 dead and missing) by the end of August. Two months later, the average overall crew strength was 2,963, while average monthly aircrew losses were 10.7 per cent (318).

The losses were heavy but the prime problem was logistics, traditionally the Wehrmacht's Achilles' heel. With Russia largely devoid of hard-topped roads, the rail network was vital for supplies, but the need to change the lines to the Western European gauge made it difficult to bring forward not only food, fuel and ammunition, but also basic necessities such as spares and lubricating oil. Despite this the Luftwaffe was extremely active until October, flying on average 1,200 sorties per day, and sometimes 2,000, with *Stukagruppen* displaying an average sortie rate of 75 per cent of unit establishment, *Jagdgruppen* 60 per cent and *Kampfgruppen* 40–45 per cent. This level of activity, and frequent movements, came at a price, and overall serviceability declined to 1,544 on 10 July, 1,654 a month later and 920 by the end of August.

The huge moves made by the Luftwaffe squadrons aggravated the problem. In keeping pace with the Panzers, Richthofen's headquarters moved 18 times by December, and during the first three weeks five of his *Gruppen* advanced 600 kilometres. Supply bases were established every 300 kilometres, but even this was inadequate for Luftgau zbV 4, which reported average daily fuel consumption per month between July and October of 50, 167, 111 and 85 tonnes. When *Barbarossa* began only four *Transportgruppen* were available, soon reinforced by five more, but their combined strength was barely 450 aircraft and they could support only the spearheads. This forced the *Luftflotten* to use *Kampfgruppen* and even gliders for resupply missions.

The *Heeresflieger*, and especially the *Nahaufklärungsstaffeln* that probed up to 50 kilometres behind enemy lines, suffered especially badly and withered away because they were too small to impose their will upon the overstretched supply system. There was a steady stream of losses, with 173 aircraft destroyed by enemy action to the end of 1941. The situation was exacerbated by Hs 126 production being run down in favour of the Fw 189. Halder noted as early as 10 July that some of Bock's *Staffeln* had no aircraft, while *Nachtaufklärungsstaffel* 2 had only two serviceable Do 17Ps and many *Nahaufklärungsstaffeln* were using Storchs or trainers. The crisis continued until October, when *Nahaufklärungsstaffeln* were bundled together to create *Aufklärungsgruppen* (Reconnaissance Groups, AufKlGr) for *Heeresgruppe Nord* and four of the more exposed army headquarters (2, 6, 11 and 17 *Armees*), which proved encouraging enough to stimulate the creation of *Nahaufklärungsgruppen* (Short Range Reconnaissance Groups, NAGr) three months later.

The Luftwaffe's personnel faced many hardships and usually lived in tents over pits during the summer campaign. Later, wooden huts were provided, but during the winter more substantial shelter was needed, which was easier if they were based near a town or city. Then they would sleep on couches or sleeping bags, but if nothing else was available they would share the verminous homes of the peasants. However, when they returned to the Reich with their little 'guests' the epidemic-fearing local authorities became hysterical and permitted the men to return to 'civilisation' only after they were thoroughly deloused.

In the morning, officers and men would complete their ablutions then go to the mess (*Fliegerhorst Kasino*) to collect their cold rations, including a third of a loaf of bread, cured sausage, cheese, an apple or tomato and some jam and butter. They would also collect a meal ticket that would be for a hot lunch, the cold rations being used for breakfast and dinner, although flight crews often received a breakfast egg, all washed down with coffee or 'indescribable' Ersatz coffee.

After breakfast crews would go to the command post for daily orders and briefings, with strike crews receiving written orders and target descriptions from the *Fliegerkorps*. Fighter crews would either go to the dispersal 'huts' (usually a tent) or climb into their aircraft if they were on standby, while their friends sat in deckchairs around the dispersal 'hut' to doze, read or play cards. After the morning's operations there would be lunch at the mess. This would consist of a substantial meal of fresh or canned meat, vegetables, fruit and powdered potatoes, or poultry from the peasants, usually made into soups or casseroles, but during periods of intense operations replaced by sandwiches. There would be a Sunday roast (*Sonntagsbraten*) with beef and vegetables, and while both quantity and quality of rations declined as the war progressed, the Luftwaffe generally ate well.

In the summer heat food went off quickly, while the Wehrmacht's standards of field hygiene were generally lower than those of the British and Americans. As a result men would suffer intestinal problems, and often have to resort to the 'Thunder Bench' (*Donnerbalken*), where they would pass time and much more.

At the end of the day the crews might chat, and listen to records or the radio. If the weather 'frogs' decided the conditions for the following day would be bad, aircrew were allowed alcohol. The conquest of France meant there were substantial quantities of spirits and wine available, but many men wound down with German beer – this was often Airmen's Beer (*Fliegerbier*), with only one per cent alcohol – and then would go to bed.

Meanwhile, the VVS was still adapting to its heavy losses, which meant the gradual disbandment of Frontal Aviation divisions and the growing assignment of regiments to army and front headquarters, together with RAGs. On 20 August the Defence Ministry reduced each regiment to two squadrons of nine aircraft, and two aircraft for the regimental headquarters, which would remain the basic establishment until 1943. In fighter regiments the reduction in numbers saw pilots forced to operate increasingly in pairs, although the *Zveno* remained official policy. In an effort to boost morale, units that had distinguished themselves were designated Guards (*Gvardii*), with higher pay scales and greater access to new aircraft.

By 1 October the VVS in the West had 1,540 aircraft on the main battle front supported by 472 DBA bombers and 697 PVO fighters, but increasingly numbers were made up of obsolete aircraft in the night bomber role. On that same date NBAPs, also called Light Night Bomber Regiments (LNBAP), were authorised throughout the West, with 71 formed with U-2s in October–November 1941, together with 27 regiments with R-5s and five with SBs. They were often manned by flight school students or even *Osoaviakhim* flying clubs, and by the end of the year the total had risen to 90 regiments.

With much of the aircraft industry in western cities, the Russians had to evacuate plants to new sites in, and behind, the Urals, where hundreds volunteered to serve in them. While the Luftwaffe was aware of this activity, it was unable to interfere. With many factories on the move, and therefore unable to renew production until the autumn at the earliest, the VVS would largely have to live off its 'hump'. General-maior Nikolai Sokolov-Sokolenok, commandant of the aviation engineering academy, was appointed head of VVS rear services, and he began to sort order out of the chaos. This took time, however, and for months fuel and ammunition supplies were erratic – the VVS lost 70 per cent of its stocks – while the shortage of mobile workshops and spares meant repairs were slow.

To support *Taifun* Kesselring received reinforcements from Löhr and welcomed back Richthofen. He now had 1,320 aircraft at his disposal, which was approximately half the Luftwaffe's strength in the East. Richthofen was not enthusiastic about supporting Bock's left (9 *Armee* and 3 *Panzergruppe/Panzerarmee*), enveloping the West and Reserve Fronts, because the previous month's operations had halved his strength. Loerzer's mission was to support Bock's right (Guderian's 2 *Panzerarmee* and 4 *Armee*), enveloping thr Bryansk Front, using Fiebig's 14 single-engine *Gruppen* for close air support while the *Kampfgruppen*'s 400 bombers isolated the battlefield. The offensive was preceded by a successful campaign against airfields, which left West (Michugin), Reserve (General-maior Evgenii Nikolaenko) and Bryansk (General-maior Stepan Krasovskii) Fronts with a total of only 568 aircraft on 1 October, augmented by part of 6th IAK and five DBA divisions with 158 serviceable aircraft.

The offensive began on 30 September, with Guderian, supported by 40 *Flivos*, striking towards Orel, which, despite opposition from every available Russian bomber, fell three days later. This allowed Loerzer to fly in supplies for Fiebig, including 500 tonnes of fuel. Already the second stage of the offensive was underway, as Bock's left punch was thrown on 2 October, with 1,387 sorties, followed by 971 the next day. These helped the Panzer spearheads to meet at Vyazma on 7 October, supported by some 800 bomber sorties. A Russian heavy bomber squadron at Vyazma was saved when ad hoc pilots, including a flight engineer and a paratrooper, flew out all the aircraft. The remaining Soviet personnel were mopped up by 20 October, with Luftwaffe help.

In the aftermath of this defeat uncertainty created panic in Moscow, and from 15 October thousands fled. When Golovanov drove from the city centre to a nearby airfield he was angry to be informed by a newly arrived Er-2 pilot of Moscow's capitulation. Towards the end of October the NKVD executed dozens of generals in its custody, including most of the VVS and PVO leaders. A desperate Stalin frequently rang Zhigarev's headquarters, only to receive soothing, but inaccurate, responses from the VVS commander. Air operations were further hindered by his frequently conflicting orders. Zhigarev coordinated a 937-sortie campaign against airfields between 11 and 18 October to relieve the pressure upon the encircled troops, but without noticeable effect, and used TB-3 transports to send supplies to the front.

As the situation deteriorated it was Sbytov, now the Moscow District VVS commander, whose fighter regiments ended the uncertainty with tactical reconnaissance missions. One patrol discovered the enemy breakthrough on 5 October, and 95 aircraft, including a squadron made up of instructors, struck the spearhead. So great was the threat, however, that Russian groundcrews carried grenades to defend their airfields.

By 10 October, 6th IAK, which was defending Moscow from both air and ground attack, was down to 344 serviceable fighters. Some were flying five to six sorties per day – a pace maintained due to the surplus of pilots. The corps would be the first to benefit from foreign aid when, on 12 October, its 126th IAP became operational on American-made Tomahawk fighters delivered by the British, although their vulnerability to Russian winters made them a slender reed. Five days later a Kalinin Front was created on West Front's right, with General-maior Nikolai Trifonov hastily cobbling together the air support. By 1 November he had only 89 aircraft, including 56 fighters.

The Russians claim the VVS flew 26,000 sorties to the end of October, 80 per cent in direct support of the troops, but suffered heavy losses due to other problems. Contact with Moscow was frequently lost, partly due to the shortage of radios, which hindered air strike coordination and establishing FEBA location. On 6 October Zhigarev demanded his subordinates establish command posts alongside those of the armies, with clear maps of the situation, but often VVS officers could discover the FEBA only by flying over the front in a U-2.

By now the temperature was dropping noticeably, with rain and sleet turning Kesselring's airfields into bogs and reducing activity to an average 554 daily sorties on 21–25 October. This gave the *Schwarzmänner* the chance to maintain aircraft, and when the weather improved there was a remarkable scale of effort, especially by Stukas. But the *rasputitsa* impeded the advance and the Russians resisted every inch of the way; and yet ObdL was determined to reduce its forces in the East. On 5 November Kesselring informed Loerzer they would both soon depart for the Mediterranean. When Bock learned this he protested vigorously to Halder, and emphasised this would demoralise his men, but on 11 November he was formally informed that Kesselring would depart within a week. The following day Loerzer began handing over his sector to Fiebig as Bock desperately attacked to exploit the air power that was fading before his eyes.

Loerzer's withdrawal involved 13 *Gruppen* that had flown 40,000 sorties since the beginning of the campaign, as he proudly proclaimed in an order of the day that also noted the expenditure of 23,150 tonnes of bombs and the destruction of 3,826 aircraft (2,169 in the air), 789 tanks and 14,339 vehicles. There had been 3,579 attacks upon railways in which 159 complete trains and 304 locomotives had been destroyed. He did not forget his signallers, who had laid 3,000 kilometres of wire and transmitted 40,000 radio and 30,000 teletype messages – figures that may be taken as typical of all the *Fliegerkorps* in the East.

The Russians kept the Wehrmacht outside of Moscow, having flown 51,300 sorties since *Taifun* started, 14 per cent by 6th IAK. By 5 December they had lost 293 aircraft, and there was serious congestion because only 43 of the 120 airfields around the Soviet capital were suitable for combat operations – many of these belonged to 6th IAK. But on 29 November Kesselring departed for Dresden, and the next day Richthofen assumed command of the Luftwaffe's Moscow front, including Fiebig.

Progress on the ground was slow, while muddy German airfields were frozen and the airmen usually flew in low cloud, fog, snow and rain with the constant threat of icing. There were 919 sorties from 30 November to 2 December, but on 6 December *Taifun* formally ended. Two days later *Weisung Nr 39* placed the Wehrmacht on the defensive because of 'the severe winter weather that has come surprisingly early'. The Luftwaffe, which had had 489 aircraft destroyed and 333 damaged since 28 September, was ordered to create a defensive infrastructure and to disrupt the recovery of enemy forces 'as far as possible'. Hitler anticipated no significant Russian action before March 1942 because he knew they had suffered heavy losses – 6,100 combat and 11,800 second-line aircraft according to Russian documents. Nevertheless, Stalin demanded an active defence from his equally exhausted forces, and on 5 December his skeletal armies had begun counter-attacks to save Moscow. The VVS had 1,658 combat aircraft on the main front and many in NBAPs, nearly a third of which were unserviceable, while the PVO had some 633 fighters and the DBA 273 bombers.

The main blow was delivered by the Western, Kalinin and Bryansk Fronts supported by a total of 1,376 aircraft, including some from 6th

IAK, the DBA and Moscow District. Some fronts managed to fly an average of 211 sorties per day. The determination to push back the invader meant U-2 biplane bombers occasionally operated in daylight, but only when visibility was reduced to about 500 metres, which forced them as low as 25 metres. Richthofen, outnumbered, at the end of an overstretched supply line and facing severe weather, reacted to each new crisis as best he could, and often with success, for the Russians suffered similar problems. Nevertheless, the featherweight push was a psychological hammer-blow to the equally exhausted Germans, who lacked air support. To their own surprise, the Russians made rapid progress despite Richthofen's units flying 494 sorties during 5–9 December and 388 combat and seven transport sorties during 12–14 December. Bock's over-extended defences collapsed, his troops retreating to bring down the neighbouring fronts like a house of cards as the wings of panic beat in many headquarters.

On 16 December Hitler issued his 'stand fast' order, and three days later dismissed Brauchitsch to become Commander-in-Chief of the Army. Despite the Führer's order the Wehrmacht was in full retreat, yet during the winter of 1941–42 both dictators were driving the war on 'empty', with virtually no reserves of men and materiel. With Siberian winds chilling the air to -46°C, freezing Russian soil and burying it under metres of snow, only strength of will kept the front aflame as gangs of desperate, hungry, exhausted men fought on under the banners of divisions and brigades. The situation was reflected on the battle maps, with the front, especially west of Moscow, evolving into a series of exposed salients that neither side had the strength to eliminate.

The Russians tried to finish off the Wehrmacht especially around Moscow, where, on 1 January 1942, the Kalinin and West Fronts had just 331 aircraft, including 218 bombers, of which 160 were night bombers. Blizzards and fog reduced air operations, although Kalinin Front flew 2,866 sorties during January and 6,667 in February, while 318 transport sorties supported the spearheads. To aid West Front operations General-maior Aleksei Levashev's 4th Airborne Corps was dropped some 320 kilometres behind enemy lines from the morning of 27 January, but the

Luftwaffe struck its behind-the-lines airfield and destroyed seven of the 65 transports there. Then, on the night of 26/27 February, a Bf 110 intercepted Levashev's TB-3, and the badly damaged aeroplane landed at Moscow with a dead General-maior onboard.

The fate of Germany's Eastern Front pivoted on the central sector, where Richthofen juggled ten under-strength *Gruppen* that shielded the army and flew more than 5,000 sorties between January and March. ObdL provided him with four *Kampfgruppen* and, to supply isolated or retreating troops, five *Transportgruppen* under Oberst Friedrich-Wilhelm 'Fritz' Morzik, who had been appointed Luftwaffe Quartermaster Air Transport Commander and Instrument Training School Command (*Lufttransportführer beim Generalquartermeister der Luftwaffe und Kommando der Blindflugschule*) on 1 October, then received another four on Hitler's orders while Löhr sent other *Transportgruppen*. These were aspirins to cure cancer, however, for the Wehrmacht retreat continued in the following weeks.

But the Russians were too weak to exploit the situation, while VVS operations were hampered by the fragmentation of their scarce resources, for more than half the regiments were attached to armies. On the West Front Mishugin had 34 of 41 regiments attached to nine armies, while on the Kalinin Front, under Rudenko from 4 January, 23 of 27 regiments were with six armies. The Luftwaffe still concentrated its forces in multi-role task forces that helped to restrict the Russian advance during the winter, with close air support and attacks on communications. A monthly average of 14,000 tonnes of bombs was dropped on such targets from December 1941 through to April 1942. Yet the price was high, and between 7 December 1941 and 8 April 1942, 859 aircraft in the East were destroyed and 636 damaged.

Luftwaffe strength on the main front declined from 1,546 combat aircraft on 10 January to 1,537 on 14 February then began to rise to 1,550 on 14 March, although the bomber and fighter forces averaged 509 and 423 aeroplanes, respectively, with an average 41 per cent serviceability. As the situation eased, Luftwaffe strength rose to 1,716 aircraft by 18 April – almost half the strength it had on 22 June 1941.

Keeping aircraft airworthy during the winter months was a new Labour of Hercules. Metal tools became brittle and not even pre-heating them made them reliable, engine oil froze, hydraulic fluids became like glue and rubber in seals and tyres crumbled. Engines had either to be turned over regularly, consuming the limited stocks of petrol and oil, or enclosed in heated sheds or 'alert boxes'.

By March mutual exhaustion and the spring *rasputitsa* helped to stabilise the central front, but from the Luftwaffe's viewpoint the most significant event took place in *Heeresgruppe Nord*'s sector following the envelopment by Northwest Front of Generalleutnant Walter Graf von Brockdorff-Ahlefeldt's II *Armeekorps* with 95,000 men around Demyansk on 9 February 1942. Simultaneously, 5,000 men under Generalmajor Theodor Scherer were surrounded at Kholm, to the southwest. No major airlift was initially envisaged for Brockdorff-Ahlefeldt until Halder's formal request to Jeschonnek on 13 February.[11]

Keller's two *Transportgruppen* were already supplying the corps a trickle of supplies, but nowhere near the basic daily requirement of 300 tonnes. Hitler promised Keller 337 transports within a week, and on 18 February ordered Morzik to supervise the operation. He arrived at Pskov-West airfield with a small staff that same day as Air Transport Commander East (LTF Ost). Morzik was a former Junkers test pilot who had flown airliners in Russia. Within three weeks he had received 15 *Transportgruppen*, mostly by mobilising schools. Arctic weather reduced serviceability to about 30 per cent, forcing Morzik to pull strings with his Lufthansa and Junkers contacts in order to acquire spares and aircraft such as Fw 200s and Ju 86s, which would have been difficult to obtain through official channels.

Morzik benefited from the fully equipped bomber base at Dno and from *Fliegerkorps* I's air superiority over Demyansk. The *Transportgruppen* would fly 7,572 sorties supporting 16 *Armee* in March and 5,870 in April. The transports flew mainly from Pskov and Ostrov, a distance of 250–260 kilometres or 90 minutes flight time, and by the end of February Morzik was established and meeting minimum requirements. To reduce losses, his transports flew in 'pulks' of 20–40 at 1,800–2,400 metres. From 4 March he was able to meet the army's 300-tonne target.[12]

The Northwest Front commander, General-polkovnik Pavel Kurochkin, recognised the importance of the airlift before his air chief, General-leitenant Timofei Kutsevalov, who concentrated upon ground support and used fighters against the transports only from the end of February. This threat was contained by *Jagdgruppen*, although bombers occasionally struck Demyansk's airstrips. Morzik's main bases were left untroubled, however. In April Stavka belatedly sent 6th Shock Air Group (*Udarnaya Aviatsionnaya Gruppa*, UAG) with six fighter regiments, but this failed to penetrate the German fighter screen. Morzik gradually raised deliveries to 544 tonnes a day.

A ground offensive opened a corridor to the pocket on 18 May, and the airlift was gradually reduced, although three *Gruppen* continued to support II *Armeekorps* until Demyansk was evacuated in January 1943. By then Morzik's *Gruppen* had flown 33,086 sorties, bringing in 64,844 tonnes of supplies and 30,500 men (24,303 tonnes and 15,446 men by 18 May), while 35,400 men, most of them sick or wounded, were evacuated. The cost was high, with 125 transports being lost (the loss of Ju 52/3ms being equivalent to half the aircraft's annual production) and 140 badly damaged, while 387 aircrew were killed.

Kholm, with its tiny airstrip under artillery fire, depended upon Go 242 and DFS 230 gliders, which landed in the gloom of dawn or dusk, their flights sometimes covered by a *Kette* of Ju 88s. They were supplemented by supply drops from as low as 200 metres using bombers and transports, which provided 1,024 tonnes in one three-day period. In May the pocket was relieved after a 103-day siege in which 27 transports were lost.

The airlifts succeeded because of the bases' proximity to the pocket and the weak aerial opposition that they faced, but their relief from the skies convinced Hitler that any isolated garrison could hold out against the Bolshevik hordes. The general backslapping that ensued would raise expectations and ignore the terrible effects the airlift had on multi-engine aircrew flight training in particular. Not only did it destroy aircraft earmarked for training, it also killed both instructors and promising students alike. Finally, these flights consumed 42,155 tonnes of fuel – a third of total monthly production.

Throughout the winter Moscow suffered intermittent bombing. As early as 8 July 1941, Halder had noted Hitler wished to destroy Moscow and Leningrad through air attack, and five days later Richthofen stirred the pot by claiming Moscow's destruction would help the Wehrmacht's advance. But permission was not given until *Weisung Nr 33* on 19 July, when Loerzer received three *Kampfgruppen* from the West (61 bombers) to bring Kesselring's force to 11 *Kampfgruppen*. The following day he briefed his commanders on the new operations, which would be supported by X-Geräte beacons to support KGr 100's pathfinders.

The defence of Moscow was the PVO's prime mission, and for this task 6th IAK PVO was created two days before the invasion with 389 fighters, including 175 new LaGG-3s, MiG-3s and Yak-1s and 68 nightfighters. It also had some experienced pilots, a few of whom had 400 hours in their log books. ObdL sent a reconnaissance aircraft so high over Moscow on the first day of the war that it was not detected, and from 8 July the reconnaissance effort intensified. There was tension between IAK commander Polkovnik Ivan Klimov, who wished to direct the fighters from his command post, and his superior, the PVO area commander General-maior (General-leitenant from 28 October 1941) Daniil Zhuravlev, who wanted him to operate from the regional headquarters. Yet Zhuravlev's command still relied largely on wire communications, which slowed reaction times, with cloth panels used to direct fighters in daylight, as in World War I.

The first raid by 195 bombers on the night of 22/23 July used burning Smolensk as a beacon, and dropped some 200 tonnes of bombs. It briefly forced Stavka into a Metro station, from whence it re-emerged as the bombing eased. Raids were detected by a RUS-2 radar manned by experts, and this led to about 175 sorties by single-engined fighters. Nevertheless, the Germans lost only six bombers. The following two nights saw raids by some 225 bombers, but there was a lull during August, apart from 83 bombers striking on 10/11 August, while Kesselring built a chain of 16 radio navigation beacons and Zhigarev stripped eight IAPs from Klimov to reinforce 6th IAK. In an attempt to restrict the Germans the Russians despatched Pe-2s and Yak-4s to trail the bombers to their bases, which were then subjected to attack. The Luftwaffe would repeat this concept, with spectacular success, against the Russians and their American allies in the summer of 1944.

Anti-aircraft artillery was the backbone of the PVO throughout the war, with fighters assigned a complementary role. Partly for this reason, and partly because it was newly established, 6th IAK lacked equipment when Germany invaded – it had only 39 engine starters out of an establishment of 110 and 40 petrol bowsers instead of 165. Only 147 pilots were combat trained, 88 on new fighters, and eight of them were qualified to fly nightfighters. In mid-July test pilots were hastily assembled to form two nightfighter squadrons, equipped with SBs and Pe-2s. Klimov tried to bring order out of chaos, but his bullying attitude, with frequent threats of court martial, was resented. In fact the decision to split the Moscow air defence area into four sectors for fighters reportedly came from Stalin himself. With the eyes of Stalin upon him, Zhigarev built up the Moscow PVO, which had 719 fighters on 17 July and was promptly reinforced by four regiments of veteran pilots from the front.

The Luftwaffe's effort against Moscow gradually tailed off, and while there were 23 raids involving 289 sorties during October, these were minor irritations rather than serious attacks. The Luftwaffe's lack of bombers, rather than Soviet resistance, was the key to Moscow's success, with the last night raid on 5/6 April 1942, concluding a campaign of 11 day and 76 night attacks – six by 50 aircraft and 59 by less than a dozen bombers. There were another 94 sorties flown over Gorki from 4 to 6 November.

The PVO generated 1,015 nightfighter sorties in July and 840 in August (out of 8,065 and 6,895 nationally, respectively), with most Soviet nightfighters being single-engined aircraft which, like the RAF in 1940, depended upon the bravery and skill of their pilots for success. They were crudely converted with flame-dampers, but none had radar, while the few illuminated runways often remained dark because groundcrews feared attracting the enemy. Development of a 'Peshka' fighter, the Pe-3, began during August 1941, although production would be diverted to both bomber and reconnaissance regiments and a radar-equipped version would not be evaluated until April 1942. By then Klimov had gone, possibly a victim of his conflict with Zhuravlev and general dislike within the PVO, and he was replaced on 8 November by Polkovnik Aleksei Mitenkov.

From January 1942 observer posts began to receive radios for GCI, and each fighter sector had a RUS-2 radar to help provide information on the tactical situation. During the first year of the war these radars guided 149 interceptions in which 73 victories were claimed, aided by the introduction of RUS-2S, which had a height-finder capability.

To improve overall defence, on 9 November 1941, the GKO created the post of Deputy Minister (Commissar) for Air Defence or Commander of the PVO and appointed General-leitenant Mikhail Gromadin, the former Moscow air defence chief, to the position. He controlled all air defence apart from Leningrad, which was overseen by Leningrad Front, with ten PVO regions west of the Urals and the northern Caucasus. During 1941 the PVO flew 90,991 sorties, of which 65 per cent (59,145) were patrols and only 3,173 were scrambles. In supporting the Red Army the PVO flew 27,516 sorties (30 per cent) while fighter sweeps amounted to only 30 sorties.

The Soviet Union did not develop a real interest in strategic bombing, with 'attacks upon administrative, political and military sites in the hinterland' being of lesser importance than striking enemy ground forces 'throughout the Operational and Strategic depth'. At first the DBA provided direct support to the hard-pressed Red Army with attacks upon troop and armoured concentrations as well as communications targets, all within 200 kilometres of the front line. The planned long range escort forces were never created and the bombers flew alone in daylight, with catastrophic consequences.

Supporting the North Front and attacking both Königsberg and Danzig was 1st AK DD (General-maior Vladimir Izotov), while 3rd AK (Polkovnik Nikolai Skripko) supported West Front and struck facilities around Warsaw, and 2nd AK (Polkovnik Konstantin Smirnov) and 4th AK (Polkovnik Vladimir Sudets) supported Southwest Front together with Polkovnik Aleksei Duboshin's 18th AD. In the first three months of the war the DB bomber flew 11,186 sorties, 70 per cent in daylight, of which 2,112 were from 22 June to 10 July. Almost all were against troops at low level in the late afternoon. Losses were so heavy that on July 3 Zhukov banned large formations from unescorted daylight operations, and also demanded high-altitude night bombing. Golovanov's 212th AP DD with its expert navigators attempted to strike Warsaw on 23/24 June but hit nearby towns, with two aeroplanes being forced to land by Russian fighters whose pilots had never seen a DB bomber before!

Between 22 June and 10 July DBA strength in the West fell from 1,339 bombers to 688, while the number of crews dropped from 931 to 722. By October 1 it was down to 472, the air corps being disbanded on 20 August. During 1941 the DBA flew 20,741 sorties and dropped 11,162 tonnes of bombs, but lost 389 aircraft to fighters and 206 to flak. Most of the effort, 15,408 sorties (74 per cent), was against enemy troops, 1,506 sorties (7 per cent) were against airfields and 1,346 against transport, while 1,478 were for transport.

Königsberg and Memel were attacked by 1st AK on 22 June, but little damage was inflicted and such raids were soon abandoned. While Stalin wanted to bomb Berlin, only the Baltic Fleet's 1st Mine-Torpedo Regiment (*Minno-Torpednyy Aviatsionnyy Polk*, MTAP) was immediately capable of such a mission – it was personally organised by the VVS-VMF commander General-leitenant Semen Zhavoronok. A successful reconnaissance from Muhu (Moon) Island, near Oesel, on 5 August was followed on 7/8 August by a 13-sortie mission against Berlin, and another 20 sorties on 13/14 August. The regiment's prime targets, however, were coastal towns, which involved 53 sorties until 22 October.

In early July 1941 two ADD regiments were created to strike targets deep in the enemy rear – 412th Heavy Bomber Regiment (TBAP) with the four-engined TB-7, and 420th Long Range Bomber Regiment (*Dahl'niy Bombardirovochnyy Aviatsionnyy Polk*, DBAP) with DB-3s and the new Yer-2. On 9 August they were assigned to the new 81st AD DD under well-known polar pilot and children's author Kombrig Mikhail Vodopyanov, who was ordered to strike Berlin with incendiaries – he despatched bombers to bases in the Leningrad area.[13] Only seven of the

18 bombers sent to Berlin on 9/10 August reported reached the target. Four were lost to friendly fire and accidents, one of them Vodopyanov's, although he survived. Another seven raids involving 46 sorties were staged up to 4/5 September, with several aircraft lost to engine failure. The latter caused a crew flying a lone raid to Berlin on 8/9 November to bail out after the pilot put the bomber on autopilot. Astonishingly, the aircraft landed safely, was recovered and repaired.

Zhigarev blamed the failure upon poor leadership and planning, so Stalin summoned Golovanov to Moscow and appointed him commander of 81st AD on 17 August, but Vodopyanov remained as a pilot at his own request. Golovanov largely agreed with Zhigarev, especially noting the crews' inexperience with radio navigation aids. He brought in experts from his 212th DBAP, and with their assistance he made the division the only one in the Soviet Union that could use navigation aids to help them safely make the round trip.

The only DBA strategic bombing campaign was against the Romanian oilfields, but again it was in the wake of the navy. Navy Minister Admiral Nikolai Kuznetsov had ordered attacks by noon on 22 June 1941, at a time when the VVS was banned from crossing the Romanian border. Daylight attacks on Romanian ports often fell foul of Constanta-based III./JG 52, which claimed most of the 31 bombers lost to 24 June. This effort left half of its fighters unserviceable, however. Casualties and a lack of results led Kuznetsov to end this campaign on 26 June, and on the night of 30 June–1 July, the bombers began minelaying. By the end of July the VVS-ChF bomber force had been halved, despite the addition of an NKVD bomber squadron.

Kuznetsov also ordered night attacks upon Ploesti's oilfields, but the usual weaknesses – only 30 VVS-ChF crews were night-qualified – meant few bombers found the target. From 9 July Ploesti became the priority for both the Navy and 4th AK DD, which opened the DBA campaign on 25 June by warming up with attacks on ports. Only 79 sorties were flown against Ploesti during July, including a daring 'Peshka' dive-bombing mission on the 13th. An unusual feature of this campaign was the use of the Combined Dive-Bomber (*Sostavnoi Pikiruyuschii*

Bombardirovschik, SPB) TB-3 'Aerial Mothership' (*Aviamatka*), carrying a pair of I-16s – each armed with two 250kg bombs – against a Danube bridge, which suffered five *Aviamatka* attacks during August. At about this time Golovanov also participated in a programme to develop radio-controlled TB-3s, SBs and DB-3s packed with explosives. These would be guided to their target by escorting aircraft after the pilot had bailed out. The Americans later developed a similar weapon in Project Aphrodite and, like them, the Russians abandoned the project due to fusing and control problems.

From mid-August VVS-ChF bombers supported beleaguered Odessa, although there were some morale-boosting missions against Bucharest during September. While the DBA now bore the brunt of the campaign against Ploesti, the navy did stage occasional raids, some by GST (licence-built Catalina) GVF flying boats. Soviet sources indicate there were 2,651 sorties against Romania, mostly harassing operations. The naval 2nd MTAP flew 295 sorties (92 against Ploesti) and dropped nearly 219 tonnes of bombs (75.3 tonnes on Ploesti). The Russians did damage Romania's oilfields, but the Luftwaffe and the FARR made them pay a heavy price, claiming 143 victories by 21 October, including 73 by *Jagdflieger*.

DBA strength continued to contract, and by 22 October, with Moscow under threat, it had 439 aircraft including 92 TB-3s, nine Pe-2s and 28 fighters. By 22 December this figure had dropped to 226 serviceable aircraft (182 DBs and 84 TB-3s and a number of TB-7s and Er-2s). In October it struck troop concentrations and airfields but then increasingly switched to communications, especially the rail network, bombing 32 stations during 7–18 December. Early in January 1942, as the Red Army advanced westward, Stavka ordered a campaign against the rail network around Smolensk, the prime supply base on the Moscow front. During a four-night campaign that was judged successful, some 200 sorties were flown. The campaign was extended to road communications and continued into April. Golovanov's men, renamed 3rd AD DD, also tried to decapitate *Heeresgruppe Mitte* by striking its headquarters – an operation similarly judged a success, although it was actually another failure.

Stalin was increasingly dissatisfied with the DBA's results, especially as the British trumpeted Bomber Command's growing successes. The idea of an elite bomber force may have come from Beria through the head of the Leningrad NKVD. In a report analysing air attacks upon Leningrad, Pavel Kuprin recommended the creation of a dedicated long range bomber force under Stavka control.[14] Stalin discussed with Golovanov the idea of reviving the Armies for Special Employment (*Armiya Osobogo Naznachiya*, AON), but decided instead to reorganise the DBA, centralise its command under Golovanov with Skripko as his deputy and make it answerable to Stavka.

Long Range Aviation (ADD) was created on 5 March 1942, with 341 bombers and 367 aircrew, of whom 57 per cent were qualified for night operations – their high quality was due to the fact that 87 per cent of the pilots and navigators assigned to ADD were from the pre-war VVS. Golovanov immediately began improving training, for which he acquired two or three Li-2s that were converted into navigation trainers. He also expanded his command, although Zhigarev must have resented losing control of the long range bombers while Golovanov took the cream of aircrews. Golovanov's bases were all to receive concrete runways, and he was awarded higher priority in terms of aircraft, engines, bombs and spares. This guaranteed supply of essential equipment would owe much to Golovanov's good relations with Stalin, which allowed him to get men out of prison camps, including Tupolev. This irritated Beria, as did the fact that ADD crews who were shot down behind enemy lines and escaped were not subjected to Smersh checks.

The ADD's role was identical to the DBA's, although now Golovanov would select the targets and his staff would then work out the details. However, the ADD's commitment to supporting the Red Army meant Golovanov spent much time flying to front headquarters, and his bombers still operated in penny packets. The ADD, like Bomber Command, would also be involved in supporting partisan operations. In April it began to create transport regiments, beginning with 101st Transport Aviation Regiment (*Trahnsportnyy Aviatsionnaya Polk*, TAP – later 101st AP DD) under female commander Major Valentina

Grizodubova, a famous GVF pilot who had been pressing for some months to join the long range force. Stalin, who was probably aware of her NKVD file and her close, if not intimate, relations with senior Party figures, queried the appointment. Golovanov correctly argued she was a capable pilot, only to discover, two years later, the truth of Oscar Wilde's comment that 'no good deed goes unpunished'.

Heavy losses in both battle and territory forced the Russians to use women more extensively than any other country. In addition to their traditional clerical, domestic and medical roles, they flew combat missions often alongside men, serviced and armed aircraft, acted as signallers and played a major role in supporting air operations. Women laid down most of the metal matting for runways supporting US bombers around Poltava in 1944, where nurses shielded wounded American airmen with their own bodies when the bases were bombed.

The influx of huge numbers of women into the armed forces bemused military leaders, and the Russians were no exception. Soviet society theoretically regarded men and women as equals, but in chauvinist times Russian men were more chauvinist than others. Yet Russian aviatrixes persuaded Stalin and Novikov to form three all-female regiments – fighter, assault and night bomber – in the vain hope of creating an all-female division, and all distinguished themselves, especially the 46th GvNBAP. But 'the beautiful girls', as Voroshilov called them, did not like female commanders, who were usually replaced with men.

It appears that in the early years of the war women had to adapt male uniforms, including underwear, although these problems were gradually overcome. Yet clothing was often in short supply, and in a summer parade of one fighter regiment in 1944 the irate *polkovnik* noticed a female member in a great coat. When she was ordered to remove it she had only her underwear on. The gallant *polkovnik* allowed her to put the coat back on, and later married her!

Some married couples served together, not always with happy consequences. The divisional signals officer of 205th IAD accidentally landed behind enemy lines and was captured. Interrogated by the Germans, she later escaped and returned to Soviet territory. Interrogated by Smersh, she admitted she had talked, which resulted in her husband and division commander, PolkovnikYurii Nemtsevich, being sent to the rear on 28 April 1944. Yet many couples who married later met in aviation regiments, although the mixing of the sexes in dangerous conditions so far from home inevitably caused sexual problems. Promiscuous girls could be sent away for 're-education', while many more were sent home pregnant. Relationships often began when male aircrew asked women to wash or sew their clothes, and few regimental commanders tried to ban them. Often couples were permitted to live together as 'soldiers' wives'. Indeed, female fighter pilot Lidiya Litvyak lived with Alexei Solomatin, who was her 'slave' in combat. Sometimes the relationship was formalised if the girl became pregnant.

There were more women in the support battalions, and as one assault regiment (*Shturmovaya Aviatsionnaya Polk*, ShAP) pilot noted, 'One could spend time with nice girls' from such units, relationships whose preliminaries involved dropping a greatcoat onto the ground. An IAP pilot noted that many pilots were too 'free' with women in the regiments, which led to 'excesses', including beating up one woman or pursuing another into a Party meeting, both perpetrators being sentenced to penal battalions.

The problems certainly concerned air army political departments. In the case of Papivin's 3rd Air Army (*Vozdushnaya Armiya*, VA), there were meetings between operational and Party commanders about 'disrespectful attitudes' to female troops, while Papivin himself demanded a 'special' attitude toVVS women. But Grizodubova put the boot on the other foot in the spring of 1944, accusing Golovanov of condoning sexual harassment.

Grizodubova made several landings behind enemy lines supporting partisans, but used her Party connections to complain that her regiment had been denied Guards status by both her divisional commander, General-maior Vasilii Kartakov (1st AD DD) and corps commander, General-leitenant Viktor Nestertsev (7th GvAK DD). Grizodubova claimed her superiors had refused to nominate the regiment because she would not sleep with them, and that Golovanov had condoned this conduct.

Nestertsev and Kartakov told Georgii Malenkov, Head of the Central Committee's Personnel Department, the regiment was denied the accolade because of its poor discipline and high accident rate, and that they had publically rebuked Grizodubova. Golovanov was not informed because Grizodubova was a name-dropper who always suggested an intimate connection with senior Party members and made unauthorised trips to Moscow. Despite (or because of) this, Malenkov was clearly leaning towards Grizodubova, who then claimed Golovanov and Kartakov were brothers-in-law, and for this reason in 1941 Golovanov had promoted him from *Maior* to *Polkovnik*.

When he heard this Golovanov laughed with relief, and when he said the promotion was recommended by Stalin, Malenkov shot out of the room. He returned to dismiss Grizodubova's complaints, warned she would face a tribunal and indicated she would lose her Party membership. A weeping Grizodubova was replaced in May 1944 by Maior Stepan Zapylenov, who turned around the unit that became 31st GvAP DD by the end of the year.

As the spring *rasputitsa* ended the winter fighting, Stalin took stock, and the VVS did not escape his attention. It had achieved much, but there was no escaping the fact that usually the Luftwaffe dominated the skies and the buck stopped at Zhigarev's desk. This may explain why Zhigarev left so slight a footprint in the sands of time, for he is mentioned in few memoirs and usually in lists of 'spear carriers' who contributed to the success of offensives.[15] In part this was because, like most Russian managers, he cringed before his superiors and cowed his subordinates. On one occasion Novikov was visiting an airfield when a TB-7 – an aircraft he had never seen before – landed, and as he inspected it he encountered VVS Commissar Pavel Stepanov, who introduced him to Zhigarev. Novikov asked if there was anything he could do to help, and was brusquely told, 'Mind your own business. We can do without you.' Zhigarev then drove off.

Whatever his lack of social skills, Zhigarev was a hard worker and skilled administrator. Rudenko, one of his few friends, said he had a penchant for research. He undoubtedly played a major role in keeping the VVS together in trying times along with his chief-of-staff from August 1941, General-maior (General-leitenant from 29 October)

Grigorii Vorozheikin, a former, and future, 'guest' of the NKVD. It is likely that reforms driven by his successor Novikov were based upon Zhigarev's foundations, but the former Leningrad air commander had powerful friends in Zhukov and Andrei Zhandov, as well as being a more dynamic personality.

The cause of Zhigarev's dismissal on 11 April 1942, was a dispute between him and Aviation Minister Shakhurin over the former's failure to provide pilots to pick up new aircraft from factories. Zhigarev claimed the aircraft had not been formally accepted, but when General-leitenant Nikolai Seleznev (the VVS Supply Director) was called in he confirmed the aircraft simply lacked pilots to ferry them. A furious Stalin called Zhigarev a scoundrel and told him to go. Yet Stalin appreciated his skills, and he was neither demoted nor disgraced, instead being given command of the Far Eastern VVS, where he was briefly an air army commander during the 1945 war with Japan.

Zhigarev's post-war career waxed as Novikov's waned, for in succession he commanded the ADD and then the VVS, before becoming Defence Minister. In 1959, as head of civil aviation, he signed an agreement establishing civil air links between London and Moscow. On the day he was relieved as VVS commander he left it a legacy by authorising evaluation of the LaGG-3 fitted with the M-82 radial engine. The resulting combination soon became the outstanding La-5 fighter.

CHAPTER 3

THE TIDE TURNS
May 1942 to February 1943

Novikov faced challenges as the spring *rasputitsa* ended the winter campaign and everyone looked towards Kharkov as the fulcrum for 1942's operations. Stalin was delighted by his successes, yet he recognised his forces needed to remain on the defensive due to material shortages. Nevertheless, he demanded an active defence.

Stalin wished to shield Moscow while simultaneously eroding enemy strength and expanding reserves for a strategic offensive at a later date. To improve the line Stalin wanted pre-emptive strikes, and received two plans from Timoshenko and Zhukov. Timoshenko proposed advancing from the Izyum Salient upon Kharkov, the lynchpin of the Ukrainian rail network, while Zhukov preferred eliminating the German Rzhev Salient. Stalin accepted both, together with a number of smaller operations, despite Stavka's fears this would disperse the country's scarce resources, such as Soviet air power.

On 1 May the VVS-KA had 3,700 aircraft on the main battle front, although 70.5 per cent of them were assigned to army and front headquarters. But it had only 3,146 pilots, which meant 16 per cent of the aircraft could not be flown, while less than 35 per cent of its pilots were qualified to fly at night. Augmenting the VVS were 329 ADD bombers, 1,051 PVO fighters and 448 VVS-KBF/ChF naval aircraft. The situation posed serious problems for Novikov, who was a short,

41-year-old widower with a surviving son. He had joined the VVS in 1933, and during the Purges of 1937 he was cashiered. Reinstated in June of the following year, Novikov was rapidly promoted.

He had studied air power, and especially the theories of Aleksandr Lapchinskii about the importance of gaining air superiority and using air power to support the army. This, together with his administrative skills, ensured he had played a significant role during the Winter War, while in 1941 he would concentrate his forces for greater effect. However, the strain of command under Stalin meant that Novikov, like many Soviet military leaders except Zhukov, was a heavy drinker, and by the end of the war he was an alcoholic.

Probably building on Zhigarev's foundations, Novikov reformed not only the front but also the training and supply organisations, while strengthening Stavka's reserve. His efforts to improve communications for command and control were aided by the Director of Signals Directorate, General-maior (General-leitenant from 30 April 1943) Georgii Gvozdkov. Beginning in the Stalingrad sector, from September 1942 they would establish radio networks at all levels down to regimental, and would introduce GCI into the VVS based upon command posts, initially manned by 25 reserve regiment commanders, some two to three kilometres from FEBA and at eight- to ten-kilometre intervals. These could call up fighters by radio, or telephone, in response to reports from a screen of forward observation posts.

Novikov sought to concentrate his limited air power rather than disperse it in penny packets. To shield Moscow, on 5 May 1942, he ordered the formation of the first Air Armies (VA) containing a fifth of the VVS, and he also planned reserve Fighter Armies (*Istrebitelyenaya Aviatsionnaya Armii*, IAA) and Bomber Armies (*Bombardirovochnaya Aviatsionnaya Armiya*, BAA). The first air armies were created from 10 to 16 May under former frontal air commanders General-leitenant Kutsevalov (West) and General-maiors Krasovskii (Bryansk) and Mikhail Gromov (Kalinin).

The air armies were multi-role commands consisting of air divisions, each of which were roughly equivalent to a *Geschwader* with three or four regiments – usually dedicated fighter, bomber, night bomber and assault formations, although some were mixed. They were created by stripping regiments from fronts and armies, although to allay Red Army fears about air support, many army commands were left with the comfort blanket of a Mixed Regiment (*Smeshannaya Aviatsionnaya Polk*, SAP), which included a fighter squadron, or NBAP regiment. The creation of air armies was extended into the southern fronts between 22 May and 15 November and into the northern fronts between 14 June and 1 December, when 14 VA was created to support the Karelian Front – the tenth formed in the West, while four more were created in the Far East.

The disruption of the training organisation and its shortages of resources hindered the flow of replacements, leaving Novikov to continue Zhigarev's policy of using NBAPs both for replacements and as the cadres for new units. During 1942 the VVS disbanded 39 and converted 58 to new roles – 28 as ShAPs and 22 as SAPs, while the remainder became transport units. The migration of NBAPs continued over the next two years, most becoming ShAPs, but one became an IAP, four became BAPs (including 970th NBAP with Bostons), while others became transport or liaison units.

Meanwhile, the Wehrmacht, including the Luftwaffe, also prepared for the summer campaign. Railways had been converted to the European gauge, and while roads remained rutted cart tracks, they could now be used to distribute fuel, food, ammunition and spares for the forthcoming offensive. Heavy losses forced Hitler to cut his coat to suit his cloth, and while he planned to smooth out the front line to economise in manpower, he hoped the Wehrmacht would quickly regain its old vigour, and this was reflected in OKW *Weisung Nr 41* published on 5 April.

In the Crimean Peninsula Manstein's 11 *Armee* was to eliminate the Kerch bridgehead (*Unternehmen Trappenjagd*) then take Sevastopol (*Unternehmen Störfang*). Bock's *Heeresgruppe Süd* was then to eliminate the Russian Izyum Salient (*Unternehmen Fridericus*) using General Friedrich Paulus's 6 *Armee* and *Armeegruppe Kleist* (17 *Armee* and 1 *Panzer Armee*). This would set the stage for the main campaign, *Unternehmen Fall Blau* – a series of envelopments to take the Wehrmacht to Stalingrad and Rostov, which would open the way for the occupation

TABLE III-1: LUFTWAFFE FUEL SITUATION 1942 (TONNES)

Quarter	Production	Consumption
Q1 1942	281,000	272,000
Q2 1942	333,000	388,000
Q3 1942	417,000	412,000
Q4 1942	441,000	354,000

TABLE III-2: SOVIET AIR POWER FUEL CONSUMPTION 1942

Branch	Tonnes
VVS-KA	3,030,121
ADD	510,085
VMF	235,523
GVF	37,638
Total	3,813,367

of the Caucasian oilfields. Once this was achieved Manstein would join *Heeresgruppe Nord* to take Leningrad.

Oil remained the Wehrmacht's Achilles' heel, with Romania and, to a lesser degree, Hungary the prime natural sources augmented by synthetic production in Germany. Luftwaffe consumption during 1941 outstripped supply to force ObdL to cut back non-operational flying times, but this ensured that during 1942 production exceeded total Luftwaffe consumption by 156,000 tonnes; yet the training organisation's allocation was further reduced, with adverse effects upon the students (see Table III-1). By contrast Soviet air power consumed 2.75 times more than the Luftwaffe at 3,965,382 tonnes, even when the Caucasian oilfields were threatened (see Table III-2).

Weisung Nr 41 assigned the Luftwaffe its usual range of Tactical and Operational Level tasks, although noting, 'The possibility of a hasty transfer of Luftwaffe units to the central and northern fronts must be borne in mind, and the necessary ground organisation for this must be maintained as far as possible.' Richthofen's Smolensk-based

Fliegerkorps VIII, which had supported *Heeresgruppe Mitte* during the winter, was to play a major role in the new offensive, but it needed a rest. Greim's *Fliegerkorps* V was reformed at Smolensk on 1 April and, after a brief handover, Richthofen and his staff returned to Germany on 10 April for four weeks' well-earned leave, while Greim's command was upgraded to *Luftwaffenkommando Ost*. Two days later Greim split the front into Generalleutnant Fiebig's *Fliegerdivision* 1 at Dugino in the north and former *Flfü Afrika* Generalleutnant Stefan Fröhlich's *Fliegerdivision* 2 in the south at Bryansk.

Richthofen had little time to enjoy his leave, for Jeschonnek telephoned on 18 April to inform him that, at Hitler's behest, he would be deployed autonomously to the Crimea – a move that angered Löhr. When Richthofen was briefed by Jeschonnek at *Luftflotte* 4 headquarters in Nikolayev, Löhr demanded that *Fliegerkorps* VIII should join Pflugbeil's *Fliegerkorps* IV supporting the main operation. Jeschonnek rebuffed him, and on 28 April Richthofen arrived in the Crimea, set up headquarters near Feodosia and assumed command of Wild on 30 April.

The Luftwaffe squadrons in the East required major reorganisation and re-equipment. Between 7 December 1941 and 8 April 1942, 859 aircraft were destroyed and 636 damaged, and by 30 March first-line strength was only 1,766 aeroplanes. The *Gruppen* had to be reorganised, their lost aircraft and crews replaced and the exhausted survivors given leave. First-line strength continued to drop to 1,746 combat aircraft by May Day, but in succeeding weeks units flooded back, and by 1 June strength had reached 2,324. There were few new aircraft apart from the Bf 109G fighter, the Ju 87D dive-bomber and the underpowered, twin-engined Hs 129 armoured ground-attack aircraft.

Geschwader stripped their *Ergänzungsgruppen* to provide extra crews, although some were not fully trained. Tactical air support was strengthened through the creation on 13 January of *Schlachtgeschwader* 1 under Oberstleutnant Otto Weiss, this unit being equipped with fighter-bombers (*Jabos*) and Hs 129s. The ground infrastructure was not neglected, especially in the south, where all-weather airfields were built, maintenance facilities improved and signal networks extended.

The reconnaissance arm needed the most urgent reforms because the *Heeresflieger* had withered on the vine, so administrative necessity drove changes. A third of the 55 *Nahaufklärungsstaffeln* were disbanded and the remainder, largely re-equipped with the Fw 189A, were grouped in May 1942 into *Nahaufklärungsgruppen* raised from *Koluft* and *Gruppenfliegerstäbe* to provide tactical reconnaissance. The army also lost its *Fern-* and *Nachtaufklärungsstaffeln*, which were grouped with Luftwaffe *Fernaufklärungsstaffeln* in July to form *Fernaufklärungsgruppen*.

As the ground dried out *Trappenjagd* (Bustard Hunt) began in the Crimea on 8 May, influenced by Richthofen's earlier lecture to Hitler on the value of air power in ground operations. Richthofen expanded the airfield system to reduce bomber sortie times and, because he was fascinated by the SD 2 anti-personnel bombs known as 'Devil's Eggs', he had more than 6,000 canisters of them delivered by the end of April. Manstein was delighted at the prospect of what the XXX *Armeekorps* war diary would describe as 'concentrated air support, the like of which has never existed', but shocked to be informed on 16 April by Hitler that he would personally oversee the air campaign. Manstein's first meeting with Richthofen on 22 April proved reassuring, and they began a close working relationship, despite the latter's propensity to play armchair general.

The slow return of *Gruppen* from Germany delayed *Trappenjagd* for three days, but when it began Richthofen had 20 *Gruppen* with 740 aircraft, plus some seaplanes, while Pflugbeil provided an extra two *Kampfgruppen*. Facing them on 1 May were 404 aircraft under General-maior Evgenii Nikolaenko, who had become Crimea Front air commander on 28 January, only to discover that most of his regiments were under army command. His few airfields were overcrowded and some aircraft were based on the Taman Peninsula.

Sitting in the front command post and terrifying everyone was Red Army political chief Lev Mekhlis, who micromanaged operations and demanded fighters scramble to meet every Luftwaffe intrusion. This exhausted pilots and left many aircraft unserviceable. Between 12 February and 7 May, 44th Army's 743rd IAP flew 2,160 sorties and lost 11 I-153s and six pilots, including the commander. It was duly left to face *Trappenjagd* with just a single serviceable fighter. The front and VVS-ChF lost 50 aircraft during April, while the latter had its commander, Nikolai Ostryakov, killed on 24 April when his visit to a repair facility coincided with that of Stukas. He was replaced on May Day by Ermachenkov, who would remain in this position until the end of the war.

From the first day the Luftwaffe dominated the air, with 'Messers' orbiting Russian airfields, yet the Russian air commanders initially failed to recognise the scale of the impending disaster. Torrential rain proved a greater obstacle to Richthofen than the Russians, and with his Stuka airfields turned to swamps, he had to use KG 55's He 111s on low-level missions to scatter SD 2s and wreak havoc, but this cost the *Geschwader* eight bombers. The Russians were destroyed by 20 May, by which time Richthofen's units had flown some 5,500 sorties and lost 37 aircraft – the Russians lost 417. Nikolaenko, who alone lost 315, was dismissed on 12 May and never again held a front line command. He was replaced by ADD Deputy Commander Skripko.

Support for *Trappenjagd* severely dropped from 12 May because Timoshenko launched his offensive from the Izyum Salient towards Kharkov. For Novikov it was bad timing because his reforms had barely begun. Indeed, Vershinin, commander of the South Front's 308 aircraft, learned on 7 May that his forces would become 4th VA on 22 May. While preparing for this change he would have to support the secondary attack as Southwest Front launched the main blow, supported by 618 aircraft still under General-leitenant Falaleev's command. All the regiments were severely under-strength with total establishments of 600 and 680 aircraft, respectively.

Falaleev, who would celebrate an unhappy 43rd birthday on 31 May, was a former deputy commander of Far Eastern air forces, VVS Inspector General and then VVS Main Directorate's First Deputy. He had distinguished himself at the front by concentrating his forces, but for this offensive 285 aircraft, including 153 fighters and 57 night bombers, were in task forces under army command, leaving 333 aeroplanes, including 117 fighters and 121 night bombers, under his authority.

The Russian attack on 12 May surprised General Friedrich Paulus's 6 *Armee*, which planned to launch *Fridericus* in the same area a week later. The ADD began to strike rail communications and airfields from the night of 9/10 May, Russian intelligence having estimated Pflugbeil's strength at 330 combat aircraft. On 1 May Pflugbeil had 507 aeroplanes, but then surrendered 360 to Richthofen, leaving him only 147 aircraft, including a *Stukagruppe*, to meet the threat. Paulus was pushed back as Falaleev flew 563 sorties and Vershinin 100 on the opening day, the 'Ilyushas' proving especially effective against enemy morale.

Once Hitler recognised the seriousness of the situation he ordered Richthofen to return Pflugbeil's *Gruppen* and also to dispatch 150 of his own aircraft. The arrival of 15 *Gruppen* from 13 May gave Pflugbeil 650 aircraft to interdict the battlefield, as Kleist prepared to lance into the Izyum Salient from the south. From 14 May the pendulum began to swing in the Germans' favour as their fighters savaged poorly escorted bomber and attack missions.

Luftwaffe strike forces hit troop concentrations and communications with such effect that Russian fighters were ordered on 15 May 'to clear the skies of German bombers'. That day, a noon conference completed details for the German riposte, and two days later, under clear, bright, skies, Kleist began driving north with massive Luftwaffe support from *Gefechtsverband Süd*, created the previous day with 11 *Gruppen*. The Luftwaffe provided air support 'most effectively' as the 1 *Panzer Armee* war diary observed, and within 20 minutes of a request for air support the troops would hear the sound of German aircraft. By now VVS strength had been slashed, with many regiments down to six aircraft, yet commanders demanded more missions, which exhausted and demoralised the men.

The Luftwaffe established air superiority, and on a hot, humid 17 May *Kampfgruppe* crews flew up to seven sorties. Falaleev lacked day bombers, his 'Ilyushas' suffered poor serviceability and in desperation he ordered fighters to be fitted with RS-82 unguided rockets for ground-attack missions, making them vulnerable to the *Jagdgruppen*. Intensified ADD attacks on rail and airfield targets from 18 May failed to slow down the German advance, and Timoshenko later reported, 'From the second day of our offensive the enemy achieved air superiority, and by means of continuous strikes by a large quantity of aircraft our forces were deprived of freedom of manoeuvre on the battlefield.'

On 19 May the rest of Pflugbeil's squadrons supported Paulus's counter-offensive against the northern face of the salient, while the next day Stukas struck the Donets crossings to destroy five bridges and damage another four in order to prevent the enemy retreat. On 21 May Löhr ordered Pflugbeil to support Kleist, adding, 'The objective is to wear down enemy forces by ceaseless attacks, to cause him heavy losses by bombing and strafing and thus hasten his final destruction.' The previous day, with the arrival of II./SchG 1 with 24 Hs 129s and two Hs 123s, ObdL asked Löhr to report on the effectiveness of Hs 129Bs armed with 30mm MK 101 cannon against tanks – during the battle they were credited with 25 destroyed.

By 24 May the two spearheads had met, and within four days the flames of Russian resistance were extinguished in a battle that cost Löhr some 150 aircraft. Pflugbeil had flown 15,648 sorties and dropped 7,700 tonnes of bombs, together with 383 supply canisters, for the loss of 49 aircraft and 110 aircrew, while transport aircraft flew 1,545 tonnes of supplies to forward airfields and isolated troops. A typical *Kampfgruppe*, III./KG 55, which joined him from *Fliegerkorps* VIII on 13 May, averaged 49 sorties a day and dropped 77.75 tonnes of bombs between 14 and 17 May.

The Russians, who lost 542 aircraft, failed due to a combination of decentralised control, aircraft shortages, inexperienced pilots and poor communications and tactics. Falaleev, described by Rudenko as 'thoughtful and considerate', was the scapegoat, being severely criticised for burdening his fighters with rockets. In June he was relieved by General-maior Timofei Khryukin, a veteran of air combat in both Spain and China. However, Novikov recognised Falaleev's strengths and in July appointed him VVS Chief-of-Staff, where he remained until April 1946. Promoted to Marshal in August 1944, by which time he was Deputy Commander, Falaleev became commandant of the VVS Academy post-war, before retiring due to ill health in 1950 and dying five years later.

Pflugbeil now supported *Unternehmen Wilhelm* and *Fridericus* II so as to secure jump-off lines for *Blau*. Richthofen was originally scheduled for the latter mission but Jeschonnek decided to allow him to complete *Unternehmen Störfang* (Sturgeon Trap). Operations from 10 to 25 June were hindered by rain, which frequently grounded the Luftwaffe, and on 23 June a staff officer carrying plans for *Blau* I ignored security regulations and flew to the front, landed behind enemy lines and was killed. The plans fell into Russian hands, but Stalin dismissed them as a hoax and continued to believe the main blow would again be towards Moscow. The Germans encouraged this with a deception operation, *Kreml* (Kremlin), but *Blau* I was renamed *Braunschweig*, *Blau* II became *Clausewitz* and *Blau* III became *Dampfhammer*.

The blow fell on Khryukin, who was informed on 9 June that his command was to become 8th VA, although it was not established until 13 June. Nevertheless, he and Vershinin's 4th VA destroyed or badly damaged 20 of Pflugbeil's aircraft on the first day of the offensive, half of them *Zerstörer*, although Khryukin's own losses were also heavy. The completion of *Fridericus* II on 25 June brought few prisoners for the Germans in a disappointing swansong for Löhr.

Meanwhile, preparations for *Störfang*, the assault upon Sevastopol, were hastily completed. Returning units gave Richthofen a dozen *Gruppen* with 449 aircraft on 1 June, with the *Fliegerkorps* providing tactical air support while Wild, with 70 aircraft plus seaplanes, interdicted Soviet shipping. Sevastopol was defended by Polkovnik Georgii Deyuva's newly formed 3rd Special Air Group (*Osobaya Aviagruppa*, OAG) VVS-ChF, which had 98 aircraft on 20 May but only limited support from former teacher General-leitenant Sergei Goryunov's 5th VA in the North Caucasus and the VVS-ChF.

The German airmen acted as siege gunners when preparations began on 2 June with 723 sorties to drop 570 tonnes of bombs on the port, while Deyuva could fly only 70 sorties. By 7 June Richthofen had flown 3,069 sorties, some bomber crews flying 18 times a day, to deliver 2,264 tonnes of bombs excluding incendiaries but including SC 1400, SC 1800 and SC 2500 heavy bombs. The supply system, especially with fuel, could not keep pace with such intense operations and the sortie tempo declined with a daily average of 1,000 for 8–11 June and 780 for 13–17 June. Deyuva received 28 Yak-1 fighters during 10–11 June, but the pilots flying these new aircraft were inexperienced and contributed little to the port's defence. On 20 June his bombers and flying boats were withdrawn, leaving him with just 31 aircraft by 4 June.

The Russians continued to bring in men by sea, but it was becoming increasingly hazardous, and Wild accounted for two destroyers, two minor warships, 11 merchantmen (22,591grt) and a salvage vessel from May to July, while a destroyer and a merchantman (2,787grt) were lost to Luftwaffe-laid mines.[1] The Russians stopped sending large vessels on 27 June, while the GVF flew 288 Li-2 night supply flights from 21 June to 1 July, Black Sea Fleet commander Vitse-Admiral Filipp Oktyabrskii taking one of the last flights out.

With German bomb stocks running low, precision delivery was vital, with some targets facing 30 attacks daily. On 23 June *Fliegerkorps* VIII departed, leaving Wild in command, and the pace declined to 400 sorties a day. Wild toured the airfields cajoling unit commanders and raising the average daily sortie rate in the last five days of the campaign to 961, including 1,329 on 29 June. The following day Deyuva's surviving aircraft departed, leaving the skies open to the enemy, having flown 3,144 sorties from 25 May to 1 July, including 1,621 ground attack, for the loss of 69 aeroplanes.

The last defender fell on 4 July, by which time the Luftwaffe had flown 23,751 sorties, lost only 31 aircraft and dropped 28,528 tonnes of bombs at a time when the monthly average expenditure for ordnance during 1942–43 was 27,100 tonnes. The level of effort owed much to the dedication of the *Schwarzmänner*, who ensured a serviceability rate of 64 per cent. Yet the success would prove a poisoned chalice for, like Demyansk, it raised army expectations, which the Luftwaffe failed to match, exacerbating future relations between the two services.

Richthofen was transferred to Kursk to support the main campaign, but he would not lead *Fliegerkorps* VIII for much longer. Sevastopol demonstrated he was overdue for promotion, and on 28 June – the day

Braunschweig began – he formally relieved Löhr as commander of *Luftflotte* 4 while also leading the *Fliegerkorps*. There was a week of intense activity as Richthofen provided Tactical Level support to clear the passage of tanks while Stalino-based Pflugbeil flew Operational Level missions to strike enemy headquarters, reserves and communications – the long days allowed even bomber crews to fly five sorties a day. Richthofen coped thanks to Löhr's capable chief-of-staff, General Günther Korten, and on 4 July Fiebig replaced him at *Fliegerkorps* VIII.

For *Braunschweig* the Luftwaffe assembled 2,690 combat aircraft (including Spanish and Croatian *Staffeln*) on the main front – its largest concentration in the East since *Barbarossa* and never later equalled, with Richthofen having 59 per cent (1,582 aircraft). He received 20 *Gruppen* from the West and the Mediterranean and three from his northern neighbours, which were augmented by 265 Hungarian, Italian, Romanian and Slovak combat aircraft, while Greim, with 496 aircraft, would support the *Kreml* deception from mid-June by increasing reconnaissance flights around Moscow.

The VVS had 3,613 combat aircraft on the main front by 1 July, supported by 377 ADD bombers, 1,190 PVO fighters and 452 naval aircraft. Stavka's reserve had dropped since May to 377 in 51 regiments, which, on establishment, should have had 1,122 aircraft. Neither industry nor the training organisation could match the losses, and between 1 July and 1 November 1942, an average of 118 regiments a month were resting, re-equipping or forming – a loss to VVS strength of nearly 2,600 aircraft.[2] Opposite *Luftflotte* 4, which had 1,758 combat aircraft and 250 Allied, were Timofei Khryukin's 8th VA, Krasovskii's 2nd VA, Vershinin's 4th VA and Goryunov's 5th VA, with Ermachenkov's VVS-ChF – a total of 1,856 combat aircraft. In addition the fronts could call upon the PVO, notably 65 fighters of General-maior Ivan Yevsevyev's 101st IAD PVO behind Bryansk Front, and the ADD to give a slight numerical superiority over the Germans. The VVS was extremely active striking enemy airfields while the PVO intercepted as many reconnaissance flights as possible, bringing down two aircraft with Taran tactics.

Low clouds and heavy rain delayed the launch of *Braunschweig* by 24 hours, but it opened on 28 June with a Luftwaffe assault upon communications for the loss of 15 aircraft, while the Russians lost 23. In a 17-hour period on the first day there was the usual intense activity, with crews flying up to six sorties. *Gefechtsverband Nord*, based upon KG 76, was created here under Generalmajor Alfred Bülowius, an 'Old Eagle' who had been in the 'England *Geschwader*' and then served in the army until he transferred to the Luftwaffe in 1934. However, he had been running training units for the past two years.

The Russians hastily pulled back behind the Don river and tried to rally around Voronezh, which Pflugbeil struck with every available bomber despite the efforts of Yevsevyev's fighters. Krasovskii was apparently made a scapegoat and replaced at 2nd VA on 4 July by General-maior Konstantin Smirnov, the former Volga District VVS commander. To stabilise the Voronezh situation General-maior Yevgeniyy Beletskii's new 1st IAA was committed on 5 July with 231 fighters, including American P-39 Airacobras dubbed Kobras by the Russians. The VVS constantly struck the German troops, but 'Ilyusha' losses were heavy and local commanders ignored Novikov's instructions to use their fighters only against bombers. Made into fighter-bombers with 250kg bombs, the aeroplanes roamed up to 30 kilometres behind enemy lines, sometimes on armed reconnaissance missions.

On 4 July Paulus established a bridgehead across the Don, and this forced back Khryukin's 8th VA, with just 342 sorties during the next three days. In mid-June Moscow demanded that the 'Ilyusha' fly with full bomb loads, but 4th VA had only nine Il-2s and numerous 'horseless' pilots, so regiments sought to raise bomb loads by 200kg.

On 7 July the Voronezh Front was created from part of Bryansk Front, retaining Smirnov's 2nd VA. However, a shortage of officers meant General-maior Ivan Pyatykhin's 15th VA joined Bryansk Front as late as 22 July. The fighting cost the Russians dear. Khryukin flew 3,546 sorties between 1 and 11 July and lost 91 aircraft, while in six days Beletskii lost half his command – 93 fighters destroyed and 23 badly damaged. From 28 June to 31 July Yevsevyev's aircrew flew 2,413 sorties and claimed 47 victories, while the ADD flew 3,125 sorties and dropped more than 4,000 tonnes of bombs to support the Voronezh defenders. A further 1,246 sorties were flown against communications links from 5 to 31 July.

With the front line now anchored in the north at Voronezh, Hitler sent troops, including five *Kampfgruppen*, south to support *Clausewitz*, leaving German and Hungarian troops supported by Bülowius with two *Gruppen* and Colonel Sándor András's 2nd Hungarian Air Brigade. Still convinced that Moscow was the objective, Stalin demanded a counter-offensive around Voronezh, which was launched on 20 July without success, although bridgeheads were established along the Don. In response five *Kampfgruppen* returned to Bülowius, with crews flying up to four sorties a day. The lone *Jagdgruppe* lost eight fighters from 28 June to 31 July, but helped destroy 283 of Smirnov's aircraft, halving his command and bringing total Russian losses between 28 June and 24 July to 783.

To contain the threat around Voronezh Richthofen despatched *Fliegerkorps* I headquarters, which had arrived from *Luftflotte* 1 on 19 July. He wanted Pflugbeil to command it but was persuaded to give it to Korten on 24 August, despite regarding him as 'too young'. The headquarters was redesignated *Luftwaffekommando Don* on 26 August and arrived in Kharkov two days later, initially with eight *Gruppen* and a few Allied squadrons. Korten's Luftwaffe element was soon halved, and by 1 September he had only 151 aircraft augmented by 110 Hungarian and Italian aeroplanes, the latter under General Enrico Pezzi. Korten was forced to rely upon brains rather than brawn, and established headquarters at each end of his sector, switching forces to meet crises.

Meanwhile, Fiebig supported *Clausewitz*, which proved an anti-climax because three days before the Germans struck, on 9 July, Stalin ordered a withdrawal to avoid envelopment. Yet there was still aerial fighting, and in this, and earlier operations, Fiebig had lost 110 Stukas and *Schlachtflieger* by 10 July. Just as *Clausewitz* began, Hitler split Bock's *Heeresgruppe Süd*, which was supported by both of Richthofen's *Fliegerkorps* – Bock's *Heeresgruppe B*, supported by Fiebig would advance on Stalingrad, while *Heeresgruppe A*, under Generalfeldmarschall Wilhelm List and supported by Pflugbeil, would drive into the

Caucasus. The Russian withdrawal caused Hitler to abandon *Blau* III/*Dampfhammer* on 13 July and order the two *Heeresgruppen* to strike across the lower Don in a bid to envelop the enemy, while 6 *Armee*, still supported by Fiebig, advanced on the northern flank as Bock was replaced by Weichs.

To take Rostov, the gateway to the Caucasus, Hoth's 4 *Panzerarmee* joined List, with Fiebig briefly joining his comrade for this operation before thunderstorms washed away *Clausewitz*. The squadrons, especially those controlled by Fiebig who had most of the single-engined units, moved forward so rapidly that their new airfields were sometimes still under artillery fire. Most of Fiebig's twin-engined aircraft went to Pflugbeil, who could support them more effectively from his established bases. The Luftwaffe was very active operationally, striking airfields and communications (especially bridges), although the usual combination of extreme activity and lengthening supply lines reduced sortie levels – III./KG 55 flew an average of 23 per day to drop 29 tonnes of bombs between 24 and 31 July.

Khryukin's aircrew flew 3,546 sorties between 1 and 11 July, most lasting 30 minutes, and dropped nearly 263 tonnes of bombs. Nevertheless, on 14 July he was ordered back across the Don; but retreat caused all the air armies serious problems. They had few vehicles, most of which were worn out and kept breaking down, so it was difficult to supply airfields, while there were serious shortages of low-loaders and tractors. Khryukin dropped from 217 to 138 serviceable aircraft between 2 and 11 July, stores could not be evacuated and as personnel marched eastwards Khryukin had to use 272nd Night Bomber Aviation Division (*Nochnoy Bombardirovochnyy Aviatsionnaya Diviziya*, NBAD) to keep track of squadrons. His headquarters moved every day between 4 and 8 July, with his 235th IAD moving three times in five days. Vehicles and dumps were destroyed, including most of Khryukin's tyres, but heavy rain slowed the German advance and made it difficult to supply its spearheads. III./KG 4 was forced to fly supply runs, while on 12 July, Ju 52/3ms flew in 200 tonnes of fuel.

Paulus reached the Chir, a subsidiary of the Don, on 17 July, and two days later he was ordered to take Stalingrad. To defend the city

Khryukin, on 22 July, had 337 serviceable aircraft augmented by Stalingrad's 102nd IAD PVO, under Podpolkovnik Ivan Krasnoyuchenko to 15 October then Polkovnik Ivan Puntus. This had 50 to 60 fighters, mostly 'Ishaks' and 'Chaikas', supported by three *Permatit* radars. Fiebig had some 250 aircraft augmented by 33 Italian fighters. The 'Ilyushas' proved so troublesome, picking off trucks during late July, that Lützow's JG 3 made them a priority target. Supply shortages brought the German advance to a stop north of Kalach, some 75 kilometres west of Stalingrad, as the Russians averaged 550–600 sorties a day.

On 30 July a major Soviet counter-attack around Kalach briefly isolated XIV *Panzerkorps* headquarters, which was soon relieved, after major air battles in which Khryukin's aircrews flew more than 1,000 sorties but his bombers tended to operate in poorly escorted penny-packet formations. The new Bf 109G, with its twin 20mm cannon, proved to be very effective against 'Ilyushas', which accounted for 18 of Khryukin's 27 losses on 31 July. The battles also saw the front deputy air commander General-maior Rudenko directing GCI from the 8th VA command post using visual observation reports. Although this form of control showed potential, fighter pilots were reluctant to accept instructions from the ground, preferring to patrol the FEBA, where targets were plentiful.

Meanwhile, Pflugbeil supported an advance into the Donets Bend to secure jump-off points for a thrust into the Caucasus, nearing Rostov by 20 July. The Luftwaffe's prime opponent was Vershinin's 4th VA, whose headquarters moved 11 times between 11 July and 10 August, and flew only 630 sorties between 9 and 12 July due to the disrupted infrastructure and loss of material – one pilot managed to save his damaged fighter by commandeering a team of oxen to tow it to the airfield in a four-day Odyssey! By 20 July Richthofen had 718 serviceable aircraft, including 36 with ShG 1 and 86 *Zerstörer*, while to shield the Caucasus Vershinin and Goryunov had a total of 160 aircraft. Rostov fell on 23 July in a battle that saw Wild's torpedo-bombers drop SC 1800 bombs, the aerial battle bringing VVS losses on this front to 783 between 28 June and 4 July. To prevent the enemy exploiting their success the

VVS and VVS-ChF harassed every German attempt to cross the Don around Rostov with 2,431 sorties between 20 and 28 July, some being made by MBR-2 flying boats.

These were dark days for the Soviet Union, and they placed great strain on the political officers or commissars who headed the Party organisation and who had a separate code of conduct. Until 'unitary command' was established on 9 October 1942, the commissar was also the deputy unit commander. Not only did he have to counter-sign all orders, he also had to perform the roles of evangelical priest, guard dog and welfare officer.

Relations with officers and men varied from unit to unit, often depending upon whether or not he was an airman – one artillery observation pilot noted he had never met a decent commissar during the war. A commissar would exhort pilots to ever greater feats and berate them if he deemed they had failed, which could be particularly galling. When one 'flightless' commissar called a fighter pilot a coward for not taking off when 'Messers' strafed his airfield, the pilot retorted, 'Fuck you. If you want to fight take the aeroplane up yourself', and the regimental commander backed him. Yet many flying commissars were respected or even liked, although all remained wary of them for they were the eyes and ears of the Party, ready to denounce 'cowards' and 'defeatists'. Newcomers were warned to be careful what they said when the commissar was around.

The commissar organised Party lectures – officially 'meetings' to 'discuss' the military or political situation, but even Party members found them boring. He would exhort airmen before offensives to new peaks of endeavour, often through public pledges, and sometimes organised unit parades. He also controlled access to the Party, one assault regiment pilot putting in his application before take-off and having it endorsed by the time he had landed. Many aircrew, even those who had suffered from Party decisions, were anxious to join it, and membership certainly helped win the commissar's recommendations for honours or awards.

A GvIAP commander was killed in July 1944 when the regimental commissar, his 'slave', abandoned him. He was punished by being sent to a penal battalion for cowardice. This was a common punishment for infractions of the military code, with such units having a high mortality rate. Sometimes men were sent to a penal battalion for mission failure, such as providing inadequate fighter escort or bombing their own troops, yet it did provide official redemption to survivors, or for those who distinguished themselves with the reinstatement of rank and honours. From 9 September 1942, penal squadrons were formed in the Stalingrad Front's 8th VA, with another on 22 September in 5th VA. These were fighter, attack and night bomber units that were used to maintain both discipline and air strength. They apparently withered away by early 1943.

Meanwhile, the day Rostov fell, Hitler again demonstrated his strategic incoherence with *Weisung Nr 43*, which assumed the Russians in the south had been annihilated and that the Donets was secure. List was ordered to complete the destruction of enemy forces in the north Caucasus then seize the eastern coast of the Black Sea to neutralise the Soviet Black Sea Fleet, while simultaneously taking the oilfields in *Unternehmen Edelweiss*. However, he lost Hoth to Weichs, who was to continue his advance on the Don, take Stalingrad then advance down the Volga to Astrakhan. While providing the strongest support for List, Richthofen was also to help Weichs, although 'the early destruction of the city of Stalingrad is especially important'. He was to interdict enemy oil transport but not bomb the oilfields unless List's operations made this 'absolutely essential'. From 25 July Pflugbeil began to interdict traffic on the Volga and by the end of the month he had virtually cut oil traffic. From 26 October to 15 November his attacks in the Caspian sank two tankers, a large tug and two barges (total 6,709grt) to create major problems for Soviet oil distribution into the summer of 1943.

Richthofen bitterly complained to ObdL about supporting diverging *Heeresgruppen* with inadequate resources. In June and July he lost 740 combat aircraft destroyed or badly damaged, 391 of them to enemy action, while 177 aircraft were sent back for overhauls. Only 668 replacements were received, leaving him with barely 1,500 aircraft because the Luftwaffe was already overstretched. This forced Richthofen to juggle his limited assets over the next five months.[3] At first he focused upon the advance to Stalingrad, probably because it was easier to support, leaving Pflugbeil as the poor relation supporting List and Wild, who also sank seven merchantmen (21,541grt) between 1 July, 1942, and 2 July, 1943. On 20 August Richthofen regretfully informed List that he was transferring most of his aircraft to Stalingrad on Hitler's orders, and when List's chief-of-staff, Generalleutnant Hans von Greiffenberg, asked OKH on 28 August when the *Heeresgruppe* would receive air support, he was told tersely, 'When Stalingrad is taken, or given up as impossible.'

The Wehrmacht advance on Stalingrad was bitterly opposed, Stalin having issued his 'Not one step backwards' order on 28 July. Three days later Pflugbeil's bombers were ordered to bomb the city while Paulus and Hoth renewed their advance in early August to force the Russians to divide their forces. Novikov planned to create 16th VA, authorised on 6 August, from 8th VA to defend Stalingrad's southern approaches, but it was difficult to find enough men for the new headquarters. Eventually most of 1st IAA's staff were assigned to the new air army, but in the meantime Khryukin had to cover both fronts. Rudenko established an air group within 8th VA to support the southern approaches, and when 16th VA was formed on 4 September he became operational commander, although the nominal commander was former commissar and gifted administrator General-leitenant Pavel Stepanov. He had just organised Khryukin's infrastructure, building 19 airfields east of the Volga to bring the total to 50 and providing 3,100 tonnes of fuel. The new air army would reflect the two officers' strengths, but even before its formation Stepanov knew his roles were purely administrative and temporary.

These were hard times for Khryukin, who lost 230 aircraft from 20 July to 10 August, with serviceable aircraft grouped under experienced commanders. From 20 July to 17 August he received 21 full-strength regiments (447 aircraft), of which 75 per cent had modern combat aircraft and from mid-August another 30 from training centres, although in the 220th IAD only a third of the pilots were trained in formation flying. The reinforcements included 287th IAD on 20 August with 57 new La-5 fighters, which suffered teething troubles and initially proved inferior to the Bf 109F/Gs. Nevertheless, Russian airmen, flying 300–350 sorties a day and 100–150 at night, inflicted a steady trickle of losses upon the Luftwaffe, while 'Ilyushas' eroded truck strength. However, they could not stop the next onslaught on 21 August, supported by Fiebig's 600 aircraft.

'Ilyusha' losses were high partly because the aircraft had no tail gunner, the average pilot at Stalingrad lasting three sorties. From early August Khryukin augmented them with LaGG-3-37 fitted with 37mm cannon and deployed fighter-bombers. Moscow was reluctant to develop a two-seat version of the 'Ilyusha' for fear of disrupting production or reducing performance, but regiments began to convert aircraft with a crude tail-gunner position, often using a leather belt as a seat. This reduced losses to fighters, and production of the two-seater Il-2m3 began in the summer of 1942. The aircraft debuted on 30 October, at a time when regiments were developing shallow dive-bombing tactics to compensate for poor bombsights.

On 23 August Richthofen assembled 1,200 aircraft to support an advance through Stalingrad to the banks of the Volga as the *Kampfgruppen* began a 24-hour bombardment with 1,600 sorties. Khryukin and Krasnoyuchenko had 260 serviceable aircraft, as well as 100 ADD bombers. They could not prevent 1,000 tonnes of German bombs, including incendiaries, falling from as low as 2,000 metres to turn Stalingrad's log-cabin suburbs into a forest of stone chimneys, leaving the city centre under a thick pall of smoke. Only three bombers were lost because Krasnoyuchenko lacked experienced pilots capable of defending Stalingrad from such attacks.

Things began to improve from late August when two radars were assigned to provide Russian fighters with GCI, initially from the division command post and then from the bases of 572nd (Yak-1) and 629th (Kittyhawk) IAPs. They operated 18–20 hours a day and could detect aircraft at 3,000 metres some 120 kilometres away and at 5,000 metres up to 150 kilometres away. Nevertheless, the system failed to gain pilot confidence until November. During July–December 102nd IAD would fly 68,813 sorties and be credited with 647 victories.

The bombing helped Paulus's spearheads reach the banks of the Volga, where they were briefly isolated and sustained by fuel and ammunition brought in by 300 Ju 52/3ms and He 111s. There was then a brief pause to bring up supplies and to concentrate the Wehrmacht for the assault upon Stalingrad. Hungarian and Italian troops, followed by 3rd Romanian Army, were now holding the 500-kilometre Don line south of Voronezh, and added some 150 aircraft to Korten's strength. The Romanians then sent General Ermil Gheorghiue's *Gruparea Aeriană de Luptă* (GAL) with 180 combat aircraft, which deployed from 6 September.

Khryukin's headquarters had been forced across the Volga but continued its dynamic, although ineffective, defence at the cost of 201 aircraft between 23 and 31 August to leave it with 192 serviceable machines, including 57 fighters. The situation was so serious that as Stalingrad burned, Novikov arrived to coordinate air operations. The following day Golovanov sent him five more bomber divisions to join the DBs and Il-4s of 50th AD in a task force under his deputy Skripko, who had 143 bombers, including TB-3s and Li-2s, by 25 August, and immediately began to strike the Don crossings.[4] During the pause Fiebig received most of Pflugbeil's bombers for another 24-hour aerial bombardment of Stalingrad from 3 September to support Paulus's advance into the city. He established a command post with a panorama of the battlefield, while an army observation battalion provided an up-to-the-minute picture of the situation. Stukas flew four sorties a day in *Staffel*-size missions against targets selected from small-scale maps. Indeed, Richthofen was to comment in his diary on 1 November that his aircraft were dropping bombs within grenade-throwing range. During this period Hs 129s largely removed their cannon and were used as light bombers because pilots were sceptical about the effectiveness of the MK 101 cannon against tanks.

Gruppe-size attacks were only for Paulus's major thrusts, and he agreed in late September that *Kampfgruppen* should be confined to striking artillery on the Volga's eastern bank and to interdicting river traffic. Yet Richthofen seized every opportunity to criticise Paulus's leadership, even persuading OKH to despatch five combat engineer battalions in a vain effort to turn the tide of battle. As late as 16 November he was complaining about Paulus to Army Chief-of-Staff Generaloberst Zeitzler, who replaced Halder on 25 September.

The open steppes made it easy for Fiebig to build airstrips for his squadrons, with *Stuka-* and *Schlachtgruppen* established between the Don and the Chir within sound of the battle, *Jagd-* and *Zerstörergruppen* within the Don Bend itself and *Kampfgruppen* operating from Morozovskaya and Tatsinskaya, 200–250 kilometres from Stalingrad. A typical *Kampfgruppe*, III./KG 55 flew 288 day missions between 28 September and 24 October, these being largely short-range sorties with maximum loads to deliver 2490.25 tonnes of bombs. A further ten long-range night sorties delivered 12.5 tonnes.

On 4 September the VVS and PVO had 738 aircraft, including 313 fighters and 241 'Ilyushas', to defend Stalingrad, augmented by 150–200 ADD bombers. Khryukin's men resisted as best they could, flying 22,691 sorties from 13 September to 18 November and dropping 5,063 tonnes of bombs. On 1 September he had only 97 serviceable fighters, and from the next day had priority for Yak-1 production, augmented during September by the first Yak-7Bs. To make the best use of them, on 5 September Polkovnik Boris Sidnev, commander of 268th IAD, directed pairs of fighters orbiting at 5,500 metres, with bombers, their priority.

Fighter and 'Ilyusha' units shared airfields for closer cooperation, with the former ordered to tighten their formations and remain with the Il-2s until the end of the mission, rather than flying home individually. Day bombers now struck from below 5,500 metres, while night bombers would approach with idling engines, then attack from 400–500 metres, often dropping flares to illuminate the target. Russian losses were heavy – 556 in September alone, 36 of them Krasnoyuchenko's aircraft and the remainder evenly split between Khryukin and Rudenko – yet by 1 October Khryukin had 437 combat aircraft, of which 246 were serviceable, although his airmen were exhausted. Richthofen's position was little better for he had lost 103 aircraft in September. From 5 to

12 September his units flew 7,507 sorties, a daily average of 938, but after 11 weeks of operations he was down to 950 aircraft, and by 20 September he had only 232 bombers.

Rudenko had to hammer the small and inexperienced core of 1st IAA into 16th VA, but he was an extremely experienced front-line commander. He did not formally assume command until 28 September, starting with only 152 serviceable aircraft including 31 night bombers, and there was an inauspicious debut from 4 September. He lost 50 aircraft in the first four days – one 'Ilyusha' every 20 sorties. His fighter divisions lost 157 aircraft and 83 pilots during September in a month when his airmen flew 5,225 sorties, of which 992 were strike, and he was steadily reinforced to have 232 aircraft, including 13 night bombers, by 1 October. Rudenko also tried to introduce GCI but was handicapped by a shortage of both transceivers and experienced fighter pilots to act as controllers.

Skripko's men were also active and flew 6,523 sorties in September, striking targets within and without the city, crews sometimes flying up to three sorties a night. Such attacks over the city itself soon became almost impossible due to smoke, so the bombers switched to rail targets, although experienced crews made occasional low-level afternoon attacks on Stalingrad, where, by 6 October, the central and southern parts were in German hands. Paulus's men were exhausted and awaited reinforcements, while Luftwaffe strength in the East had now dropped by almost 11 per cent after four months of continuous operations. During October seven *Gruppen*, including three transport, and several *Staffeln* either returned to the Reich or were transferred to the Mediterranean theatre.

The autumn evenings were growing chillier and rain showers became more common as Paulus renewed his attempt to take Stalingrad from 14 October. Richthofen recalled most *Gruppen* from the Caucasus but faced Soviet pressure along the whole front, thus depriving them of rest. Nevertheless, Luftwaffe support helped to ensure that by 7 November the Russians were left with their legs dangling in the Volga in a tiny bridgehead against which StG 2 flew 1,208 sorties during 23–26 October. The VVS did what it could, Khryukin extending GCI and making occasional attacks upon airfields, aided by Skripko from the end of October, but with little effect despite high claims. The weather disrupted both sides' operations, although Rudenko flew 5,718 sorties during October and lost 61 aircraft.

Russian night bombers were especially active during October, with Khryukin's crews flying up to ten sorties a night, each delivering 350kg of bombs leading an OKH liaison officer to note on 15 October that their night air superiority was assuming 'intolerable proportions'. They were also used to supply the remaining Stalingrad bridgeheads, flying 1,008 sorties between September and December and dropping 200 tonnes of food and ammunition in bags.

Each air army was supported by transport aircraft, 65 from the GVF for Khryukin, but they were banned from approaching within 50 kilometres of the FEBA during the day. The ADD flew 5,634 sorties in October and 3,334 to mid-November, bringing the total for the Stalingrad campaign (17 July–19 November) to 11,317, or almost half of ADD sorties, to drop 12,025 tonnes of bombs. Russian historians state that from 14 September to 19 November their airmen flew 45,325 sorties and dropped 15,440 tonnes of bombs around Stalingrad, but the cost was high. From 17 July to 19 November, 2,063 aircraft were lost, but it had bought Stalin time and, ominously, VVS activity was growing as Luftwaffe reconnaissance began to provide evidence of preparations for a major offensive.

During the late summer and autumn of 1942 Novikov and Golovanov continued reforming and reorganising their forces. With many fronts relatively quiet, it was also possible to expand both, although VVS casualties during 1942 were high – 8,168 combat aircraft to enemy action, 3,888 fighters (47 per cent), 1,145 day (14 per cent) and 1,307 (16 per cent) night bombers and 1,676 (20.5 per cent) attack. The losses of aircraft, infrastructure and production facilities prevented Russian air power from recovering until late in 1942, although until mid-1943 it conducted an active defence largely with Tactical Level air support and limited Operational Level capability. Factories were now producing aircraft that could match, or exceed, their enemies' performance, including La-5, Yak-7B and, from December, Yak-9 fighters, the two-seat Il-2 and the new Tu-2 medium bomber. Russia's Western allies were also supplying growing numbers of aircraft, and while the Hurricane, Spitfire, Kittyhawk and Airacobra fighters received mixed reviews, the American Boston and Mitchell bombers were highly regarded.

During the latter part of the year fighter regiment establishments were raised to three squadrons with a total of 32 aircraft. Novikov believed in concentrated air power and he began to pair divisions into fighter, bomber, assault and mixed air corps (*aviatsionnyy korpus*), with the first three formed on 10 September. Soon eight would be at the heart of a powerful Stavka strategic reserve, which by the beginning of November had 20 divisions and 71 combat regiments and would soon be committed to a mighty riposte.

Novikov joined the evening briefings and planning meetings usually held in Stalin's Kremlin office, presenting analyses of the previous day's operations prepared by General-maior (General-leitenant from 7 August 1943) Nikolai Zhuravlev, his operations head. During one such review on 12 September there was talk of threatening Paulus's communications. As they looked at the maps Zhukov and General-polkovnik Aleksandr Vasilevskii, Chief of the General Staff since June 1942, murmured that 'another solution' might be found, implying something on a larger scale. Stalin overheard them and asked, 'And what does "another solution" mean?'

This question was like a pebble landing in a pond to send out ripples. The options produced the following day saw Vasilevskii preferring to strike the Stalingrad Salient – *Operatsiya Uran* (Uranus) – while Zhukov advocated a complementary attack, *Operatsiya Mars*, upon the Rzhev Salient to end the threat to Moscow. Again Stalin accepted both plans on 26 September, starting with *Mars* in mid-October to confuse the enemy. But preparations were disrupted by weather, and at the end of October it was decided to reverse the schedule, with *Uran* beginning in mid-November followed by *Mars* about 24–25 November. *Uran* envisaged the envelopment of the Stalingrad Salient followed by *Operatsiya Saturn* to destroy the 8th Italian and 3rd Romanian Armies, then drive towards the Donets to isolate *Heeresgruppe A* in the Caucasus. As preparations began Stalin conserved his strength, feeding the fire within the city that bore his name with just enough resources to continue pinning down the enemy.

Stalin regarded air support as vital and insisted the offensives be postponed if it could not be guaranteed, but Zhukov and Novikov informed him the air armies would be fully ready by 15 November. They were over-optimistic, for an acute shortage of trucks made the transport of supplies extremely difficult. By the second week of November the VVS was down to two rations of fuel, with severe shortages of ammunition and spares.

A front was created in the north under General-leitenant Nikolai Vatutin supported by the new 17th VA under Krasovskii, who was now restored to favour. He had to create his new command from almost nothing, Novikov making frequent visits to assist him. However, with the Volga icing up, he and his neighbour, Rudenko, had difficulty building up supplies at airfields – a problem exacerbated by the lack of local railways and vehicle shortages. Stavka reserves raised Krasovskii's strength to 477 combat aircraft, including 66 Il-2s converted by 1st Mixed Air Corps (*Smeshannyy Aviatsionnyy Korpus*, SAK) workshops into two-seaters, but there were too many new pilots within 17th VA who needed training. His squadrons also required new airfields and 982 tonnes of fuel.

Despite these shortages, Rudenko was excited and elated when front commander General-leitenant Konstantin Rokossovskii informed him of *Uran*. He continued to augment his 'Ilyushas' with LaGG-3-37s, but received few new regiments and had to build only six airfields. By 19 November he had 342 aircraft, including 93 night bombers and 14 liaison aircraft. He also faced a unique problem with mice that gnawed wiring in aircraft then contaminated food and water, leading to an outbreak of mouse cholera or tularemia on 9 November that gave many of his staff officers high fevers, killed two and at one point left only Rudenko and an Operations Department lieutenant on their feet. The sick were soon nursed back to health and the aircrews remained unaffected.

TABLE III-3: BALANCE OF COMBAT AIR FORCES FOR *URAN*

Formation	Fighters	Bombers	Attack*	Reconn	Total
17th VA	118/14	133/15	166/22	6/0	423/51
16th VA	117/19	102/35	107/25	3/1	329/80
8th VA	183/65	166/78	123/73	27/16	499/232
ADD	–	375/118	–	–	375/118
PVO	88/65	–	–	–	88/65
Luftflotte 4	203/125	139/64	230/136	155/72	727/397
Romanians	Unknown	Unknown	Unknown	Unknown	150/100

Notes: First figure total, second figure unserviceable.
*Luftwaffe figure includes Ju 87s, *Schlacht* and Bf 110s.

Khryukin had the hardest task supporting General-polkovnik Andrei Eremenko's defence of Stalingrad while planning missions to aid the offensive. Fighter cover was provided for barges bringing fuel from Astrakhan and two transport regiments aided his build-up, although few of the new airfields were ready when the offensive began.

By 19 November the VVS had 5,014 combat aircraft on the main battle front, but there were only 4,819 aircrew of whom just 958 were fully trained. The Navy had 439 aircraft while the ADD had 479 bombers, all supported by 837 PVO fighters. Although *Uran* was the prime theatre, it received only nine Stavka reserve regiments together with 1 SAK headquarters and two divisions, while *Mars* received 28 air regiments together with five air corps headquarters and nine divisions. Some 1,714 aircraft were assigned to the offensive, facing 877 Axis aeroplanes (see Table III-3).

Between May and October the Luftwaffe in the East lost 1,757 aircraft to enemy action and 1,356 to accidents, while its strength steadily declined from 2,142 at the beginning of September to 2,034 two months later partly due to overstretched supply lines associated with the offensive against Stalingrad. There, the Luftwaffe received four trains a day to the Chir railhead, 100 kilometres from Stalingrad, and had priority over Army traffic. On 1 November Richthofen proposed to Weichs and Paulus that some of his railway space be allocated for Army ammunition because with fighting at such close quarters 'the Luftwaffe cannot be very effective any more'. Since 10 August he could also call upon up to ten *Transportgruppen*, with 506 aircraft on 1 September, initially under Morzik's LTF Ost, established on 11 June. On 20 October three (some 135 aircraft) were transferred to the Mediterranean, and it would appear Morzik's command was then broken up and the remaining *Gruppen* scattered, with Fiebig receiving four under *Stab* KG zbV 1.

By mid-November these aircraft had brought in 42,630 tonnes of supplies and 27,044 personnel, while evacuating 51,018 casualties. Most of these supplies were for the Luftwaffe, including 20,173 tonnes of fuel, which allowed Richthofen to build up what proved to be a very valuable reserve. The distribution of this manna was eased by Richthofen's early rationalisation of his motor-transport resources, which not only allowed him to create a reserve but also increased the 'lift' of supplies from 2,000 tonnes to 5,000 tonnes.

Korten's forces were steadily milked and by 1 November he was down to 140 combat aircraft, with just a single bomber. Then on 7 November his *Jagdgruppe* was transferred to the Mediterranean, although it was replaced by one from Fiebig. During November Richthofen lost six *Kampfgruppen* (155 aircraft) withdrawn for rest or sent to the Mediterranean, whose malign influence meant nine *Gruppen* were transferred there from the Eastern Front together with two sent to re-equip in the Reich. To offset this loss of strike power the Luftwaffe began to emulate the Russian night bombers by undertaking nuisance raids on ammunition dumps, headquarters, artillery batteries and even individual vehicles. Attacks by these 'Sewing Machines' (*Nahmaschinen*) were usually little more than pinpricks that killed or wounded a couple of troops, hit one or two vehicles or supply dumps. Their cumulative effect was only gradually appreciated by the Luftwaffe, and the origins of the German equivalent are obscure.[5] It probably began with young pilots demanding to copy their enemies and grew in scale until on 7 October ObdL authorised each eastern *Luftflotte* to create their own

Auxiliary Bomber Squadrons (*Behelfskampfstaffeln*) of ten aircraft to operate up to 60 kilometres behind enemy lines. *Fliegerkorps* VIII created two manned by NAGr personnel, and the same pattern was probably followed by the other *Luftflotten*. The new formations were renamed Disruption or Harassment Squadrons (*Störungkampfstaffeln*) from 10 to 30 November, and by early November Richthofen had 25 such units equipped with Ar 66s, Go 145s and Hs 126s. Trainers and obsolete *Nahaufklärungsstaffeln* aircraft were the backbone of these units, augmented by W 34 and Fw 58 light transports. At the other end of the scale, at the end of December, 1./*Störkampfstaffeln Luftflotte* 1 had two Fw 200 Condors assigned, thus making it the Luftwaffe's first Eastern Front four-engined bomber unit.

The Russians' Volga build-up was shielded by fog, rain, sleet and snow showers that sharply reduced Luftwaffe activity, but FAGr 4 photographs showed that 3rd Romanian Army faced a major blow, although signs of a threat to Paulus's southern flank were ignored. Fiebig lacked the strength for major strikes, while as a precaution Richthofen assembled supplies for two *Gruppen* at Bokovskaya airfield near the junction of the 8th Italian and 3rd Romanian Armies. He also prepared a contingency plan for Pflugbeil to move north in the event of a crisis, leaving Caucasian air support under the I *Flakkorps* commander, General Otto Dessloch. By the beginning of November Fiebig had 487 aircraft and Pflugbeil 484, which dropped to 441 and 297 respectively by 19 November.

On 18 November low cloud and drizzle reduced visibility to two to three kilometres but Soviet meteorologists anticipated clear skies and cold weather when *Uran* began the next day. On this basis Novikov carefully organised a campaign in which bombers would strike airfields, headquarters and troop concentrations, while 'Ilyushas' supported troops. These plans were wrecked when a warm front suddenly arrived from the Caucasus, causing a thaw, low cloud, dense fog and temperatures just above freezing during 19–20 November.

Vatutin pulverised 3rd Romanian Army on 19 November as Krasovskii and Rudenko flew 546 and 82 sorties, respectively, although two-thirds of the latter failed to find their target, while Fiebig flew only 120, mostly in *Kette* strength and GAL was grounded. Richthofen wrote in his diary,'We must have good weather soon, otherwise there can be no hope', but the following day only the most experienced 'Ilyusha' pilots were despatched on reconnaissance missions, flying almost on the deck. The weather failed to stop the Red Army, however, and a momentary break in the clouds allowed a low-flying *Nahaufklärungsflieger* to spot huge tank columns driving through 4th Romanian Army in the south, with Hoth narrowly escaping encirclement.

A brief improvement in the weather on 21 November saw both sides' aircraft more active, with three *Gruppe*-size missions by I./KG 100, while StG 2 flew 141 sorties. The weather deteriorated again on 22 November, when Fiebig flew 150 sorties but had to abandon his forward airfields, allowing the Russians to link up east of the Don Bend on 23 November. The poor weather from 19 to 23 November meant that air power played little part in *Uran*'s success, during which the VVS averaged 200 sorties a day, including supply drops into the Stalingrad bridgehead, and the Luftwaffe averaged 100.

The Germans cobbled together a line along the Chir under the Luftwaffe's Generalleutnant Alfred Mahncke, an 'Old Eagle' who had served under Thomsen, but in the Luftwaffe had performed only administrative duties.[6] Behind it the Luftwaffe regrouped at Morozovskaya, Tatsinskaya and nearby Oblivskaya, and used Richthofen's assembled supplies to fly 150 sorties a day on 22 November. Some supply drops were flown to isolated groups of Axis troops struggling westward, while the Luftwaffe signals network ensured that Fiebig's headquarters monitored the situation as Paulus decamped to a new command post nearer Stalingrad. Some 250,000 men were encircled in a pocket 50 kilometres long and 40 kilometres wide, including 2,000 air- and groundcrew in two *Jagdgruppen*, a *Stukastaffel* and the remnants of three NAGr operating from four airfields, primarily Pitomnik and Gumrak.

Richthofen had long telephone conversations with Jeschonnek seeking reinforcements and supplies, but it was a fortnight before he received the former, and these were from Korten. Clear skies on

November 25 helped the Luftwaffe to contain Vatutin and secure its new airfields while VVS operations were restricted by fuel shortages at Russian forward airstrips. Nevertheless, the VVS was beginning to despatch sweeps or 'hunters' (*okhotniki*) in *para* (pair) or *zveno* (flight) formations, which helped to increase Luftwaffe losses on this front from 19 November 1942 to 1 January 1943, to 278 aircraft.

Paulus and his corps commander wanted to break out, but national prestige and the Demyansk experience created a consensus within OKH that he should await relief, despite opposition from Manstein, whose newly created *Heeresgruppe Don* was to relieve the pocket in *Unternehmen Wintergewitter* (Winter Thunderstorm). Those closest to the front recognised that the Russians were far stronger than a year earlier, while a potential source of protein in the form of Paulus's transport horses had moved westwards a month earlier due to a shortage of fodder. Everything depended upon an airlift, but when Paulus raised this prospect with Fiebig on the evening of 21 November, the latter replied with considerable perception, 'That's impossible! Our aircraft are heavily engaged in Africa and on other fronts. I must warn you against exaggerated expectations.'

Hitler's decision that Paulus stay in Stalingrad was underpinned by Göring's assurances, made in good faith after telephone discussions from Italy with Jeschonnek and *Generalquartiermeister* von Seidel, that the Luftwaffe could meet Paulus's daily requirement of 700 tonnes. After the catastrophe Göring blamed both and threatened them with courts-martial, but Seidel retained his post until the end of June 1944, when he commander of the training *Luftflotte* 10.

They were all wrong. Morzik calculated the task required 1,050 Ju 52/3ms, but on 1 November the total number of transports in the East, excluding medical evacuation aircraft, was just 429, of which Richthofen had 298. Half the 23 *Transportgruppen* were in the Mediterranean, and the aircraft of those recalled to the East needed modifications at Berlin-Staaken for the Russian winter. The He 111 *Kampfgruppen*, in which each aircraft could carry 1.5 tonnes, were increasingly given the transport role, while 600 aircraft were mobilised from the *Fliegerschulen* to make up the shortfall. Even long range anti-shipping units, some with He 177s, were pressed into service. By 4 December the transport fleet had 17 *Gruppen* – 11 with Ju 52/3ms, four with He 111s and two with Ju 86s, with some 285 aircraft augmented by a few Romanian and Italian transports. One of the latter, piloted by Italian Air Corps commander General Enrico Pezzi, vanished on 29 December while evacuating wounded.

Richthofen's transports were nominally capable of bringing in 288 tonnes a day, but if more Ju 52/3ms arrived then the 700-tonne target was easily attainable, assuming ideal weather, maintenance and organisation. However, there was an ominous absence of clear leadership. On 30 November, *Fliegerkorps* VIII was made responsible for the transport effort into Stalingrad, with Fiebig delegating the task of Air Supply Commander (*Luftversorgungsfüher*) to Tazinskaya base commander Generalmajor Viktor Carganico, whose role was solely to assemble supplies. Only on 2 January 1943 did Fiebig receive supreme authority as LTF *Luftflotte* 4, although he was simultaneously fighting the enemy. It remains a mystery why Morzik was not brought in, rather than remaining in Berlin. Responsibility for moving the supplies was delegated to two *Geschwaderkommodoren*, each with four or five *Gruppen* – Oberst Hans Förster of KG zbV 1 at Tazinskaya with Ju 52/3ms and Ju 86 and Dr Ernst Kühl of KG 55 at Morozovskaya with bombers.

The transports flew day and night, escorted whenever possible, although the presence of the escort often attracted Russian fighter attention. When the *Jagdgruppen* were diverted to support *Wintergewitter*, the transport 'pulks' were left at the mercy of massed anti-aircraft guns as well as enemy fighters. Bases were also attacked, leaving Fiebig pessimistic about the airlift's prospects yet desperate for success. He wrote in his diary on 17 December, 'it must succeed! The alternative is unthinkable.' Snow, sleet, low cloud and fog meant only 60 per cent of the transports despatched reached the pocket, pilots sometimes making seven attempts to land, while only 30–40 per cent returned.

Pitomnik was suitable only for single-engined aircraft, and Paulus rejected Luftwaffe requests to expand Gumrak because of its proximity to his new headquarters. While justifiably complaining about the failure to provide sufficient supplies, he failed to organise the reception or distribution of supplies and dumped the responsibility upon flak division commander Generalmajor Wolfgang Pickert. The latter used a *Flakregiment* to create order from the chaos, while signallers lashed together a navigation system that operated in the face of Russian jamming.

Not until 4 December did Novikov give priority to cutting the aerial supply line, but already, on 26 November, Rudenko and Khryukin had begun to coordinate blockade operations. Later establishing dedicated command posts for this role, Rudenko had the north and northeast and Khryukin the south and southwest, with both using pairs of interceptors. In December radio-based GCI was introduced, with fighters ready to scramble to reinforce standing patrols that forced the transports under 3,000 metres, where they were concealed in the haze. While Luftwaffe losses were nowhere near the VVS's inflated claims, Russian air superiority over the pocket cut the quantity of supplies being flown in. On 30 November they inflicted a 23 per cent loss rate on the *Tante Jus*, while on 25 December, after a 48-hour hiatus, the transports brought in only 78 tonnes and lost five aircraft. When part of 16th VA was ordered south on 19 December, the reduced opposition allowed the Germans to bring in 561 tonnes in two days, with no transports lost and only five damaged.

The VVS also supported Red Army operations to reduce the Stalingrad pocket and drive back potential relief forces, while the ADD flew 962 sorties from 20 November to 31 December that saw its aircraft drop 900 tonnes of bombs on communications links and airfields. By 1 December Khryukin was moving to the Volga's west bank with 761 aircraft, but from the start of the offensive to the New Year he had lost 133 aircraft. Indeed, by 16 December he was down to 492 serviceable combat aircraft, including 53 U-2s. Rudenko, on 1 December, had just 258, but he was soon reinforced, and during December he flew 4,125 sorties and lost 64 aircraft.

Wintergewitter began on 12 December, supported by Pflugbeil flying 350 sorties a day using some *Kampfgruppen* transferred from transport duties. But the advance ran out of steam only 55 kilometres from the pocket within 12 days, although the weak local VVS forces were unable either to disrupt the German build-up or contain the threat. Part of Khryukin's 8th VA was pulled from the pocket and sent south, where it fiercely contested the skies, flying more than 1,700 sorties between 17 and 23 December and dropping 282.6 tonnes of bombs not only to stop Manstein but also to support a thrust towards Rostov. From 19 December some of Rudenko's squadrons joined the battle as Richthofen's forces were nearing their limits with only 599 combat aircraft available on 20 December. Indeed, his five *Jagdgruppen* lost 91 fighters during December and received only 34 replacements.

Richthofen's close air support resources were also extremely limited because aircraft, together with many *Schwarzmänner* and signallers, their vehicles and equipment, had been driven into the pocket. A new clutch of muddy airfields was established west of the Chir, but groundcrews there lacked even basic tools, which led to much squabbling over the limited resources. The handful of available aircraft were extensively used, sometimes flying 14 individual sorties a day. The disruption of the landline signal network by enemy advances meant orders were either transmitted by radio (making them vulnerable to interception by the enemy) or delivered by Storch – a time-consuming business.

Hitler still refused to authorise Paulus to break out, leaving Richthofen at his wits' end. He moaned in his diary on 18 December that he had been unable to speak to anyone and had given up telephoning Jeschonnek, who ignored him and broke promises. Göring had finally reached Hitler's headquarters at Rasternburg on 10 December after a 'tour of inspection' in Italian art galleries. He was so shocked at the situation that, when briefing Kesselring on the Mediterranean situation, the mention of Stalingrad left him in floods of tears.

Wintergewitter forced the Russians to divert resources to meet the threat and doomed plans for *Saturn*, forcing Stalin to accept a smaller offensive. In *Malyi Saturn* (Little Saturn) Vatutin would smash through the 8th Italian Army then join a double envelopment of Manstein's *Heeresgruppe Don*, with the spearheads meeting at Tatsinskaya and

A Ju 87B-1 of 6./StG 77 taxis out at a Ukrainian airfield in the summer of 1941. It was piloted by the *Staffelkapitän* Hauptmann Herbert Pabst, who, on 1 September 1941, became *Staffelkapitän* of the *Ergänzungsstaffel*. He then specialised in training, becoming *Kommandeur* of two training *Gruppen*. (*EN-Archive*)

A Ju 88A-4 of 9./KG 51 prowls over the southern section of the Eastern Front. The Ju 88 and He 111 were the prime Luftwaffe bombers in the East, and this *Staffel* was part of Generalleutnant Curt Pflugbeil's *Fliegerkorps* IV from September 1941 to May 1942. In October 1944 it became a *Nachtschlachtstaffel*. (*EN-Archive*)

This attempt to camouflage a Bf 109G to conceal it from Russian attacks merely made it look like a collection of Christmas trees were draped around the fighter. (*Der Adler*)

Drums of fuel are delivered to an airfield by truck, rolled off the back and then rolled to the *Tante Ju* on the left. Fuel production and supply were the key to success during World War II. (*Der Adler*)

For Generalfeldmarschall Albert Kesselring the glass was always half full, hence his nickname of 'Smiling Albert'. Unlike the other *Luftflotten* and *Fliegerkorps* commanders, the Bavarian Kesselring was no 'Old Eagle', having never been an airman in the Great War. (*Der Adler*)

As Russian fighter and anti-aircraft defences grew stronger good preparation was vital to the planning of Stuka operations. Here, the commander gives his men a last-minute briefing. (*Der Adler*)

BELOW • Twin-engined He 111s and Ju 88s were the backbone of the Eastern Front *Kampfgruppen*, and this photograph shows a Heinkel at rest. Its wide fuselage made the aeroplane easy to load with supplies, which is why He 111s were increasingly used more as transports than bombers as the war went on. (*Der Adler*)

A line of Bf 109Fs from II./JG 54 prepares for a patrol during the winter of 1941–42. This photograph illustrates why groundcrews were called 'black men' (*Schwarzermänner*) – the one in the foreground apparently has a fire extinguisher in case of emergencies. (*EN-Archive*)

A He 111H-16 of 8./KG 53 comes in to land after a mission in the summer of 1942. This *Gruppe* was part of *Luftwaffenkommando Ost*, which conducted some strategic bombing at about this time and later became part of the strategic bombing force, *Fliegerkorps* IV. (*EN-Archive*)

Two Fw 190A-5s of I./JG 54 in flight over the Soviet Union wearing the *Geschwader* 'Grünherz' (green heart) emblem below their cockpits and the *Gruppen* emblem on the nose. I./JG 54 began to replace its Bf 109Gs with the Fw 190, known to the Russians as the 'Fokker', from November 1942. (*EN-Archive*)

A Bf 110E of the *Gruppenstab* of I./StG 1, showing yellow lower wingtips and a yellow fuselage band around the fuselage, taxies out in the snow during the winter of 1942–43. With the reorganisation of Luftwaffe ground-attack units in October 1943 I./StG 1 became I./SG 1 and disposed of its Bf 110s. (*EN-Archive*)

While petrol bowsers were the fastest means of refuelling aircraft, they were in short supply in the East. Instead, as with this Ju 88, the 'black men' had to use hand-pumps to transfer fuel from drums to the aircraft's petrol tanks – a clumsy and time-consuming process. (*Der Adler*)

Airfield installations are blown up just before the Luftwaffe abandons them. Where possible, most of the runways would be ploughed up, allowing aircraft to operate from them until the final demolitions. The site would also be seeded with mines. (*Der Adler*)

A bomb-aimer's view from a diving Ju 88. Dive-bombing was a Luftwaffe obsession, and it was demanded for the four-engined He 177. (*Der Adler*)

General der Flieger Martin Fiebig was a bomber group commander in World War I and distinguished himself with close air support commands until he was promoted to succeed Richthofen as commander of *Fliegerkorps* VIII. He ended the war commanding *Luftwaffekommando Nordost*, which evolved from *Fliegerkorps* II. (*Der Adler*)

German bombers had many advantages over their Russian enemies, including armour and self-sealing fuel tanks. But their armament was much weaker, the Luftwaffe tending to rely upon the 7.9mm MG 15, such this one manned in the nose of a He 111. (*Der Adler*)

A formation of He 111s pass over a Russian river which the bomb aimer is observing. The Heinkels were used for long range bombing because they had a superior radius of action when compared with the Ju 88 – 1,900 kilometres to 1,700 kilometres. (*Der Adler*)

A Bf 109G-6 of III./JG 54 receives a major service in a rural area on the northern Russian Front in the spring of 1943. In March of that year the *Gruppe*, under Hauptmann Reinhard Seiler, was one of the first transferred to the West. (*EN-Archive*)

Three Fw 190A-4s of 5./JG 54 bask in spring sunshine at Siverskaya in the late spring of 1943. Recently freed of their winter scheme white, many II. *Gruppe* aircraft were given a distinctive new camouflage scheme combining what has been described as tan, or brown, with two shades of green. Note that both *Geschwader* and *Gruppe* badges are still being worn, and also black *Staffel* numbers. 'Black 5' was the mount of Austrian Oberleutnant Max Stotz, who was promoted to *Staffelkapitän* of 5./JG 54 later that same summer, only to be reported missing in action near Vitebsk on 19 August 1943. All bar 16 of his 189 kills were gained with II. *Gruppe*. (*Eddie Nielinger*)

Bf 109G-6 'White 10' of 1./JG 52 at Kharkov-Rogan during *Unternehmen Zitadelle* in the summer of 1943. The acting *Gruppenkommandeur* at this time was Hauptmann Johannes Wiese, a *Ritterkreuz*-holder who ended the war as *Kommodore* of JG 77. (*EN-Archive*)

'Black men' gingerly install a bomb into the cradle of a Stuka. Bomb handling was not without its dangers, and the electric fuses of some German bombs were notoriously unreliable. A number of bombers were seen to explode without warning. (*Der Adler*)

A 'black man' completes work on the middle engine of a IV./TG 3 Ju 52/3m. The *Tante Ju* was an extremely robust transport aircraft that could take a variety of loads, and while plans existed to replace it they never succeeded. (*Der Adler*)

Burning vehicles after a Luftwaffe bombing raid. Air power destroyed relatively few tanks throughout the four-year conflict in the East, but the loss of 'soft-skinned' vehicles could be even more devastating, depriving armies of much-needed supplies. (*Der Adler*)

An eclectic collection of aircraft abandoned near Stalingrad. In the foreground is a He 111 of KG 53 beside a He 111F communications aircraft that had been pressed into transport duties. Behind it are a Bf 109 and a Hs 123. (*Der Adler*)

A remarkable photograph taken from underneath a diving Ju 87 after the bomb cradle has released the bomb. The Stuka would normally carry a 500kg or 250kg bomb, but the Ju 87D could carry a 1,800kg bomb for specialised, short-range operations. (*Der Adler*)

Russian troops stroll past a downed Fw 189 tactical reconnaissance aircraft that they especially loathed because they were associated with artillery retribution. Their twin-boom configuration led the Russians to call them 'Frames' (*Rama*), as in window frames. (*Der Adler*)

Oberst Hans-Ulrich Rudel flew 2,530 sorties in the East – probably more than anyone else on either side. On seven occasions he landed to rescue downed comrades, yet his love of keep-fit did not endear him to subordinates who said of his teetotal habit, '*Oberst Rudel trinkt nur Studel*' (Colonel Rudel drinks only soda water). (*EN-Archive*)

Wolfram von Richthofen, shown here as a *General der Flieger*, spearheaded the Third Reich's offensives and was closely associated with both army support operations and the Ju 87. He was also a notorious armchair general, and could be thoughtless to his subordinates, leading one JG 77 pilot to dub him 'a real dickhead' (*ein gewaltiger Knallkopf*). (*EN-Archive*)

A 'black man' scuttles out of the way as a '*Y-Gerät*'-equipped aircraft of 4./KG 53 runs up its engines prior to take-off. That single 50kg bomb seems somewhat lost under the broad expanse of the machine's port wing. (*via John Weal*)

The groundcrews had it the hardest of all. These 'black men' of KG 55 at least have the benefit of a warm-air blower to make working on that port engine a little easier. (*via John Weal*)

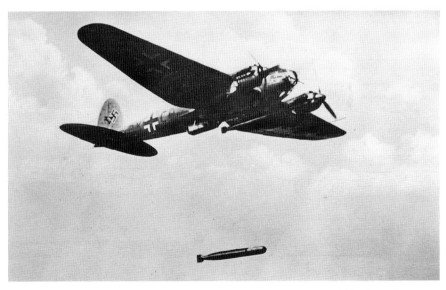

A He 111 launches the first of two practice torpedoes. In combat it would be suicidal for the machine to remain at this height for long. (*via John Weal*)

A *Staffel* of *Luftflotte* 6 StG 1 Ju 87Ds heads eastwards protected by a Bf 109 escort. The Russians called the latter 'Messers' and the Stukas either 'Clog' (*Bashmakov*) or *Lapteshnik*, a derivative of *lopati*, the wooden sandals made from lengths of platted lime bark commonly used in the countryside. (*Der Adler*)

The small fires quickly taking hold in the tinder-dry fields and scrubland below suggest that this attack is being carried out either with antipersonnel bombs or clusters of incendiaries. (*via John Weal*)

Bridges would feature high on the Stukas' list of targets throughout the war on the Eastern Front. Having demolished the road bridge in the background, this unit – note the Ju 87 pulling up and away at top right – was recalled several days later to destroy the pontoon bridge the Soviets had constructed to replace it. (*via John Weal*)

With bombs already detonating off to the left, these two Stukas of II./StG 77 (bottom right) are intent on another target. The two black dots immediately above them are Soviet armoured vehicles that have left the convoy on the road in the centre of the picture and are seeking the 'safety' of open fields – according to an accompanying report, neither made it. (*via John Weal*)

Almost symbolic in its simplicity, a classic shot of a winter-dappled 'Dora' of StG 2 setting out on yet another mission to try to stop the tide of Soviet armour from flooding westwards across that flat, frozen, landscape far below. (*via John Weal*)

A *Gruppe* of Ju 88s en route to their target in tight formation was an impressive sight. (*via John Weal*)

A *Staffel* of KG 51 machines in tight formation low over the rolling landscape of the central Crimea. (*via John Weal*)

The commander (right) of a Pe-2 reconnaissance aircraft briefs his crew in preparation for a combat sortie. This machine has already seen some action – note the repair patch on the fuselage over the star insignia. (*Dmitriy Khazanov and Aleksander Medved*)

Morozovskaya. These bases were vital to the Luftwaffe to supply Stalingrad and prop up the Chir River line, now under General Karl Hollidt's command.

Korten had about 100 aircraft, including 23 *Störkampfflieger*, the Italians were down to 87 aeroplanes, but were desperately short of supplies, while the FARR had only nine serviceable fighters. Krasovskii had been reinforced to give him 632 combat aircraft, a third of them R-5 and U-2 night bombers, and he was given operational control of Smirnov, who would fly 505 sorties to the end of December. The offensive, which began on 16 December, pulverised the Italians. However, while Krasovskii flew 3,672 sorties from 16 to 31 December, 2,067 against the Italians, his support was undermined by weather that see-sawed between cold clear days and warm foggy ones, turning roads and airstrips into marshes. By this time Hs 129 pilots were beginning to restore the MK 101s to their aircraft, and it was noted that six of them in II./SchG 1 claimed ten tanks. By New Year's Day they had flown 3,138 of the *Gruppe's* 6,508 sorties in 1942, while the Hs 123s had flown 1,523.

Krasovskii faced fierce resistance as Richthofen received two *Kampfgruppen* from Greim and transferred other *Gruppen* from Fiebig and Pflugbeil to raise 280 aircraft – most based at Millerovo – to meet the threat. They harassed the Red Army advance, which forced Millerovo to be hastily abandoned on 20 December, leading Hitler to authorise the evacuation of other bases in the Russians' path, but only if they were under fire. Most now organised their own defence, and one held out for a week before it was evacuated. However, as the Russians approached Morozovsk and undefended Tatsinskaya, temporary home of Fiebig, the latter dithered because he realised Hitler's orders would disrupt the Stalingrad supply run. When the Russians reached Tatsinskaya on the morning of 24 December the airfield was crammed with aircraft, which took off amid chaotic scenes, Fiebig's being one of the last off the ground.[7] However, 54 aircraft were lost, including 46 transports together with most of the supplies, a train with 50 damaged aircraft, 300 tonnes of fuel, spares and vehicles to hamper operations for many weeks.

Morozovsk was luckier because Kühl transferred his transports in time and the approaching Russian tanks ran out of fuel. Clear skies the next day allowed Stukas to use the base to drive off the enemy as the He 111s returned, while a German counter-attack retook Tatsinskaya on 28 December. But these airfields were too exposed and were abandoned by 3 January for bases 350–400 kilometres from the pocket, ending Ju 86 operations and reducing the He 111s to one sortie per day.

The collapse of the Don line and the need to reorganise the transport effort meant that on 2 January Fiebig transferred his single-engined units to Mahncke's specially-formed *Fliegerdivision Donez*, which received increasing support from *Kampfgruppen*. They reverted to their traditional mission under the recently established *Kampfführer*, *Luftflotte* 4, and with their aid as well as most of the Hs 129 and Bf 110 ground-attack aircraft, Mahncke covered the retreat westwards behind the Donets, although this stretched the air ferry to breaking point.

Meanwhile, on 30 December, Rokossovskii and Rudenko were ordered to destroy the Stalingrad pocket in *Operatsiya Koltso* (Ring), launched on 10 January. Rudenko had 525 combat aircraft, including 87 night bombers, but with the ADD delivering a rain of bombs he helped compress 6 *Armee* tighter into its tomb, and even the commitment of Ju 290 four-engined transports brought no surge in supplies. The few German transports that did manage to land and take off in these days were often stormed by desperate men seeking safety. On 13 January Fiebig wrote in his diary, 'The 6 *Armee* is fighting its last battle', and the remaining airfields were soon lost.

Hitler demanded the supply of 300 tonnes daily to help 6 *Armee* tie down the largest possible Soviet force, but only on 18 January was a single command, *Sonderstab Milch*, established to organise every aspect of the airlift. Milch had the dynamism and administrative flair to improve the situation, and by 29 January he had assembled 363 aircraft and 14 fighters with long-range tanks that made a sweep over the pocket the following day. Low cloud and poor serviceability restricted operations, and with Richthofen's airfields under frequent attack, all fighters were assigned to conventional operations.

On 23 January the pocket had been split in two, and they could be supplied either by parachute or by simply throwing out food and ammunition from as low as 50 metres. Nothing could prevent the inevitable, however, and on 31 January Paulus was captured, followed, three days later, by the last of 91,000 Germans as 12 He 111s flew forlornly overhead.

The Luftwaffe had delivered 8,250 tonnes of supplies and evacuated some 11 per cent of the German troops, 24,760 wounded and 5,150 key personnel. It was an impressive effort, but amounted to only nine per cent of Paulus's requirements. The daily average number of sorties was only 68, with 111 tonnes of supplies – indeed, Paulus's 300-tonne requirement was met on only four days. The cost was high with 279 aircraft (including 174 Ju 52/3ms) lost and 215 damaged, while personnel losses were also heavy (114 between 28 December and 5 January). Many *Tante Jus* were drawn from schools, along with instructors and advanced students, leading Göring later to comment that their destruction and the loss of 67 He 111s from the *Kampfgruppen* meant that 'There died the core of the German bomber fleet.'

Soviet air power played an important role in the victory, with Rudenko flying 8,741 sorties in the final phase to bring total Russian sorties since the beginning of the offensive to 35,929, including 3,334 by the ADD. The GVF was also very active during this phase, flying 46,000 sorties to bring in 31,000 troops and 2,587 tonnes of supplies. The cost, however, was high, with 706 aircraft lost from November to February, while the Luftwaffe lost 919 to enemy action and 587 to accidents, the majority on the Southern Front. This left Richthofen with 624 combat aircraft by 1 February. In addition, the Italians and Romanians lost 153 aircraft.

The VVS's growing strength prevented the Luftwaffe from disengaging units for refitting, and it was forced to rationalise. Its strength was down to 1,616 aircraft at the beginning of February, with an acute shortage of long-range reconnaissance aircraft to cover a 300-kilometre-long front. Serviceability was low because of intensive operations, frequent moves, inadequate repair facilities and groundcrew exhaustion, and therefore many unserviceable aircraft had to be abandoned. But the VVS had its own problems, including an acute fuel shortage during the first two months of 1943, with many 'thirsty' forward units in the south. The ADD was called in, using Li-2s of 1st AD and TB-3s of 53rd AD to fly in fuel. This was little more than a trickle, however.

As 6 *Armee* died Manstein slowly retreated, but from 29 January he was threatened with envelopment as a new Russian offensive, *Skachok* (Gallop), fragmented the remnants of *Heeresgruppe B* in the north. Korten, with some 220 aircraft, provided only token air support, with the Hungarians down to 15 serviceable fighters. Mahncke shielded Manstein's left while Pflugbeil covered the right as Hoth and Kleist withdrew towards Rostov and dedicated train-busting *Kampfstaffeln* struck the rail system. Khryukin had 220 serviceable combat aircraft out of 640 during the advance on Rostov, flanked by Rudenko in the north and Vershinin in the south. Khryukin would fly some 5,900 sorties during this period, but the frequent changes of base caused the Russians 'enormous difficulties'. Yet by the end of February Manstein faced a crisis that seemed set to dwarf Stalingrad, with everything depending upon Hoth reaching Rostov from the Caucasus.

Stalingrad helped reverse Russian fortunes in the Caucasus. When the Germans crossed the Don at Rostov the Wehrmacht easily drove the enemy into the mountains, but not before they wrecked most of the oilfields. List split the Russians into two but resigned on 9 September, leaving Hitler personally to direct *Heeresgruppe A*'s operations. Pflugbeil's squadrons were hard-pressed to keep pace with the Panzer spearheads. Indeed, from 28 July 3.(H)/14 had eight bases in four weeks. At the beginning of August Pflugbeil had 500 German and Romanian combat aircraft but lost some 150, including five of seven *Kampfgruppen*, one of two *Stukagruppen*, to Fiebig to support the assault upon Stalingrad, and another 50 to other Eastern Front commands.

Vershinin's 4th VA supported operations in the north Caucasus, although on 28 July it had only 126 serviceable aircraft, half of them night bombers. Goryunov's 5th VA shielded the southern and western Caucasus with 90 serviceable aircraft, some regiments being down to eight aircraft, but he could count upon 216th VVS-ChF aircraft. Goryunov was an infantryman who switched to the VVS in 1922, fought the Japanese in 1938 and the following year was one of the few who distinguished himself during the Winter War.

The air armies fought back vigorously and Goryunov flew 5,127 sorties during August but lost 29 aircraft, 14 in striking airfields, before being split into two task forces. Vershinin lost 149 in August and September, his and Goryonov's airmen having an operational life expectancy of just four weeks. By 5 September Goryunov had 139 aircraft, and during the month flew 2,905 sorties but lost another 27 aircraft. Three days later Vershinin was promoted to command the Trans-Caucasus Front's air support and was replaced by General-maior Nikolai Naumenko.

The VVS had to requisition tractors, horses or oxen to tow damaged aircraft to safety. Where possible abandoned airfields were ploughed and mined, while surviving ones were given supplies for just a day's operations. Lack of spares restricted 'Peshka' units, while 'Ilyushas' were used as light bombers, ignoring doctrine that said they should strike armour with guns and rockets. Many of the flying schools evacuated to the region the previous year saw their students drafted into the Red Army, where they remained for more than a year.

Until early October Richthofen's support for *Heeresgruppe A* was half-hearted and Pflugbeil's strength dropped to 195 combat aircraft. Then a petulant Richthofen temporarily reinforced Pflugbeil with six of nine *Kampfgruppen* and one of the two *Stukagruppen*, a total of 175 aircraft, when there was a pause at Stalingrad pending a new assault. When Göring emphasised the supremacy of the Stalingrad Front, Richthofen ignored him and the decision was left to Hitler, who met both men and Jeschonnek on 15 October. A good-humoured Führer rubber-stamped Richthofen's decision, partly because he believed that the Stalingrad battle was in its last phase. But the arrival of reinforcements did not improve the situation, the support being described as 'adequate, but not lavish', allowing a few bomber sorties against the Grozny oilfields. Mountainous terrain and heavy rain meant that the Army could not exploit Luftwaffe attacks and, in a fit of pique, Richthofen refused to increase air support. Mist, fog and rain shielded the Russians from the full effects of Pflugbeil's reinforcement and the pressure eased when the bombers returned north.

Goryunov flew 6,252 sorties in October and 2,465 in November, as there was some growth in VVS strength, although by mid-November he had only 148 aircraft while Naumenko had 281, the Navy had 231 and 50th AD DD had 44 bombers.

Uran forced Pflugbeil, who had just lost three *Kampfgruppen* to the Mediterranean, to transfer almost all his forces northwards, and as compensation flak officer and former Bavarian fighter pilot Dessloch created *Luftwaffekommando Kaukasus* from I *Flakkorps* headquarters on 25 November with some 150 aircraft. While Pflugbeil was willing to provide some bomber support, Dessloch was essentially on his own, although General Konrad Zander's *Flfü Krim*, established on 15 October and disbanded on 15 March 1943, helped. Wild's command was renamed *SeeFlfü Schwarzesmeer* in December 1942.

Hitler transferred command of *Heeresgruppe A* to Kleist, who was ordered to retreat north through Rostov, although by 1 December his air support was down to some 120 aircraft. The pursuing Russians flew 5,800 sorties, 2,000 by naval aircraft, during December but did not seriously interfere with the retreat because of their own supply problems. Goryunov's 763rd NBAP flew 314 tonnes to armies and evacuated 338 wounded during November and December. December also saw the Russians lose 60 aircraft, bringing their total losses in the Caucasus since 25 July to 644 aircraft.

In early January 1943 the Red Army was within 30 kilometres of Rostov, but Naumenko was falling behind. The shortage of vehicles meant captured airfields received only a trickle of supplies, while bad weather forced Naumenko's formations to fly in penny packets. A shortage of cable meant that wired communications also lagged behind the advance, making control difficult as there were few radios. During the first fortnight of January Naumenko flew 5,840 sorties, of which 4,042 were ground support. By using bombers to pin down the enemy Pflugbeil gained time for 1 *Panzerarmee* to escape, but 17 *Armee*, still sheltered by Dessloch, retreated westwards into the Taman Peninsula, where it established a bridgehead behind the Goth's Head Position (*Gotenkopfstellung*). Goryunov and the VVS-ChF also faced supply problems, and at one point they maintained attacks using StG 77's captured bomb dump.

Luftwaffenkommando Kaukasus became I *Flakkorps* on 7 February and was subsequently replaced by *Fliegerkorps* VIII, which used a Condor *Transportgruppe* to provide 254 tonnes of supplies while returning with 1,887 men and 12 tonnes of copper. In mid-February this was replaced by six *Transportgruppen* of 180 *Tante Jus*, together with glider *Gruppen*. These flew up to three sorties a day until the end of March, bringing in 5,418 tonnes of supplies and evacuating 15,500 men. Goryunov and the Navy tried to interfere with this traffic but with little success.

By the beginning of February Richthofen was reeling, having lost 775 combat aircraft since the start of the Soviet offensive, 300 in accidents. He was left with 624 combat aircraft (excluding 125 bombers on transport duties) to support Manstein, although the battered *Kampfgruppen* were reverting to their traditional role. Combat units received 329 replacements, and eight weak *Gruppen* returned to the Reich to reorganise while Pflugbeil (with Mahncke) and Korten supported Manstein. Korten's command became *Fliegerkorps* I on 17 February and moved to Poltava, while the infrastructure was rebuilt to give the Wehrmacht some grounds for optimism after a dreadful winter.

While all eyes turned to the Russian Southern Front during the second half of 1942, fierce defensive battles were fought by Generalfeldmarschall Günther von Kluge's *Heeresgruppe Mitte* as Stalin sought to neutralise perceived threats to Moscow. From 30 July a third of the VVS, some 1,340 aircraft, supported attempts rumbling on until early October to envelop the Rzhev Salient, losing more than half of its men. Kluge's success owed much to Greim's support. He exploited excellent command facilities and communications, including a rail-based mobile command post provided by his old friend Göring. From the start the front was split between *Fliegerdivision* 1, now under Generalleutnant Alfred Schlemm, and Fröhlich's *Fliegerdivision* 2, which compensated for numerical weakness – 354 combat aircraft at the beginning of May, 473 in August, 571 in September and 459 in November, which forced *Ergänzungskampfgruppen* to be used against partisans. The August battles cost Greim 194 aircraft (52 in accidents) in battles that saw the Eastern Front debut of the Fw 190, which the Russians dubbed the 'Fokker'.

Gromov's 3rd VA supported the western attack, while the eastern was supported by 1st VA, but with Kutsevalov transferred to the Far East on 17 July to form an air army it was now under the command of General-leitenant Sergei Khudiakov, an experienced staff officer. Together, they had 1,000 aircraft, supplemented by the ADD, which inflicted much damage. However, this success came at great cost. When losses were combined with transfers to Stalingrad, the combined force of 3rd and 1st VA had been reduced to 570 aircraft by 1 October. The ADD tried in vain to reduce the German threat by attacking airfields, as well as flying 1,527 defensive sorties.

Stavka reinforcements for *Mars* brought Gromov's force back up to 1,030 aircraft, but Khudiakov had only 624. Furthermore, the disruption of communications to the Caucasus oilfields severely restricted fuel and air support for the offensive. Greim, who had nearly 500 combat aircraft, had detected Russian preparations and so was waiting when *Mars* was launched on 25 November. However, *Fliegerdivision* 2 was transferred to France on 1 November to act as an anti-shipping command, and on the same day Bülowius relieved Oberst Plocher at *Fliegerdivision* 1, which was now defending the Rzhev Salient.

Mars also began in thick fog, which restricted air support mostly to attacks upon German defences. While Velikiye Luki and Kholm were isolated, initial success in the Rzhev Salient turned into disaster and Stavka shut down operations on 16 December after losing 120 aircraft in Zhukov's worst defeat, which cost him half his men. Despite low cloud and blizzards, Greim's airmen were extremely active, reinforced by bombers from *Luftflotte* 1. One Russian observer noted how groups of bombers would attack and as they departed 'over the smoky horizon' another would be beginning its bombing run. During this operation the Luftwaffe came close to a spectacular success when a bomber struck West Front headquarters while Zhukov and Golovanov were visiting. Golovanov was injured by a near-miss on a sauna while a hut allocated as Zhukov's accommodation was struck, fortunately before he occupied it.

Greim's casualties are uncertain but units reported 88 aircraft lost to enemy action in November and December and 60 to accidents. He now supported the 7,000-man garrison at Velikiye Luki through supply drops and later gliders, but the operation cost the Luftwaffe 55 aircraft and few of the garrison reached German lines following a breakout on 15/16 January.

By the beginning of February Greim was down to some 330 combat aircraft and facing a new crisis, for on 24 January 1943, the Russians, supported by Naumenko, struck Kluge's left near the boundary with *Heeresgruppe B* and annihilated 2nd Hungarian Army. Richthofen assumed responsibility and assembled 300 aircraft, with operational control of several of Greim's *Gruppen*. The bombers made low-level attacks upon troops on the open steppe, joined by Fw 190 *Jabos* that were making their debut, to inflict heavy losses leading the Red Army to make bitter protests about the absence of Naumenko's support, which was due to inexperienced pilots and fighter bases far in the rear.

Stalin reacted to the failure by increasing the pressure, and from 2 February launched *Operatsiya Zvezda* (Star) from Voronezh, supported by Smirnov, to take Kharkov and Kursk. Greim was able to contain this threat, but a new one emerged north of the Rzhev Salient on 22 February when Rokossovskii was brought north with Rudenko and Khudyakov to recapture Orel. Khudyakov's squadrons had not recovered from *Mars*, and Luftwaffe air attacks cut bloody swathes through the Russian ranks. Nevertheless, with Rudenko's support Rokossovskii made good progress despite rain, fog and heavy snow.

Short of resources, Hitler reluctantly sanctioned the evacuation of the Rzhev Salient from 1 March in *Unternehmen Büfel* (Buffalo), but it was too late to save Kharkov or Kursk. This was completed in mid-March, covered by Bülowius, who then supported counter-attacks from

11 March and made successful strikes against Rudenko's airfields. Despite reinforcements Rudenko was exhausted and Moscow temporarily abandoned plans to take Orel but was determined to hold the great salient around Kursk as the *rasputitsa* ended large-scale operations. Greim retained airfields around Orel and Smolensk, but he had suffered heavy losses – 1,062 combat aircraft from May 1942 to March 1943, 615 to enemy action.

German fortunes had also failed in the north, where *Heeresgruppe Nord*, backed by Keller's *Luftflotte* 1, became a backwater and was steadily milked of resources for other fronts. Förster's *Fliegerkorps* I launched two offensives against the Baltic Fleet, *Unternehmen Eisstoss* (Ice Blow) during 4–5 April and *Götz von Berlichingen* during 20–30 April, involving 596 sorties that sank a training ship and damaged two battleships and two cruisers, 11 destroyers, six submarines and five auxiliaries. This brought the total sorties that month to 9,047 for the loss of 29 aircraft. The defenders, including the newly created Leningrad PVO Army, were greatly aided by seven radars, which also helped to contain Förster's assault on Leningrad's communications around Lake Ladoga in May. The failure of this operation helped to shape ObdL's decision to transfer *Fliegerkorps* I to *Luftflotte* 4 on 19 July. The most significant offensive action that followed was a minelaying offensive around Kronstadt from 27 May to 14 June involving 306 sorties.

From July to September 1942 the Leningrad and Volkhov Fronts launched offensives designed both to improve Russian positions and to divert forces from the south, and Keller flew 21,986 sorties. By 19 August General-maior Stepan Rybalchenko had 185 serviceable aircraft supporting Leningrad Front, former bomber pilot Zhuravlev's 14th VA formed on 27 July to support Volkhov Front having 213 aeroplanes while Samokhin had 187 serviceable naval aircraft. The offensives achieved little, although Russian air strength remained constant between 1 July and 19 November, with the combined strength of the Leningrad and Volkhov Fronts at 281 and 295 aircraft, respectively, while 7th IAK on both dates had 84 fighters. Naval air strength during this period was 202 and 208 aircraft, respectively.

Hitler still regarded Leningrad as a prime objective, and on 23 July 1942, his *Weisung Nr 45* included *Unternehmen Feuerzauber* (Magic Fire) in which Manstein's 11 *Armee* would storm the city, and it appears ObdL decided to give Richthofen operational command of *Luftflotte* 1 for this attack. The first step came in August when *Flfü* 1 under Oberst Torsten Christ arrived with 11 *Armee* to prepare air support for the projected assault upon Leningrad. On 8 September Richthofen flew in, and in a meeting with Manstein they agreed with Hitler's view that 'Leningrad should be forced to surrender through Luftwaffe terror attacks (*terrorangriffe*).' The following day Richthofen met Keller and went to Berlin, but by then Manstein was fully committed, meeting a Russian attack from the east. *Feuerzauber* disappeared in a puff of smoke.

Christ supported Manstein's efforts, and in October *Flfü* 1 resumed night raids on Leningrad but the following month lost most of its bombers to Greim. On 15 January 1943, Christ departed to become *Fliegerkorps* IV Chief-of-Staff under Oberst (Generalmajor from 1 March) Herbert Rieckhoff, a former observer and policeman who had been Keller's chief-of-staff since 13 October 1941. *Luftflotte* 1's strength had dropped from 475 combat aircraft in May 1942 to 341 by the New Year, its losses to that date from 1 May being 639 aircraft, 339 to enemy action.

Meanwhile, Moscow prepared to exploit its successes in the south and permanently relieve Leningrad in *Operatsiya Iskra* (Spark) by Leningrad and Volkhov Fronts, the former receiving 13th VA on 20 November under Rybalchenko. Planning began on 25 December, with Voroshilov as Stavka coordinator facing many problems. For Rybalchenko, these included the need to fly supplies into airfields often under air or artillery fire, while air- and groundcrews, despite being high priority, were on short rations and were slowly wasting away from dystrophy. The evacuation of most aircraft plants made the repair of damaged aircraft difficult, and staff from them had to be brought in to support maintenance and repair work. There were also fuel shortages, which, on one occasion, forced the VVS to use oil-based additives that sometimes composed a quarter of a barrel of fuel. There was some release when the ice road reopened on 20 December, and by March 1943 this had brought in 214,000 tonnes of supplies and evacuated 89,000 people.

However, Rybalchenko's 12 regiments were severely under-strength and instead of 330 combat aircraft they had only 128, of which 108 were serviceable. For this reason he was given overall operational control of Zhuravlev, with 374 aircraft (282 serviceable) and Samokhin's 223 (195 serviceable).[8] Also available were Erlykin's 7th IAK PVO with 79 fighters (43 per cent of them Warhawks and Hurricanes), although it should have had 128 fighters. There was a severe shortage of day bombers with only 60 available, including 15 SBs and 20 DB-3/Il-4, augmented by 88 night bombers including 13 MBR-2 flying boats, while at least a third of naval aircraft (82) were obsolete 'Ishaks', 'Chaikas', SBs and R-10s. *Iskra* was also supported by 815th DBAP with only ten bombers, all of them serviceable.

Despite their weaknesses the Russians had overwhelming air support with 814 aircraft against an estimated 150. Vorozheikin coordinated operations and 13th VA, army and division staffs wargamed operations while the airmen were trained to fly in bad weather. Rybalchenko conducted crude photo-reconnaissance using hand-held cameras from the rear seat of 'Ilyushas' while 'Peshkas' conducted deeper reconnaissance.

Iskra was launched on the morning of 12 January in low cloud and visibility down to 500 metres, which restricted Rybalchenko's airmen to only 159 sorties on the first day, troops lighting bonfires in the FEBA to prevent friendly fire incidents. Improvements in the weather allowed for greater VVS support, but the Red Army made slow progress through the web of enemy strongpoints, although Keller could do little to stop the advance. He was able to fly 2,449 sorties including 931 strike, in January, but the Russians drove a corridor to Leningrad south of Lake Ladoga to end the siege, although skirmishing continued until the end of January. Rybalchenko flew 2,426 sorties and lost 27 aircraft, Zhuravlev flew 4,565 and lost 120, the Navy flew some 1,900 sorties and lost 34 while Erlykin's fighters flew 702 sorties without loss. Keller lost 51 aircraft during January, of which 31 were to enemy action.

With the spring of 1943 Greim pondered strategic attacks, having conducted some half-hearted attacks on factories after the bombing of

Moscow ended in April 1942. ObdL was clearly interested, for on 28 February 1942, it requested reports on airfields suitable for the He 177 heavy bomber, yet the bombing achieved little. Plocher, who commanded *Fliegerdivision* 1 in October 1942, wrote revealingly after the war:

> Since none of these attacks resulted in the actual destruction of the source of enemy power, it would have been far more advisable to have committed these few planes in support of the Army. Because these unsystematic attacks made no tactical impact whatsoever at the front, they were literally senseless and could be considered a typical example of inefficiency and waste in military operations.[9]

The PVO was reorganised again on 5 April 1942, with a PVO front created for Moscow, while the capital and Leningrad each received a PVO army, another subsequently being added to shield Baku. The remainder of European Russia was divided into six districts with 11 regions, and on 1 May 1942, the PVO had 1,254 fighters. PVO units were used in ground offensives, and by mid-November their strength had dropped to 989 fighters. Furthermore, only 502 aircrew were trained for night operations.

While the PVO would receive more radars, its greatest weakness was the absence of airborne radar, despite development work beginning in 1940. In April 1942 the PVO issued instructions on radar-based GCI, while for night operations 6th IAK equipped MiG-3s of 34th IAP with British Identification Friend or Foe (IFF) equipment in June. During the winter of 1941–42 development began on a radar for the 'Peshka' fighter version, the Pe-3, as *Gneis* (Origin), and this entered service as the 200 MHz Gneis-2a in December 1942. A total of 230 were produced, some being installed in single-engined fighters such as Yak-9s and Yak-3s, while the Leningrad-based 2nd GvIAK (formerly 7th IAK) equipped ten Hurricanes with radar in May 1943, but these aircraft were replaced by Spitfires a month after. Russian air defence was also boosted by the arrival of a British GL Mk II fire control radar in January 1942, which was quickly reverse-engineered to produce SON-2a (Sleep). Examples entered service in December 1942.

Limited radar support meant only 16 per cent of PVO sorties were scrambles, and during the second half of 1942 PVO fighters flew some 136,000 sorties in the European theatre and claimed 1,284 victories, 76 at night. The PVO lost 513 fighters, mostly over Leningrad and Stalingrad, but new fighters reached its regiments, although 'Ishaks' and 'Chaikas' remained in service with some units until mid-1944. At the beginning of 1942, 59 per cent of the PVO's fighters were older models, but this was reduced to a third by May 1942 and less than a quarter by April 1943, in part by using Anglo-American aircraft.

The ADD was steadily expanded during 1942 from 329 bombers (114 heavy) in May to 479 (63 heavy) in November. The heavy bombers, combined in May into 45th TBAD (45th AD from 15 June), declined due to TB-3 fleet attrition and limited production of the Pe-7, but there was some compensation with the arrival of American Mitchells in the summer, bringing total deliveries to 564 bombers. During 1942 the ADD flew 39,692 sorties and dropped 42,091 tonnes of bombs at a cost of 477 long range bombers and 320 crews. More than half the sorties (20,026) were army support, including 13,874 around Stalingrad from mid-July 1942 through to early February 1943. The average sortie was 3.6 hours in length, with the best crews leading each mission and marking the target with parachute flares. Ranges were extended with cardboard drop tanks on external bomb racks.

Like Bomber Command, the ADD adopted a streaming approach with aircraft at various heights, each crew receiving the exact time, course and height to and from the target, while target location was aided by radio direction finders. One bomber returned to discover its base covered in fog and the radio operator had to bail out, go to the airfield and arrange fires along the runway, which allowed the bomber to land safely.

Less than three per cent of sorties (1,114 in total) were flown against 'strategic' targets, but in late June Stalin summoned Golovanov to discuss attacks upon Berlin without explaining the reason. A reluctant Golovanov was eventually browbeaten to guarantee a date on which they would take place. Coastal targets such as Königsberg, Libau, Memel and Tilsit were initially struck by 325 sorties in July for the loss of two bombers. Berlin was finally attacked by heavy bombers operating from forward airfields in August and September, 212 sorties being flown. Two raids (122 sorties) were made on Budapest in September and one (46 sorties) on Bucharest, but the campaign then fizzled out.

In part the ADD's expansion was to support the Partisan movement, a task assigned to 1st Transport Aviation Division (*Trahnsportnyy Aviatsionnaya Diviziya*, TAD), specifically 101st, 102nd and 103rd AP DD under Polkovniks Ivan Filippov to 4 July, then Nestertsev, which became 101st AD DD on 28 July. During 1942 529 sorties were flown, which delivered 494 tonnes of cargo and 895 personnel to the partisans, while 1,000 wounded were evacuated. The division also supported NKVD operations, for which it flew 138 sorties, delivering 63 tonnes of cargo, 527 people and evacuating 32 agents. ADD bombers also had a transport role that involved 2,067 sorties to deliver nearly 1,480 tonnes, while evacuating 6,919 wounded in another sign of the recovery of Soviet air power – one which boded well for the following campaigning seasons, but there would be an initial setback.

CHAPTER 4

THE RUSSIANS ADVANCE
March 1943 to April 1944

The winter campaign concluded with the recapture of Kharkov on 16 February 1943, yet each step forward consumed supplies that were difficult to replenish. The Red Army offensives in late 1942 had torn a great gap in the German lines south of Voronezh, and from 29 January Krasovskii's 17th VA weakly supported *Skachok* (Gallop) to isolate German forces east of the Donets by hitting troop concentrations, rail junctions and airfields.

Meanwhile, Richthofen ended his subordinates' private wars on 5 February and instructed them to support Manstein's *Heeresgruppe Don*, renamed *Süd* on 13 February; but two days later the Russians were approaching Manstein's headquarters at Zaporozhe. Stavka was worried because the spearhead, General-leitenant Markian Popov's Mobile Group, was running on fumes, yet Stalin would not rein in the Red Army. Manstein's intelligence organisation and Luftwaffe comint discovered that 'Gallop' had slowed to a walk because Soviet troops were exhausted, and he decided to envelop Popov with a counter-offensive. Richthofen kept most of his forces in the Rostov area until 10 February, and was then involved in three days of conferences with Göring, Jeschonnek, Martini, Milch and Zeitzler, before flying to Zaporozhe for three more days of conferences, with Manstein planning this riposte. His aircraft began regrouping to support Manstein from

10 February, but they still had to shield an overstretched 400-kilometre-long line.

Richthofen was enthusiastic about supporting the counter-offensive and rushed to reorganise and rationalise his forces, sending the eight weakest *Gruppen* to rest and re-equip. Their departure not only allowed the remaining units to be strengthened but also reduced both the strain on the infrastructure and airfield congestion. Serviceability improved to more than 50 per cent because the Luftwaffe was returning to the excellent bases built the previous year near major supply depots, which accelerated re-equipment of *Stuka-* and *Schlachtgruppen*.

With 928 aircraft Richthofen retained control of the *Kampfgruppen*, but moved Korten's *Fliegerkorps* I to Poltava to support Manstein's left. Fiebig's *Fliegerkorps* VIII was transferred to the Crimea, while Pflugbeil's *Fliegerkorps* IV was in the centre at Dnepropetrovsk as his subordinate, Mahncke's *Fliegerdivision Donetz*, covered Manstein's right from Stalino, together with *Gefechtsverband Hozzel* – the Stuka force concentrated under StG 2 *Kommodore* Oberleutnant Paul Hozzel.

On 19 February, 4 *Panzer Armee* and Korten began the counter-stroke northwards towards Kharkov, while Pflugbeil used Mahncke as his spearhead to help 1 *Panzer Armee* isolate and crush Popov. Richthofen flew 1,145 sorties on 21 February and 1,486 the following day, with one *Stukagruppe* of 23 serviceable aircraft tallying 130 sorties. Korten and Pflugbeil concentrated upon Tactical Level support and were encouraged to operate across command boundaries, the daily average sortie rate reaching 1,000 as Hozzel supported the spearheads. Richthofen was also advised on *Schlachtflieger* by Weiss, who led *Versuchskommando für Panzerbekämpfung* (popularly known as *Panzerjägerkommando* or Anti-tank Command Weiss) with cannon-equipped Ju 87Gs and Hs 129Bs, which had greater success against armour than Stuka bombs.

The offensive drove into the left of Voronezh Front, which was supported by Smirnov's 2nd VA and quickly reinforced by four corps, while Krasovskii received two to bring his strength to 700 aircraft. But Kharkov was recaptured on 15 March and Belgorod three days later before the *rasputitsa* stopped Manstein and left the Russians with a huge salient around Kursk and bridgeheads over the lower Donets. Air operations were wound down, and by the end of March Pflugbeil was reduced to 184 aircraft as the VVS, which lost only 420 aircraft between 13 January and 3 April, withdrew units to rest and re-equip. This success saw Richthofen's units reporting the loss of 305 aircraft to enemy action and 250 to accidents in February and March.

Across the lines Zhukov investigated the defeat and replaced Smirnov with Krasovskii on 26 March, transferring 17th VA to former 1st Bomber Corps (*Bombardirovochnaya Aviatsionnaya Korpus*, BAK) commander Vladimir Sudets. He had entered the VVS as a mechanic in 1925 and later fought both the Japanese and the Finns in a career that saw him fly 45 types of Russian combat aircraft.

Meanwhile, South Front, supported by Khryukin's 8th VA, reached the river Mius by mid-February just as Richthofen's bombers struck the rail networks supporting the front, which went onto the defensive. Aerial skirmishing continued until the end of April, when Khryukin transferred substantial forces to the Caucasus, which became the new aerial flashpoint in the East. On 28 March Stavka demanded an offensive to drive 17 *Armee* into the sea just as Richthofen began supporting the Kuban bridgehead, which was ostensibly a springboard for a future offensive against the Caucasian oilfields.

In anticipation of the summer campaign Fiebig and Korten swapped sectors on 31 March, the latter arriving as the *Gotenkopfstellung* was struck by the Russians from 4 April until the end of May. Korten initially had 250 German, Romanian, Croatian and Slovak aircraft, and this number had been reinforced to 490 by early May, including five Croatian, Romanian and Slovak squadrons. The Russians deployed Naumenko's 4th VA, Goryunov's 5th VA and Ermachenkov's VVS-ChF, augmented by 60 ADD bombers, for a total of 570 aircraft, with Vershinin acting as air coordinator, and he too would be reinforced with 234 aircraft in mid-April to match German reinforcements.

There were reported to be tensions between the two air army commanders, for whom this would be their Caucasian swansong. For the summer campaign Novikov transferred Goryunov to Voronezh on 24 April and sent 256 aircraft to Naumenko, but on May Day he too went north to command 15th VA, with Vershinin replacing him. By then Stavka had further reinforced the Caucasian air forces with some 300 aircraft, while Ermachenkov doubled his contribution to bring total support for the front to 848 aeroplanes (719 in 4th VA), which increased to 924 by the end of May. The ADD sent another 140 bombers, and on May Day created 6th AK DD (General-maior Georgii Tupikov), while Skripko acted as air coordinator. Their operations were handicapped by the distance of bases from the FEBA – 50–100 kilometres for the VVS and VVS-ChF and 300–350 kilometres for the ADD, which was most severely affected by the thaw – to aggravate congestion problems. To counter the enemy over the Kerch Straits, Izotov commanded two fighter divisions and a night bomber division that flew some 1,200 sorties between 17 and 23 April.

The initial attack saw Korten fly 2,151 Stuka sorties between 17 and 19 April and average 400 sorties daily, while *Panzerjägerkommando Weiss* also distinguished itself, but from mid-May Korten lost most of his *Gruppen* as the Luftwaffe reorganised for the summer campaign. His *Staffeln* recorded the loss of 192 aircraft to enemy action during April and May and 132 to accidents, although some may have been outside the Taman Peninsula. By the time the Russians broke off their offensive Naumenko had flown 10,250 sorties and Goryunov 2,299, half being close air support. Russian sources indicate the two men lost 240 aircraft to enemy action, with 4th VA having a further 851 damaged and withdrawn to repair depots where 471 were repaired, 308 cannibalised and 73 scrapped. The ADD flew 2,419 sorties between 17 April and 23 May, 1,141 against airfields and the remainder against enemy troops and defences. The campaigns consumed 12,000 tonnes of fuel and needed 93 transport aircraft to support operations.

The offensive helped the VVS adopt more flexible fighter tactics based on *paras* and *zvenos*, while forward radio control posts constantly updated the airmen about the tactical situation on the ground and in the air. Offensive air power was increasingly concentrated in narrow sectors, with the 'Peshkas' often seeking command posts, while artillery observers in 'Ishaks' and 'Chaikas' circled over the battlefield like hawks. Russian records indicate a third of the bombers were obsolescent, 40 per cent of the fighter regiments retained the LaGG-3 or earlier aircraft and 11 per cent of Russian air strength in the Caucasus consisted of imported aircraft.

The spring *rasputitsa* restricted air operations, although Richthofen struck airfields and communications as far east as the Volga between March and July 1943, while both sides considered the summer campaign. Manstein wished to lance the boil of the Kursk Salient quickly by striking north from the Kharkov Salient to regain the Operational Level initiative. However, Hitler envisaged the offensive as a means of regaining the Strategic Level initiative with a double envelopment of the Kursk Salient – *Unternehmen Zitadelle* (Citadel) – with Kluge's *Heeresgruppe Mitte* striking from the Orel Salient in the north.

During the spring and early summer the Luftwaffe refitted its Eastern Front units, whose main front combat strength steadily rose from 1,616 combat aircraft in February to 1,998 in April and 2,334 by June, despite the loss in the East of some 1,725 aeroplanes, including 940 to enemy action. Milch's reforms saw qualitative improvement, with more Fw 190s in *Jagdgruppen* and the creation of more *Panzerjäger* units. Allied and satellite formations also benefited from growing German production to cover secondary fronts, allowing the Luftwaffe to concentrate on key sectors.

Across the lines Zhukov concluded as early as 8 April that the 'Fascists' would strike the Kursk Salient and convinced Stalin to adopt a strategy of temporary strategic defence followed by an offensive to take the Orel Salient. The Russians frantically began to fortify the Kursk Salient, but their biggest problem was to discover when *Zitadelle* would begin. Probing by reconnaissance aircraft accelerated during the second half of June when cameras were introduced to improve tactical reconnaissance, usually by small fighter formations during the afternoon. Night reconnaissance missions by U-2s and R-5s reported large convoys moving up to the front, and these reports were confirmed by ADD-backed partisans.

Novikov continued to concentrate VVS formations, and during the second half of 1942 he began to strip regiments from army headquarters in the northern and central theatres – he accelerated this process from mid-February. Of 30 SAPs, 19 were disbanded and 11 converted to new roles, including six which became IAPs, the spare resources being absorbed by the air armies who were joined by the first Allied air unit, the French 1st IAP 'Normandie', although exiled Spaniards were already in its ranks. VVS main front strength increased to 8,491 by 1 July, although 852 were obsolete U-2s, SBs, Ar-2s, Su-2s and R-5 night bombers, while 83 of the 1,239 day bombers were Il-4s, the majority in 15th VA. The Navy could add 843 aircraft, the PVO had 1,079 fighters supporting or behind the main front, while the ADD had 740 bombers. Yet there were only 5,732 aircrew because the training organisation had still not recovered from the setbacks of 1941–42.

At the beginning of the war there were 73 schools, but most were withdrawn eastwards and the number was reduced to 48. Despite receiving 3,160 *Osoaviakhim* aircraft, most of which went to training units, the Russian air training organisation remained at around 6,000 aeroplanes throughout the war because many U-2 (Po-2 from August 1944) trainers were used for combat or support roles. With few advanced trainers produced in Russia much use was made of worn-out aircraft from the front. There was also a shortage of instructors as many of the best had been transferred to the front, often at their own request because they felt they were shirking in the rear, while there was also a serious shortage of fuel. In 1942 the schools received only 55 per cent of their requirement, and the disruption of supplies meant this dropped to 52.5 per cent in 1943, before rising in 1944 to nearly 68 per cent. In 1942 there were 5,735,768 training sorties, which dropped to 3,717,443 the following year, before it rose to 5,783,631 in 1944. These flights averaged only 15 minutes' duration or less.

The combination of these factors sharply reduced both training quality and numbers. In 1942 it was planned to train 23,260 pilots, in

1943 19,770 and in 1944 21,350, but the actual figures were 13,383, 12,277 and 14,765, respectively, and the desperate need for them meant the 'foals' (*sherebyat*) went to reserve units for operational training sometimes with as little as three flying hours in their log books, while others as late as 1943 had just 15–20 hours. There was little gunnery or aerobatic training, which some schools banned, and to increase their flying hours 'foals' ferried aircraft. Even operational training was restricted to an average 12.5 hours for a combat pilot (fighter, assault, bomber) in 1942, rising to 17 in 1943 and 20.5 in 1944. Novikov was well aware poor training was behind his heavy casualties, but only in January 1943 did he establish the Main Directorate of Combat Training for Frontal Aviation under General-maior (General-leitenant from 5 January 1943) Daniil Kondratiuk, former commander of 6th VA, who remained in post until the end of the war. His efforts had limited effect.

Another problem was the students' low priority for rations – one pilot reported he and three comrades had to share a loaf of bread and a tomato, while others survived on weak pea soup that left them without the strength to fly. At one gunnery school students lived on cabbage leaves and potato peel taken from bins, although the food situation in central Asia appears to have been better, with some students reporting receiving three meals a day, although this included camel meat and barley so hard it was called 'shrapnel'.

When regiments sent 'merchants' (*kuptsii*) or 'traders' (*torguvtsii*) to reserve units to select the best replacements they often found the newcomers a burden.[1] Hungry, the new pilots often had to be fattened up before they could be sent aloft. Barely able to take off and land, they required more flying hours and rushed courses in navigation, formation flying and combat at a time when the regiments were supposed to be resting. This put a strain on the experienced airmen – often a handful of survivors after intense fighting – yet the process was repeated before every offensive until war's end. In May 1943 half of Rudenko's pilots were 'foals', while in Sudets' 237th ShAP/305th ShAD all but two airmen were flying their first combat mission. When Krasovskii received 256th IAD from Stavka reserve during the Kursk campaign it had 96 fighters, including 43 of the new Yak-9s, but the pilots were so ignorant of navigation that sometimes half would get lost.

When *Barbarossa* began the Luftwaffe had 41 basic and 22 advanced/ instrument training schools with 4,300 aircraft, of which 14 per cent were Bü 131 basic trainers. Despite shortages of both instructors and fuel, students still logged some 300 hours each during 1942 – far more than the 'foals'. In July 1943 Generalmajor Werner Kreipe, a participant in the Beerhall Putsch of 1923, became head of training (*General der Flieger-Ausbildung*) and rationalised the organisation to 27 basic training schools by 1944, but he expanded advanced and instrument training to 29 schools, insisting there be no reduction at this level, which he said was 'the most important aspect of the entire training process'. He almost doubled the training fleet to 8,000 aircraft, and while fuel shortages steadily reduced flying hours to about 250 hours in 1943, 175 hours and then 110 hours in 1944 – still more than the enemy – the schools produced 14,500 pilots in 1943 and 29,050 in the 12 months after Kreipe's appointment, although by the end pilots went solo after ten flights instead of 50 as pilot quality undoubtedly declined.

The Russians had greater success than their enemies in the field of production, although direct comparison can be restricted to 1942–44, with annual production figures shown in the Appendix. In numerical terms the Russians outstripped the Germans with a 37 per cent increase in production in 1942, but increases in 1943 and 1944 were almost identical at about 15.25 per cent. Yet heavy losses meant obsolete aircraft such as the SB, 'Chaika' and Su-2 remained in front line service even into 1944, while the 14-year-old U-2/Po-2 remained the backbone of the NBAPs.

These increases were achieved by focusing upon single-engined aircraft, which required less material and fewer man-hours to build than multi-engined aircraft, unlike their British allies. British production between 1942 and 1944 rose by only 16.3 and 1.57 per cent, but multi-engined aircraft amounted to more than 54 per cent of the aircraft built each year with the percentage of four-engined aircraft representing 9, 18 and 23.25 per cent of total production. Only 14 per cent of Russian production in 1942–43 consisted of multi-engined aircraft and this dropped to nearly 11 per cent in 1944, while in 1942–43 the percentage of multi-engined aircraft emerging from German factories declined from 48.5 to 40.87 and finally 22.5, while aircraft of three or more engines accounted for only 5.0, 6.5 and 2.5 per cent of total production.

Russian production was augmented by imported Allied aircraft, although this amounted to only nine per cent of the total number of aircraft delivered to the Soviet air forces in 1942 and 12.5 per cent in 1944, after peaking at 17.75 per cent in 1943. Yet fighter deliveries were 15–20 per cent of acceptances in 1942–44, peaking at nearly 24 per cent in 1943, while in medium bombers the figure rose from 45 per cent in 1942 to 48 per cent in 1943–44.

Soviet industry increased production, despite half the workers being unskilled and working in conditions of very great hardship, by rationalising types of aircraft and slashing man-hours – the Il-4, for example, needed only 12,500 hours to build in 1943 compared with 20,000 the previous year. Several designs, notably the Li-2 and U-2/Po-2, were multi-use, with the former produced as both transport and bomber while the latter served as a trainer, night bomber, artillery observation post, light transport and, in the S-2 form, as a medical evacuation aircraft. The need to produce existing designs, although they were frequently updated, meant many Yak IAPs had mixes of aircraft (even late in the war a single IAP might have Yak-1s, Yak-3s and Yak-7s, the equivalent of Spitfire Is, Vs and IXs). In fact the Russian aviation industry would produce only three entirely new combat aircraft designs during World War II, namely the Il-10, La-5 and Tu-2. Production of the Tu-2 – the best Russian bomber – was halted by Stalin from January to December 1943 but restored after a clamour from the front. Stalin ordered production restored and rebuked Shakhurin, saying, 'You should have complained about me to the Central Committee!'

The continued shortage of aluminium, despite substantial imports from Russia's allies, who also supplied machine tools, meant most communist combat aircraft featured wood in their airframes. The low-skilled workforce produced poor quality aircraft and engines to the point where each Yak-1 was unique, sometimes with different length landing gear! Aircraft often had ill-fitting parts, with rags filling the gaps, and tools were occasionally left behind within the airframe. Aircraft also suffered from leaky engines and unreliable hydraulics, with imported aircraft being superior in terms of engine reliability and internal fittings.

The dubious quality of Russian aircraft was graphically underlined on 3 June 1943, when Yak-9 fighters built at Factory 153 in Novosibirsk began shedding their skins – a fate soon shared by Yak-3s and Yak-7s, as well as Il-2s from Factory 30 in Moscow. The fault was traced to an unauthorised modification to camouflage paint, which reacted to the glue and poor quality timber in the wings, causing delamination under stress. When the matter was brought to Stalin's attention he muttered darkly of 'sabotage', and no doubt the NKVD discussed the problem with the official who made the unauthorised changes. Prompt action to restore the paint composition resolved the problem, but hundreds of aircraft had to be modified and the problem would still occasionally re-occur, although on a smaller scale.

Under Milch, production steadily increased, although the German aviation industry still preferred craft- rather than mass-production. He failed to exploit production facilities outside Germany apart from in Moravia, which was the western rump of Czechoslovakia absorbed into the Reich, where factories produced trainers, communications aircraft and transports. Between 1942 and 1944 the main plants in France and Moravia produced 4,941 aircraft, including 479 Fw 189s and 602 Ju 52/3ms as Milch switched non-combat aircraft production abroad to allow German factories to concentrate upon combat aircraft.

Milch created a Fighter Staff (*Jägerstab*) under engineer Otto Sauer to meet the growing need for fighters, but the two were soon locking horns. In May 1944, while reporting on *Jägerstab* activities, Milch revealed he had ignored Hitler's instructions to produce the Me 262 jet fighter as a bomber and was 'shot down in flames'. Surprisingly, Göring tried to dissuade Hitler from appointing Albert Speer as head of aircraft production but he replaced Milch on 20 June. He imposed mass-production techniques and rationalised production by following the Russian example of concentrating upon single-engined aircraft, especially fighters. However, Speer faced identical problems to the Russians, and many new aircraft were of poor production quality.

Meanwhile, Hitler planned to execute *Zitadelle* from late April 1943, but heavy rain, supply problems and difficulties rebuilding the Panzer divisions led to several postponements until 5 July, with Jeschonnek vainly objecting during a conference in Munich on 4 May to delays as he claimed the Luftwaffe was completely prepared. However, Richthofen was already facing strong enemy pressure.

In anticipation of *Zitadelle* the Soviet air forces were striking airfields and rail networks. The first Russian operation by all the air armies around the Kursk Salient struck 17 airfields during 6–8 May, with planning confined to a small group to achieve surprise. The aim was to catch aircraft while they were being serviced, and air army commanders were notified only 24 hours before D-Day, with some regimental commanders briefed only four hours before take-off. The three-day offensive involved 1,392 sorties, with formations streaming through narrow sectors under radio silence to surprise and saturate the defences. The operation claimed 506 aircraft, 373 on the ground, for the loss of 122, but German losses were actually five aircraft destroyed and 20 damaged. Radar-supported defences took a heavy toll on the attackers, who switched to night operations for the next attacks conducted against 28 airfields by the ADD, with some VVS assistance.

Following a Stavka directive to neutralise enemy airfields from 8 to 10 June, the ADD flew 2,330 sorties and would claim 580–750 aircraft for the loss of 25 aeroplanes, but the Germans lost only eight, half of them Storchs, while 11 were damaged. The Luftwaffe largely focused upon rail targets, but also struck airfields such as Kursk, where bombs fell within 600 metres of Novikov's headquarters. This skirmishing eroded VVS strength – Rudenko flew 14,309 sorties from April to June, including 5,480 by night bombers, while between 1 and 5 July his strength dropped from 1,108 to 1,052 serviceable aircraft, fighters and assault aircraft suffering the heaviest losses.

The Luftwaffe used the lull to reshuffle the Eastern command. Göring was growing tired of Jeschonnek and wanted to exchange him for Richthofen. A delighted Jeschonnek arrived at *Luftflotte* 4 headquarters to familiarise himself with its situation but Richthofen recognised he was being offered a poisoned chalice. He opted to assume command of *Luftflotte* 2 in the Mediterranean instead, departing with Bülowius and Mahncke on 13 June. Jeschonnek's hopes were dashed by Manstein's alarm at the prospect of an inexperienced commander at a crucial time, and to allay his fears Göring replaced Richthofen with Dessloch, initially as acting commander (*Chef*) rather than commander-in-chief (*Oberbefehlshaber*). This may have raised Jeschonnek's hopes, for he was at Dessloch's headquarters when *Zitadelle* commenced, but when he realised he would continue to be Göring's whipping boy he grew depressed and eventually committed suicide on 18 August. He was replaced by Korten and former *Luftflotte* 3 Chief-of-Staff Generalmajor Karl Koller, another Bavarian 'Old Eagle' and post-war policeman, who were determined to reform the Luftwaffe.

Greim's command was upgraded on 5 May to *Luftflotte* 6, with Generalmajor Josef Punzert's *Fliegerdivision* 4 controlling air operations in the north from June, while *Fliegerdivision* 1 (under General Paul Deichmann from 26 June) operated in the south. On 11 June Korten had been appointed *Chef* of *Luftflotte* 1 in succession to the retiring Keller, leaving Mahncke as acting commander of *Fliegerkorps* I, his *Fliegerdivision* having been dissolved on 31 March. When Korten's long overdue promotion was confirmed on 26 June, Mahncke handed over to Generalleutnant Karl Angerstein. On 18 May Fiebig was transferred to *Fliegerkorps* X in the eastern Mediterrean, his previous position being filled on 22 May by Generalmajor Hans Seidemann, who had spent several years as Richthofen's chief-of-staff.

Meanwhile, both sides prepared for the forthcoming trial of strength. Within the salient Rudenko's 16th VA shielded the north, Krasovskii's 2nd VA was in the south and Goryunov's 5th VA was in reserve. Facing the northern part of the Orel Salient were General-leitenant Mikhail Gromov's 1st and Naumenko's 15th VAs, while opposite the Belgorod–Kharkov Salient in the south were Sudets' 17th and Khryukin's 8th VAs.[2] Stavka stripped its reserves to strengthen the Kursk Salient, including sending 20 air corps, leaving it with only 108 aircraft.

TABLE IV-1 – SOVIET AVIATION FUEL CONSUMPTION, 1943

Branch	Tonnes
VVS-KA	5,205,944
ADD	831,702
VMF	125,092
GVF	7,931
Total	6,170,669

Within the salient the three air armies on 1 July had 3,036 combat aircraft, including 268 night bombers. Opposite Orel the two air armies had 2,036 aircraft (including 262 night bombers), while opposite Kharkov were 1,253 aircraft. A major weakness was the day bomber arm, with only 556 aircraft – mostly 'Peshkas', which had smaller bomb loads than the Heinkels and Junkers – making the Russians more reliant on their 803 'Ilyushas'. The PVO provided 280 fighters, together with three radars, while the ADD deployed 500 bombers in 26 of its 34 regiments.

Although there remained serious problems distributing both fuel and additives, Soviet air power generally received adequate stocks, and during 1943 consumed some six million tonnes (See Table IV-1). Each airfield received fuel and ammunition for eight to nine days' operations, together with a three-day emergency supply, while the new PTAB 2.5kg, hollow-charge, anti-tank bombs were flown into 'Ilyusha' regiments at the last minute.

Novikov supervised planning from May onwards, aided by his deputies General-polkovnikii Vorozheikin, now First Deputy Commander-in-Chief, and former 1st VA commander Khudiakov, VVS Chief-of-Staff from 1 May, who set up their command posts near front headquarters. Vorozheikin appears to have taken the lead in coordinating operations, but would share Novikov's post-war fall from grace with Khudiakov, who would be executed. Novikov wanted Rudenko and Krasovskii to launch a pre-emptive strike on the heavily defended airfields, but both men feared heavy losses that would compromise long-term air support. Rudenko could point to the fact he lost 35 aircraft on the first day of the May airfield offensive, possibly due to poor planning, and in view of his close professional relationship with front commander Rokossovskii, he rejected the idea outright. On the eve of *Zitadelle* Vorozheikin put pressure upon Krasovskii to strike airfields, a move supported by front commander Vatutin, but Krasovskii's agreement was conditional on joint attacks with Sudets.

Vorozheikin and Zhukov agreed air counter-attacks would be in two stages – when the enemy formed up and when they struck the defences – but the plan was never implemented. They envisaged each fighter and strike aircraft would fly 3–4 and 2–2.5 sorties per day, respectively, or 6,800–8,400 sorties in five days. They appear to have benefited from comint information, learning on 23 June that ObdL regretted the repeated postponement of *Zitadelle*. But there remained uncertainty almost to the last minute about when the attack would be launched, and all the Russian leaders were clearly relieved when they had confirmation of H-Hour. Golovanov was ordered on 3 July to coordinate ADD operations in the north of the salient while Skripko worked in the south, but on the night of 4/5 July he was in Stalin's dacha outside Moscow when Rokossovskii rang to say the Germans would attack the next day. Golovanov immediately flew to the front.

VVS intelligence put the strength of *Luftflotten* 4 and 6 at 2,050 aircraft, but it was actually 2,132, compared with 2,690 for *Braunschweig* a year earlier. Seidemann had 1,100 aircraft, reinforced by 40 from András's 2nd Hungarian Air Brigade, while Greim assigned Deichmann's *Fliegerdivision* 1 with some 730 aircraft to support Kluge's spearhead, Generaloberst Walter Model's 9 *Armee*. Dessloch also had 1st Romanian Air Corps at Mariupol with 100 aircraft to cover Manstein's right.[3] The *Luftflotten* suffered fuel problems because the Luftwaffe's monthly allocation in the East was only 160,000 tonnes while consumption could be up to 350,000 tonnes. Greim noted increased activity consumed 8,634 tonnes of B4 bomber fuel but only 5,722 tonnes were delivered, leaving 4,886 tonnes in his fuel dumps. The situation for C4 fighter fuel was even worse with 1,079 tonnes consumed but only 441 tonnes delivered. With overall fuel consumption exceeding supply, available

TABLE IV-2: LUFTWAFFE FUEL SITUATION (TONNES)

Quarter	Production	Consumption
I/43	407,000	429,000
II/43	483,000	471,000
III/43	515,000	538,000
IV/43	512,000	387,000
I/44	535,000	413,000

stocks would dictate mission sizes, and during *Zitadelle* Greim consumed 9,713 tonnes but received only 6,163 tonnes. A surge in operations in both the Russian and Mediterranean fronts saw consumption exceed supply in the first and third quarters of 1943 by more than 20,000 tonnes each, while savings from late 1943 reflected the withdrawal of *Kampfgruppen* in the East (See Table IV-2)

From early April the FAGrs probed the Kursk Salient, Greim's flying 1,638 sorties photographing the entire 18,600-square-kilometre salient and noting much incoming traffic. Greim lost a quarter of his reconnaissance force to raids on Orsha South in April, and when the enemy build-up was discovered, Kluge demanded reinforcements, creating another delay for *Zitadelle*. Comint also discovered a profusion of Russian ground and air units in the salient, but on 20 June Hitler set A-Tag for 5 July, and in a vain attempt to achieve surprise many *Staffeln* flew to their bases on the evening of 4 July. The Russians learned the Germans were assembling during the night and responded with powerful artillery bombardments, which forced both Deichmann and Seidemann to abandon plans to strike airfields in favour of counter-battery missions. Rudenko thought this was preliminary softening up and took five hours to respond to the offensive, while Krasovskii struck enemy airfields and suffered the predicted heavy casualties.

Long, bright summer days ensured the Luftwaffe provided good air–ground cooperation, with some pilots flying up to eight sorties a day as Seidemann's *Flivos* reported the situation every two hours. By contrast Rudenko had provided few liaison officers to the armies while Krasovskii totally neglected this task. On the first day the Luftwaffe was the more active, flying 4,462 sorties against 3,385 and losing 45 aircraft compared with 258, but human and mechanical exhaustion together with heavy consumption of supplies meant this effort faded by 11 July. Heavy rain on the night of 7/8 July continued into the morning to cause fog, there were often storms during the afternoon and this pattern continued until 12 July, sometimes grounding both sides. Generally, the Luftwaffe was able to contain Soviet airmen and to inflict heavy losses both in the air and on the ground, but this could not prevent the Russians striking targets 25 kilometres behind the FEBA.

While the focus was upon daytime operations, both sides also operated extensively at night. The ADD sometimes used Pe-8s carrying up to four tonnes of bombs over the front, with some crews flying four sorties a night, while night bomber regiments or specially picked 'Ilyusha' crews carried smaller loads but flew more frequently. On the southern face they flew 544 sorties between 6 and 8 July, often when the ADD could not fly, and on 9 July Skripko was ordered to make greater efforts. German *Störungkämpfer* were very active, while bombers occasionally struck marshalling yards and train-busters prowled the lines.

The ADD suffered heavy losses, many to Hauptmann Heinrich Prinz zu Sayn Wittgenstein's IV./NJG 5, which was credited with 49 victories in July – the prince alone claiming 20 – as Greim's *Nachtjagdstaffeln* flew some 150 sorties. On one occasion four out of seven bombers were shot down, and on 19/20 July three Pe-8s fell. Airfields such as Lipetsk were also interdicted. Between 4 and 15 July the VVS flew 4,095 night sorties and dropped 2,800 tonnes while the *Kampfgruppen* flew some 200 night sorties until 18 July, yet the Red Army was disappointed by its air arm. Rudenko mismanaged the early days then made near-hysterical demand for reinforcements, and Zhukov's obvious annoyance with him left the air army commander displaying nervous anxiety. Krasovskii was later criticised for command and control failures on the first day, although like Rudenko he quickly recovered.

Yet such was Novikov's alarm at how the offensive was going that on 7 July he despatched inspection teams to all air armies and air corps and soon discovered they had suffered heavy losses, often through ignoring doctrine – especially in 'Ilyusha' regiments. Sudets' 306th ShAD suffered a 31.6 per cent loss rate, mostly to ground fire, as formations fell apart during attacks to expose individual aircraft. Fortunately, on the second day of the offensive, units seemed to follow Novikov's demands that they operate in large formations and that rear-gunners retain a third of their ammunition for the return flight. Both measures helped cut 'Ilyusha' losses.

Many casualties were due to poor planning and reconnaissance, with commanders more interested in generating sortie numbers to impress their superiors rather than effective mission planning. Aircrew were denied initiative, there was poor coordination between the arms and poor radio discipline, so Novikov demanded air armies delegate mission planning to division commanders who could use their initiative to respond to changing conditions.

On the first day Rudenko's combat air patrols were overwhelmed, leaving him with weaker escorts. A disastrous attempt the next day to intervene on the battlefield with a massive blow brought his fighter casualties to 143, with 6th IAK down to 48 serviceable fighters. In the south, Krasovskii's inadequately prepared GCI organisation was swamped. To improve fighter performance Novikov replaced defensive regimental-size missions with *para*-sized patrols over enemy lines, with the best pilots encouraged to make sweeps. GCI proved a disappointment because at first the command posts were 50–60 kilometres from the FEBA with badly installed aerials. Although they were later moved forward, decisions were still made on the basis of conflicting radio reports from pilots or front line troops

Both sides gave wildly optimistic figures for the destruction of enemy armour, the Germans with their cannon and the Russians with the PTAB. Deichmann claimed the destruction of 74 tanks, mostly from 2nd Tank Army, between 5 and 11 July, but only nine of 138 tanks lost were due to air attack. Seidemann claimed 116 tanks between 7 and 8 July, but many of the 'burning' tanks were making smoke to conceal themselves by pumping diesel into their exhausts. The Russians opposite Seidemann later concluded that during the German offensive only a quarter or a third of their tanks were knocked out directly or indirectly by bombs. It was stated by 1st Tank Army that only ten of 530 knocked-out armoured vehicles were due to aerial attack, but 66 per cent of its vehicles were recorded as 'burned', many after being targeted from the air.

A third of Krasovskii's 'Ilyushas' carried the PTAB, compared with just 16 per cent of Rudenko's Il-2s, but the average bomb load per aeroplane was only 269kg due to the design of the bomb-bay. The bombs were certainly effective against 'soft-skinned' vehicles, but only a few armoured vehicles hit by them were burned out. Indeed, a 1944 survey of 31 Panthers found destroyed on the road to Belgrade, in Yugoslavia, discovered the PTAB accounted for only one. RAF examinations of armour after the Normandy campaign also suggested that few armoured vehicles were destroyed by aircraft.

The *Zitadelle* campaign came to a climax in the south around the village of Prokhorovka on 12 July when *Operatsiya Kutuzov* struck the Orel Salient and forced Kluge to break off his offensive. A successful counter-attack prevented Manstein piercing the last line of defence, by which time Krasovskii had only 472 serviceable aircraft (half of them fighters), while Sudets had 350. The Germans were exhausted too, but bloody skirmishing continued for a few more days. In an ominous sign of the times, on 15 July Seidemann had to switch most of his support to help the Romanians defend the river Mius on Manstein's southern flank.

Yet Hitler was more concerned about the Allied landing in Sicily, and on 13 July he halted *Zitadelle* and transferred forces to Italy, including Dessloch's I./KG 55, which arrived on 28 July and was returned to him on 19 August without having flown a mission in the Mediterranean! Between 5 and 11 July Deichmann flew 8,920 sorties, 341 at night, while Rudenko flew 7,463, 1,164 at night, and there were 778 ADD sorties. Seidemann flew 16,185 sorties between 5 and 18 July, 563 at night, while Krasovskii and Sudets flew 16,170, including 4,712 at night, and the ADD flew 1,521.

From 5 to 31 July Greim lost 229 aircraft, while Seidemann lost 192, a total of 421. In the same period 16th VA lost 439 aircraft, 2nd VA 372 and 17th VA 244, a total of 1,055, or a third of their strength – figures which reflect the greater experience of Luftwaffe airmen. But this quality was rapidly being eroded – the Stuka arm lost eight *Ritterkreuz-* holders during July while the Jagdwaffe's emphasis upon *Experten* meant its effectiveness declined because the 'Young Hares' lacked their experience. The Russians suffered the same problem, with Krasovskii's *Shturmovik* regiments losing 209 aircraft in July – the average 'Ilyusha' pilot was lasting just six sorties (or 13 hours). By comparison, the average fighter pilot lasted 15 sorties (11.5 hours) and bomber pilots 62 sorties (almost 70 hours).

Zitadelle set a pattern for both air forces. During the defensive phase – 5–11 July in the north and 5–18 July in the south – ground support was the VVS's prime role. Of the 23,721 sorties flown, 47.5 per cent of Rudenko's were ground attack and 51 per cent were air supremacy, while Krasovskii's were evenly split at 47.5 per cent for army support and air supremacy. Some 90 per cent of ADD sorties were against enemy defences and troop concentrations and only 217 against rail and airfield targets. In the same periods the Luftwaffe flew 24,852 sorties, of which 70.5 per cent were army support and 24 per cent were for air supremacy. The figures clearly show the Luftwaffe was now committed to Tactical, rather than Operational, Level missions to act as flying artillery, thus violating pre-war doctrine. This trend would not be reversed until the end of the year.

The Kursk victory set off a series of Russian offensives that exploded along the front like a string of firecrackers. For *Kutuzov*, Novikov and Golovanov coordinated operations after reinforcing Gromov and Naumenko with five air corps, but they, and especially Naumenko, were plagued by inexperienced regimental commanders. Each Russian army headquarters received an air army liaison team, but the shortage of 'Ilyushas' meant Naumenko had to use three regiments of Yak-9Ts with 37mm cannon. The ADD's 113th BAD was also forced to change roles, using its Il-4s to augment the dwindling number of 'Peshkas'. Golovanov also committed some 450 bombers to *Kutuzov*, including all the remaining Pe-8s.

The ADD heralded the start of the offensive on the night of 11/12 July with 542 sorties against the German rear, while at dawn VVS air attacks augmented the massive artillery bombardment. Some 'Ilyushas' were used to lay smoke to conceal the movement of assault troops. The two air armies flew 1,605 sorties on the first day (2,174 if 16th VA is included), and their operations each featured a massed 'Ilyusha' strike to help the troops penetrate deep into the defences. Greim had 866 aircraft, but poor weather restricted Deichmann's response and caused 96 strike sorties to be abandoned – his crews still flew about 1,000 to contain the threat, however. He was aided by two *Luftflotte* 1 *Jagdgruppen* to give him the equivalent of eight *Jagdgruppen*.

The Germans' experience told, and the two air armies lost 59 aircraft – 1st GvIAK had 25 fighters destroyed and 19 pilots killed or captured, while Deichmann lost ten aeroplanes. He flew another 1,000 sorties on the second day, but fuel shortages cut this to around 700 on 14 July. By then Gromov's fighter shield was proving more effective against Luftwaffe strike sorties. The German situation became more desperate when 16th VA supported an attack northwards from the Kursk Salient on 15 July after a five-day rest. Rudenko's units flew 1,000 sorties on the first day but they would suffer 'considerable' losses. The 15th also saw Naumenko launch three massive strikes of 300–400 aircraft over the battlefield, and with Soviet pressure growing, Kluge began building the *Hagenstellung* (Hagen Position) at the salient's base.

By now ObdL had stripped Seidemann of another five *Gruppen* and Meyer's *Panzerjäger* of some 200 aircraft in order to reinforce Deichmann, despite ominous signs of a Russian offensive along the Donets. On 15 July the *Kampfgruppen* briefly reverted to their traditional role at night against communications hubs, especially rail targets, but daylight operations were too hazardous. The following day the Luftwaffe made some 1,500 sorties to prevent the enemy from isolating the defenders, but much of this effort was wasted because the Russians were advancing through dense forest, which made them difficult to detect. By now Naumenko had flown 4,800 sorties and Rudenko 5,000, with half harassing the retreating enemy, against Deichmann's 6,000, but neither side had air superiority and each was able to strike the enemy rear.

As pressure grew Hitler sanctioned the evacuation of the Orel Salient in *Unternehmen Herbstreise* (Autumn Journey) on 26 July, although heavy rain delayed this from commencing until 1 August. The VVS reacted promptly with 5,000 sorties, aircraft sweeping the roads in attacks that also cut most wired communications. However, they were unable to interfere significantly with the withdrawal. The Germans also withdrew large quantities of material, some flown out in more than 3,000 transport sorties between 21 July and 17 August, when *Kutozov* was ended because the Germans had occupied the *Hagenstellung*. During the offensive the Russians flew 60,995 sorties, dropped 15,000 tonnes of bombs and lost 1,104 aircraft, while Deichmann's men had flown 37,421 sorties, dropped more than 20,000 tonnes of bombs and lost 199 combat aircraft.

Hard on the heels of the retreating Germans, the Russians retook Orel on 5 August and tried to move aircraft onto captured airfields. ObdL demanded abandoned airfields be thoroughly destroyed, although they were still to be used until the last moment. Buildings were generally demolished and most runways ploughed up, then mined, leaving one in commission until the final sorties took off, often as shells fell on the boundary while flak batteries held off the enemy as the final demolition was completed. The Russians responded by sending in engineer teams to clear mines and booby traps, often under enemy fire. Recovery teams would then restore the basic facilities so that airfields could receive regiments often within three days of them being liberated.

During late July a severely reduced Seidemann flew only 1,855 sorties from 19 July to 1 August, and he was dependent upon the Crimea-based Angerstein whose units aided him with 2,700 of his 10,500 sorties during this period to bring Dessloch's total to 13,746. Without Angerstein's support Seidemann had to rely upon the slender reed of the Hungarian Air Brigade with 45 aircraft. As it became obvious a Russian offensive against the Belgorod–Kharkov Salient was imminent, reinforcements brought Dessloch to 1,138 combat aircraft by 3 August. The new offensive was supported by 1,450 combat aircraft under Rudenko, Krasovskii and Goryunov, coordinated by Falaleev, a General-polkovnik since March. The Russians' slender numerical superiority was eroded by poorly trained aircrew, half of Goryunov's pilots being 'foals', but there was a good omen in a unique incident. On the night of 20/21 July a 7th GvAP TB-3 was hit by flak, set ablaze and the crew bailed out. The pilot managed to extinguish the fire, however, and he soon spotted his crew in a cornfield, landed, picked them up and returned to base.

The ADD softened up the defences on 2/3 August, and that morning's attack saw Krasovskii and Goryunov fly massive strikes, the former despatching 300 sorties two hours before the assault troops jumped off. The Russians were showing increasing sophistication in the way they supported offensives, with fighters working with radar (although there remained problems), strike forces hitting the rear more frequently and assault forces concentrating on narrow fronts to aid breakthroughs, with dedicated radio networks to direct them to targets. Polkovnik Ivan Poblin's 1st BAK, which reinforced Goryunov, provided the usual support, but retained a reserve for targets-of-opportunity. During September the PVO supported the Red Army by transferring some of its radar-equipped 'Peshkas' to the VVS, who in turn used them to fly nocturnal patrols over Ukrainian bomber bases to provide early warning for Russian night fighters of departing Luftwaffe bomber formations.[4] Many Russian fighter pilots in the late summer were more interested in attacking the enemy than escorting aircraft, and this cost Goryunov 30 'Ilyushas' and 'Peshkas'. Many fighter sorties were also wasted on patrols due to a continued general lack of confidence in radar-controlled GCI. This all helped the vigorous Luftwaffe response as Seidemann was reinforced by Deichmann and Pflugbeil, but Belgorod still fell on 5 August. So intense were the German air attacks that Goryunov successfully requested permission to divert from front support to attacking airfields.

Meanwhile, Falaleev ordered an ADD campaign against rail targets around Kharkov, which led to 2,300 sorties being flown between 6 and 17 August. Seidemann's crews flew up to 1,000 sorties a day, and even used SC 1800 'Satan' blockbusters against the Russians, but he was unable to stop them. By 20 August they were approaching Kharkov, and when enemy columns were spotted fleeing the city some 1,300 strike sorties were generated before the city fell the next day. During this operation the VVS lost 153 aircraft, but flew 28,265 sorties to 23 August, of which more than half (14,668) were by Goryunov while another 4,133 were flown by Sudets against enemy communications.

South of the Belgorod–Kharkov Salient the river Mius front faced probing attacks from 17 July, and these became a full-scale offensive supported by Khryukin's 8thVA from 18 August. Pflugbeil's *Fliegerkorps* IV supported the front, together with the Romanian Air Corps (95 aircraft), while his comint played a major role in the defence, alerting the troops to enemy intentions. However, they were unable to hold the line and began retreating, covered by Pflugbeil until he was appointed commander of *Luftflotte* 1 on 4 September and replaced by General Rudolf Meister. Rudenko, Krasovskii and Goryunov, together with Sudets and Khryukin, maintained the pressure, but they and the ADD lost 420 aircraft. The IAPs and ShAPs frequently shared airfields, the latter increasingly targeting river crossings while 'Peshkas' concentrated on rail targets after battlefield support – Poblin's crews increasingly flew dive-bomber attacks at angles up to 60 degrees.

During August and September, with his whole front off its hinges, Manstein slowly retreated towards the River Dnieper and the sanctuary of the *Wotanstellung* (Wotan Position). Dessloch was heavily engaged and the *Kampfgruppen* suffered badly – 100 bombers lost to enemy action out an average strength of 314. With an average strength of 214, the *Stukagruppe* had 107 Ju 87s shot down and the *Schlachtflieger* lost 25 from an average force of 59. Luftwaffe strength was also eroded by other factors such as American bombing raids on the Reich, which caused the transfer westward of six *Jagd-* and *Zerstörergruppen*. Overall fighter strength in the East dropped to 330 by 1 September and 390 by 1 January 1944, as the VVS grew in strength and quality.

During 1943 experienced bomber and 'Ilyusha' crews made greater use of radio navigation aids to the point where veteran Il-2 crews could show 64 per cent hits in a 200 × 200 metre area, compared with half this in 1941. General-leitenant Vasilii Ryazanov's 1st Assault Corps

(*Shturmovaya Aviatsionnaya Korpus*, ShAK) developed a tactic called the 'vicious circle' (*porochnyi krug*), with circling formations sending down aircraft to stage continuous attacks for up to half an hour. Radar support for fighters continued, while Krasovskii and Sudets used intruders in low-level attacks (100–700 metres) on trains to block the lines. Reconnaissance regiments standardised on 'Peshkas' for Operational Level sorties up to 300 kilometres behind the FEBA and came to supply hourly reports on advances. From September 1943 a fighter-equipped squadron was added to each regiment for tactical reconnaissance, with the 'slave' shielding the 'master' who acted as the eyes.

During September regiments changed base up to four times, and while some sites were captured airfields, many regiments operated from stubble-covered fields that had just had their crops harvested. There were major supply problems because the few rail lines were stretched to breaking point, which slowed the pace of operations. Yet in August Khryukin flew 15,642 sorties and the following month 16,230, while Sudets flew 16,188 sorties in August alone. The ADD was also active, flying 6,254 sorties and dropping 6,820 tonnes of bombs, of which 3,585 sorties and 4,454 tonnes were against rail targets.

At the end of September Manstein entered the *Wotanstellung*, with the Russians hard on his heels. They established several bridgeheads along the Dnieper to act as wedges for breaking through the defences but then paused for a fortnight to reorganise and to regroup. General Ivan Konev would later criticise Goryunov's subordinates, especially air corps commanders, for failing to cover the crossing in good weather and in particular General-leitenant Ivan Podgorny (4th IAK) for taking so long to provide continuous fighter cover over his bridgehead. In an attempt to expand its Dnieper bridgehead at Bukhin, the Voronezh Front dropped two paratroop brigades (5,000 men) using 180 Li-2s of the ADD and GVF. Poor visibility doomed the hastily organised operation on 23/24 September and the troops were scattered. Front commander Vatutin had vetoed Skripko's request to postpone the operation, and when he tried to name scapegoats Stalin told him the disaster was his own fault. Golovanov would study the failures closely after the war when he headed the reformed airborne forces.

After a brief pause the Russians prepared to break through the *Wotanstellung* and the VVS assembled 2,850 aircraft in the Ukraine, where Dessloch, on 10 October, had 819 combat aircraft augmented by 167 in Hungarian, Romanian and Slovakian squadrons, although the latter unit was plagued with defections. Hard probing began on 9 October and Seidemann reacted vigorously, flying 867 day and 158 night sorties on 10 October alone. Three days later, masked by poor weather and low cloud, Goryunov (442 aircraft) and Sudets supported a new offensive that broke through Manstein's right. Meister helped but, to relieve the burden, Angerstein's *Fliegerkorps* I was transferred from the Crimea on 14 October to cover Kleist's forces on the northern shores of the Black Sea.

By 20 October the *Wotanstellung* was pierced, exposing the excellent bases at Krivoi Rog, but Dessloch exploited the *Kampfgruppen* mercilessly with two sorties a day here and a third some 300 kilometres to the north defending Kiev. Utilising other airfields, the Luftwaffe flew up to 1,200 sorties a day to support a timely counter-attack that saved Krivoi Rog until February 1944. However, on 3 November, Krasovskii, with 603 aircraft, helped a breakthrough that headed for Kiev. Dessloch used every *Panzerjäger* aircraft available but could not prevent the city's fall on 6 November, although aided by 370 sorties, the Germans retook Zhitomir 11 days later. The Russian advance beyond Kiev came close to splitting *Heeresgruppen Mitte* and *Süd* until all available Luftwaffe units were committed to a counter-attack in rain, low cloud and fog, which temporarily halted the enemy on 23 November. A reinforced Seidemann, whose *Kampfgruppen* used Y-Gerät electronic aids for some night attacks, was fortunate the VVS did not exploit the congestion at his handful of all-weather airfields before poor weather largely grounded both sides for nearly a month.

The Kiev offensive caught Manstein off guard, for he believed the greater threat would come from the south where, on 23 October, Khryukin with 900 aircraft supported an attack upon Kleist's left that by the end of the month had isolated the Crimea. The scale of Russian activity may be gauged from the fact Goryunov flew 10,165 sorties and dropped 975 tonnes of bombs during October while Khryukin flew 12,380 sorties. The Russians continued to be plagued by inexperienced pilots, however – a major cause of the 47 fighters lost by General-maior Aleksandr Outin's 7th IAK, which amounted to 65 per cent of Goryunov's total losses. Khryukin received 6,328 tonnes of fuel and lubricants, together with 2,730 tonnes of ammunition, but they were quickly consumed, leaving his air army, like the others, running on empty. During December the weather deteriorated, with flying on Khryukin's front possible on only two days and three nights. This gave ObdL time to withdraw Meister's headquarters and some *Kampfgruppen* as the cadre for a strategic bomber force.

The frequent abandonment of bases, depots, repair workshops, aircraft parks and command posts with their landline networks compromised Luftwaffe operations. Yet it spearheaded the Wehrmacht's efforts to contain breakthroughs in what were dubbed 'Fire Brigade Tactics' (*Feuerwehr Taktik*) through tactical strikes that tried to blunt the spearheads detected by the *Nahaufklärungsstaffeln*. Their successes were usually temporary, with strike forces often flying unescorted in daylight to suffer heavy wastage from fighters and ground fire. Indeed, during October and November the *Schlachtflieger*'s losses amounted to nearly 30 per cent of establishment and more than 20 per cent of total Luftwaffe losses to enemy action in the East. New crises would often draw away the *Gruppen* before they had completed their missions, so airmen were frittered away through incoherent solutions to local crises.

The Luftwaffe's transition to a Tactical Level force was underlined on 18 October when the distinctions between the dive-bombers (*Stukagruppen*), fighter-bombers (*Schlachtgruppen*) and anti-tank units (*Panzerjägerstaffeln*) were abandoned, with all organised into *Schlachtgeschwader*. The surviving Hs 129s were concentrated in IV./SG 9, while the remainder of the *Schlachtgruppen* had the Ju 87, although II./SG 2 also retained a few Hs 123B biplanes until May 1944. Both the Ju 87s and Hs 123s were gradually replaced by *Jabos* from April to December 1944, apart from III./SG 2 and the *Panzerjägerstaffeln*. Many of the Stukas would be transferred to the *Nachtschlachtgruppen*, simultaneously renamed from *Störkampfgruppen*, which represented 30 per cent of the Eastern Front strike force by New Year's Day 1944.

Schlachtgruppen usually operated around the FEBA within 150 kilometres of their bases and flew at 1,800 metres to make shallow dive attacks with anti-personnel and armour-piercing bombs against weapons, armour concentrations, transport and signal centres. From late 1943 they benefited both from radio beacons and improvised radio-telephone communications. The *Panzerjägerstaffeln* would usually operate in *Staffel* formation while *Nachtschlachtgruppen* would fly individually to strike batteries, transport and troop concentrations.

The *Kampfgruppen* focused upon troop and artillery concentrations, such missions having the advantage that they often lasted only an hour. Indeed, one pilot noted that of the first 100 of his 312 sorties, only seven per cent involved more than ten minutes over enemy territory.[5] This put greater strain on the machines and often meant two sorties a day, at the end of which many *Kampfgruppen* were down to six serviceable bombers. They were also increasingly used as transport units because they had the firepower to protect themselves and their precious cargoes from fighters. The one area where they retained an Operational Level role was interdicting the enemy rail system, with three dedicated, train-busting *Staffeln* supported by FAGr 100. Illustrating the success these units had in the East, the commander of 9.(*Eis*)/KG 3, Hauptmann Ernst Fach, was credited with destroying 216 locomotives.

The erosion of the Eastern Front bomber force was completed by Korten and Koller, whose pleas for a strategic bombing force were sanctioned by Hitler and Göring on 26 November. In December Meister's *Fliegerkorps* IV was withdrawn from *Luftflotte* 4, redesignated the Eastern Replenishment Staff (*Auffrischungsstab Ost*) and gradually assigned most of the Eastern Front *Kampfgruppen*. *Fliegerkorps* I, under Deichmann, from 8 November, was now given responsibility for the southern sector, leaving an operational headquarters in the Crimea.

Between 1 September and 31 December the Luftwaffe lost 1,012 aircraft, of which 553 fell to enemy action while another 100 were destroyed on the ground (37 to air attacks). By the end of the year the

Luftwaffe's first-line strength in the East had dropped to 1,732 combat aircraft on the main front, of which Dessloch had 966 – nearly 56 per cent – and 216 transports, augmented by 90 Hungarian and Romanian aircraft. Despite the loss during 1943 of no fewer than 9,543 aircraft, including 4,642 fighters and 3,515 'Ilyushas', the VVS had 4,815 aircraft on the main front, with another 3,996 in Stavka reserve, augmented by 742 naval, 885 PVO and 1,003 ADD bombers. For operations in the Ukraine there were 1,953 VVS (40.5 per cent of strength) and 429 VVS-ChF aircraft.

By the end of 1943 Manstein and Kleist were extremely exposed, with few natural defences. Stavka was determined to exploit the situation, ordering the destruction of enemy forces in the Ukraine. Goryunov supported the first offensive in this region on 24 December from Kiev, flying 1,100 sorties to take Kirovograd on 8 January and thus depriving the Luftwaffe of a major airfield complex. Dessloch was forced to disperse to airstrips that were boggy during the warm spells, then withdraw to permanent airfields at the end of January. The main offensive began on 5 January, but fog and low cloud restricted air support while frequent warm spells caused aircraft to ice up as they climbed, yet Krasovskii, with 503 serviceable aircraft, and Gornyunov, with 551, would fly 14,739 sorties that month. Ice hampered command and control, cutting telephone wires, so most communication was by radio.

Lack of aircraft restricted the Luftwaffe response, although Dessloch correctly anticipated that the first blow would come from Kiev. He reinforced Seidemann, who received tactical control of Deichmann's *Kampfgruppen* (which remained in their southern bases) as well as 100 of Angerstein's *Schlachtflieger*. Bad weather, poor airfields, frequent moves and the transfer of the infrastructure to central Poland (650 kilometres away) reduced maintenance, so there were barely 300–350 sorties per day. By 20 January Dessloch was down to 849 combat aircraft augmented by 132 Hungarian and Romanian aeroplanes, while the effort wore down the *Schlachtgruppen* and dashed hopes of re-equipping both the *Stukagruppen* and the Fw 189-equipped *Nahaufklärungsstaffeln*.

Russian progress was slow until 29 January, when there was a double envelopment of XLII and XI *Armeekorps* with 56,000 men around

Korsun. Seidemann immediately deployed three *Transportgruppen* to the concrete runways of Uman to support the pocket, but heavy snow and low cloud impeded operations and Dessloch's chief-of-staff, Generalmajor Karl-Heinrich Schulz, warned it was almost impossible to fly in supplies. In the first five days 44 aircraft were lost, two full of wounded, and they had to parachute in supplies. Manstein organised a relief operation, *Unternehmen Wanda*, on 8 February, while Seidemann organised a new transport effort from the following day. The Russians responded by bringing in, from 9 February, General-maior Leonid Rybkin's 10th IAK PVO to reinforce Krasovskii's aerial blockade, and they inflicted heavy casualties on the German and Hungarian fighters.

The Germans had built an airfield on firmer ground by 9 February, but only 100–185 tonnes a day could be flown due to rain and fog hindering the transports. A blizzard on the night of 17/18 February allowed the Germans to break out, and some 36,200 reached safety while another 4,161 wounded were flown out. The *Transportgruppen* flew 1,500 sorties to bring in 2,026 tonnes of supplies and to evacuate 2,400 wounded, but 32 aircraft were lost and 113 damaged. During the offensive Krasovskii's airmen flew 6,081 sorties, while Goryunov flew 3,212, losing 74 and 49 aircraft, respectively. Rybkin flew 143 sorties without loss. Novikov was sent to this front by Stalin to supervise anti-armour operations, and on 21 February he was joined by Zhukov, who received a telephone call from Moscow. He put down the telephone and informed Novikov that he had been promoted to become the first Chief Marshal of Aviation, having been promoted to Marshal in March 1943.

Despite the struggle to supply the Korsun pocket, most of Dessloch's strength was initially assigned to Deichmann's *Fliegerkorps* I as the Russian left began offensives from 10 January. Although Deichmann had to return many of Seidemann's aircraft for operations around Korsun, he helped *Fliegerkorps* VIII to stage heavy attacks, which, together with muddy roads, brought the northern Russian offensive to a halt. But his task was still hard, as during February Khryukin alone flew 6,093 sorties, with two-thirds being close air support until an early thaw created low clouds that forced Russian airmen into the mouths of flak batteries. Their supply lines were also becoming increasingly strained, Khryukin receiving 10,700 tonnes of fuel and ammunition at forward airfields in January and February, while 2,160 tonnes were flown into Sudets' airfields by 300 Li-2s and U-2s during mid-February.

The supply problems were due to poorly bedded rail track that restricted trains to speeds of only 2–4km/h. NBADs were used for aerial resupply, carrying a 180–210kg load including a bag or fuel tank under the fuselage, a crate in the navigator's positions and shells under the wings. Krasovskii's 326th NBAD flew 822 sorties between 8 and 16 February to deliver 49 tonnes of petrol and 65 tonnes of ammunition. The Russians also suffered from poor airfields, some made by peasants who trampled straw and reeds into the ground, but mud hamstrung aircraft whose engines overheated. Most airfields were also so narrow that they restricted operations. Finally, there were too few support units, and they lacked vehicles and spare parts that in turn made it difficult to repair damaged aircraft.

There was a brief lull while both sides regrouped, but this ended on 4 March as one Ukrainian Front after another attacked. They were supported by 2,360 combat aircraft, although many units were under-strength for, on paper, they should have had some 3,400 aircraft. The Russians estimated Dessloch's strength at more than 1,460 aircraft, but his combat strength had risen from 920 in February to 990 in March, with about 100 Hungarian and Romanian aircraft, while his transport strength fell from 331 to 275 and then rose to 568. Dessloch's unit lost 469 combat aircraft during January and February – only 245 to enemy action – and 95 transports (48 to enemy action), but there were continued difficulties delivering replacement aircraft and crews.

The Russians now carved great gaps in the German line, with the Luftwaffe's primary roles being army support and transport. However, with the *Kampfgruppen* down to 99 bombers the Luftwaffe frittered its resources in penny packets to provide the illusion of air support. The *Stukagruppen*, especially, struggled for survival, with many *Experten* failing to return, and by early March Manstein's left had been split, with General Hans-Valentin Hube's 1 *Panzerarmee* facing envelopment. On 23 March the city of Ternopol was isolated, but its 4,000-man garrison held out until 15 April, supported by five transport and two glider *Gruppen*. Dessloch's response was hindered by the need to return a *Jagdgruppe* to *Luftflotte* 1 as the Russians pushed back the Wehrmacht from the gates of Leningrad. This operation also absorbed most of Golovanov's bomber regiments until later in March, when they returned to fly 1,830 sorties mostly against rail targets, before switching to supply operations.

On 24 March Hube, with 300,000 men, was finally isolated, but pushed westwards into Poland, partly to exploit VVS weakness and Luftwaffe strength. A substantial transport force was available in Odessa to support the Crimea, but this was too far from Hube, so Morzik, as *Transportfliegerführer* 2 *der Luftflotte* 4 (TFF 2), moved to Krosno, in Poland, to support him. Here, he assembled 150 Ju 52/3ms, with 100 of Meister's bombers, at bases with concrete runways. The supply mission began in snow, low cloud and poor visibility, but as the weather improved crews flew up to five sorties a night. Preparations for supporting the aircraft, as well as receiving and distributing supplies, were far better because Stalingrad veteran Hube had learned lessons from past campaigns, and his men could live off the land. Transport operations improved when Kamenets-Podolskiy airfield was secured on 1 April, and three days later Hube was saying that the supplies, largely of ammunition and fuel, were adequate.

The Russians were unable to eradicate Hube's pocket because they were flying from boggy airstrips, while Dessloch used permanent bases to fly 20,868 sorties during March. A relief offensive linked up with Hube on 7 April and the newly arrived troops stabilised the southern Poland front. The well-organised operation was responsible for 8,000 of the 11,149 sorties flown by Dessloch in March, which saw some 3,500 tonnes of supplies delivered. Dessloch lost 25 transports during March, 18 to enemy action, bringing his total transport losses since November to 238 aircraft destroyed or badly damaged, 129 to enemy action. Tragically, while flying back to his troops after receiving the Diamonds to his *Ritterkreuz*, Hube was killed in an air accident in Austria on 21 April.

During early March Manstein's right retreated towards Romania, his line at one point propped up by the move of part of a division in Me 323

Gigant transports. Dessloch used both Deichmann and Seidemann to support the southern flank, and they flew an average of 700 sorties each day (and more than 1,000 on five occasions). From 17 March the peril facing Hube meant 2nd Romanian Air Corps (120 aircraft) was brought in, but it could not prevent the fall of Nikolaev on 28 March and Odessa on 10 April. The Luftwaffe was almost exhausted, Dessloch having 997 combat aircraft in April and his *Jagdgruppen* only 42 serviceable fighters on 20 March. Fortunately, the Dniester provided the necessary breakwater, and by mid-April the Russian fury had abated. On 8 March Dessloch moved his headquarters to Morzyn, in Hungary.

The Ukrainian campaigns had cost *Luftflotte* 4 a total of 2,149 combat aircraft between September 1943 and May 1944, 1,202 to enemy action, and a further 204 transports, 98 to enemy action. Despite reaching sanctuary, Manstein and Kleist were relieved and their commands renamed *Heeresgruppen Nordukraine* and *Südukraine*.

The last Ukrainian campaign, from 24 December to 17 April, saw the VVS regiments fly 31,836 sorties, including 13,176 against enemy troops, drop 7,000 tonnes of bombs and lose 676 aircraft. They were now well placed to renew the offensive along the whole front during the summer, for the Germans had few natural defences. The PVO returned to western Ukraine, with 450 fighters shielding the rail network as army support became a growing PVO mission. Transport was a major feature of Russian air operations during the latter stages of the campaign, with 15 per cent of Krasovskii's 400 daily sorties involving supplying fuel and ammunition to the spearheads. During the first fortnight of April Goryunov flew 4,817 transport sorties that brought in 670 tonnes of supplies. The GVF was also mobilised, and during March it supplied forces facing Hube with 790 tonnes of fuel. It also moved 3,500 tonnes of cargo to the Ukrainian fronts during March and April. The ADD was also increasingly diverted to the transport role, and in April flew 1,500 sorties in support of forces in southern Poland to provide 2,300 tonnes of supplies, including 600 tonnes of fuel.

In the summer of 1943 the Taman Peninsula remained a backwater, but in September the Red Army renewed pressure with support from

Vershinin's 4th VA, with 599 combat aircraft, and Ermachenkov's VVS-ChF, with 450. On 8 September Hitler authorised the evacuation of the *Gotenkopfstellung*, which was completed on the night of 9/10 October after the *Transportgruppen* moved 15,661 men and 1,154 tonnes of equipment. Russian air power totally failed to disrupt the evacuation and sank only three small naval vessels, while in revenge Stukas sank three destroyers attempting a bombardment of the Crimean shore on 6 October.

In anticipation of a major campaign against the Crimea on 1 November, a beachhead was secured on the Kerch Peninsula and shielded by 229th IAD. The latter set up a radar and comint station, the station being created by adapting a tank radio receiver. In February 1944 the PVO created the North Caucasus PVO Divisional District for this task, and within a month it had two radars and 96 fighters. Meanwhile, the VVS harassed the enemy and supported Crimean partisans by flying 409 sorties between October 1943 and April 1944. These delivered 215 tonnes of supplies and evacuated 952 wounded in 80 landings.

To support the Crimean garrison of 17 *Armee* and Romanian troops an airlift was organised from 5 December and placed in the reliable hands of Morzik as TFF 2 at Odessa with seven *Transportgruppen* (200 aircraft), many transferred in from the Mediterranean, operating from Odessa then Foscani, in Romania. When *Fliegerkorps* I left the Crimea it created, in December, *Fliegerkorps* I *Crimea* Operations Staff (*Einsatz Stab Fliegerkorps I/Krim*) from *SeeFlfü Schwarzes Meer* under its commander, Oberst Joachim Bauer. By late March 1944 the Russians were clearly preparing to regain the Crimea and Germany lacked the resources to hold it. Hitler refused to abandon it because its air bases might be used to strike the Ploesti oilfields, which were already being pounded by the Western Allies. In March Stalin ordered an offensive to retake the territory from the north, supported by Khryukin's 8th VA, which had been reinforced with two air corps to give it 662 combat aircraft, and the Kerch Peninsula, supported by Vershinin (538 combat aircraft), plus Ermachenkov who contributed 64. This gave the Russians an overall strength of 1,264 aircraft, which were augmented by the ADD.

Khryukin, who had received some of the new Yak-3s, prepared 33 airfields for the offensive (some of these came under mortar and artillery fire while being built), together with a largely female forward command post. The average air army required 500 tonnes of fuel and 158 tonnes of bombs per day, and he had to assemble a week's worth. A forward radar had already been established, and between January and March it detected 1,614 targets that led to 135 interceptions. Bauer had just 127 combat aircraft based upon a *Jagd-* and two *Schlachtgruppen*. A third of the pilots in Gerhard Barkhorn's II./JG 52 were *Experten* with more than 40 victories apiece, while most of their opponents flew lumbering LaGG-3s. The Germans would be reinforced by a *Kampfgruppe* and a *Panzerjägerstaffel*, but these 35 aircraft made no difference to the outcome of the campaign.

Probing attacks began on 8 April, with the main offensive launched from the north, supported by 108 'Ilyushas', the following day. An additional 100 Il-2s supported the Kerch attack. Vershinin's airmen discovered the Germans were evacuating the Kerch Peninsula, but his reports were dismissed and he had to go to Stavka coordinator Voroshilov to authorise attacks on the columns. The captured Kerch airfields were sprinkled with SD 2s and Vershinin also suffered a serious fuel shortage after his aircraft consumed 1,412 tonnes in the first three days and he then found it difficult to bring reserve stocks in across the Kerch Straits.

Between 8 and 17 April the Luftwaffe flew 2,390 combat sorties over the Crimea, but with little effect, while the VVS flew 8,874 and dropped 655 tonnes of bombs, Khryukin's men performing the lion's share of the work with 6,847 sorties. Bauer, who lost his right eye in an air attack, clearly could not cope and was evacuated to receive a *Ritterkruez* for his efforts. Deichmann moved his headquarters to the Crimea on 11 April to coordinate missions with Romanian bases, as bombers and transports, shielded by a *Zerstörer* detachment, brought in ammunition and evacuated both wounded and 'useless mouths'. German airfields were under heavy attack, and on 11 April Khryukin's 2nd GvNBAD moved into the Crimea to use captured bombs against their former owners. The following day an unofficial evacuation began and

Ermachenkov interdicted the sea lanes. His bombers sank only six merchantmen (11,083 grt) and five small warships while his mines sank three small warships.

The Germans were pushed into Sevastopol under unrelenting air attack, which left Deichmann with 37 combat aircraft and nine seaplanes by 25 April. With the issue no longer in doubt, Vershinin's headquarters was withdrawn to Belorussia, leaving Khryukin to finish off the enemy with 1,023 aircraft. From 30 April to 4 May the VVS struck positions around Sevastopol, dropping 2,000 tonnes of bombs. On 5 May the last stage began as Khryukin and Ermachenkov overwhelmed the enemy. The last Axis fighter missions were flown over Crimea three days later, after which the surviving 13 fighters departed, carrying groundcrew in their fuselages. Fighting in Sevastopol continued until 14 May, by which time Deichmann had flown 1,678 combat sorties over the previous ten days.

In supporting the assault upon Sevastopol Khryukin had flown 30,875 combat sorties and the ADD 1,865 sorties to drop 43,565 tonnes of bombs, while another 1,219 sorties were flown against Romanian ports. The Crimea campaign cost the Russians 266 aircraft and the Germans 97, including 76 abandoned and blown up, while some of Dessloch's losses of 173 transport aircraft, 73 to enemy action, were here and the rest while supporting Hube. The Axis evacuated 142,310 men, of whom 21,547 were flown out on the night of 10/11 May.

Good pre-planning meant Kluge's *Heeresgruppe Mitte*, supported by Greim, had a less traumatic time. The *Wotanstellung* had been extended along the Dnieper and Desna to the Baltic as the *Pantherstellung* (Panther Position), occupied by the beginning of October 1943 and held until the following summer. On 23 August, when the Russians launched *Operatsiya Suvorov* towards Smolensk, Kluge was west of the line, but having already anticipated a threat to the northern flank, Greim, in June, created *Fliegerdivision* 4 at Smolensk. It was led by Plocher until 25 August, when Oberst Franz Reuss took over. Plocher faced General-maior Nikolai Papivin's 3rd VA, Gromov's 1st VA and part of Naumenko's 15th VA with some 1,100 aircraft. Papivin, who once guarded Lenin's Kremlin apartment and office, had been deputy commander of 1st VA after commanding fighter and assault divisions prior to getting his own air army on 26 May 1943, but he had only 205 aircraft. The Russians were also aided by the ADD, which would fly 7,533 sorties against defences in front of Smolensk.

Suvorov was poorly planned and executed, so Plocher and Reuss contained the brief threat, which was renewed on 6 September and used by Kluge as an excuse to withdraw into the *Pantherstellung* from 18 September. Reuss covered the withdrawal with daylight delaying actions complemented by systematic night harassing operations against communications. The recapture of Smolensk on 24 September was of personal interest to Novikov, whose wife and younger son were buried there, but the campaign was not officially closed until 2 October, by which time the Russians had lost 303 aircraft.

Papivin then supported an assault north of Smolensk from 6 October that drove down the *Heeresgruppen Nord* and *Mitte* boundary near Nevel. Greim had 760 aircraft to meet the threat, and between 10 and 15 October Reuss flew 3,701 sorties including some major daylight bomber missions, but heavy rain played a major role in the German success. Papivin was reinforced to support unsuccessful attempts to take Vitebsk and Orsha, which lasted into January 1944, and Reuss held Papivin.

Deichmann also faced pressure in the south, where Rudenko helped the Red Army push back Kluge's right and Manstein's left, despite serious problems getting supplies from bases 300–400 kilometres in the rear. A lack of support meant unit strength melted away, which forced Rudenko to concentrate his aircraft into a shock group with a nominal eight fighter, assault and bomber divisions. This received priority as the other units withered away, allowing Deichmann to briefly contain the threat. A new effort began on 15 October, and Deichmann was soon involved in heavy aerial fighting, with both sides suffering significant losses. Indeed, during October SchG/SG 1 lost 45 aircraft, 19 to enemy action. During this period Kluge was replaced by Generalfeldmarschall Ernst Busch, while Deichmann transferred to *Fliegerkorps* I on November 7 and was replaced by anti-shipping specialist Generalmajor Robert Fuchs.

There was another pause, then the Belorussian Front began pushing Busch's southern flank in the Pripet Marshes from 2 January 1944. A weak Fuchs replied as best he could, aided by snow, fog and low clouds that forced the Russians to operate in small formations, although they made a major effort to disrupt the rail network. Rudenko flew 11,400 sorties during the first quarter of 1944, but the Russians made little progress. On 24 February General-leitenant Fedor Polynin's 6th VA was brought in to continue the advance along the southern marshes to Poland. Polynin was an extremely experienced officer who had held senior staff positions before receiving 6th VA in January 1943, and he helped surround Kovel until a reinforced Fuchs held him. During March *Luftflotte* 6 flew 6,499 sorties and a German counter-attack on the 30th of that month, aided by a *Jagdgruppe* transferred from Dessloch, relieved Kovel. Stalin was furious and demoted Polynin's 6th VA to become Rudenko's subordinate.

Between September 1943 and April 1944 Greim lost 615 combat aircraft and about a dozen transports, but his losses to enemy action were relatively light at 311, or an average of 44 a month. Russian losses are unknown, but were undoubtedly heavier. With partisans plaguing *Heeresgruppe Mitte*'s rear, anti-partisan operations played a role during this period, sometimes amounting to 12 per cent of sorties during lulls. In addition to *Kampf-* and *Schlachtverbände*, anti-partisan sorties gave training units operational experience, even torpedo-bombers! The partisans were supported by both the VVS and the GVF, and during 1943 there were 3,708 sorties flown by U-2s and R-5s behind *Heeresgruppe Mitte* to deliver 270 tonnes of ammunition and 1,500 personnel, while 2,000 sick and wounded were evacuated for the loss of six aircraft and seven aircrew.

In the aftermath of *Iskra* Keller's strength continued to decline to 247 aircraft by the beginning of March 1943, and during the year he flew 45,187 sorties, 23,613 of them strike missions. Rieckhoff, on 23 February 1943, received full-time command of *Flfü* 1, which was upgraded to *Fliegerdivision* 3 in December 1943. By contrast, by mid-1943 13th and 14th VA had 489 aircraft, including 88 day bombers, while the Baltic Fleet had 229. On 7 July, 7th IAK PVO was renamed 2nd GvIAK PVO, under Polkovnik Nikolai Antonov from 24 June, 1943, and during the year its pilots flew 5,664 sorties and claimed 36 aircraft.

Luftflotte 1 saw a rapid turnover in commanders, with Korten relieving Keller on 26 June, but his elevation to ObdL saw him replaced on 4 September by Pflugbeil. The year also saw desultory air combat, with *Luftflotte* 1 on the defensive, its strength having dropped to 221 combat aircraft in July 1943 and then steadily increased to 433 by the beginning of the year. The ADD waged a three-month campaign on the Leningrad Front from June to August, flying 5,356 sorties and dropping 6,533 tonnes of bombs. As usual enemy positions attracted the most activity, but 1,210 tonnes were dropped on long-range artillery batteries shelling the city, while rail and airfield targets attracted only 671 tonnes.

Luftflotte 1's shortage of resources meant its *Nachtschlachtgruppen* were used in daylight to support counter-insurgency operations on the army group boundary and also to create the Luftwaffe's 'Foreign Legion'. A *Staffel* of Estonian airmen was used for coastal patrol from February 1942, and in April 1943 it became AufKlGr 127 (*See*) (later SAGr 127) and proved encouraging enough to become NSGr 11 (*Est*) in October. Latvian airmen were then recruited for NSGr 12 (*Lett*) in February 1944; but an even greater pool of manpower was captured Soviet airmen. General Andrei Vlassov was the figurehead for recruiting Russians to fight for the Germans, and in December 1943 *Ostfliegerstaffel* I was created with U-2s. There were ambitious, and ultimately vain, plans to create an air force under the former head of the Yalta Aeroflot sanatorium, Oberst Viktor Malcev. It possessed a single *Nachtschlachtstaffel* that flew a few sorties before it was disbanded in the summer of 1944. Malcev fell into Russian hands at the end of the war and was shot.

In September 1943 the Leningrad Front began planning a major offensive to drive back the invader. It was a formidable problem for the front was strongly fortified, with the *Pantherstellung* in the rear. The offensive was based upon enveloping the enemy left, 18 *Armee*, from the Oranienbaum bridgehead and from Leningrad itself, while pinning down the right, 16 *Armee*. Supplying the VVS forces was easier for this operation, although Samokhin and Antonov had to ensure the safety of convoys into the Orianenbaum bridgehead. At the beginning of the month Rybalchenko had 324 aircraft, Zhuravlev 256 and Samokhin 313, while Naumenko's 15th VA had 599. The ADD provided the Il-4s of 1st GvAK and the Li-2s of 5th, 6th and 7th AK for a total of 442 bombers. Rybalchenko's airmen practised ground-attack tactics on a dummy system north of Leningrad, and there was considerable training in bad weather flying.

The Russians estimated Pflugbeil's strength at about 150 aircraft when it was actually 433, which rose to 450 by the end of the campaign, with *Fliegerdivision* 3 under General Walther Boenicke from 6 January 1944. Pflugbeil had received *Jagd-* and *Schlachtgruppen* from Finland and Greece, together with a train-busting *Staffel*, but his only other bomber force consisted of an operational training unit. Worse, just before the Russian offensive he had to surrender a *Jagdgruppe* to defend Bulgaria.

The offensive, heralded by 250 Li-2 night bombing sorties that dropped 876 tonnes of bombs, began on the morning of 15 January. Operations were disrupted by cloud down to 100 metres and snow and mist that cut visibility to 100–500 metres, so only individual pilots or small formations could operate. Rybalchenko's men flew just 13 sorties while Zhuravlev's were grounded all day. By the end of January the two air armies had flown 4,500 sorties, 70 per cent of them ground attack, as the Red Army threatened to envelop two *Armeekorps*, which eventually escaped. On 19 January naval bombers hit Boenicke's headquarters, while the next day the Leningrad Front demanded the airmen strike enemy communications. By the end of the month 18 *Armee* was on the verge of collapse and JG 54's old base at Siverskaya was in enemy hands.

Although Pflugbeil received few reinforcements due to the greater crises in the Ukraine and Italy, he helped restrict the advance until mid-February, when permission was given to withdraw into the *Pantherstellung* in early March. The Russians were hindered by poor weather, as well as the usual difficulties in moving forward supplies to captured airfields. Once on site, restoration teams removed 629 bombs, 233 booby traps, 14,145 mines and 4,000 shells. During the offensive Rybalchenko's airmen flew 14,389 sorties, of which 7,356 were ground attack and 1,450 artillery support. Fighter missions accounted for 4,875 sorties, but only 146 were flown against airfields and 506 against rail targets. The latter were usually attacked by the ADD, which flew 8,555 sorties in support of the offensive. Pflugbeil lost 201 aircraft, of which half were to enemy action, while the Russians lost 260 in a campaign that pushed the Germans back 180 kilometres to deprive the Luftwaffe of bases that had been assigned an important role in Meister's strategic bombing campaign.

The early part of 1944 saw changes in both sides' air forces. On 13 February the disbandment of Volkhov Front saw Zhuravlev's army briefly joining Leningrad Front for ten days, then being withdrawn into Stavka reserve, leaving some regiments with Rybalchenko. On 11 April ObdL and the Air Ministry (RLM) were finally merged as Air Force Supreme Command (*Oberkommando der Luftwaffe*, OKL) to bring the Luftwaffe in line with the other services, *Fliegerkorps* IV returned to duty, while the *Schlacht-* and *Nahaufklärungsgruppen* received Fw 190s. However, by June 1944, of 19 *Schlachtgruppen* (excluding the Hs 129-equipped SG 9) only half were fully equipped with Fw 190F/Gs, the remainder flying Ju 87D/Gs, while of 22 *Nachtschlachtstaffeln* in the East only nine were fully equipped with the Ju 87. Air–ground liaison was improved, however, with Air Control Teams (*Fliegerleittruppe*) providing direct radio contact with the aircraft from an armoured half-track or even a command tank.

ObdL/OKL had been giving serious thought to strategic bombing in the East since 1943 when delays with *Zitadelle* allowed Greim to indulge his interest in the subject. On 12 May 1943, his *Kampfgruppen* began a campaign against targets, especially railways, up to 300 kilometres behind the lines, with his prime targets being the GAZ vehicle plant at Gorkii (now Nizhni Novgorod), the Yaroslavl rubber plant and Saratov oil refinery. They were defended by General-maior Alexei Osipov's Gorkii District PVO Corps with 105 fighters, two *Permatit* search radars and two SON-2 fire control radars, but it appears there were no radar-equipped fighters – nightfighter pilots depended upon searchlight support. The *Permatit* search area was restricted by mountains and most communication was by telephone.

The GAZ plant was struck from 4/5 to 22/23 June, with the bombers arriving in a 'Crocodile' (*Krokodil*) stream. The target was severely damaged, only returning to full production on 18 August. However, it made T-70 light tanks (although the chassis was also used for the SU-76 self-propelled gun), so the raid had little impact upon Soviet tank strength. Among other targets hit during 1,813 sorties was Factory 292 in Saratov, the prime producer of Yak-1s, which some sources state was destroyed or severely damaged on 22/23 June.

The defence against these attacks was a shambles, with the bombing cutting landlines to disrupt command and control, leaving the interceptor pilots on their own. Once airborne, the latter usually engaged targets beyond the range of their guns. Eight attempted Taran tactics, of which three were reportedly successful. The PVO flew 431 sorties and claimed 52 interceptions, while the *Kampfgruppen* lost some 20 aircraft – a 3 per cent loss rate. To disrupt further attacks the VVS staged an offensive against airfields during 8–10 June 1943, but suffered heavy casualties. The imminence of *Zitadelle* eventually forced Greim to abandon his campaign, which needed four-engined bombers with longer range and greater payload to be truly effective.

During the spring of 1943 bombers pounded rail networks, with many Luftwaffe raids in daylight, but casualties were heavy. On 22 May a raid by 111 strike aircraft lost 11 aircraft, although it disrupted traffic at Kursk junction for 10–12 hours. On 2 June the Luftwaffe staged the unsuccessful *Unternehmen Carmen* with 596 sorties, but lost 17 bombers – many to some 300 enemy fighter sorties. The following night raid by 202 bombers was also unsuccessful. These failures led ObdL to decide against repeating daylight raids.

After Stalingrad, Stavka ordered attacks on rail networks from the night of 24/25 January, and these continued until March 1943. On two nights in mid-March there were 579 sorties against targets in central Russia, guided by primitive navigation devices, including partisan bonfires, but they severely damaged Orel station. From March Stavka extended the campaign to road communications and Golovanov's chief-of-staff, General-leitenant Mark Shevelev, drew up plans that paid greater attention to the bomb-load mix based upon examination of targets now in Red Army hands. This campaign began on 4 April and involved 9,400 sorties until 4 July, of which 3,000 were against targets opposite the Kursk Salient. The scale gradually increased until the bombers were striking targets up to 300 kilometres from the FEBA. Crews increased bomb loads and reduced fuel so Il-4s carried 2.5 instead of 1.5 tonnes and Pe-8s 5.4 tonnes instead of four tonnes, including two one-tonne bombs or anti-personnel bomb containers under the wings. For long range raids in late April and early May the Mitchells were given extra fuel tanks.

From January to July 1943 the ADD flew 15,328 sorties against rail targets, concentrating upon Bryansk, Orel and Gomel, which attracted 44 per cent (6,818) of sorties. Krasovskii and Rudenko joined this campaign in early May and flew 1,909 sorties in roving missions that were judged to be very successful. Some attacks were extremely effective, with 109 bombers that struck Orsha on 3/4 May destroying three ammunition trains with 300 wagons and attacks on Bryansk during 3–11 May destroying 1,200 tonnes of ammunition. However, Kluge's rail transport officer, Oberst Hermann Teske, noted 94 air attacks on his system in April, 159 in May and 123 in June, but said they had limited effect.

The ADD continued to expand, and on 30 April 1943, it was reorganised into four (later seven) corps, with two divisions, usually of two regiments, including the heavy bomber 45th AD. Together with independent regiments, its strength rose from 700 bombers in April to 740 on 1 July and 1,003 on 1 January 1944. A quarter of the aircraft were Li-2s, which could carry a one-tonne bomb load, while the number of heavy bombers dropped from 50 to 20 between July and January. The TB-3 was phased out, but Mitchell numbers rose from 88 to 111 as the ADD received 1,200 Western aircraft during 1943. Nevertheless, the Il-4 remained its backbone.

The ADD's Strategic reconnaissance role was extended to 600 kilometres, and it also flew 652 sorties on Operational and Tactical Level reconnaissance during 1943. To support this, and its traditional roles, the ADD was authorised to have 1,200 crews, and Golovanov expanded his navigation training organisation and received VVS repair workshops. The use of electronic navigation aids was broadened to include enemy beacons, although the Germans sometimes moved them.

The ADD's prime role remained directly supporting the Red Army. Indeed, Stavka seemed to regard it as an aerial fire brigade. Such missions accounted for 39 per cent (29,416) of the 74,956 sorties it flew in 1943, followed by 36 per cent (27,437) against transport and 11.5 per cent (8,674) against airfields. During the bombing sorties, which averaged 3.8 hours, 78,613 tonnes of ordnance was dropped. For airfield attack missions the bombers were augmented from October 1943 by two intruder regiments, 112th and 113th AP NOB DD, later joined by a third, with Mitchells and A-20G Bostons. Total losses during the year were 687 bombers, of which 516 appear to have been due to enemy action. Many of these losses were later described as 'unjustified' because of last-minute demands for ADD support that disrupted training. The missions would be organised by liaison teams that would visit army commanders. Another reason for such losses was due to the hasty arranging of long range missions, often with little information on the defenses and with too little account of the crews' state of training.

Following a Stavka directive in April demanding attacks 'on military–industrial and administrative centres deep in the enemy rear', there were 1,027 sorties flown during 1943 at a time when Russia's Western allies were intensifying such operations. Golovanov concentrated upon East Prussian and Pomeranian targets that were beyond the range of his allies, and he helped undermine enemy feelings of security. The campaign began on the night of 12/13 April, and included 920 sorties against Königsberg, where 788 tonnes of bombs were dropped, including five-tonne ordnance. It ended on 13/14 May with little tangible effect, although Moscow did not appreciate this because bomb-damage assessment was poor. Like RAF Bomber Command until 1941, the commanders relied too much upon vague debriefing reports of fires and explosions. General Staff representative Polkovnik Filip Tikhonov eventually expressed his concerns to Golovanov, who followed the RAF example and fitted cameras and illumination ordnance to his bombers in the spring of 1943 for assessment purposes.

There were other parallels with the RAF in the growing concern over strengthening defences, especially nightfighters, although ADD's losses were only 1.3 per cent of the aircraft taking part in the missions. Like the British, the ADD adopted looser formations, with every regiment split into weather reconnaissance, target illumination and target photographic groups from the best crews. Greater flexibility in routing, timing and altitude were important factors in reducing losses, but the key factor to crew survival was alert gunners. If a nightfighter was spotted the pilot would adopt a violent evasive manoeuvre similar to the British 'Corkscrew' called 'The Snake' (*zmyera*), which was well suited to the robust Il-4.

Golovanov appears to have been late to appreciate the threat from radar, as he only began studies of enemy ground and airborne radars during the autumn of 1943. He would wait until the spring of 1944 before considering the use of metal strips, known in the West as 'Window', to confuse radars, but only after the Germans deployed *Düppel*, their equivalent of 'Window'. He also lost bombers to meteorological conditions partly because weather briefings were based upon British meteorological information until Golovanov established his own organisation.

Luckily missions into the Reich were abandoned in July 1943 just as the Germans were completing the last section of what the British called the Kammhuber Line after nightfighter head General Josef Kammhuber. Known as the Four-Poster Bed (*Himmelbett*) system, it consisted of radar-based GCI with a Freya 125 MHz search radar to detect the target and two Würzburg 500 MHz fire control radars to direct interception by fighters orbiting radio beacons. During the spring of 1943 the system was extended into Poland and East Prussia, but it was never completed – although *Nachtjagd Raumführer* 112 was established at Königsberg-Devau.[6] The system supported Wittgenstein's IV./NJG 5 based in Insterburg with 33 Bf 110s, Do 217s and Ju 88s on 1 March and 48 on 1 May – half of these aircraft, and possibly 75 per cent, had Lichtenstein 485 MHz airborne radar.[7] The brief ADD campaign cost Golovanov 14 aircraft, while Wittgenstein was credited with five victories between 16 April and 3 May. None of his comrades had any success, although contemporary *Luftflotte* 6 *Nachtjadgschwarm* or 10(N)./ZG 1 claims may also have been from this campaign.[8] The ADD also flew supply missions that accounted for 7,750 sorties during 1943 to meet growing demands from the partisan headquarters. Golovanov had long argued he could not meet both bomber and supply requirements with his existing force, and the burden was eased in July 1943 when Stalin gave him operational control of the GVF. This provided more aircraft, a pool of skilled airmen and further technical support facilities, GVF head Astakhov becoming an ADD deputy commander. During 1943 the GVF flew 16,328 sorties behind enemy lines, delivering 4,551 tonnes of material and moving 15,473 people. The merging of its role with the ADD meant it also flew 795 bombing sorties and dropped 337 tonnes of bombs.

Meister's *Auffrischungsstab Ost* (also *Fliegerschuldivision* 6) prepared for strategic bombing, but first it rested its *Kampfgeschwader*, often at former training bases, before rigorous training that the crews accepted with relish. Most missions would be at night, and Meister imitated Bomber Command tactics, with KG 4 providing a proficient Pathfinder force. Training, however, was disrupted by bad weather, as Greim informed Korten on 1 February 1944, as well as the diversion of *Kampfgruppen* to aerial resupply in the northern Ukraine during April and May, which cost 57 bombers to enemy action. Yet Meister's force grew from 286 aircraft on New Year's Day 1944 to 471 by 1 June.

Even before *Fliegerkorps* IV was withdrawn Greim's staff had begun outline planning for the campaign, assisted by 1./ObdL, which included Ju 86P high-altitude reconnaissance aircraft, and by military intelligence agents (*Abwehr V-Männer*). Many *V-Männer* flew from Greim's bases, although one Ju 86P was shot down in the first action by a Russian-operated Spitfire VB. Meister began detailed planning in February 1944 and optimistically calculated that 50–80 per cent of productive capacity could be eliminated with a comprehensive programme for striking production and material reserves. One plan was to use a Do 217 *Gruppe* with the anti-shipping F-X guided glide bombs to strike targets as far east as Gorki from Finnish airfields.

But enemy preparations for an offensive, and Korten's eagerness to use the force, redesignated *Fliegerkorps* IV on 31 March, meant they were quickly deployed in *Unternehmen Zaunkönig* (Wren), an offensive against the western Ukraine rail network. This began on 27/28 March, and there were 45 missions involving some 7,000 sorties by mid-June, with 17 missions assessed as 'very good' or 'good' and a one per cent loss rate. Meister aped Bomber Command with electronic navigation and support systems, although the *Kampfgruppen* preferred to operate in bright moonlight, and flew in Crocodiles to flare-marked targets using *Düppel* against radars. There were 180–190 sorties a night delivering 200 tonnes of bombs, with the largest effort on 30 April/1 May involving 252 sorties. In late May high-altitude daylight operations with the He 177 began from East Prussia in formations of up to 87 aircraft, the pilots avoiding engine fires through careful use of the throttles.

Nightfighters had been a growing threat to Russian bombers since June 1941, with home defence units claiming five victories to August 1942, one over Berlin, but a nightfighter detachment sent to the East in the summer of 1941 had little success. The Luftwaffe had to extemporise a response to the night threat to the front-line troops (*Feldheer*) in Russia, and *Schlacht-* and *Kampfgruppen* and 3./*Nachtaufklärungsstaffel* were credited with seven victories between July 1941 and May 1942 and four more in 1942–43. However, the greatest night successes during 1942 were by JG 54, which used the short, light nights to claim 59 victories in 1942 and six more in 1943.

The need for dedicated nightfighter units was obvious by late 1942, and on the recommendation of Major Wolfgang Falck, the father of the *Nachtjagdflieger*, *Nachtjagdschwärme* were created in each *Luftflotte* during early 1943, together with 10(N)./ZG 1. Initially they relied upon visual detection, but one *Schwarm* was diverted to ground-attack missions and in January 1943 absorbed by a train-buster *Staffel*. Although their strength never exceeded 40 aircraft, they were credited with 31 victories, including two Pe-8s, during the first half of 1943. However, after an inspection by Kammhuber it was decided to extend *Himmelbett* along the Eastern Front.

On 26 June Wittgenstein's IV./NJG 5 joined Greim, supported by five rail-mounted radars, but it did not become operational until 17 July. By the time of the unit's withdrawal to Germany on 10 August it had been credited with 61 victories, including eight heavy bombers – 28 by Wittgenstein – for the loss of two fighters in accidents.

This system was extended along the front, and the nightfighter force expanded to about 60 aircraft by the end of the year. They were credited with another 129 victories during the rest of the year, mostly Il-4s and Mitchells, but including four Pe-8s. Nightfighters remained effective into the summer of 1944, when they buckled under the strains of constant retreats and fuel shortages. Although credited with 328 victories in 1944 and 55 in 1945, the nightfighter force rarely downed slow-flying U-2/Po-2s.

The Gorkii raids demonstrated the serious deficiencies in the PVO's nightfighting capabilities, which were not addressed when it was reorganised on 29 June 1943. Following the abolition of its central command, the nightfighter force was again placed under the control of Red Army gunnery chief Voronov. It was now split into West and East Fronts, the latter covering Gorkii, Saratov and the USSR east of the Urals and the Caucasus, the boundary running north–south and east–west through Arkhangelsk, Kostroma and Krasnodar. Each front had its own training and support organisation. The West Front under General-polkovnik Gromadin absorbed the Moscow air defences including 1st IIA PVO, but not Leningrad PVO Army, which remained under Leningrad Front control. The East Front was under General-leitenant Gavriil Zashikhin, a former naval air defence commander and NKVD 'guest' who headed the Leningrad PVO Army until July 1943.

On 1 July 1943, the PVO had 2,124 fighters and 1,693 aircrew, of whom 770 were night qualified, with Gromadin having 1,012 fighters. Excluding units in the Arctic Circle and including some of Zashikhin's Western units, the PVO probably had some 1,500 fighters around the main front. By 25 August, 18 per cent of the PVO's fighters were assigned the protection of Red Army lines of communication while 75 per cent shielded cities and industrial areas.

The Red Army advance in 1943 reduced the strategic bombing threat and PVO resources were increasingly switched to protect newly reconquered territory by stripping the quieter PVO sectors, despite a shortage of telephone cable for communications. Only in mid-1943 were the first radio battalions established for the observation service (VNOS), while there remained major problems coordinating air defence with the front commands. The fighters themselves, as with the VVS, increasingly received transceivers, while the end of the year saw the introduction of improved versions of RUS-2 radar in the form of Redut 43 and *Permatit* R-2. During the year PVO fighters flew 40,604 sorties and lost 278 aircraft. While the main role remained homeland defence, eight per cent of sorties (3,355) were supporting the Red Army, three per cent (1,213) were escort missions and there were also 358 sorties in fighter sweeps, some 12 per cent in all. Despite radar, nearly two-thirds of sorties were patrols and only a quarter were scrambles.

By 1 January 1944, Far Eastern reinforcements helped expand the PVO to 2,380 fighters, but the number of crews dropped to 1,459, of whom 697 were night qualified. Gromadin had 1,528 fighters, many supporting the Red Army, but the advances of 1943–44 forced a further reorganisation of the PVO. On 29 March the two fronts were replaced by the Northern (Gromadin), Southern (Zashikhin) and Transcaucasian (General-leitenant Petr Gudymenko) Fronts, each with its own support organisation, with the Northern and Southern Front boundary running east–west through Pugachev, Petrovsk Michurinsk Elec, Dmitriev, Sevsk, Novgorod-Seversky, Nizhin, Korosten and Luck. While the new organisation would face no major threats in the coming year, it would face a major scare.

CHAPTER 5

RED STAR TRIUMPHANT

May 1944 to May 1945

In the summer of 1944 Stalin prepared a grand settling of accounts with Hitler and began to strike what the Russians later described as 'The Ten Great Blows'. The first struck Finland from 10 June, which changed sides on 19 September, the re-establishment of the Russian Embassy in Helsinki having an influence upon Russian Long Range Aviation. The hardest blow, *Operatsiya Bagration*, would strike the great German Belorussian salient running 700 kilometres from Vitebsk past Mogilev and Bobruisk then east to west through the Pripet Marshes. To deceive the enemy the Red Army ostentatiously concentrated south of the Pripet Marshes.

By the beginning of June the VVS had 9,843 combat aircraft (excluding reconnaissance) on the main front, with a Stavka reserve of 1,535. They were supported by 1,281 of the PVO's fighters, while the ADD had 1,195 bombers, including 30 Pe-8s and 212 B-25s. The Navy had 1,184 aircraft on the main front, but part of the VVS–KBF's 494 aircraft were operating on the Finnish front.

Novikov urged his air army commanders to delegate authority for more flexible operations and told them on 15 May that their subordinates would now decide how to execute missions based on daily mission statements from VA headquarters. Red Army support, especially of mechanised formations, remained the prime VVS role, with almost 40 per cent of sorties in 1944 being close air support, while six per cent involved attacks upon targets in the enemy rear. Army fighter cover accounted for 14.5 per cent of sorties, and 18 per cent were escort missions. As the Luftwaffe fighter shield evaporated more than 53 per cent of VVS sorties in 1945 would be close air support. The short range of Novikov's strike force made it difficult to project air power deep into the enemy rear, for the 'Ilyushas' and 'Peshkas' could reach no more than 600 kilometres behind the lines with bomb loads of 600kg. But Bostons could strike 800 kilometres with 900kg, and during the winter Novikov redistributed some regiments so that eight of his 19, later 20, day bomber divisions had a Boston presence to give them a longer 'reach'.

Bagration involved, from north to south, 15th, 3rd, 1st, 4th, 16th and 6th VA. Khryukin had taken over 1st VA when Gromov became head of Frontal Aviation training while Vershinin's 4th VA had arrived from the Crimea. Naumenko and Papivin still commanded 15th and 3rd VA, respectively, although the former would have no immediate role in the offensive. Rudenko had the largest concentration, and also had operational control of Polynin's 6th VA, possibly because Novikov still had doubts following the failures in April. There are conflicting figures from Russian sources about their air strength for *Bagration*, from 5,327 (including 2,318 fighters, 1,744 'Ilyusha' and 655 day and 431 night bombers) to 5,417 (see Table V-1) to 5,700. In addition 1,007 ADD bombers, or 84 per cent of its strength, would support the offensive, which would include some 47 per cent of VVS strength on the main front. The PVO assigned 500 fighters to cover the communications hubs of the *Bagration* fronts.

The priority was to rebuild battered forces, some of Rudenko's divisions being down to 40 aircraft in April. 'Foals' and regimental and squadron commanders all benefited from rigorous training in the lead-up to the offensive. Group tuition often took the form of conferences where aircrew shared their combat experiences. Of 48,000 non-combat sorties flown from April to 22 June, 27,000 or more than 56 per cent were training. There was also a major effort made to strengthen navigation training over the densely forested terrain, aircrew making greater use of navigation aids, both visual and electronic. In fact as losses

TABLE V-1: SERVICEABLE AIRCRAFT AT THE BEGINNING
OF *BAGRATION*

Type	3rd VA	1st VA	4th VA	16th/6th VA	Total
Day Fighter	399	984	193	952	2,528
Day Bomber	–	340	–	297	637
Night Bomber	79	80	121	155	435
Assault	371	530	196	636	1,733
Reconnaissance	36	30	18	–	84
Total	885	1,964	528	2,040	5,417

Source: Hardesty & Grinberg (p. 301)

declined the overall quality of Soviet airmen slowly improved, and during 1944 it began to overtake that of its enemies, although the 'foals' remained a problem until the end of the war.

From May into mid-June there was an extensive reconnaissance effort, which shaped Stavka directives issued on 31 May and also VVS planning, coordinated by Novikov, Golovanov, Falaleev and Skripko. Their first objective was to establish air superiority so that the strike force could wreck the enemy throughout his Tactical Level depth. No wire communications were permitted during planning, with corps and division commanders briefed five to seven days before the attack while regimental commanders had only a few hours notice. The physical strain was so severe that shortly before *Bagration* Golovanov collapsed with nervous exhaustion, and while he followed Stalin's advice to rest at home and drink vodka, Skripko bore the brunt of ADD planning.

Assembling supplies proved the usual challenge, especially for Rudenko (see Chapter 1), whose supply line extended 500 kilometres to the east and left him short of vehicles and spares. His airfields eventually assembled up to eight 'fills' of fuel and ten of ammunition, but many units had to scour the countryside for food. Rudenko divided 16th VA in two – he commanded 1,259 aircraft including all his 'Peshkas' and Bostons, while his deputy, General-maior Mikhail Kosykh, commanded the remaining 726 aircraft.

Their aircrew were billeted in huts and villages up to ten kilometres from the airfield, sleeping in bunks or on straw mattresses, and often sharing their rations with their hosts. Groundcrews lived in smoky dugouts with improvised stoves and had sleeping bags. All would rise before dawn, wash and clean their teeth with their finger, but airmen usually did not shave, then walk to the mess for breakfast of tea or coffee, rolls or black bread, sometimes with sausage, then go to the airfield.

Forward airstrips would have a command-post bunker (and dispersal hut) and two bunkers for airmen and one for groundcrews. Pilots would then check that their aircraft were combat ready, before reporting to the regimental command post to meet their crews or gunners. The aeroplane check was needed to watch one's rear in more than one sense, for carelessness or exhaustion might mean the groundcrews had forgotten to service or refuel the aircraft. During Stalingrad an LaGG-3 pilot got five days in the guardhouse when engine failure caused his fighter to force-land – his crew chief got 20 days.

After a mission briefing they would set off and return to have a light lunch at the mess, often buckwheat porridge but sometimes tea and sandwiches. They might then fly another sortie, and at the end of the working day return to the mess for dinner – the main meal. Aircrew had Level 5 rations (3,450 calories a day) including meat (0.5 kilogrammes) and 100 grammes each of butter and sugar, augmented with two bowls of buckwheat porridge or mashed potato. Some hunted for the pot, and they also received a block of chocolate a day that they tended to accumulate until the end of the week. Groundcrews had Level 6 rations (2,954 calories), with less meat and sugar, and millet often forming a major part of their diet. Aircrew often gave them their leftovers, although this was officially frowned upon, but support units were often half-starved.

Generally there was plenty of bread and soup but the quality of food may have varied from front to front depending upon its importance. Tins of Tushonka, also called 'Mystery Meat', were a staple and earned their name because they could be pork, chicken, beef or even horse! As the Red Army advanced, regiments expected to receive less rations from the rear and augment them from captured stocks or from villagers. From

Lend–Lease, food such as sausage and canned meat was highly prized, together with flying jackets and boots. Shirts were often of 'English cloth', and because their issue scarves were rough, causing boils that made it difficult to turn their heads, pilots would seek out silk scarves from captured aircrew or make them from old parachutes.

After a combat mission aircrew were entitled to a tot of 100g (or 0.1 litre) of vodka or 200g of wine before dinner, or 50g for novice pilots. Some men augmented this ration with moonshine, and there were certainly some alcoholic pilots, notably Stalin's son Vasilii, but the wise pilot did not fly while intoxicated. One fighter pilot who did so was transferred to a bomber regiment as a navigator. Socially, the aircrew did not mix outside the squadron, and within a regimental mess each squadron had its own table, as did gunners. Pilots, who received 30 packets of cigarettes a month, would often share them with the groundcrews. There were different brands for different ranks, with regimental commanders smoking 'Kazbek', pilots 'Beloe Morye' (White Sea) and groundcrew 'Prostoi' (Easy).

There was a widespread superstition among aircrew that shaving, or having a haircut, during the morning was unlucky, so they would wait until the end of the day's missions. It was also considered unlucky to be photographed before take-off. In one Guards assault regiment it was said any man who had sex with one of the women groundcrew would not survive his next mission. Aircrew also believed that once they had completed a series of operational missions – 3rd–4th, 13th–14th and 33rd–34th – they had a better chance of survival.

In bad weather they would remain in a dispersal hut playing cards, draughts, dominoes or chess, although some regiments such as 1st GvIAP banned cards. They might listen to a gramophone or live music, for each regiment had a good accordion player, or even dance with girls in the regiment. At the end of the day men would chat and write home, then go to bed.

Money was sent home or used to buy food or luxuries such as sausage, canned food, chocolate and cakes. Pilots washed once every 20–30 days in drums of hot and cold water, using wet straw as a washcloth, while clothes were often doused in drums of petrol then dried. One assault regiment pilot recalled that during the summer of 1943 he did not wash himself until his unit reached the Dnieper. When relieving themselves men and women would squat in holes and then use newspaper.

At the beginning of June the Luftwaffe had 2,169 combat aircraft in the East together with 265 Hungarian and Romanian aeroplanes, excluding home defence forces. Soviet deception convinced Hitler that the main blow would come south of the Pripet Marshes towards the Romanian oilfields, with the result that Greim had 836 aircraft (38.5 per cent of total strength), but Meister's 681 bombers were nearby. To meet the perceived threat the Germans strengthened their forces in southern Poland and Romania. There were less than 400 single-engined fighters in the East, and such was the complacency that at a conference on fighters and fighter production on 15–16 May the *Inspektor der Jagdflieger*, Generalmajor Adolf Galland, noted that only 11 per cent of total fighter operations were in the East during April, compared with 24 per cent over Western Europe and 38 per cent over the Reich.

Greim knew a Russian offensive was imminent but did not realise the main blow would strike him, although he split his forces into three to meet anticipated attacks. Reuss's *Fliegerdivision* 4 in the East supported 3 *Panzer* and 4 *Armee*, while Punzert's *Flfü* 1 in the centre (including three *Einsatzgruppen* of the *Fliegerschuledivision*) and Fuchs' *Fliegerdivision* 1 in the West supported 9 *Armee* and 2 *Armee*, respectively. Fuchs had Greim's 100 *Schlachtflieger*, which were also ready to aid Generalfeldmarschall Model's *Heeresgruppe Nordukraine* in southern Poland. The fighters were with Oberst Karl-Gottfried Nordmann's *Jagdabschnittführer* 6, formed on 1 May with 85 serviceable aircraft, having benefited from Dessloch's last-minute transfer of two *Jagdgruppen*.

The Luftwaffe also faced a growing fuel crisis as Allied bombers pounded production facilities. An OKW report covering August 1943 to 6 June 1944, noted that in April Romanian oil transport was halved, while monthly production dropped 60 per cent from 400,000 to 240,000 tonnes. The impact upon the Luftwaffe during 1944 is shown in Table V-2, with operations increasingly shaped by fuel shortages, especially

TABLE V-2: LUFTWAFFE FUEL SITUATION JULY–DECEMBER 1944

Quarter	Production (tonnes)	Consumption (tonnes)
Q1 1944	535,000	413,000
Q2 1944	386,000	541,000
Q3 1944	91,000	311,000
Q4 1944	105,000	138,000
Total	1,117,000	1,403,000

TABLE V-3: SOVIET AIR POWER FUEL CONSUMPTION 1944–45 (TONNES)

Branch	1944	1945
VVS-KA	11,071,584	7,045,003
DBA/ADD	417,263	99,077
VMF	77,957	19,360
GVF	1,311	5,290
Total	11,568,115	7,168,730

during the second half of 1944 when consumption outstripped supply by 55,000 tonnes. This led to drastic cuts in consumption, with training reduced to 100 hours and fighter pilot training cut to 35. By contrast, the American delivery of several refineries and the recovery of the Caucasian oilfields meant Russian air power consumed twice as much fuel in 1944 compared with 1943 (see Table V-3). Virtually all of this was for the VVS, with consumption for Golovanov's bombers and the Navy cut from 417,263 tonnes compared with 831,702 tonnes and from 125,092 tonnes to 77,957 – drops of 50 and 35.5 per cent, respectively.

To pull, or at least blunt, the Bear's claws, Greim flew 6,777 sorties in April and 8,989 in May, with night attacks accounting for nearly 37 per cent. The scale increased during the first 15 days of June, when 5,995 sorties were flown, but he had only 3,800 tonnes of fuel. To counter this the ADD flew 1,472 sorties against airfields between 13 and 18 June and dropped 1,450 tonnes of bombs, while intruder regiments also harassed airfields. Ten days before *Bagration* was launched a campaign involving 1,472 sorties struck German communications, with the ADD using their equivalent of Window some 70–80 kilometres from the target. This, and alert crews ready to 'snake' if a nightfighter was spotted, reduced losses, but Pe-8 crews sometimes joked that they faced three enemies – flak, nightfighters and the moon.

The ADD and GVF also flew 533 supply drops to partisans, with 139 sorties involving landing, although German counter-insurgency operations captured many airstrips. The GVF alone would fly 800 sorties behind enemy lines, with 307 tonnes and 1,000 people moved, including women and children – one Po-2 of 97th OAP GVF carried ten children in a single flight.

The storm struck from 23 June, with Vitebsk and Mogilev enveloped to push back 3 *Panzer Armee* and isolate 4 *Armee*, while a thrust northwards sliced the Belorussian Salient like a joint of meat to envelop 9 *Armee* at Bobruisk on 26 June. The 4 *Armee* tried to fight its way westwards, but on 2 July Russian spearheads met near Minsk to complete its isolation. From 26 June, as the armies faced envelopment, Meister's bombers switched from attacking communications and airfields to close air support, but ground fire and fighters accounted for 72, including ten He 177s. Bombers also supplied isolated garrisons and troops, because even with a second *Transportgruppe* Greim had only 66 transports on 1 July.

The pockets were squeezed out piecemeal and few of *Heeresgruppe Mitte*'s troops escaped, but by mid-July the Germans were beginning to rally around Kaunus, Bialystok and Brest-Litovsk as the Russians drove westwards. Meanwhile, from 23 June, another offensive began to widen the gap and pushed *Heeresgruppe Nord*'s 16 *Armee* northwards as it tried to bar the route to the Baltic, with 1st and 4th VAs using reconnaissance aircraft to radio target details for 'Ilyushas' and 'Peshkas'.

Russian regiments flew into forward bases under low cloud on 20–21 June, but the sunny weather of 22 June was followed that night by rain. Despite Skripko confidently informing Stavka coordinator Zhukov, and Novikov, that the ADD programme would be executed as planned, they witnessed the bombers aborting after an hour because their crews could not see the visual beacons. Fortunately, the skies cleared in the morning to allow massive air support. Each assault army was provided by 1st and 3rd VAs with a single division of 'Ilyushas' and fighters, while attacks hit positions and reserves. These strikes were so intense that even flak gunners deserted their posts. Massed bomber strikes were used against any obstacle to the advance, while the VVS fighter screen held back most *Schlachtflieger* attacks. Vershinin's bombers blasted lanes through wire and minefields then destroyed most batteries, while specially trained 'Ilyusha' crews hunted down the assault guns, which were the German infantry's prime source of armoured support.

Greim responded vigorously with 2,162 sorties on the first day, while massed *Schlachtflieger* attacks raised this to 5,319 the next day. He received five *Gruppen* (280 aircraft) from his neighbours and four from France and Italy, virtually all Pflugbeil's fighters and *Luftflotte* 2's last strike force, to give him 1,109 aircraft by 26 June. The *Schlachtflieger* flew four or five sorties a day but Greim's airmen rarely reached their potential of 3,000 sorties a day due to fuel shortages and were soon overwhelmed. Despite receiving 170 reinforcements, including two *Jagdgruppen* from the Reich, Nordmann had little impact and by 1 July he was down to 259 fighters. The rapid Russian advance compounded Greim's problems, forcing units to abandon airfields and repair shops – I./JG 51 moved seven times to 1 July and 1./NSGr 2 eight times to the end of July.

Increasingly, the VVS interdicted communications at the Operational Level to turn the German retreat into a Calvary and paralyse every counter-attack in a mirror image of June 1941, especially Rudenko, whose regiments did not join the fray until 24 June after an inauspicious start. A night attack by one of his bombers saw front commander Rokossovskii's headquarters attacked in error while Zhukov was visiting, both men being lucky to escape unscathed. The airmen involved were fortunate to escape with minor punishments because a furious Rokossovskii wanted to send them to penal units, but he was persuaded to relent. Rudenko soon redeemed himself, and on his first day the full weight of 16th VA, with 3,291 sorties, fell on the luckless Germans. A post-operations report by the Wehrmacht noted the severity of the strikes from the sky led men to throw themselves to the ground even if a Storch appeared, while much equipment was abandoned or destroyed by fleeing troops.

On 26 June Khryukin's 'Ilyushas' struck the rail lines between Minsk and Orsha, while Vershinin's massive air attacks accelerated the destruction of 4 *Armee* as Rudenko's 'Ilyushas' and 'Peshkas' roamed along the river Berezina striking targets of opportunity to isolate 9 *Armee* at Bobruysk and prevent a joint breakout. The next day Vershinin told Novikov that 4 *Armee*'s massive retreating columns offered an excellent opportunity for the VVS, and requested, and received, assistance from Rudenko and Khryukin. On 29 June Rudenko's 'Peshkas' downed a bridge at Beresino to cause a massive traffic jam that was lashed by regimental-size formations of 'Ilyushas', who killed two corps and a divisional commander and thousands of troops. However, Rudenko's prime target on 27 June remained the 9 *Armee* pocket, which he pounded relentlessly despite dense clouds of smoke and dust obscuring the battlefield. A post-operation investigation found 150 AFVs, some 6,300 motor vehicles and hundreds of wrecked guns and carts, and as a result of his success Rudenko was given a gold watch.

Khryukin and Vershinin continued to pummel 4 *Armee*, whose men cowered in the dense forests where fighters, 'Ilyushas' and U-2s sniffed them out like hunting dogs and swarmed over them in packs. Soviet air superiority confined German aerial resupply to parachuting supplies on the short nights, but even this was abandoned on 4 July and four days later the survivors surrendered.

From 27 June the air armies moved into 'deloused' captured airfields led by Li-2 and U-2 supply aircraft, although a German attack at Minsk on 5 July forced one fighter unit to scatter like frightened birds. By 4 July the VVS and ADD had flown 55,000 sorties in support of *Bagration*, of which 6,053 were by the ADD, which continued to hit defences and concentrations. From the night of 26/27 June to 4 July, 3,200 sorties were flown against rail targets within the salient, which received 3,500 tonnes of bombs, while another 2,646 sorties and 3,027 tonnes of bombs were used against rail targets leading to the west.

When the Russians reached Minsk the Germans expected them to end their offensive, but on 5 July Stavka ordered an advance upon Warsaw and pushed back the remnants of *Heeresgruppe Mitte*, now under Model, who tried to keep contact with Generalfeldmarschall Ferdinand Schröner's *Heeresgruppe Nord*. His defence was further undermined by the defeat of *Heeresgruppe Nordukraine* in mid-July, and on the 25th of the month the Russian spearheads reached and then crossed the Vistula but were now outrunning their supplies. The ADD flew 2,106 sorties to supply the three Belorussian fronts with 2,563 tonnes of supplies during July, including 951 tonnes of fuel, and they were augmented by NBAPs and the GVF. However, as their Western allies soon discovered, aerial resupply could never match consumption and was costly in aviation fuel.

On 23 July Polynin had only 830 tonnes left, sufficient for one 'fill' per aircraft, although more soon arrived and he flew 12,000 sorties between 18 and 31 July. A shortage of motor vehicles aggravated the VVS problems, and although Li-2s were bringing in supplies from bases 500 kilometres in the rear, by the time Rudenko reached Warsaw he was left with 'very modest reserves of fuel'. Supply shortages and poor weather weakened Soviet air power from mid-July and Rudenko flew 7,591 sorties (542 daily average) from 18 to 31 July compared with 4,265 (609 daily average) from 1 to 17 July. His forward command post moved almost every week while fighter and night bomber regiments moved up to eight times in July and the *Sturmoviks* about six times. Even the 'Peshka' units moved four times, with the regiments usually leapfrogging their way forward, with half moving while the remainder supported the army. Most of the captured airfields by the beginning of August were far behind the FEBA, and with radio networks saturated most non-essential communication was by courier in aircraft or vehicles.

Greim began July with 1,186 combat aircraft, but he had to surrender many to his neighbours. On 14 July he reported that Reuss, shielding East Prussia, had two *Jagd-* and three *Schlachtgruppen*. Fuchs, near Warsaw, had a *Jagdgruppe* and a *Stukagruppe*, but the *Jagdgruppen* were down to 256 fighters (140 serviceable) and he had consumed most of his fuel. Indeed, he had enough for only three days of major operations. However, as Russian fighter screens weakened from late July the Luftwaffe became a growing threat to their advance, despite being reduced to 500–600 daily sorties. Meister combined Tactical and Operational Level missions, striking spearheads and communications with a powerful He 177 raid that devastated Lublin on 24/25 July, while another near Brest-Litovsk hit the headquarters of 80th Rifle Corps, killing the corps commander. But fuel shortages led to Meister's *Kampfgruppen* being withdrawn from operations on the morning of 29 July. The ADD, on the other hand, flew 5,590 sorties during July, supporting operations in Belorussia and northern Poland, including 2,302 sorties against rail targets.

The retreat brought the Luftwaffe closer to its bases and supplies, and when Model began a counter-offensive at the end of July it was supported by 200 of Greim's 1,327 aircraft, with bombers making night attacks upon bridges. Model regained some ground and stabilised the front by mid-August, although Russian bridgeheads remained north and south of Warsaw at Magnuszew and at Sandomierz–Baranow. Rudenko and Polynin were hamstrung by poor command and control, together with fuel shortages and few supplies, but the situation improved during the second half of August and radars, together with fighter reinforcements, shielded the Vistula bridgeheads to force Greim to use fighters for tactical reconnaissance missions.

Between June and August Greim lost 852 combat aircraft, 553 to enemy action, and most units were exhausted. JG 51 was left with 19 serviceable aircraft at the end of July, and by 31 August it had lost 43 pilots killed and missing, with another 14 wounded, since *Bagration* began. By contrast the Russians lost 822 aircraft to enemy action from 23 June to 29 August.

The German defence was further handicapped by the Warsaw Uprising, which lasted until 2 October and attracted much aerial activity during August and September. The Western Allies tried to support the insurgents from Italy, with the RAF and its Polish squadrons flying 213 sorties from the night of 4/5 August, but they suffered a 16 per cent loss rate (34 bombers). On 11 September Stalin permitted USAAF supply missions from Poltava and Mirgorod, and on 18 September the Americans flew 107 sorties to drop 1,248 canisters for the loss of one B-17. Little of this largesse reached the insurgents, who were under occasional Luftwaffe attack, because they lacked secure landing zones and had poor communication with the outside.

Two women from Warsaw reached 1st Belorussian Front headquarters on 13 September and met the Polish-speaking commander, Rokossovskii, who agreed to provide immediate support, but communications problems reduced its effectiveness. Increasingly hazardous supply missions were undertaken by 9th GvNBAD and 1st Polish SAD and by 1 October they had flown 3,475 sorties and dropped 115 tonnes of supplies, although little reached the insurgents. Russian and Polish fighters tried to intercept German strike aircraft over Warsaw while 'Ilyushas' sought out troop concentrations, but it was very much hit-and-miss.

Desultory air combat continued through the late summer and autumn, with Greim's airmen flying an average of 300 sorties a day – 5,980 day and 425 night sorties in October alone, losing 108 aircraft – but with little influence on operations. Fuel remained the key problem, and in August Greim calculated he needed nearly 157 tonnes of B4 and 26.4 tonnes of C3 per day. By 6 August consumption had risen to 212 tonnes and 106.4 tonnes, respectively, forcing him to cut the daily ration to 150.4 and 21.6 tonnes a day. As supply lines improved the VVS became more active, Rudenko flying 13,034 sorties in September and 14,648 in October, but on 5 September Polynin's 6th VA was withdrawn. It was nominally disbanded three weeks later then resurrected as the Polish Army Air Force Command to support the Polish Army Air Force (*Ludowe Lotnictwo Polskie*), whose 1st SAD (4th Polish SAD from 1 November) had reached the front on 23 August.

The Russian advance towards the Baltic and East Prussia was opposed by Pflugbeil and Greim's *Fliegerdivision* 4 under Reuss, who faced Papivin and Khryukin, the latter overcoming growing supply problems to help take Vilnius on 15 July, despite the garrison being reinforced by a paratroop drop. Papivin supported the advance on Riga, which continued in the following weeks, his air army being reinforced by 467 aircraft and a Tu-2 ADD division that struck rail networks.

Pflugbeil had 364 combat aircraft by 20 June, although this number had been reduced to 233 within six days by the despatch of an ad hoc air group *Gefechtsverband Kuhlmey* to Finland, to meet the first of the Ten Great Blows. There Pflugbeil flew 6,300 day and 970 night sorties during June. He and Reuss struggled to contain the Russian advance towards the Baltic, which threatened to split Model from *Heeresgruppe Nord*'s Schörner despite Reuss receiving 140 aircraft from Greim, including a substantial number of his *Schlachtflieger*. Attacks involving five *Schlachtgruppen* with 160 aircraft delayed the advance on Riga but at heavy cost, the units losing 40 aircraft to enemy action in July, and futilely, for on the 30th of the month the enemy reached the Baltic near Riga. However, an airlift by 86 Ju 52/3ms reinforced Schörner with an infantry division. Papivin flew 11,431 sorties during July and dropped 1,161 tonnes of bombs, but his airfields fell further behind the FEBA, and with severe fuel shortages he had to seek help from Khryukin, whose ranks included the French Normandie-Niemen Regiment.

Meanwhile, Pflugbeil faced a new front when the Russians struck into Estonia on 10 July supported by Naumenko's 15th VA with 546 aircraft, but no day bombers. The Russians were soon held by the *Pantherstellung*, and their supply columns, confined to a few roads through marshes, were exposed to *Jabos*. Bombers also struck their bases, notably on 19/20 July when 70 He 177s targeted Velikiye Luki railway station. Yet Pflugbeil was now stretched to breaking point, with only 321 combat aircraft by 1 August. There was brief relief for Schörner and Pflugbeil when *Heeresgruppe Mitte*, now under Generaloberst Hans Reinhardt, launched *Unternehmen Doppelkopf* (Twin Head) into Lithuania from East Prussia on 16 August, supported by Reuss, who was reinforced with five *Gruppen* and a *Schule-einsatzstaffel* to give him 301 aircraft with 1,152 tonnes of fuel.

With their aid, a 30-kilometre-wide coastal corridor was opened to Schörner on 20 August, but simultaneously Pflugbeil faced new offensives in Estonia, supported by Rybalchenko's 13th VA and Zhuravlev's 14th VA. The former, with 379 aircraft reinforced by 78 PVO fighters and 120 naval aircraft, was forced by rain, fog and low cloud to operate in penny packets on the first day, but improved weather saw massed strikes reinforced by ADD Il-4s. While the Russians took Narva, Schörner contained the threat. Zhuravlev, with some 270 aircraft, was too weak to significantly influence the battlefield against Pflugbeil, who had 521 serviceable combat aircraft by 20 August.

On 14 September Pflugbeil faced a massive Russian sweep westwards towards the Baltic supported by 3rd, 14th and 15th VAs with 2,643 aircraft. Papivin, a General-polkovnik since 19 August, had 1,180 combat aircraft, including 100 night bombers, and that month flew 16,340 sorties. Rybalchenko, who had been forced to transfer two divisions to the Arctic-based 7th VA, still had 429 combat aircraft as well as VVS-KBF support. From 17 September to 23 November he would fly 9,459 sorties, of which 4,187 were close air support. This pushed back Schörner, who faced a new attempt to isolate him, supported by Papivin's 1,404 combat aircraft, from 5 October. Dense fog hindered air operations at first, but during October Papivin flew 16,110 sorties to drop 2,500 tons of bombs, which helped cut the coastal corridor near Memel, while Pflugbeil flew 4,237 sorties, with night activity of 1,464 sorties exceeding all the other eastern *Luftflotten*, and lost 22 aircraft.

This Russian pressure forced Hitler to authorise Schörner's evacuation of Estonia and most of Latvia and retreat into the Courland Peninsula on the west of the Gulf of Riga, with Riga itself falling on 13 October. Pflugbeil's trouble-shooter, Generalmajor Sigismund Freiherr von Falkenstein and *Fliegerdivision* 3, who controlled some 400 aircraft including 160 *Jabos*, inflicted heavy casualties but lost about 50 of their own aircraft. Following the capture of Riga, Zhuravlev's headquarters went into Stavka reserve, where it remained until the end of the war. This brought no relief to Pflugbeil whose command was milked as Russians neared East Prussia, leaving him only 219 serviceable combat aircraft by 10 October.

Reuss had some 350 aircraft to defend the province but lost 75 to enemy action together with 50 *Schlachtflieger* sent to prop up the Western

Front – the latter were joined by another two *Gruppen* once the crisis passed in early November. Falkenstein and his *Fliegerdivision* were also sent westwards on 2 November, and while they returned to the east in January 1945, they went to Greim. The crisis also saw the disbandment of two Baltic State *Nachtschlachtgruppen*, NSGr 11 on 4 October after several Estonian crews fled to Sweden, and the Latvian NSGr 12 on 17 October because it was tarred with the same brush, although a few pilots transferred to JG 54 to defend their homeland.

Naumenko and Rybalchenko would pin down Pflugbeil in Courland with 1,106 combat aircraft at the beginning of 1945, this number having been increased to 1,600 in February in preparation for a new offensive. By contrast Pflugbeil had 189 combat aircraft by 20 December, which briefly rose to 237 on 10 January, then slumped to 170 on 9 April as OKL provided just enough resources to keep alight the flame of resistance. The Russians slowly compressed the Courland bridgehead, which remained in German hands until the end of the war both to tie down enemy troops and shield training grounds for new U-boats, which Hitler vainly hoped would turn the tide in the Atlantic. In the face of Soviet air superiority *Luftflotte* 1 was downgraded on 17 April 1945, to *Luftwaffenkommando Kurland*. When Germany surrendered on 9 May a few pilots escaped Russian captivity by flying to Sweden, each *Jabo* of III./SG 3 carrying three *Schwarzmänner*! A last-minute attempt to evacuate wounded and fathers of large families in 35 Ju 52/3m transports ended in disaster when fighters intercepted the returning formation and only three aircraft survived.

The VVS-KBF under Samokhin, a General-polkovnik from 5 October, supported these operations and later those along the western Baltic coast by interdicting sea lanes using 625 combat aircraft by 1 January. He sank the anti-aircraft cruiser *Niobe*, 12 minor warships and ten merchantmen (22,203grt) during the second half of 1944, and in 1945 13 small warships and an auxiliary, together with 31 merchantmen (93,425grt). Samokhin's minelaying efforts were less successful, with 651 laid between 1941 and 1943, 666 in 1944 and 961 in 1945, of which 95.5 per cent were ground mines.[1] They sank few ships, especially when compared with the RAF, whose 'gardening' in 1945 alone harvested eight merchantmen (71,281grt).

For the Luftwaffe, crises flared southwards like bushfires during the summer. In mid-July Greim faced one in southern Poland, where Dessloch engaged Rudenko, Polynin and Krasovskii's 2nd VA with Seidemann's *Fliegerkorps* VIII. The latter had lost 80 aircraft, including half of its *Panzerjägerstaffeln*, to Greim but Dessloch compensated him with 50 from Romania. This still left Seidemann with 350 aircraft, half of them *Schlacht*, plus 30 Hungarian and 40 Slovak aeroplanes, and in the following days he would receive 200 from Greim and could call on Meister's bombers.

Krasovskii received substantial reinforcements, including four air corps, to give him 3,246 aircraft (including 1,419 fighters and 1,046 'Ilyushas', as well as three ADD divisions with Mitchells, Il-4s and Li-2s) to strike airfields. Krasovskii created two task forces – the northern with 1,200 aircraft under his deputy commander General-maior Sidor Sliusarev, and the southern of 1,500 under his own command. To the north lay Polynin with some 600 aircraft and to the south lay 8th VA, transferred from Stavka reserve on 27 June and assigned to former 13th VA deputy and Central Asia Military District VVS commander General-leitenant Vasilii Zhdanov.[2] Seidemann detected signs of a build-up, and on 10 July Model tried to pre-empt the offensive by withdrawing but, when the VVS spotted this, the Russians brought forward their offensive by two days. They struck the 4 and 1 *Panzerarmee* boundary on 13 July supported by 664 sorties that smothered the battlefield, the defenders finding enemy air power overwhelming. Seidemann, uncertain whether this was the main offensive, held back his forces and flew only 123 sorties – by comparison, 8th VA alone flew 365. The following day Seidemann generated 2,604 sorties to support a major counter-attack, but the Russian fighter screen held and powerful air strikes wrecked German armoured reserves.

A renewed German counter-attack on 15 July was supported by 2,282 sorties, but Krasovskii sent every available aeroplane against it, 2nd GvBAK carpet-bombing the enemy. The survivors were then picked off by 'Ilyushas', many in missions controlled by General-

Although a number of other types (including a single Go 242 transport glider) are also in evidence, there are at least 15 He 111s visible on this busy forward landing ground reportedly pictured early in 1942. The gradual resurgence of Soviet air power would later make such gatherings highly inadvisable – not to say downright dangerous. (*via John Weal*)

Pilots of 7th GShAP pose in front of the aircraft flown by their squadron leader, Maj N A Zub (seen here closest to the camera), on the Southern Front in March 1942. The titling on the Il-2's fuselage reads *Smert Fashistskim Okkupantam* ('Death to Fascist Invaders'). (*Oleg Rastrenin and Andrey Yurgenson*)

Pavel Fedorovich Zhigarev was the forgotten man of Soviet wartime air power. He was brought in immediately before the German invasion and the arrest of all three of his predecessors and held the VVS together. He was sent to Siberia in April 1942 in a dispute over aircraft deliveries, being given command of an air army in the Far East. (*Der Adler*)

Aleksandr Aleksandrovich Novikov would lead the VVS with distinction from April 1942, but the strain made him an alcoholic. After the war he and Aviation Industry Minister Andrei Shakhurin were jailed for ignoring defects in Soviet aircraft production following accusations by Stalin and aircraft designer Yakovlev. (*Der Adler*)

A line-up of 8th GvBAP personnel during the regiment's investiture with the Guards Banner in March 1942. The unit was commanded by Lt Col F P Kotlyar from October 1938 to February 1942, when he was replaced by Maj G S Kucherkov, who accepted the banner at the investiture. (*Dmitriy Khazanov and Aleksander Medved*)

A shot that illustrates the Luftwaffe's continuing supremacy 12 months into the air war on the Russian Front – the tail of an Il-2 shot down by future semi-centurion Oberfeldwebel Otto Wessling of 9./JG 3 on 11 June 1942. (*via John Weal*)

Cap askew, personal victory stick well in evidence, Feldwebel Rudolf Müller is congratulated on achieving II./JG 5's 500th collective kill. This photograph was taken at Petsamo in June 1942. (*via John Weal*)

Standing by the tailplane of his 'Yellow 10' at Petsamo on 30 June 1942, just four months into his operational career, Unteroffizier Hans Döbrich of II. JG 5 seems to be wondering how many more kills – over and above the 18 already booked on the rudder of the Bf 109F seen here – will be required to finish carving his still more than half-empty victory stick. (*via John Weal*)

Aircraft of the *Gruppenstab* StG 2 in the summer of 1942. The nearest machine's fuselage code, 'T6+BC', and the numeral '2' on the wheelspat, points to it being the mount of either the unit's adjutant or operations officer. The likeliest candidate for pilot of both machines is Leutnant Günther Schmid, who is known to have served as Hauptmann Dr Kupfer's *Gruppenadjutant* before taking over as *Staffelkapitän* of 5./StG 2 in late 1942. (*via John Weal*)

The commander of the pre-war Austrian Air Force, Generaloberst Alexander Löhr changed sides during the Anschluss of 1938 and was given *Luftflotte* 4, which he led until the summer of 1942 when he became a military commander in the Balkans. (*Der Adler*)

Summer 1942 in the Crimea, and the pilot of 8./KG 51's '9K+GS' runs up his engines and starts to roll. In this excellent close-up shot of the business end of a Ju 88, the additional 20mm MG FF cannon (painted white) projecting from the ventral gondola is clearly visible. (*via John Weal*)

During the summer of 1942 pilots and groundcrews of attack aircraft regiments converted single-seat Il-2s into two-seat aircraft and armed them with 12.7mm UBT or 7.62mm ShKAS machine guns for rear defence against German fighters. About 1,200 single-seaters were modified in such a way. In this photograph, Il-2 air gunner Sgt Baklar Saakyan is strapped in behind a makeshift ShKAS defensive machine gun mounting, which appears to have come from a Tupolev SB-2 medium bomber. (*Oleg Rastrenin and Andrey Yurgenson*)

Novikov's recognition of the abilities of Fedor Iakovlevich Falaleev saved him when the latter was made the scapegoat for VVS failures during the Kharkov Offensive in 1942. He became VVS Deputy Commander-in-Chief and Chief-of-Staff and was appointed Marshal in August 1944. (*Der Adler*)

A celebration of 5./KG 3's Oberfeldwebel Friedrich Kralemann's 200th mission. Kralemann (centre) flew his 260th, and last, mission on 10 September 1942 when, despite severe injuries that were to cost him his left eye, he managed to bring his crippled machine (minus cabin roof canopy and ventral gondola) back to base. Over a year later, on 29 October 1943, Kralemann was awarded the Knight's Cross, before finally succumbing to his wounds on 1 December 1943. (*via John Weal*)

Clutching a bunch of flowers, Major Dr Ernst Kupfer, *Gruppenkommandeur* of II./StG 2, shares his cockpit with a lucky piglet upon returning to Oblivskaya after completing his 400th operational mission in August 1942. (*via John Weal*)

RIGHT • Pilots run to La-5 fighters, which made their debut in the autumn of 1942. Although initially proving inferior to the enemy, the Lavochkin – particularly in La-5FN and La-7 forms – later became highly regarded. (*Courtesy of the Central Museum of the Armed Forces, Moscow via Stavka*)

BELOW • Maintaining one of the two 37mm Flak 18s under a Ju 87G anti-tank aircraft similar to that in which Rudel was credited with 519 victories. The value of heavy cannon against tanks was demonstrated by the Hs 129, although some sceptical pilots removed them in 1942. (*Der Adler*)

A petrol bowser is used during the refuelling of a VVS Boston. The Douglas 'bombing twin' equipped VVS-Frontal Aviation bomber regiments and ADD intruder regiments, and with the Mitchell made up almost half the medium bombers received by the Soviet Union between 1942 and 1944. (*EN Archives*)

A smashed He 111 transport at Stalingrad is surrounded by the bodies of its crew and probably those who wished to be passengers. The loss of Ju 52/3ms in the Stalingrad airlift disrupted Luftwaffe training because many aircraft, instructors and advanced students were lost. (*Der Adler*)

Richthofen benefited from having access to a purpose-built command train, which played a key part in supporting Manstein's counter-offensive in March 1943. Communications security was maintained by plugging the train into landlines or using couriers in Storchs like the one seen here flying overhead. (*Der Adler*)

Major Reinhard Seiler, *Gruppenkommandeur* of III./JG 54 (a post he held from October 1941 until mid-April 1943), is greeted by his dog soon after returning from a mission. Assuming command of I. *Gruppe* in the spring of 1943, Seiler was severely wounded on the second day of Operation *Zitadelle*. Retired from operations, he ended the war as *Kommodore* of training *Geschwader* JG 104. (*via John Weal*)

German bombs strike a Russian railway marshalling yard, but this picture could easily show the reverse. When *Fliegerkorps* IV staged the 'strategic' *Unternehmen Zaunkönig* most of its targets were actually marshalling yards and railway junctions. (*Der Adler*)

The bomb aimer/front gunner of a He 111 waits as the pilot runs up the engines before take-off. Bomber missions in the East grew shorter and shorter, and by 1943 could last as little as ten minutes. (*Der Adler*)

Three types of bombs are seen under the wing of this Pe-2 of 261st SBAP during the summer of 1943. The armourer to the right is resting his foot on a captured German SC 250, while the nearest bomb is a FAB-100 with a welded body. Behind it are FAB-100s with cast-iron bodies. (*Dmitriy Khazanov and Aleksander Medved*)

A group of Il-2s have their engines run up prior to flying yet another combat sortie in the Kursk sector in the summer of 1943. (*Oleg Rastrenin and Andrey Yurgenson*)

One of the ten Heinkel *Kampfgruppen* taking part in *Zitadelle* was III./KG 55. This photograph, taken in the summer of 1943, shows Hauptmann Oskar Dettke (the *Kapitän* of 9. *Staffel*) upon the completion of his 300th combat mission. Note the *Staffel's* 'Snorting bull' emblem above the celebratory garland on the machine's tail. (*via John Weal*)

A petrol bowser has drawn up to refuel a Ju 87D of Oberstleutnant Gustav Pressler's 7./StG 1. The spats, which are synonymous with the Ju 87, have been removed because they could sometimes collect mud and cause take-off or landing accidents. (*Der Adler*)

Although transformed from *Stukageschwader* into *Schlachtgeschwader* in October 1943, it was still business as usual for most Ju 87 units for many months to come. The first light dusting of winter snow has already fallen as this unidentified Ju 87D-5 prepares for take-off with a full weapon load. Note the hefty *Dinortstab* on the 250kg (550lb) underwing bomb. (*via John Weal*)

A formation of Pe-2 'Peshka' (Pike) long range dive-bombers. The aeroplane's short range meant that by 1944 bomber divisions equipped with the Pe-2 usually had a Boston regiment attached to extend their reach. (*Courtesy of the Central Museum of the Armed Forces, Moscow via Stavka*)

A squadron of Yak-9D fighters of 6th GvIAP-ChF escorts naval Bostons of 36th MTAP-ChF during an operation in the summer of 1944. The Yakovlev fighters were among the most successful in Soviet aviation history, although they were not without faults. (*Courtesy of the Central Museum of the Armed Forces, Moscow via Stavka*)

A Pe-2 of the second squadron, 12th GvBAP, in winter camouflage. This is a late-series bomber with the antennae mast relocated to the windscreen frame and individual engine exhaust stubs. Note that this aircraft has its tactical number painted on the fuselage, which was a feature unique to naval regiments. VVS RKKA Pe-2 units usually applied this number to the vertical tails of their aircraft. (*Dmitriy Khazanov and Aleksander Medved*)

The only Heinkel bombers remaining in the East during the winter of 1944–45 were those of KG 4. These late war He 111H-20s, which were fitted with a turret in place of the earlier variants' dorsal gun positions, are believed to be aircraft of II./KG 4, with the *Gruppenstab's* 'DC' in the foreground. (*via John Weal*)

In the harsh conditions of the Soviet north, reindeers were used to transport bombs to Pe-2s of 114th GvBAP. This regiment became famous through its participation in countless combat operations against German and Finnish forces in this theatre, and it ended the war with the title of Kirkenes Red-Banner and Kutuzov Order regiment, commanded by Maj A N Volodin. (*Dmitriy Khazanov and Aleksander Medved*)

Maior Grigoriy Rechkalov and his P-39Q Aircobra of 16th GvIAP. Rechkalov was very much an individualist in a collective society, and he had 56 individual and six shared victories, most in the aircraft the Russians called the Kobra. (*EN Archives*)

General der Flieger Karl Koller was the Luftwaffe's last chief-of-staff and final de facto commander. He had earlier worked with *General der Flieger* Günther Korten to develop *Fliegerkorps* IV into a strategic bombing force. (*Der Adler*)

Generalfeldmarschall Robert Ritter von Greim, was the last Commander-in-Chief of the Luftwaffe. He was flown into besieged Berlin by his mistress to receive the appointment personally from Hitler. For most of his time in the East he commanded *Luftflotte* 6. (*Der Adler*)

The Luftwaffe's largest transport was the Me 323 Gigant, an example of which is seen here ready to evacuate a load of wounded men with its forward clamshell doors open. It could carry loads of 20 tonnes (including 120 troops or 60 casualty stretchers), compared with 2–2.5 tonnes in the Ju 52/3m. (*Der Adler*)

leitenant Vasilii Ryazanov of 1st GvShAK from a forward command post. This laid the foundation for the envelopment of 42,000 troops around Brody on 18 July who were destroyed within a week with the aid of 1,538 strike sorties.

Seidemann was transferred to Greim, but the Russians reached the Vistula on 28 July, by which time Krasovskii had flown 30,500 sorties and lost 388 aircraft. Yet a post-operational analysis criticised him for not taking greater action against enemy reserves, while poor training and over-confidence led to heavy losses, especially among 'Ilyusha' units whose escorts were often found wanting. The losses meant that by late July Krasovskii was down to 2,000 aircraft and unable to move forward because retreating enemy troops threatened his supply lines. Only in August did most of 2nd VA move forward, aided by the delivery of 7,500 tonnes of fuel that had to be rationed because most was consumed defending the bridgeheads.

As Krasovskii's regiments struggled, the Red Army crossed the Vistula on 18 August to secure a bridgehead south of Warsaw around Sandomierz and Baranow. Two fighter divisions and an assault division were moved into the bridgehead while the radar screen was also extended westwards, and Greim soon reported operations over the bridgehead were almost impossible. However, across the line, supply problems forced Krasovskii to transfer several divisions to 8th VA. The offensive was officially closed down on 29 August, by which time 2nd and 8th VA had flown 48,000 sorties, dropped 6,500 tonnes of bombs and lost 289 aircraft.

With the Russians now in the Carpathian Mountains, Stalin wished to drive through them into both Slovakia and northern Hungary, and Zhdanov's 8th VA was assigned to support this attack with 666 combat aircraft, but only 84 bombers. The mountainous terrain and its mini weather systems made operations difficult, although some regiments that had served in the Caucasus were used to them. Between September and November Zhdanov's airmen flew only 7,129 sorties and dropped 2,308 tonnes of bombs against light opposition from Dessloch, with much effort providing spearheads with 11,756 tonnes of supplies. The region proved to be a backwater, although Zhdanov briefly moved to

Hungarian airfields in early January to support an unsuccessful offensive, and in March he supported a more successful thrust into Slovakia with 620 combat aircraft from Polish airfields around Krakow.

Slovak enthusiasm for the German cause had rapidly waned, and on 29 August their army led an uprising supported by 30 aircraft of the Slovak Air Force, whose defectors landed at 5th AK DD's base near Lvov. Krasovskii sent 1st Czech IAP with 25 fighters behind the lines to help the rebels from Tri Duby airfield, near Zvolen, and it flew 500 sorties before returning a month later. On 3 September Stalin diverted 4th GvAK and 5th AK DD from supporting Josef Tito's partisans in Yugoslavia to helping the uprising, their first act being, between 17 and 21 September, to fly a Czech airborne brigade of 3,000 men in to secure Tri Duby. Once this had been done, Polkovnik B. F. Chirskov, deputy commander of 53rd AD, arrived to organise transport operations. Four or five missions a night were flown, each of 15–20 aircraft, but fear of bombing meant they were unloaded with their engines running and took off as soon as they were filled with wounded.

The Russians flew more than 2,000 sorties into the airfield, delivering 1,000 tonnes of supplies. On 7 October six USAAF B-17s, escorted by 32 Mustang fighters, also landed at Tri Duby with supplies and evacuated some Allied pilots who had evaded capture. This heroic episode came to an end on 17 October with a German counter-offensive, which secured Slovakia within a fortnight.

Meanwhile, Stavka prepared to strike into the Balkans through Romania aided by Goryunov and Sudets' 17th VA with 1,759 aircraft, plus 891 of VVS-ChF.[3] Both generals had been promoted to General-polkovnik on 25 March, and for the new offensive Goryunov received two air corps while Sudets received four. Regiments were brought up to strength and operational planning focused upon the first three days supporting the spearheads to envelop *Heeresgruppe Südukraine*, after which units would respond to the military situation. Air support was aided by the proximity of airfields to the FEBA – some 20–35 kilometres for single-engined units and no more than 140 kilometres for multi-engined ones. Although Goryunov received 2,386 tonnes of fuel, he still faced a severe shortage. He hoped to use captured fuel. 'Peshkas' conducted photo-reconnaissance during the first half of August and returned with images of 104,913 square kilometres but neither front commander was happy with the quality of imagery. Camera-equipped 'Ilyushas' were then despatched to provide detailed photos of enemy defences, to help tank crews plan routes through them.

Enemy air strength was estimated fairly accurately at 810 aircraft, although Dessloch had only 232 combat aircraft, mostly under Deichmann's *Fliegerkorps* I, augmented by 436 serviceable Romanian aircraft and 40 German fighters defending the oilfields. There were another 50 maritime support aircraft under Bauer's *Seeflfü Schwarzes Meer*. The offensive began on the morning of 20 August after a two-night ADD offensive against rail targets, and Goryunov flew 3,709 sorties in the first 48 hours. There were massed blows by formations up to regimental strength against strongpoints and gun positions, with Sudets personally directing some regiments. Resistance was weak, and although 246 sorties were flown by German aircraft on the first day, the Russians claimed that not a single bomb had fallen on their troops, while Goryunov lost only two aircraft. The first days saw Sudets use low-flying 'Rippers' (*Rykhliteli*), specially converted Il-2s of General-leitenant Oleg Tolstikov's 9th SAK, to cut telephone lines by trailing wires with hooks.[4] Almost all the *Heeresgruppe* was enveloped and destroyed by 29 August because there was limited resistance from *Luftflotte* 4. The problem was not just lack of fuel and aircraft, Deichmann receiving only 60 of the latter from Greim, but also the extraordinary command decisions that saw OKL decapitate *Luftflotte* 4! On 21 August it sent Dessloch west to command *Luftflotte* 3, leaving chief-of-staff Schulz as acting commander until the appointment on 25 August of Generalleutnant Alexander Holle. Holle, who had learned to fly at Lipetsk, had served in Norway, then headed *Luftwaffenstab Greichenland* and, after a month, would exchange commands with Dessloch on 28 September.

Luftflotte 4 operations were split because Hitler demanded support for the offensive aimed at recapturing Bucharest, as well as retaliatory bombing, after the defecting Romanian government arrested dictator

Ion Antonescu on 23 August. This meant that nearly half the 945 sorties flown by Holle's airmen between 24 and 27 August were diverted away from the main threat, preventing any challenge to Russian air superiority. Indeed, Holle's first act on 27 August was to evacuate the main Romanian bases and withdraw his fighters to Hungary, where he established his new headquarters at Debreczen. Bauer was briefly given command of Luftwaffe units left behind in Bulgaria, then SAGr 125's floatplanes moved to Belgrade, where Bauer's command was disbanded on 5 September. Meanwhile, the *Transportgruppen* were active, flying 297 sorties between 22 and 28 August to bring in 2,050 troops and evacuate 300 wounded and 412 tonnes of material, while another 43 sorties from 30 August to 4 September supported survivors fleeing into Hungary.

On 29 August Stavka ordered an advance into Bulgaria and Hungary, and two days later the Russians took Bucharest. The VVS had flown 20,000 sorties in Romania from 20 to 29 August and lost only 111 aircraft, while the Germans had lost more than 150 combat aircraft, two-thirds to enemy action, although some were replaced by German-made aircraft of the FARR. Romania now became a Russian ally, and on 6 September Goryunov received operational control of 1st Romanian Air Corps with 113 aircraft. Bulgaria also switched sides on 26 August after disarming German forces within its territory, yet on 3/4 September 75th ADD aircraft dropped supplies to Bulgarian communist partisans. On 18 September a GVF regiment dropped 68 paratroops near the Bulgarian–Turkish border to seize a train carrying the German embassy staff to Turkey. Sudets moved into Bulgarian airfields and assumed operational control of his host's air force, which he inspected on 13 September. He reportedly received a warm welcome from his 'brothers', who only weeks earlier had been flying alongside the Luftwaffe. During September he flew 605 sorties and the Bulgarians 332 supporting their troops in Yugoslavia.

From 25 August the Germans began to evacuate their forces – *Heeresgruppe E* and *Luftwaffenkommando Südost* – in Greece and southern Yugoslavia. The latter unit was a counter-insurgency force under Fiebig until 1 September and then Fröhlich, and it became part of the Reich's eastern shield until Dessloch absorbed it on 22 October. Many of its squadrons were assigned to Generalmajor Walter Hagen's *Flfü Nordbalken* supporting the withdrawal and joining Dessloch's command with 90–100 aircraft to become *Fliegerdivision* 17 on 1 February 1945.

Supporting operations in the northern Balkans, initially under Fröhlich then Dessloch, was the German Air Force Commanding General in the North Balkans (*Kommandierende General der deutschen Luftwaffe in Nordbalkan*), which became *Fliegerkorps* II in November under General Johannes Fink, and then Fröhlich until it was sent north on 3 February 1945. The Luftwaffe supported the evacuation with 2,050 sorties by 31 October to bring back 30,740 troops and 1,000 tonnes of material at the cost of 100 transports destroyed or severely damaged by enemy action and seven in accidents. The allies tried in vain to harass the retreat, Sudets targeting communications between Belgrade and Salonika with 1,437 sorties between 13 and 21 September, with 306th ShAD strikes coordinated by a liaison officer with the Yugoslav partisans.

Sudets then supported Yugoslav partisans advancing northwards, and when the Russians crossed the Yugoslav border on 28 September he split his forces into a Northern Group based upon General-leitenant Oleg Tolstikov's 9th SAK and a Southern Group with two VVS divisions and 60 Bulgarian aircraft. To cooperate with the partisans the commander of 10th GvShAD created Air Group General-maior Andrei Vitruk with a fighter and an assault division which joined the successful assault upon Belgrade on 20 October. The previous day the group had become a cadre for a pro-communist Yugoslav air force, and training schools were established within Yugoslavia to produce 176 Yugoslav pilots and 2,100 groundcrews by the end of November, figures which rose to 300 and 3,400 by war's end. On 15 November the group was officially transferred to Yugoslav control, although Russian records indicate no change.

There was little aerial combat in Yugoslavia, although on 7 November Lightnings of the USAAF's Fifteenth Air Force mistook troops from 13th Rifle Corps for enemy forces and attacked them, mortally wounding the corps commander. Sudets despatched Yak fighters of 866th IAP to defend the Red Army, and there was a dogfight in which each side lost three fighters.

The Luftwaffe's main southern battleground was now over the Hungarian plains, which the Russians estimated were defended by some 550 aircraft at the beginning of September. To reduce the threat, from 14 to 15 September Goryunov's 3rd GvBAK struck airfields around Budapest. Dessloch had some 300 combat aircraft, including student crews of IV(*Erg*)./KG 2 for both reconnaissance and bombing and 150 Hungarian aircraft under their own *Flfü* 102. Fuel shortages and the need to rebuild the infrastructure reduced Luftwaffe German operations to an average 125–150 sorties a day during this period, but luckily the Russians had again outrun their supplies and for a month there was an uneasy calm, although in October *Luftflotte* 4 and *Luftwaffekommando Südost* flew 7,242 sorties, 583 at night, and lost 123 aircraft.

Goryunov was the prime VVS player in Hungary and moved into the eastern part of the country while Sudets operated in the south and from Bulgaria. The weather was poor with torrential rain frequently flooding airfields, but Goryunov flew 8,400 sorties in October, 7,667 in November and 8,245 in December. Despite shortages in both personnel and equipment, his command and control proved effective. Fighter cover was sometimes summoned within five minutes, while experienced 'Ilyusha' crews were simply directed to a map reference and told to make their own decision on how best to attack. However, poorly escorted missions led to a steady stream of casualties, with 40 per cent of the Il-2s lost falling to Luftwaffe fighters that intercepted unprotected 'Ilyushas' – Goryunov lost 35 aircraft to enemy action in November and 24 in December. Dessloch lost some 270 in the same period, 99 to enemy action.

In improved weather the Russians launched an offensive on 20 December to isolate Budapest, which housed Deichmann's headquarters. The attack was supported by Goryunov's 925 combat aircraft, including 145 bombers. Deichmann had some 600 aircraft handicapped by low fuel supplies, which reduced operations to 150–200 sorties a day. Unchecked, the Russians advanced rapidly, surrounded the city on 26 December and took most of the garrison's supply dumps, but on several occasions VVS groundcrews had to defend new bases against enemy troops. At the same time a Russian advance into southern Hungary supported by Sudets forced Deichmann to reinforce Fink, who had 120 aircraft to contain the threat.

The ferocious siege of Budapest lasted until 13 February and cost Goryunov 75 aircraft, bringing Russian losses since 29 October to 293. When the city was isolated on Christmas Day 1944 air transport expert Generalleutnant Gerhard Conrad organised an Air Supply Operations Staff (*Luftversorgungs-Einsatzstab*) with some 80 transports, including a Hungarian squadron, 85 bombers and DFS 230 gliders towed by Do 17s. On 27 December the *Heeresgruppe Süd* (renamed in September) commander, General Otto Wöhler, demanded an airlift of 80 tonnes a day (20 tonnes by parachute) into the besieged city, but an average of only 36 tonnes arrived each night

The loss of Budapest's airport forced the defenders to use main roads and a park as airstrips, with Storchs flying in to retrieve both glider pilots and Deichmann's staff, who moved to Veszprém. The last airstrips were lost on 9 January and the city followed a month later. On 8 February, when night transport operations became ever more hazardous, Dessloch was told to use *Schlachtflieger* to bring in supplies during the day, but he probably ignored this stupidity! The Luftwaffe delivered 1,515 tonnes of supplies and lost 45 aircraft and 48 gliders, as well as suffering 138 aircrew casualties, of whom 109 were dead or missing.

Throughout the siege Deichmann supported vain attempts to relieve the city, but they were outnumbered. He lost most of his *Schlachtflieger* to *Luftflotte* 6 during December, and by 10 January he was down to 175 combat aircraft while Fink had 129 and Dessloch had 40 aircraft under his direct command, together with some 100 Hungarian aircraft. But on 1 January Goryunov had 771 aircraft and Sudets 1,125, augmented by some 385 Allied aircraft, while part of the VVS-ChF with 575 aircraft was also available.

With the fall of Budapest Hitler feared the loss of his last oilfield in western Hungary and authorised an offensive, *Unternehmen Frühlingserwachen* (Spring Awakening), using troops taken from the Ardennes. Aware of this, Stavka decided to repeat the successful strategy of 1943 and absorb the attack, then smash the weakened enemy with a counter-offensive. Sudets brought ten fighter and assault regiments to support the threatened front, often sharing flooded airfields. There was a spares famine that forced him to fly worn-out aircraft into airfields, where they were cannibalised, while eight train loads of Yak-3s and La-7s came through Romania to bring Sudets' strength to 965 combat aircraft.

Dessloch had lost some 80 aircraft to Greim during February, and while he still nominally had about 850, the usual fuel shortages shackled operations as the offensive opened in low cloud and haze on 5 March. When the weather improved Sudets flew 800–900 sorties a day, while Goryunov reinforced his comrade so that by 15 March the German offensive had been held. The next day the Russians launched their own offensive after 312th NBAD flew noise barrages to cover the arrival of supporting Russian warships, but dense fog grounded both sides' airmen on the first day.

The Germans were driven back, assailed by both the VVS and the Fifteenth Air Force, with Dessloch unable to repel these aerial attacks – by 9 April he had only 430 aircraft, together with 60 Hungarian. OKL began to downgrade the forces, with Fröhlich being transferred north of Berlin on 2 April, *Fliegerkorps* I becoming *Fliegerdivision* 18 on 4 April and, two days later, *Luftflotte* 4 being downgraded to *Luftwaffenkommando* 4 under *Luftflotte* 6. Dessloch remained in command until 27 April, when he was transferred to *Luftflotte* 6 and handed over to Deichmann, while Generalmajor Paul Weitkus now commanded *Fliegerdivision* 18. Deichmann could offer only token resistance and, without fuel, he had to abandon hundreds of aircraft and disband four *Gruppen* by war's end.

On 1 April Goryunov and Sudets reached Austria as the Red Army advanced upon Vienna, whose fighter force under Oberst Gotthardt Handrich's *Jagddivision* 8 was soon absorbed into Dessloch's command. On 3 April Dessloch was ordered to concentrate operations around Vienna, but he could not prevent the city's fall on 13 April. By then Sudets' airmen had flown 24,100 sorties and dropped 5,023 tonnes of bombs, Russian losses in the campaign being 614 aircraft. Sudets continued the pursuit westwards but Goryunov was turned north to support an advance into eastern Czechoslovakia around Brno from 14 April, his units flying 16,568 sorties in April.

During 1944 the Luftwaffe flew 314,551 sorties, almost half (154,464) by *Luftflotte* 4, and lost 2,420 aircraft to enemy action, of which 1,055 (43.5 per cent) were from *Luftflotte* 4. Between July and December the day fighter force in the East flew 12,505 sorties and lost 1,733 aircraft to all causes – an unacceptable loss rate of nearly 14 per cent. The nightfighter force in the East flew 7,552 sorties and lost 366 aircraft.

The most significant development was the disbandment of Meister's strategic bomber *Fliegerkorps* IV during the summer of 1944. This decision was driven by the Luftwaffe's growing fuel crisis, but the catalyst was the failed assassination attempt on Hitler on 20 July. The bomb mortally wounded Korten, who died two days later, and with Koller busy in the West, Göring exercised his prerogatives as Luftwaffe commander. The bombers were always thirsty and the shortsighted Göring decided to conserve fuel by withdrawing *Fliegerkorps* IV to Thorn (Torun), in western Poland, on 29 July, although KG 53 was sent to launch V1s at the British Isles. The *Fliegerkorps* was disbanded on 16 September to form a new command in Denmark, while most *Kampfgruppen* were assigned to *Fliegerkorps* IX (J) on 13 November to become single-engine fighter units, the remainder switching to the transport role.

Some idea of Meister's activities may be gauged from KG 55's record of 4,250 sorties in 123 missions in the East until 12 August. Most sorties, 3,164 (46 missions), were against rail targets, which received 3,782 tonnes of bombs and cost the *Geschwader* 49 aircraft. There were 23 supply missions (535 sorties) that delivered 619 tonnes of supplies and cost 17 aircraft and 602 sorties to support the army through the dropping of almost 750 tonnes of bombs for the loss of eight aircraft. Much of this activity was for *Zaunkönig*, which ultimately proved a disappointment but Meister did have one spectacular success on the eve of *Bagration*, and that was against the Americans.

On 4 February 1944, the Russians reluctantly agreed to establish bases around Poltava at which USAAF heavy bombers flying from England or Italy could refuel and rearm, before striking targets in Eastern

Europe that might otherwise be beyond their range.[5] Dubbed Operation *Frantic*, the offensive was heavily backed by politicians back in Washington, DC, with the US government making a substantial investment in this 'shuttle bombing' concept. Indeed, it supplied all the materials to equip four bases. On 2 June *Frantic* I or *Frantic Joe* saw Fifteenth Air Force aircraft arrive from Italy and depart four days later. On 21 June the Eighth Air Force's *Frantic* II aeroplanes arrived from England. OKL was determined to interrupt this new offensive if possible, shadowing USAAF bombers to Poltava. PVO radar detected the intruder some 30 minutes after the Americans had landed, but as it was flying above anti-aircraft gun range there was a delay in despatching interceptors, which lacked oxygen and were unable to reach the enemy aeroplanes.

Meister immediately sent 180 bombers eastwards to prick American and PVO complacency, with Russian radars failing to detect the incoming threat. They could not have intercepted the German bombers in any case because they lacked nightfighters. Poltava was struck by 46 tonnes of bombs, which hit 97 aircraft and destroyed 44 B-17s, together with stores that included 360 tonnes of fuel, while SD 2 bomblets were scattered over the runways. Once they were cleared 73 surviving bombers were flown to another base, thus escaping a second raid. This time 25 PVO aircraft were hit, including a Hurricane and three U-2s. Shuttle missions never really recovered, although another five were flown until 19 September, two by fighters only. *Frantic* was abandoned after 1,009 sorties, more than half (530) by bombers.

In the following weeks 'Fatty' Göring found staff duties too onerous, and on 2 August he selected the lightweight training chief Kreipe to act as chief-of-staff, with Seidel replacing him at *Luftflotte* 10. Hitler had really wanted Greim to become de facto Luftwaffe commander, but when Göring learned this he threw a tantrum and bullied the Generalfeldmarschall into rejecting the offer. Unfortunately, Kreipe's mild manner and querulous presentations led the Führer to refer to him as 'Fräulein Kreipe'. He also accused him of treachery, which led to Gestapo surveillance. A Bomber Command raid on the night of 11/12 September so infuriated Hitler he banned Kreipe from his headquarters, and a week later he was told to resign. Although Pflugbeil was Göring's candidate, the *Luftflotte* 4 commander also preferred the perils of the Russian front to those of Hitler's headquarters, and so Koller was appointed.

Under Koller OKL still tinkered with plans to strike Russian industry, but fuel shortages meant plans for using the He 177, *Unternehmen Burgund* (Burgundy), and the Ju 290, *Unternehmen Gertraud* (Gertrude), were abandoned and Allied fighters duly destroyed half the Ju 290 force on the ground. An alternative solution involved *Mistel* (Mistletoe) or *Beethoven* composite aircraft – Ju 88 bombers packed with explosives and guided to their targets by attached fighters, which separated from their charges after aiming them. On 7 January 1945, Koller proposed *Unternehmen Eisenhammer* (Iron Hammer), which would use pilots from the Luftwaffe's special operations force, KG 200, to strike industrial targets as far as the Urals, some 2,100 kilometres east of Berlin, with the pilots returning to Courland. The plan was officially 'postponed' on 30 March when the Red Army tide was lapping at Berlin's suburbs.

By 10 January the Luftwaffe strength in the East had dropped to 2,042 combat aircraft, including only 496 day fighters and 136 bombers, *Schlachtflieger* being the basis of the strike arm. Speer had raised war production to such unprecedented heights that the Luftwaffe became a throwaway force, preferring to plunder the huge stocks of spare aircraft than repair badly damaged ones.

Increasingly, the fighting in the East took on a medieval quality, with the knights replaced by tanks and the infantry little more than poorly trained peasants. Tank destruction, therefore, had a high priority, and during the latter months of 1944 the *Panzerjäger* forces received new weapons to augment or replace the 30mm cannon of the Hs 129B or the 37mm guns of the Ju 87G, whose most formidable exponent was Rudel. From September *Jabos* began to receive anti-tank rockets based upon the bazooka-like 88mm *Panzershreck*, and then, on 16 November, the 81mm *Panzerblitz* made its combat debut with III./SG 3. A six-rocket salvo, it gave the pilot an excellent chance of destroying a tank. But there were never enough to equip all units. Indeed, by 20 April 1945, of 61 *Schlachtstaffeln* only 12 had *Panzerblitz* and two had

TABLE V-4: LONG RANGE AVIATION BOMBING STATISTICS 1944–45

Target	1944		1945	
	Sorties	Tonnage	Sorties	Tonnage
Strategic	4,466	4,813	–	–
Railways	24,134	25,492	5,251	5,061
Airfields	3,275	3,361	70	106
Ports	4,564	4,515	1,731	1,399
Troops support	16,124	17,015	7,927	8,398
Total	52,563	55,196	14,979	14,964

Panzerschreck, leaving the *Schlachtgruppen* relying upon bombs, which were best used against 'soft' targets such as enemy troops and trucks.

In contrast to the Germans, the Russian long range bomber force continued to expand, and by 1 June 1944, it had 1,195 aircraft, including 413 Li-2s. During the spring ADD had created 14 new regiments, including a third Mitchell-based intruder unit, together with a matching infrastructure. Yet OKW reported ADD attacks upon the rail system in the east were less serious than those in the west and south, both because the system was less vulnerable and because the Russians lacked the offensive firepower of the Western Allies. ADD's prime role continued to be the direct or indirect support of the Red Army, with 30 per cent of its sorties and bomb loads striking defensive positions (see Table V-4). There was also greater emphasis placed on indirect support, with attacks on communications and airfields accounting for nearly 61 per cent of sorties flown and bombs dropped.

Although strategic bombing accounted for less than 8.5 per cent of sorties flown, in December 1943 Stalin ordered Golovanov to prepare a night offensive against Helsinki to coincide with a diplomatic effort to push Finland out of the war. The campaign began on 6/7 February 1944, and there were three 'massive' raids on 26/27 February involving 1,980 sorties and 2,386 tonnes of bombs. A further 396 ADD sorties hit Finnish ports between 10/11 and 22/23 February, while VVS bombers flew 850 sorties against Helsinki, which was defended by a *Gruppe* of 'Wild Boar' single-engined nightfighters. The raids occurred at ten-night intervals, with the weather scouts acting as pathfinders and target markers while the bombers followed in streams, the crews reporting numerous fires and explosions at 'military facilities'. Yet there appears to have been limited photographic bomb-damage assessment and the crews' word was accepted largely without question.

The last attempt at a Douhet-style offensive was in September 1944 when Golovanov sought to knock Hungary out of the war. During September there were four raids on Budapest involving 1,129 sorties with Il-4s and Mitchells, some involving flights of 875 kilometres, while Hungarian factories, rail targets and airfields were attacked by more than 900 bombers, bringing the total bomb load to 3,100 tonnes. By contrast, during that same month the Fifteenth Air Force flew 1,605 bomber sorties against Hungarian targets while the RAF flew 149.

By the time the last of the Hungarian raiders landed, Stalin was re-evaluating the ADD's contribution to the war effort following startling information from opposite flanks of the front. Industrial teams followed the Red Army into Romania hoping to spirit away plant and machinery from the Ploesti oilfields to Russia found a wasteland of charred metal, brick and stone as a result of Allied bombing. This was the first Russian experience of the power of their allies' strategic bombing and it spurred research on the 'uranium bomb' under Beria. If Golovanov's airmen were correct, Soviet diplomats returning to Helsinki should have found it in a similar condition. They reported that it was almost untouched.

Stalin now re-evaluated the need for strategic bombing and authorised work on the Tu-4, a B-29 clone, and the 'uranium bomb' for use in the post-war world, but he decided Golovanov's bombers were now better employed supporting the Red Army. His decision might have been influenced by Golovanov suffering a second breakdown after being given added responsibility for the airborne forces, and on 6 December – Finland's Independence Day – the GKO disbanded the ADD and restored autonomy to both the GVF and the airborne forces. The bombers were transferred to the new 18th VA, still under Golovanov, who had 1,185 aircraft by New Year's Day, including 407 Li-2s, with some compensation for the loss of the Pe-8s through increasing numbers of Yer-2 medium bombers, which had resumed production in 1943 following a two-year hiatus in favour of Il-2s. Golovanov would fly 20,115 sorties during the final months, of which nearly 15,000 were made by bombers. Half of these were flown in direct support of the Red Army, with aircraft expending 100kg bombs, and he lost 186 bombers, including 93 Il-4s.

The GKO may also have been influenced by the resources and manpower required to build the Pe-8, of which only five were produced in 1944. During the year the casualty rate increased to one per 46 sorties, compared with one per 103 in 1942, and by 1944 52 of the heavy bombers had been lost, 14 to enemy action. By July 1944 30 remained in service, this number having dropped to 18 by the end of the war. In order to boost their ranks, a number of obsolete TB-3s had to be returned to first-line service from training units. In July the heavy bomber regiment 45th AD DD converted to Mitchells, and on the night of 1/2 August the Pe-8 flew its last operational sortie.

But the disaster at Poltava had a silver lining for Golovanov, for 22 B-17s were repaired and entered service with 890th AP, and they were joined by more damaged aircraft that landed behind Soviet lines. From March 1945 B-24s joined the inventory, and altogether 73 American heavy bombers would serve in Soviet regiments. While none saw action, they helped train the core of a post-war reborn ADD.

Transport continued to be important for the Long Range Aviation and in 1945 there were 3,500 sorties that brought in 4,117 tonnes of cargo and 19,357 people and evacuated 10,307 wounded. They also flew many special operations missions in support of the fronts – 326 in 1944 and 180 in 1944 – while to support the fronts they inserted 196 GRU and NKVD personnel in 132 sorties in 1944 and 72 personnel in 73 sorties during 1945. During 1944 ADD flew 10,011 special operations sorties, carrying 11,952 tonnes of cargo together with 27,552 personnel and evacuated 6,996 wounded, but in 1945 there were only 300 sorties flown.

Increasingly, the ADD and GVF were used to support foreign communist guerrilla movements. Returning from Tehran in December

1943, Stalin paused at Baku to telephone Golovanov, demanding he fly supplies to Tito's Yugoslav partisans. These flights began from the Kiev area in February 1944 with Li-2s of the former GVF 10th Guards Transport Division (*Trahnsportnyy Aviatsionnaya Diviziya*, GvTrAD), which later transferred to Vinnitsa. There were numerous difficulties, not least the navigation of a 2,600 kilometre round trip, poor liaison that meant many drops failed to reach the partisans and the threat from enemy fighters in Hungary that sometimes meant intruder support was required.

In January 1944 a Russian military mission under GRU General-leitenant Nikolai Korneev flew to Bari, in Italy, and then to Yugoslavia. This improved liaison, while responsibility for delivering supplies was transferred in May 1944 to the Mitchells of 5th GvAD DD. By the time this division moved to Romania in September it had flown 1,930 sorties to Yugoslavia and delivered 1,758 tonnes of supplies. It reverted back to a bomber role when in June 1944 Moscow secured an agreement to base an ADD detachment – the Air Group for Special Duties (AGON) under Polkovnik Vasilii Shchelkunov – in Bari with 12 C-47s and Li-2s, later supported by a Yak fighter squadron and four Po-2s. Shchelkunov delivered 3,000 tonnes of supplies and 5,000 personnel and evacuated 1,500 wounded without losing a single aircraft.

The Luftwaffe's KG 200 was also involved in special operations, usually dropping agents, although this became increasingly unsuccessful. On the night of 22/23 May 1944, a Ju 290 flew 30 *V-Männer* from Romania to the Caucasus to start an insurrection in *Unternehmen Salzsee* (Salt Lake). The transport was tracked by radar, strafed by Hurricanes after it landed and then the NKVD arrived to capture both aircraft and agents. A plan to assassinate Stalin in Moscow (*Unternehmen Zeppelin*) saw an Ar 232B transport written off as it brought in the *V-Männer* on the night of 4/5 September 1944, and again the NKVD rounded up everyone.

With the PVO increasingly supporting the army, home defence forces were stripped of resources, although regiments moved only with Stavka permission. This weakening of the home defence forces was slowed by the need to shield the over-burdened rail system, while PVO front commanders were also reluctant to lose assets for fear of repercussions if Germany struck. The army was not always grateful, and on 30 January 1944, Rokossovskii complained the PVO was slow to organise the defences of recaptured cities and would not guarantee the necessary resources to do so. There was also the problem that the army and PVO air observer organisations operated on different radio wavelengths and so could not coordinate tracking.

On 1 June 1944, the PVO had 2,790 fighters in the West, of which half (1,412) were imported aircraft – largely Kobras and Kittyhawks, augmented by some Hurricanes and Spitfires. Novikov simplified VVS logistics by using Russian aircraft to replace foreign ones, which were then used to update the PVO's inventory. During 1944 the PVO flew 29,715 sorties, of which ten per cent were battlefield support and some 20 per cent (5,979) were escort missions, and these probably accounted for most of the 131 fighters lost to enemy action that year. In homeland defence, 42 per cent (12,250) of sorties were combat air patrols and 25.6 per cent (7,626) were scrambles, yet the threat diminished after *Bagration* as the PVO faced only individual reconnaissance aircraft, with one radar-based victory for every 18 sorties compared with one for 40 sorties two years earlier.

Yet Moscow's air defence concerns actually increased during the summer of 1944, influenced by events in Western Europe. On 12/13 June the first V1 cruise missile hit London, and Moscow feared it would be next, so on 19 July the Red Army Artillery's Military Council approved plans similar to those of the British to meet this threat based upon a three-zone system. The first was a barrage balloon barrier five to ten kilometres from potential targets, then an anti-aircraft artillery zone 15–20 kilometres deep and beyond that a fighter zone.

The PVO Northern Front together with the Leningrad and Moscow PVO Armies were reorganised to meet this threat, but unlike the Leningrad PVO Army, the capital's defences were split into two belts. An outer one in Smolensk linked the Nevel, Vitebsk, Orsha and Mogilev sectors, including 328th IAD, with 556 guns and eight Pegamatite radars. Closer to Moscow was a gun belt with 834 guns with SON fire control radar and 360 barrage balloons. The radar network was extended, but there were many areas where coverage was patchy, which forced the PVO to rely extensively on patrols. Radar-equipped nightfighters were in short supply, and their tactical zone was 20 kilometres in front of the guns, although they could range up to 100 kilometres to the west.

In December 1944 the western PVO received its final wartime reorganization, with the Northern and Southern Fronts replaced by the Western (General-polkovnik Daniil Zhuravlev), Southwestern (Zashikhin) and Central (Gromadin) Fronts to provide greater flexibility of strategic defence while supporting the army. By 1 January 1945, PVO strength had risen to 3,149 aircraft, of which 52 per cent (1,640) were foreign designs. The year saw only 1,738 PVO sorties around the main front, with nearly 75 per cent (1,213) of them being combat air patrols and ten per cent (254) scrambles. Only four fighters were lost to enemy action.

The VVS remained the prime element of Soviet air power, and during 1944 it flew 768,893 sorties on the main front and lost 11,952 aircraft (including those destroyed on the Finnish front), while another 2,594 worn-out aeroplanes were withdrawn. The ADD flew some 48,097 sorties while carrying out Operational Level missions and lost 696 aircraft, including 410 bombers. VVS losses included 7,897 aircraft (68.4 per cent) to enemy action and 3,641 (31.5 per cent) in accidents partly due to flying in poor weather and from inadequate airfields, while 36.5 per cent of all fighter losses were caused by accidents. Production matched the losses and quality steadily increased. The LaGG-3 was finally phased out, together with the Hurricane and Warhawk, while the Yak-3 and La-7 reached the front line, as did the improved Il-10 'Ilyusha'.

At the beginning of 1945 the VVS had 12,265 combat aircraft on the main front (excluding 13th and 15th VAs) while Stavka had another 575. There were 4,501 serviceable day fighters, 1,727 serviceable 'Peshkas' and Bostons and 3,524 'Ilyushas', with the Il-10 about to enter service. These figures include French, Czech and Polish squadrons, and the Russians could now also count upon 200 Romanian and Bulgarian aircraft and 18th VA. The PVO had some 720 aeroplanes supporting the Red Army, while the VVS-KBF could also support the winter offensives north of the Carpathians. However, it was obvious to Novikov that

Soviet air power was far behind that of the Allies, its potential post-war opponents, with fighters based upon old-fashioned construction techniques. There were no jet aircraft close to reaching front line service, and strike forces lacked range and payload.

Yet to prepare for the next campaign, the VVS flew 1,759 reconnaissance sorties over Poland, despite only nine flyable days from November 1944 through to mid-January 1945, and covered 109,200 square kilometres. These were to help Stavka plan a single blow to knock Germany out of the war by advancing from Warsaw to Berlin. To this end Krasovskii and Rudenko had 4,772 aircraft, of which Rudenko had 2,421, and there was considerable planning effort expended to move regiments forward – for which 20 per cent of each air army's stock of spares was allocated. Radars were distributed to fighter fields to keep German reconnaissance aircraft out of an 80–100 kilometre exclusion zone.

The VVS faced Greim's *Luftflotte* 6, which had Generalmajor Klaus Uebe's *Fliegerdivision* 4 covering East Prussia, Fuchs' *Fliegerdivision* 1 shielding northern Poland and Seidemann's *Fliegerkorps* VIII covering central and southern Poland. Uebe was supported by the nightfighters of Hauptmann Egbert Belau's *Jafü Ostpreussen*, while *Flfü* 6 under Oberst Karl Stockmann controlled Baltic anti-submarine and mine-countermeasures units, reinforced from 2 February by training units. Greim had 1,079 combat aircraft on 1 December and 1,075 by 10 January, including 421 *Schlacht-* and *Nachtschlachtflieger* as well as 94 nightfighters, but only 18 bombers. He also received nearly 45 per cent of the replacement aircraft sent to the East in the last two months of 1944.

Dense fog and blizzards thwarted VVS plans when the Russians struck on 12 January, yet Krasovskii, south of Warsaw, sent artillery observers over the German positions in low-flying Po-2s to discover which defences required a second bombardment, while experienced 'Ilyusha' crews struck potential barriers to the tanks. Despite the weather he also demanded large-scale missions, with some 'Ilyushas' striking 4 *Panzerarmee*'s headquarters to facilitate a breakthrough. Both Rudenko and Greim were largely grounded on the first day, but during the next Rudenko got into his stride while Krasovskii flew some 700 sorties, almost half against armoured reserves. His fighter sweeps, as much as the weather and fuel shortages, again restricted Greim, to whom OKL sent 20 *Gruppen* from the West, home defence and *Luftflotte* 4 – a total of some 460 fighters and 100 *Schlachtflieger*.The desperate need for ground-attack aircraft meant that from 13 January, nightfighters and long range reconnaissance aircraft were pressed into this role, while *Nahaufklärunggruppen* Fw 189s augmented the *Nachtschlachtgruppen*.

The weather improved only from 15 January, allowing Rudenko to lash communications and drop a key bridge outside Warsaw to block fleeing columns, while Krasovskii threw regimental-size strike missions at retreating troops. Only from 16 January did Greim's resistance really begin with 587 sorties, including 414 *Schlacht*, as SG 77 claimed success with *Panzershrek*. The following day Polish troops recaptured Warsaw, supported by 1st Polish SAK, while Golovanov began a ten-day, 600-sortie campaign against the rail network.

By 17 January Krasovskii and Rudenko had flown 11,748 sorties and Greim 2,184 but, as the Germans collapsed, a thaw brought fog and low cloud to restrict both air forces and cause Russian 'friendly fire' incidents. When the weather cleared the VVS mercilessly interdicted German communications, destroying motor and equine transport and blasting bottlenecks together with counter-attacks.The *Schlachtflieger*, in groups of 20 to 50 aircraft, desperately struck spearheads, destroying a few tanks here and some vehicles there. But it was like trying to stop a tsunami with a stone, and at great cost, with seven *Ritterkreuz*-holders being killed in January alone, while between 20 and 22 January SG 77 lost 26 aircraft.

From 20 January theVVS regiments began to move forward, although sometimes the progress of the advance was threatened by isolated enemy troops. Indeed, when 402nd IAP landed at Sochaczew airfield, west of Warsaw, it discovered that the Germans held the western perimeter! New airfields remained a problem, with many turned to bogs by the thaw. This meant that accidental losses initially exceeded those to enemy action. However, as the Russians entered German territory they turned some autobahns into airfields, filling the gap between the lanes with bricks and gravel.

The Russian advance split in two the German front in Poland, and the Red Army overran 130 Luftwaffe airfields – some with concrete runways – including major ferrying points for replacements. Greim abandoned damaged aircraft together with repair and storage facilities, while the general disruption of transport starved units of supplies. The *Fliegerschule*, under Seidel's *Luftflotte* 10 since 1 July, had been driven to Polish sanctuaries by prowling US fighters and it now fled to Leipzig and Denmark.

Krasovskii supported the advance into Silesia – the last untouched industrial area, including aircraft assembly and component plants. The Russian advance cut Fw 190 production by 25 per cent, seriously affecting *Jagd-*, *Schlacht-* and *Nahaufklärunggruppen*, although this was offset in the short term by large stocks of reserves. Also captured was V1 test site *Erprobungsstelle Udetfeld* near Katowice (Kattowitz), together with intact missiles. Seidemann's *Fliegerkorps* VIII, briefly renamed *Luftwaffenkommando Schlesien* between 24 January and 2 February, fought desperately to restrict the effectiveness of the enemy's upper Oder bridgeheads – units flew 280 sorties on 24 January alone, but suffered heavy losses. Seidemann received some relief in January when Falkenstein's *Fliegerdivision* 3 returned from the West to cover the mountain approaches into the Sudetenland and Moravia on his right. On 24 January the *Heeresgruppen* were again renamed – *Mitte* became *Nord* and 'A' became *Mitte*, while *Heeresgruppe Weichsel* was created under Himmler to defend West Prussia and Pomerania, supported by *Fliegerkorps* II, now under Fiebig, which Dessloch transferred on 3 February.

Meanwhile, Rudenko supported the advance that approached the lower Oder 75 kilometres from Berlin, leading Stavka, on the night of 28/29 January, to demand Berlin be taken by 15–16 February. But the defence was consolidating and by 4 February the Russians held only bridgeheads, despite Rudenko flying 11,193 sorties, including 1,058 in fighter sweeps, with most of his losses due to flak. The Luftwaffe on the entire Eastern Front flew only 7,338 sorties between 29 January and 4 February and lost 158 aircraft. By 1 February Greim was using pre-war air bases with concrete runways, although barely half of his 1,300 combat aircraft, including 750 day fighters, were serviceable. A thaw disrupted Soviet supply lines and forced vehicles to travel on the few hard-topped Polish roads, where they were vulnerable to the *Schlachtflieger*, which claimed 800 in one day. Because of this problem, and limited airfield space, Rudenko was restricted to 624 sorties between 1 and 10 February, of which 43 per cent between the 1st and the 3rd were aerial resupply.

OKW ordered all aircraft fuel reserves be concentrated in the East, commenting, 'Air operations in all other theatres of war are, compared with the Eastern Front, of absolutely negligible importance.' Retreats exacerbated fuel problems, and with small dumps scattered to protect them from air attack, petrol bowsers drove long distances to pick up a few tonnes so that even home defence units found difficulty assembling the 20 tonnes they needed for a mission. On 27 January the 2,000 aircraft on the whole Eastern Front flew only 1,403 sorties, with 608 the following day, mostly by *Luftflotte* 6. Incomplete data from the OKW war diary indicates Luftwaffe activity in the East dropped from 7,300 sorties per week in the first half of February to 5,100 in the second half, with 2,900 in the first half of March and 2,600 in the second half. From 31 January to 2 February the Luftwaffe in the East flew 3,300 combat sorties, many against Oder bridgeheads, but lost 107 aircraft (three per cent). It was a measure of Luftwaffe ineffectiveness that the Russians supporting the main offensive, who flew 54,000 combat sorties, lost only 343 aircraft from 1 January to 3 February.

By 20 February fuel shortages had led OKW to order that aircraft be used only against decisive points in the advance, yet by mid-March Greim was down to 64–72 tonnes of fuel per day. On 1 February, as the enemy advanced upon Berlin, he was given command of all operational, training and support units, as well as testing facilities. His eyes, however, were on the material riches of Generaloberst Hans-Jürgen Stumpff's home-defence *Luftflotte Reich*, and on 3 February he gained operational control of Stumpff's *Jagddivisionen* 1 – Berlin's shield. Three days later, when Göring asked why no day fighters had met an American raid upon Berlin, he was told OKL had ordered that all of its 445 day and nightfighters were to fly *Jabo* missions in the East. They returned to Stumpff on 24 February, but OKL earmarked eight *Jagdgruppen*, together with the division's nightfighters, for army support operations. Indeed, on 31 March Greim was again allowed to use Stumpff's *Sturmgruppen* as *Jabos*.

To coordinate fighter operations in the Berlin region Greim had created *Jafü Ost* on 26 February. By then the *Jagdwaffe* had suffered heavy losses in leaders, and in early February it had started disbanding each *Jagdgeschwader's* fourth *Staffel* and fourth *Gruppe*.

While the threat on the lower Oder was contained, it resumed on the upper Oder as Krasovskii helped a breakout from bridgeheads on 8 February. Despite Seidemann sending every available aircraft, the Russians had advanced 60 kilometres by the end of the day, and German losses were heavy. Indeed, during this campaign the indestructible Rudel was shot down by ground fire and his right leg amputated shortly thereafter. The Russians also lost a hero, for while supporting operations to isolate Breslau, the commander of 6th GvBAK, twice Hero of the Soviet Union Ivan Polbin, was shot down during his 157th mission on 11 February.

Four days later Breslau was isolated, and the next night Hitler demanded that Greim begin a major supply operation to its 35,000 defenders, although he had only 100 transports. He in turn delegated the task to Morzik, although Greim warned Hitler on 18 February that this would undermine efforts to supply Courland with the 160 tonnes of supplies it needed on a daily basis to survive. The airlift used *Staffeln* transferred from Hungary, and it was so important to Hitler that between 16 and 20 February it consumed a quarter of Greim's fuel, yet was still unable to support the garrison. Radar-guided Russian fighters inflicted heavy casualties, forcing the transports to fly at night. Even then they still suffered around a ten per cent loss rate.

From March Bf 109s and the *Nachtschlachtgruppen* dropped supply containers into the city as landings became increasingly hazardous. The last mission was made on 1 May when seven aircraft towed in gliders and two Storch light aircraft brought out the pilots and the SS garrison commander. Some 3,500 sorties were flown between 15 February and 1 May and 3,000 tonnes delivered, while 12,000 civilians and wounded were evacuated at a cost of 165 aircraft. Fighting continued in Silesia, where, on 1 March, Seidemann had 524 aircraft and Falkenstein 336, but neither could influence the outcome.

The VVS also supported secondary operations in East Prussia and northern Poland – the former by Papivin's 3rd VA and Khryukin's 1stVA with 2,029 combat aircraft, nearly 1,000 of Golovanov's bombers and Samokhin's naval airmen – in operations coordinated by Falaleev. The main blow was delivered on 14 January, but it faced the same appalling weather as in central Poland. When conditions improved Papivin and Khryukin flew massed strikes to disrupt the defenders, although Uebe responded with two large *Jabo* attacks. After a brief pause to reorganise, Papivin supported a new attack on 20 January, with his bombers striking marshalling yards, and the following day Königsberg's airfields were bombed and strafed by Khryukin.

By the end of the month Königsberg was almost surrounded, yet Uebe's command, despite being reduced to just a *Jagdgruppe* and a *Nahaufklärungsstaffel*, was upgraded on 24 January to *Luftwaffenkommando Ostpreussen* with his own *Fliegerdivision* 4 (transferred to Fiebig on 3 February), *Jafü Ostpreussen* and *Flfü* 6, the last under Oberst Ulrich Klintzsch from 1 March but transferred westward in April. With some reinforcements Uebe supported efforts, which briefly reopened land communications with West Prussia between 26 and 30 January. From 10 February the Russians pushed towards Königsberg and gradually drove 3 *Panzerarmee* onto the Samland Peninsula, where fierce air attacks had neutralised it by the end of March. That month the two air armies flew 30,000 combat sorties, most of which lasted only 30 minutes, while Uebe, down to 70 aircraft on 1 March, could do little in response.

Bombers coordinated by Novikov were now to be used as siege artillery for a set-piece assault upon Königsberg, rather like Sevastopol in 1942, with Papivin and Khryukin each receiving a bomber corps to give them 2,444 combat aircraft. Fog, drizzle and low cloud grounded the bombers as Stavka became increasingly impatient and pushed for the attack. The air bombardment began on 7 April using 246 of Khryukin's Tu-2s, covered by 232 fighters, and Novikov asked Golovanov to send in his bombers. Golovanov was nervous about committing so many aircraft in daylight, but Novikov's assurances of strong fighter support meant that 516 of his bombers delivered 550 tonnes of bombs, including two-tonne ordnance, without loss, aided by the despatch of 200 strike aircraft against airfields just before the bombers arrived.

As Golovanov's bombs fell, 300 'Ilyushas' with a strong fighter escort also struck the city while fighters circled over enemy airfields and strafed flak sites. With 5,000 sorties on the first day, the Red Army stormed the city supported by another 6,000 sorties the next day. By the time Königsberg fell on the evening of 9 April, Russian airmen had flown 14,090 sorties and dropped 4,440 tonnes of bombs.

Uebe fought on from Pillau-Neutief, his strength having risen to 147 aircraft by 9 April although he faced the usual shortages. Two days later the Russians began to mop up following a VVS offensive on 24 April, Uebe being replaced by Generalmajor Günther Sachs. The latter tried to continue the struggle, but the Germans were compressed into a fingerhold on the coast between Danzig and Königsberg and then overwhelmed, which concluded the East Prussia campaigns. Papivin had flown 18,253 sorties and Golovanov 6,652, with their combined losses during 1945 totalling 1,450 aircraft, mostly to ground fire.

Meanwhile, Vershinin's 4th VA with 1,647 aircraft supported a new offensive from 14 January through northern Poland towards the Baltic. By the end of the month the Russians had reached the Baltic east of Danzig/Gdansk, and while Fuchs' *Fliegerdivision* 1 received four of Uebe's *Gruppen*, he could do little to stop either Vershinin or the 2,766 sorties Golovanov flew against the harbours.

West of Vershinin, Rudenko supported a thrust into Pomerania and West Prussia, which was held by Himmler and supported by Fiebig, with Fuchs' *Fliegerdivision* 1 and Reuss's *Fliegerdivision* 4. Fuchs had 468 aircraft on 1 March, and supported a brief counter-offensive, *Unternehmen Sonnenwende* (Solstice), between 15 and 18 February in an attempt to isolate the Oder bridgeheads, but this provoked a new attack upon Himmler supported by Rudenko. The Red Army reached the Baltic on 4 March, and despite poor weather and the thaw, Russian airmen flew 25,764 combat sorties to bring the total since 14 February to 48,222.

Fuchs flew 2,190 sorties, while Reuss's men dropped 295.5 tonnes of bombs but could not stop the Russians. On 6 March, 46 per cent of the Luftwaffe's 429 sorties in the East were in Pomerania and West Prussia – one by a Fa 223 helicopter that rescued a downed pilot in Europe's first battlefield helicopter search-and-rescue mission. Although the Russians lost 1,073 aircraft between 10 February and 4 April, most were to flak.

Luftwaffe sorties in the East rose from 285 to 1,718 between 1 and 9 March, although the fuel situation was so critical that *Kampfgruppen* disbanded and *Nachtjagdgruppen* merged to form a *Nachtschlachtgruppe*. The silver lining in the cloud was the effectiveness of the *Panzerblitz*, with 1./SG 2 claiming 74 tanks on 3 March and III./SG 4 claiming 23 between 21 January and 16 March. To exploit the *Panzerblitz* and save fuel, Greim organised tank-detecting *Panzeraufklärungsschwarme* equipped with Storchs in late February, and their success meant that by 1 April he had five equipped with 33 aircraft.

The Oder bridgeheads remained thorns in Germany's side, and they were repeatedly attacked by *Gefechtsverband Helbig* under Oberst Joachim Helbig, *Kommodore* of LG 1, whose *Kampfgruppen* were reinforced by elements of KG 200, including those with *Mistel* and Hs 293 anti-ship missiles. His campaign began on 6 March, and at its height Helbig had 78 bombers and 29 *Mistels*, which he could augment with *Schlachtgruppen*. By mid-April he had flown some 550 sorties, 200 by bombers, which delivered a variety of ordnance including one-tonne bombs and 50 Hs 293 missiles.

The 40 *Mistels* proved the greatest asset on 31 March, however, when they downed a rail bridge at Steinau (Scinawa). While the *Mistels* were often inaccurate, and none were nearer their targets than 50 metres, they created a blast that could carve a crater 15 metres deep and 50 metres wide and destroy any building within a 150-metre radius. *Mistel* attacks continued until the end of April, but there was never sufficient fuel for them to cut traffic crossing the Oder, while USAAF strafing took a heavy toll of the *Mistel* force. Nothing could stop the Russian build-up, for the bridgeheads and communications were defended by 235 PVO fighters supported by a radar network, as well as 8,526 anti-aircraft guns.

On 9 March the Luftwaffe in the East reached a peak of 1,718 sorties, surprising the Russians, whose airfields were now drying out sufficiently enough to increase aerial support of the Oder bridgeheads as they were expanded. On 22 March there was a fierce aerial battle over Küstrin, which consumed much German fuel, leaving the Luftwaffe with only enough to power ten per cent of their 3,000 aircraft in the East and forcing Greim to disband six *Jagdgruppen* between 31 March and 13 April.

The assault on Berlin was preceded by an intense reconnaissance effort up to 60 kilometres behind the line, with Rudenko's airmen alone flying 2,600 sorties to photograph the axis of advance eight times. The 'Ilyusha' formations would initially support the infantry breakthrough, then the tank armies, for whom airfields would be a major objective. 'Ilyusha' and army units were paired and coordinated plans, while there were now plenty of short-wave radios for close air–ground cooperation. Rudenko, who was seriously ill with malaria, centralised fighter control using his 3rd and 13th IAKs, each with two or three radars to monitor the situation so he could respond in the most effective way. Rudenko requested 18,500 tonnes of ammunition and 19,000 tonnes of fuel, but at the start of the offensive he had only 16,600 and 15,300 tonnes, respectively. The fleet of 420 petrol bowsers (capacity 920 tonnes) was divided into convoys of 15–20 vehicles, with a small reserve to bring up additional supplies.

The Russians had overwhelming superiority, with the three air armies having 6,698 combat aircraft augmented by 297 Polish, while 800 of Golovanov's bombers supported Rudenko (See Table V-5) and a network of radars was established along the front to assist command and control. On 12 April Fiebig's *Fliegerkorps* II became *Luftwaffenkommando Nordost* to shield *Heeresgruppe Weichsel*'s defence of Berlin. Fiebig retained *Fliegerdivisionen* 1 and 4, which had 1,355 aircraft including 622 fighters and 451 *Schlachtflieger*. He would be joined on 15 April by a suicide attack unit, *Sondergruppe A* with 100 aircraft, *Jagddivision* 1 with some 300 fighters including Me 262s and, from 21 April, the slender reed of Klintzsch's *Flfü* 6 with 68 seaplanes. To the south lay Seidemann and Falkenstein with 791 aircraft, including 206 fighters and 339 *Schlachtflieger*.

TABLE V-5: VVS FOR THE BERLIN OFFENSIVE, APRIL 16, 1945

Air Army	Commander	Front	Strength
4	Vershinin	2 Belorussian	1,360
16	Rudenko	1 Belorussian	3,188
2	Krasovskii	1 Ukrainian	2,150

The offensive began on 16 April, but the direct attack proved a bloody shambles and made little progress, despite Rudenko's support in which 109 aircraft hit headquarters and communications targets 30 minutes before the main air and artillery preparation. The latter concentrated upon the forward lines for 20 minutes then moved to the rear as Russian infantry attacked, while 743 of Golovanov's bombers struck rear defences with 924 tonnes of bombs for 42 minutes. Fog hindered operations, and although this lifted from noon, battlefield smoke hindered visibility and forced 'Ilyusha' crews to operate in small groups.

To the south 208 of Krasovskii's bombers hit defences while 27 of his best crews, in three groups, struck enemy command posts, bringing his day's bomber total to 668 sorties. Strong resistance meant large 'Ilyusha' formations were used against counter-attacks and batteries. The first day saw Greim fly 453 sorties, including 220 *Schlacht*, which expended 74 tonnes of bombs, and 408 *Panzerblitz*, but lost 19 aircraft. By contrast Rudenko's crews alone flew 5,342 combat sorties – their greatest daily total of the war – and dropped 1,500 tonnes of bombs.

On Krasovskii's front the defence collapsed and the advance began to envelop Berlin from the south, pushing 4 *Panzerarmee* and 9 *Armee* towards Czechoslovakia. *Schlachtflieger* sent against these spearheads encountered a strong fighter screen and had little success, while Russian fighters were even used to strafe the roads as Golovanov's bombers pummelled communications. Rudenko supported new efforts to break out and on 18 April lost ten bombers and 11 'Ilyushas', but radar-supported fighters held back the enemy strike forces. On the night of 19/20 April a breakthrough was achieved east of Berlin, which now faced envelopment from the north. This threat was heralded on the night of 20/21 April when 529 of Golovanov's and 184 of Rudenko's Po-2s bombed Berlin, Golovanov following up on two nights (24–26 April) with a further 674 sorties. From the morning of 20 April – Hitler's 56th birthday – Russian shells had begun to fall in the centre of Berlin.

The Russian advance destroyed the remaining Luftwaffe infrastructure as aerial battles took place in poor visibility while the *Schlachtflieger* fought valiantly, but vainly, to stem the tidal wave at heavy cost – 19 *Ritterkreuz*-holders fell in April. On the Russian right Vershinin's airmen supported the crossing of the Oder on 20 April, although thick mist forced 'Ilyushas' to fly singly or in unescorted pairs. The Germans were now almost fighting back-to-back because the Anglo-American forces were advancing eastwards as Eighth Air Force bombers struck communications links to dash any hope of switching troops to the Russian front. American fighter-bombers destroyed ten *Schlacht-* and *Fernaufklärer* aircraft at Klentschang on 16 April, and the next day Mustang escorts caught III./SG 77 at Kamenz, north of Dresden, as it prepared to take off to strike the Red Army – 15 *Jabos* were destroyed or severely damaged on the ground.

The assault into Berlin began on the morning of 21 April from the north and east, but deteriorating visibility forced air commanders to reduce 'Ilyusha' sorties to one or two aircraft carefully picking their targets. On 22 April Jüterbog airfield in the southern suburbs was taken with 3,000 bombs, which were soon turned against their former owners. With two air armies operating over a relatively small air space, fears of confusion led to General-maior Aleksandr Senatorov (Rudenko's deputy commander and former commander of the Far Eastern 9th VA) and General-maior Boris Tokarev (6th ShAK commander) establishing command posts in eastern and northern Berlin, respectively. They were fed information from air observer posts established on every surviving rooftop and, like traffic police, controlled all air traffic to deliver precision attacks in a city where low cloud and dense battle smoke obscured visibility.

At this point Göring was relieved and replaced by Greim in farcical circumstances. With Hitler isolated in Berlin, on 23 April Göring, his official successor, sought sanction to assume the leadership, but a furious

Hitler responded by ordering his arrest. Greim was summoned to Berlin to kiss hands, flown into the beleaguered city by his mistress aviatrix Hanna Reitsch and was injured in the right foot by ground fire. After he met Hitler, Reitsch flew him out and Dessloch assumed command of *Luftflotte* 6, but Greim did not reach OKL until 8 May, so Koller was the de facto Luftwaffe commander.

The only Luftwaffe combat presence in Berlin was a fighter detachment at Tempelhof, but the Russians had air dominance. Indeed, of 328 tanks lost by 1st Ukrainian Front during the Battle for Berlin, only 27 were due to air attack as *Schlachtgruppen* increasingly flew at night. The Russians fought their way through the suburbs, and on 25 April Rudenko flew 1,368 sorties, systematically destroying strongpoints, command centres and reserves in Berlin and helping to take Tempelhof. That afternoon the Russian and American armies linked up and the following day the Red Army reached Berlin city centre, which Golovanov had earlier bombed.

Since mid-March there had been ambitious plans for 250 transport sorties a day to bring 500 tonnes of supplies into Berlin, but by mid-April there was simply not enough fuel. Furthermore, by 26 April Morzik's Armed Forces Air Transport Commander with OKL (*Lufttransportchefs der Wehrmacht beim* OKL) was down to 235 transport aircraft, 76 bombers, six helicopters, 29 glider tugs and 19 gliders. The task was assigned to Stumpff, who only had about 115 transports (including Ju 352s), which brought in troops and munitions and evacuated important personnel using roads and parks as runways until these either came under fire or were taken. The Russians monitored the activity by radar but made no serious effort to interfere, probably for fear of friendly fire incidents.

The Luftwaffe also organised supply drops, although dust, smoke and fog made it difficult to find the drop zones and the vulnerability of Ju 52/3ms to ground fire meant Bf 109s and Fw 190s were used to dump supply containers into the burning ruins from 26 April to 1 May. The transport missions involved some 200 sorties and continued until the night of 30 April/1 May at the cost of up to 30 aircraft.

On 27 April, as the last *Mistel* attack was flown against the Oder bridges, smoke and low cloud over Berlin meant only experienced strike crews were sent for pin-point attacks, while Rudenko's sorties were cut from 1,244 to 809 during 26–27 April. On 28 April, Russian fighters moved into Berlin's airfields and on May Day Rudenko's fighters recorded their last claims of the war. Berlin surrendered the next day following Hitler's suicide, with the four air armies having flown more than 92,000 sorties between 14 April and 5 May, 37,565 by Rudenko, 25,490 by Krasovskii, 26,335 by Vershinin and 3,479 by Golovanov, at a cost of 917 aircraft. There was some desultory fighting around Berlin, but from 6 May Rudenko received no combat requests and saw no sign of the Luftwaffe.

To the south Krasovskii struck 4 *Panzerarmee* and 9 *Armee*, who fought their way to the American lines aided by some supply drops. To help the defenders 36 Me 262s were sent aloft on the evening of 27 April and claimed 65 trucks and six 'Ilyushas' destroyed for the loss of three jets. JG 7 lost ten Me 262s to fighters and ground fire between 28 April and 1 May as Dessloch flew only 250 sorties.

With Germany split in two, Feibig directed a few sorties in the north while Dessloch commanded the forces in the south, Seidemann's command having being renamed *Luftwaffenkommando* VIII on 12 April as it was driven into Moravia. Barkhorn's JG 6 received 150 brand-new Fw 190D-9s from a local factory but had enough fuel for patrols by only four fighters, while OKL, which was disbanding units wholesale, did not climb onto the Führer's funeral pyre. From 4 March it transferred to the so-called Bavarian Redoubt, then to the little Austrian village of Thumersbach, where Greim joined just in time to surrender to the Americans.

On 1 May Stalin ordered an advance from the north upon Prague to prevent the enemy turning Moravia into a redoubt. The offensive began on 6 May as the Allies negotiated Germany's unconditional surrender, which came into effect at midnight on 7/8 May, yet fighting continued in the air and on the ground. On 8 May Major Erich Hartmann claimed his 352nd kill, while JG 7's Oberleutnant Friedrich 'Fritz' Stehle, in an

Me 262, shot down a Kobra of either 129th or 152nd GvIAP for the Luftwaffe's last victory in the East. The following day 100th GvIAP's Kapitan Vasilii Pshenichikov, again in a Kobra, shot down an Fw 189 for the last Russian victory, although the last aerial combat appears to have taken place on 10 May, the day before Prague surrendered. The Moravia campaign cost the Russians 80 aircraft, bringing VVS total losses in 1945 to 3,570.

Word of Germany's surrender reached the Russian front as many airmen were resting, and most learned of the news when they heard troops firing into the air in celebration. In 92nd GvIAP's quarters, the regimental commissar, who was probably drunk, walked in stark naked holding his Tokarev, which he fired into the ceiling. In 232nd ShAP a pilot who had fired his pistol was 'debagged' by his comrades. Sergei Dynda of 249th IAD, upon hearing the news, pulled his Tokarev out from under his pillow, fired into the ceiling and went back to sleep to dream like thousands of others about a better tomorrow.

ENDNOTES

CHAPTER 1

1. The building later became the Hotel Sovetskaya.
2. RAF Bomber Command suffered from the same shortcomings as Soviet Long Range Aviation at this time.
3. SB 2-M100 was officially abbreviated to SB and unofficially to SB-2.
4. Russian fighters had the RSI-4, with 20-kilometre range, while bombers had the RSB-2bis and RSB-3bis. I would again like to thank Paul Thompson for this information.
5. For Soviet aviation fuel see the Twelve O'Clock High web forum and the topic 'Soviet aviation fuel – More bang for the buck or the ruble?' from 27 August 2015. Yak-1 and Yak-7 fighters used B-92 and B-93 while Yak-9 had B-95.
6. See Mellinger, Osprey Aircraft of the Aces 56 – *LaGG & Lavochkin Aces of World War 2* (p.9), but former pilots Fedor Archipenko, Benedikt Kardopoltsev and Lev Toropov all refer to it during interviews for the I Remember website.
7. Kravchenko, a double Hero of the Soviet Union, never again held the senior position to which he was entitled by his rank and was killed in February 1943 leading 215th IAD.
8. The DBA's 1st and 3rd AK DD were north of the Pripet Marshes with 568 bombers while 2nd and 4th AK DD and 18th AD DD were south of the marshes with 762.
9. It remains a VVS base to this day, and one of its officers became President Vladimir Putin's personal pilot.
10. The Grosser Stern lay in the British Occupation Zone after World War II, but the Red Army memorial lies halfway between it and the Brandenburg Gate.
11. The sectors covered were *Luftflotte* 2 (1./ObdL), *Luftflotte* 1 (2./ObdL) and *Luftflotte* 4 (3./ObdL).

12. Khazanov and Gorbach, *Aviatsiya v bitve nad Orlovsko-Kurskoi Dugoi: Oboronitelyenyeii Period* (Appendix 9).
13. Smersh was used by Ian Fleming as the chief adversary to James Bond in the first four Bond novels. In the films based on these books it became Spectre.
14. The landing gear spats of the Stuka led Russian troops to call the aircraft the Clog (*Bashmakov*) or *Lapteshnik*, a derivative of *lopati*, the wooden sandals made from lengths of platted lime bark commonly used in the countryside. My thanks to Paul Thompson for this information.
15. Figure based on data on the *Viatory Vtoroi Mirovoi* website and its *Opganieatsinnaya Struktura* VVS-RKKA sub-site. Not included are 11th, 13th, 14th, 15th, 16th, 18th and 22nd GvBAD, which were Long Range units, while the records of 16th GvIAD/1st GvSAD, 2nd GvBAD/2nd GvNBAD/15th GvShAD are combined.
16. The top British ace in Europe was Wg Cdr James 'Johnnie' Johnson with 34 individual and seven shared victories, while the top US ace in the same theatre was Lt Col Francis 'Gabby' Gabreski with 31 individual victories and three on the ground in 166 sorties. The latter was shot down on 20 July 1944 and captured, eventually being freed by Soviet forces. Most air combat in the East took place below 4,500 metres (15,000ft), while in Western Europe and the Mediterranean engagements usually took place above this height.
17. Both sides' strike formations retained triple-aircraft units.
18. When formed on 20 June and 7 July, respectively, they had 885 and 263 fighters.
19. There would be echoes of this incident in May 1987 when German aviator Mathias Rust landed his Cessna near the Kremlin. Russian military historian Gen L. G. Ivashov noted the two incidents were linked by carelessness, a lack of coordination within the PVO and poorly trained personnel. The head of the PVO in 1987 was wartime ace Aleksandr Koldunov, who was quickly replaced. The prestige of the Soviet armed forces had been shattered, however, just as President Mikhail Gorbachov was trying to introduce reforms.
20. They were Josef Kögel to 10 March 1943, Rudolf Wodarg to 8 August 1944, and Walter Kienitz through to the war's end.

CHAPTER 2

1. This ordnance was carried in AB-23 (23 SD 2s) and AB-250 (108 SD 2s or 17 SD 10s).
2. This chapter greatly benefits from Khazanov's recently published and well-researched studies on the air war.

3. There would be 200–300 Taran attacks during the war, with the honour for the first being claimed by both Leitenanti D. V. Kokorev of 124th IAP/ Western District and I. I. Ivanov of 46th IAP/Kiev District. Some Taran strikes were due to fighter pilots misjudging the distance to their target. It was a tactic of last resort when ammunition ran out, and the trick was to survive the impact. See I Remember website interviews with 4th IAP's Viktor Kunitsyn and 196th IAP/14 GvIAP's Vladimir Mukhmediarov.

4. Pogrebov would become a cavalry commander and was missing, presumed killed, in March 1942.

5. The nickname came because they originally wore black overalls.

6. Pokryshev would be an extremely influential tactician.

7. Russian sources state that 1,702 Soviet aircraft were lost in the Baltic states and the Leningrad area between 10 July and 30 September.

8. All data on *Luftflotte* 1 here and in later chapters was kindly supplied by German aviation historian Ulf Balke.

9. The GVF also dropped agents as far west as Warsaw.

10. See website www.allaces.ru/cgi-bin/s2.cgi/sssr/struct/g/telegin.dat

11. This account benefits from Robert Forczyk's book, Campaign 245, *Demyansk 1942–1943: The Frozen Fortress*.

12. 'Pulk', the Russian word for regiment, was Luftwaffe slang for an aerial formation and was used from the first days of *Barbarossa*.

13. Until May 1940 Russian military leaders were described as 'Commanders', abbreviated to Kom, with the nominal level of command, so Kombrig was a Brigade Commander. Most were given the rank of Polkovnik and some became General-maior, but a few officers, such as Vodopyanov, retained their former ranks until 1943 when he became General-maior. His old rank might reflect reserve status.

14. Kuprin would rise to head the NKVD Third Directorate before his aircraft was shot down by fighters over Lake Ladoga in November 1942. He was one of the highest-ranking NKVD officials killed during the war.

15. There appears to be no biography of Zhigarev.

CHAPTER 3

1. In 1942–43 the Luftwaffe used 104 torpedoes and laid 430 mines in the East.

2. See Russian archive-based website avia-hobby.ru/publ/soviaps/soviaps. html and sample entries for 45th, 46th, 50th and 92nd IAPs.

3. Between 2 July and 25 August the Luftwaffe in the East lost 647 aircraft while 536 were damaged. German total losses in the East rose from 350 in

June to 438 and 436 in the next two months and then dropped to 200 and 224 in October and November.

4. The DB–3F was redesignated Il–4 in March 1942.
5. This account of Luftwaffe night attack units is largely based upon documents very generously provided by the distinguished German aviation historian Ulf Balke, to whom I owe a great debt of thanks.
6. His official records show his name as Mahnke but it was actually spelled Mahncke.
7. Robert Forczyk's Raid 30, *Red Christmas* is the best account of these events.
8. Information from 'Paul Antriebes', Axis History website, Soviet Union section 20 February 2015.
9. Plocher, *The German Air Force versus Russia 1942* (p. 97).

CHAPTER 4

1. The term 'Slave Traders' might be appropriate for these recruiters of wingmen or 'slaves'.
2. Gromov was the former 3rd VA commander, and he was transferred on 26 May.
3. The best sources for information on *Zitadelle* and its aftermath are Bergström, Khazanov and Newton.
4. Gruppa Aemorov VVS, *Sovetskie Voenno-Vozdyshnye Sily v Velikoi Otechestvennoi Voine 1941–1945* (pp. 187–200).
5. Murray, *Strategy for Defeat* (p. 249).
6. For details see the Gyges and Luftwaffe websites.
7. The *Gruppe* had 5–10 Do 217Js but it is not clear whether they had Lichtenstein.
8. All claims are based upon Foreman, Matthews and Parry, *Luftwaffe Night Fighter Combat Claims 1939–1945*.

CHAPTER 5

1. The 12 O'Clock High Forum, 'Soviet Air Force Mining in the Baltic during World War II', response by Andrey Kuznetsov, 15 May 2015.
2. Zhdanov's date of appointment is uncertain, with one source claiming it was 2 August, although Khryukin, the previous commander, held it to 2 July, when he transferred to 1st VA. The chief-of-staff, General-maior Vladimir Izotov, former commander of 1st AK DD, was probably acting commander for a month.
3. Some sources say 915 combat aircraft.
4. Erickson, *The Road to Berlin* (p. 355), and Bergström, *Bagration* (p. 83).
5. Conversino, *Fighting with the Soviets* is a valuable source for these raids.

APPENDIX

PRODUCTION

RUSSIAN, GERMAN AND BRITISH AIRCRAFT PRODUCTION 1942 TO 1944

Type	1942			1943			1944		
	USSR	Germany	UK	USSR	Germany	UK	USSR	Germany	UK
BOMBER									
Heavy	22	250	1,956	29	514	4,552	5	591	5,509
Medium	937	4,923	3,483	1,587	4,870	2,798	1,232	1,958	2,396
Light	2,564	-	1,131	2,428	-	751	2,805	-	390
Jet	-	-	-	-	-	-	-	148	-
FIGHTER									
Single-engined	9,918	4,583	7,982	14,612	9,508	7,952	17,895	25,595	7,274
Twin-engined	179	1,091	1,877	13	2,894	2,570	19	5,121	3,238
Jet	-	-	-	-	-	-	-	891*	30

Type	1942			1943			1944		
	USSR	Germany	UK	USSR	Germany	UK	USSR	Germany	UK
ATTACK	8,191	1,508	-	10,773	1,791	-	10,719	1,234	-
NAVAL	11	238	1,287	13	259	1,929	183	8	3,125
TRANSPORT	467	573	40	1,225	1,028	247	1,543	443	1,127
TRAINER	3,537	1,098	4,377	4,870	2,274	4,727	6,735	3,693	2,673
OTHER	-	1,221	225	-	1,523	485	-	647	659
Total	25,826	15,485	22,358	35,550	24,661	26,011	41,136	40,329	26,421

Bombers includes reconnaissance. Fighters includes reconnaissance and fighter bombers. Attack includes Fw 189. Naval includes shipborne aircraft and land-based flying boats.

*Includes rocket-propelled

LIST OF ILLUSTRATIONS

- Many Luftwaffe fighter pilots cut their operational teeth on Tupolev's twin-engined SB-2 and -3 bombers during the opening stages of the air war in the East. Among the hundreds brought down was this example being inspected by army troops on the central sector. (*via John Weal*)

- An impressive line-up of 'Doras' of 3./StG 77. The bareheaded figure on the left of the group is Feldwebel Herbert Rabben, who was considered by many to be one of the best pilots ever to fly with StG 77. He would be awarded the Knight's Cross after the *Geschwader's* incorporation into the *Schlacht* arm. (*via John Weal*)

- Reichsmarschall Hermann Göring and *General der Flieger* Hans Jeschonnek examine a map at ObdL headquarters. Chief-of-staff Jeschonnek was the executive commander of the Luftwaffe, which made him the whipping boy for the lazy Göring, who was always happy to take the plaudits. (*Der Adler*)

- A German bomber strikes an airfield on 22 June 1941, when the Luftwaffe enjoyed its greatest success. Russian records indicate that by 17 July the Soviet Union had lost at least 4,500 aircraft, and it took two years for the VVS to recover. (*Der Adler*)

- A *Nahaufklärungstaffeln* observer makes a last-minute check of his map while a *Schwarzermänner* runs the engine. The backbone of these *Staffeln* in 1941 was the Hs 126, nicknamed 'Crutches' (*Kostii*) by the Russians because of its metal wing braces. (*Der Adler*)

- A Stuka tail gunner photographed the successful cutting of a Russian railway line as the aircraft pulls out of its dive. With few hard-topped roads in the Soviet Union, railways were vital to both sides for large-scale transport, especially during the spring and autumn thaws. (*Der Adler*)

- The bombed rail bridge near Vitebsk in 1941. Bridges were the easiest way across Russia's great rivers, and their destruction could trap armies, as the Germans discovered in Belorussia in 1944. (*Der Adler*)

- In the early days of *Barbarossa* the *Kampfgruppen* pounded Russian installations, including barracks. Here, a Ju 88 circles burning buildings as the crew assess their success. (*Der Adler*)

- The losses suffered during the opening days and weeks of *Barbarossa* were not all

262

one-sided. This A-5 of 8./KG 76 – note the jettisoned cabin canopy in foreground – was lucky to make it back to Schippenbeil for a belly landing after being hit by Soviet anti-aircraft fire. (*via John Weal*)

- Given III./JG 3's somewhat dubious powers of aircraft recognition during the opening stages of *Barbarossa*, it would be interesting to speculate what this victorious pilot – returning to base southwest of Zhitomir, wings waggling to indicate a kill – is going to claim. In fact, on the date this photograph was taken, the *Gruppe* contented itself with a quartet of DB-3 bombers and a dozen assorted Polikarpov fighters. (*via John Weal*)

- The thaws or *rasputitsa* had a devastating effect upon air operations by reducing grass-covered airfields to marshes. Here, an airman walks across duckboards during such a period at a Stuka base. Grass-covered airfields did have one advantage – they could be used whatever the wind direction. (*Der Adler*)

- The Germans quickly learned that once the Russians had established a bridgehead across a river it was extremely difficult to drive them out. Such bridgeheads might be supplied by raft, rubber dinghies or pontoon bridges. Here, a *Panzerjäger* Ju 87G strafes a pontoon footbridge. (*Der Adler*)

- A Stuka flies low over a German tank as smoke and dust from bombed defences rises over a Russian battlefield. Close air support became a major role for the Stukas, and General Wolfram von Richthofen once claimed his Ju 87s were operating within grenade-throwing range of the German infantry. (*Der Adler*)

- The Il-2 ground-attack aircraft, usually called 'Ilyushas', were normally for close air support, striking defensive positions or hunting tanks with their 37mm cannon or PTAB hollow-charge bombs. (*Courtesy of the Central Museum of the Armed Forces, Moscow via Stavka*)

- Low-level attacks took the 'Ilyushas' into intense ground fire and aircraft frequently required patching up like this one. The robust Il-2s were very popular with their crews, despite the very dangerous work they faced daily. (*Courtesy of the Central Museum of the Armed Forces, Moscow via Stavka*)

- Before climbing into their 'Ilyusha', Assault Troopers (*Shturmoviks*) make a last-minute check of the map to determine the exact location of friendly troops and their targets to avoid 'friendly fire' incidents. (*Courtesy of the Central Museum of the Armed Forces, Moscow via Stavka*)

- An Li-2 transport ready to receive passengers at a forward airfield. The Li-2 was not a licence-built DC-3 but rather a Russianised-version with inferior performance to the few C-47s received under Lend–Lease. (*From the files of the RGAKFD in Krasnogorsk via Stavka*)

- Russian aircraft strafe Ju 88s at what appears to be a recently occupied airfield in central or north Russia, since it lacks revetments. Attacks on Luftwaffe airfields were always a gamble because they were strongly defended. (*Courtesy of the Central Museum of the Armed Forces, Moscow via Stavka*)

263

- III./KG 51 joined II. *Gruppe* at Balti at the end of August 1941 fresh from its re-equipment in the Reich. The unit's new A-4s sport the bright yellow trim indicative of a III. *Gruppe*. In KG 51's case this was applied to the front edge of the engine nacelles and as a thin outline to the *Geschwader* badge. It is believed that the spinner colours identified the *Staffel* within the *Gruppe*. (*via John Weal*)

- A pair of *Friedrichs* from III./JG 51 pictured on the central sector in the autumn of 1941. (*via John Weal*)

- 'Black men' (*Schwarzemänner*) push a Ju 52/3m free from the ice and snow so it can take off. The Russian winter proved a severe challenge for the Luftwaffe, especially in 1941–42 when engines froze and tools broke. (*Der Adler*)

- Hero of the Soviet Union Snr Lt A A Lipilin of 41st IAP. By October 1941 he had flown 112 sorties and claimed eight and three shared victories, as well as numerous targets destroyed on the ground. Flying on the northwest front, Lipilin survived the war. (*Dmitriy Khazanov and Andrey Yurgenson*)

- MiG-3 pilot Jr Lt Verkhovtsev of 72nd SAP, Northern Fleet Air Force. (*Dmitriy Khazanov and Andrey Yurgenson*)

- Inverted and in flames, an Il-2 falls to earth. The original one-man 'Ilyushas' were nicknamed 'Hunchbacks' (*Gorbatii*), but the need for a rear-gunner soon became obvious. Regiments originally modified their aircraft in the field until the Il-2m3s began to roll off the production lines. (*Nik Cornish at www.Stavka.org.uk*)

- A group of MiG-3s from 7th IAK fly in loose formation over central Leningrad. The high tower of the famous Peter and Paul Cathedral on the north bank of the Neva River can be seen below the fighters. (*Dmitriy Khazanov and Andrey Yurgenson*)

- This 9th IAP MiG-3 hit trees while making a forced-landing following engine failure shortly after take-off. (*Dmitriy Khazanov and Andrey Yurgenson*)

- Pilots of 124th IAP, which was involved in the defence of Moscow during the second half of 1941. These men are, from left to right, Dmitriy Zanin, Aleksander Pronin, Nikolay Tsisarenko and Grigoriy Ivanchenko. (*Dmitriy Khazanov and Andrey Yurgenson*)

- Aircraft production chief Generaloberst Ernst Udet (left) and his fighter chief Major Werner 'Vatti' (Daddy) Mölders. The latter was summoned to Udet's funeral following his suicide on 17 November 1941, but perished in a flying accident en route. (*Der Adler*)

- The Bf 110 *Zerstörer* (long range fighter) was increasingly used, like this ZG 1 aircraft in the winter of 1941–42, as a long range fighter-bomber. By late 1943 even this role was becoming impossible. (*Der Adler*)

- A nurse supervises the loading of a stretcher into an S-2, the medical evacuation version of the U-2/Po-2. The ADD and GVF used Li-2s to take the wounded for long-term treatment in the interior. (*Courtesy of the Central Museum of the Armed Forces, Moscow via Stavka*)

- The first winter of the war in Russia took a heavy toll on men and machines alike. Here, a seemingly endless line of railway flatbed wagons has been loaded with damaged Ju 88s for transportation to the rear for major repair work. (*via John Weal*)

- During the winter of 1941–42 personnel manning the myriad aircraft workshops immediately behind the front line laboured around the clock to expeditiously repair and overhaul MiG fighters. (*Dmitriy Khazanov and Andrey Yurgenson*)

- Stalingrad 1941–42. Troops unload supplies flown in to Pitomnik by Ju 52/3ms of *Blindflugschule* (Blind Flying School) 2. The transport crews made superhuman efforts to keep the beleaguered *6. Armee* supplied by air. (*via John Weal*)

- Commander first of *Luftflotte* 4 then *Luftflotte* 3 and finally *Luftflotte* 6, Generaloberst Otto Dessloch was a Bavarian 'Old Eagle' who commanded bomber units during the 1930s then switched to flak regiments in October 1939. His return from the 'dark side' began early in 1942. (*Der Adler*)

- Aleksandr Evgenevich Golovanov rose from Polkovnik to Marshal during the war as head of Soviet Long Range Aviation (ADD) then 18th VA. A civilian pilot, he had suffered under the Purges but was lucky to get a second chance, partly because he had once been a member of the Secret Police. (*Der Adler*)

- A stick of bombs from an aircraft of III./KG 51 goes down on Tuapse harbour, narrowly missing a row of eight Soviet submarines. This photograph is believed to have been taken during the raid of 23 March 1942, which resulted in the sinking of the 2121-ton auxiliary minelayer *Nikolai Ostrovsky*, the tug *Veshilov*, a small survey vessel (the GS.13) and an unidentified cutter. Two submarines, the *D 5* and the *S 33*, were also damaged. (*via John Weal*)

- A Ju 87B-1 of 6./StG 77 taxis out at a Ukrainian airfield in the summer of 1941. It was piloted by the *Staffelkapitän* Hauptmann Herbert Pabst, who, on 1 September 1941, became *Staffelkapitän* of the *Ergänzungsstaffel*. He then specialised in training, becoming *Kommandeur* of two training *Gruppen*. (*EN-Archive*)

- A Ju 88A-4 of 9./KG 51 prowls over the southern section of the Eastern Front. The Ju 88 and He 111 were the prime Luftwaffe bombers in the East, and this *Staffel* was part of Generalleutnant Curt Pflugbeil's *Fliegerkorps* IV from September 1941 to May 1942. In October 1944 it became a *Nachtschlachtstaffel*. (*EN-Archive*)

- This attempt to camouflage a Bf 109G to conceal it from Russian attacks merely made it look like a collection of Christmas trees were draped around the fighter. (*Der Adler*)

- Drums of fuel are delivered to an airfield by truck, rolled off the back and then rolled to the *Tante Ju* on the left. Fuel production and supply were the key to success during World War II. (*Der Adler*)

- For Generalfeldmarschall Albert Kesselring the glass was always half full, hence his nickname of 'Smiling Albert'. Unlike the other *Luftflotten* and *Fliegerkorps* commanders, the Bavarian Kesselring was no 'Old Eagle', having never been an airman in the Great War. (*Der Adler*)

- As Russian fighter and anti-aircraft defences grew stronger good preparation was vital to the planning of Stuka operations. Here, the commander gives his men a last-minute briefing. (*Der Adler*)

- Twin-engined He 111s and Ju 88s were the backbone of the Eastern Front *Kampfgruppen*, and this photograph shows a Heinkel at rest. Its wide fuselage made the aeroplane easy to load with supplies, which is why He 111s were increasingly used more as transports than bombers as the war went on. (*Der Adler*)

- A line of Bf 109Fs from II./JG 54 prepares for a patrol during the winter of 1941–42. This photograph illustrates why groundcrews were called 'black men' (*Schwarzermänner*) – the one in the foreground apparently has a fire extinguisher in case of emergencies. (*EN-Archive*)

- A He 111H-16 of 8./KG 53 comes in to land after a mission in the summer of 1942. This *Gruppe* was part of *Luftwaffenkommando Ost*, which conducted some strategic bombing at about this time and later became part of the strategic bombing force, *Fliegerkorps* IV. (*EN-Archive*)

- Two Fw 190A-5s of I./JG 54 in flight over the Soviet Union wearing the *Geschwader* 'Grünherz' (green heart) emblem below their cockpits and the *Gruppen* emblem on the nose. I./JG 54 began to replace its Bf 109Gs with the Fw 190, known to the Russians as the 'Fokker', from November 1942. (*EN-Archive*)

- A Bf 110E of the *Gruppenstab* of I./StG 1, showing yellow lower wingtips and a yellow fuselage band around the fuselage, taxies out in the snow during the winter of 1942–43. With the reorganisation of Luftwaffe ground-attack units in October 1943 I./StG 1 became I./SG 1 and disposed of its Bf 110s. (*EN-Archive*)

- While petrol bowsers were the fastest means of refuelling aircraft, they were in short supply in the East. Instead, as with this Ju 88, the 'black men' had to use hand-pumps to transfer fuel from drums to the aircraft's petrol tanks – a clumsy and time-consuming process. (*Der Adler*)

- Airfield installations are blown up just before the Luftwaffe abandons them. Where possible, most of the runways would be ploughed up, allowing aircraft to operate from them until the final demolitions. The site would also be seeded with mines. (*Der Adler*)

- A bomb-aimer's view from a diving Ju 88. Dive-bombing was a Luftwaffe obsession, and it was demanded for the four-engined He 177. (*Der Adler*)

- *General der Flieger* Martin Fiebig was a bomber group commander in World War I and distinguished himself with close air support commands until he was promoted to succeed Richthofen as commander of *Fliegerkorps* VIII. He ended the war commanding *Luftwaffekommando Nordost*, which evolved from *Fliegerkorps* II. (*Der Adler*)

- German bombers had many advantages over their Russian enemies, including armour and self-sealing fuel tanks. But their armament was much weaker, the Luftwaffe tending to rely upon the 7.9mm MG 15, such this one manned in the nose of a He 111. (*Der Adler*)

- A formation of He 111s pass over a Russian river which the bomb aimer is observing. The Heinkels were used for long range bombing because they had a superior radius of action when compared with the Ju 88 – 1,900 kilometres to 1,700 kilometres. (*Der Adler*)

- A Bf 109G-6 of III./JG 54 receives a major service in a rural area on the northern Russian Front in the spring of 1943. In March of that year the *Gruppe*, under Hauptmann Reinhard Seiler, was one of the first transferred to the West. (*EN-Archive*)

- Three Fw 190A-4s of 5./JG 54 bask in spring sunshine at Siverskaya in the late spring of 1943. Recently freed of their winter scheme white, many II. *Gruppe* aircraft were given a distinctive new camouflage scheme combining what has been described as tan, or brown, with two shades of green. Note that both *Geschwader* and *Gruppe* badges are still being worn, and also black *Staffel* numbers. 'Black 5' was the mount of Austrian Oberleutnant Max Stotz, who was promoted to *Staffelkapitän* of 5./JG 54 later that same summer, only to be reported missing in action near Vitebsk on 19 August 1943. All bar 16 of his 189 kills were gained with II. *Gruppe*. (*Eddie Nielinger*)

- Bf 109G-6 'White 10' of 1./JG 52 at Kharkov-Rogan during *Unternehmen Zitadelle* in the summer of 1943. The acting *Gruppenkommandeur* at this time was Hauptmann Johannes Wiese, a *Ritterkreuz*-holder who ended the war as *Kommodore* of JG 77. (*EN-Archive*)

- 'Black men' gingerly install a bomb into the cradle of a Stuka. Bomb handling was not without its dangers, and the electric fuses of some German bombs were notoriously unreliable. A number of bombers were seen to explode without warning. (*Der Adler*)

- A 'black man' completes work on the middle engine of a IV./TG 3 Ju 52/3m. The *Tante Ju* was an extremely robust transport aircraft that could take a variety of loads, and while plans existed to replace it they never succeeded. (*Der Adler*)

- Burning vehicles after a Luftwaffe bombing raid. Air power destroyed relatively few tanks throughout the four-year conflict in the East, but the loss of 'soft-skinned' vehicles could be even more devastating, depriving armies of much-needed supplies. (*Der Adler*)

- An eclectic collection of aircraft abandoned near Stalingrad. In the foreground is a He 111 of KG 53 beside a He 111F communications aircraft that had been pressed into transport duties. Behind it are a Bf 109 and a Hs 123. (*Der Adler*)

- A remarkable photograph taken from underneath a diving Ju 87 after the bomb cradle has released the bomb. The Stuka would normally carry a 500kg or 250kg bomb, but the Ju 87D could carry a 1,800kg bomb for specialised, short-range operations. (*Der Adler*)

- Russian troops stroll past a downed Fw 189 tactical reconnaissance aircraft that

267

they especially loathed because they were associated with artillery retribution. Their twin-boom configuration led the Russians to call them 'Frames' (*Rama*), as in window frames. (*Der Adler*)

- Wolfram von Richthofen, shown here as a *General der Flieger*, spearheaded the Third Reich's offensives and was closely associated with both army support operations and the Ju 87. He was also a notorious armchair general, and could be thoughtless to his subordinates, leading one JG 77 pilot to dub him 'a real dickhead' (*ein gewaltiger Knallkopf*). (*EN-Archive*)

- Oberst Hans-Ulrich Rudel flew 2,530 sorties in the East – probably more than anyone else on either side. On seven occasions he landed to rescue downed comrades, yet his love of keep-fit did not endear him to subordinates who said of his teetotal habit, '*Oberst Rudel trinkt nur Studel*' (Colonel Rudel drinks only soda water). (*EN-Archive*)

- A 'black man' scuttles out of the way as a '*Y-Gerät*'-equipped aircraft of 4./KG 53 runs up its engines prior to take-off. That single 50kg bomb seems somewhat lost under the broad expanse of the machine's port wing. (*via John Weal*)

- The groundcrews had it the hardest of all. These 'black men' of KG 55 at least have the benefit of a warm-air blower to make working on that port engine a little easier. (*via John Weal*)

- A He 111 launches the first of two practice torpedoes. In combat it would be suicidal for the machine to remain at this height for long. (*via John Weal*)

- A *Staffel* of *Luftflotte* 6 StG 1 Ju 87Ds heads eastwards protected by a Bf 109 escort. The Russians called the latter 'Messers' and the Stukas either 'Clog' (*Bashmakov*) or *Lapteshnik*, a derivative of *lopati*, the wooden sandals made from lengths of platted lime bark commonly used in the countryside. (*Der Adler*)

- The small fires quickly taking hold in the tinder-dry fields and scrubland below suggest that this attack is being carried out either with antipersonnel bombs or clusters of incendiaries. (*via John Weal*)

- Bridges would feature high on the Stukas' list of targets throughout the war on the Eastern Front. Having demolished the road bridge in the background, this unit – note the Ju 87 pulling up and away at top right – was recalled several days later to destroy the pontoon bridge the Soviets had constructed to replace it. (*via John Weal*)

- With bombs already detonating off to the left, these two Stukas of II./StG 77 (bottom right) are intent on another target. The two black dots immediately above them are Soviet armoured vehicles that have left the convoy on the road in the centre of the picture and are seeking the 'safety' of open fields – according to an accompanying report, neither made it. (*via John Weal*)

- Almost symbolic in its simplicity, a classic shot of a winter-dappled 'Dora' of StG 2 setting out on yet another mission to try to stop the tide of Soviet armour from flooding westwards across that flat, frozen, landscape far below.

(*via John Weal*)

- A *Gruppe* of Ju 88s en route to their target in tight formation was an impressive sight. (*via John Weal*)

- A *Staffel* of KG 51 machines in tight formation low over the rolling landscape of the central Crimea. (*via John Weal*)

- The commander (right) of a Pe-2 reconnaissance aircraft briefs his crew in preparation for a combat sortie. This machine has already seen some action – note the repair patch on the fuselage over the star insignia. (*Dmitriy Khazanov and Aleksander Medved*)

- Although a number of other types (including a single Go 242 transport glider) are also in evidence, there are at least 15 He 111s visible on this busy forward landing ground reportedly pictured early in 1942. The gradual resurgence of Soviet air power would later make such gatherings highly inadvisable – not to say downright dangerous. (*via John Weal*)

- Pilots of 7th GShAP pose in front of the aircraft flown by their squadron leader, Maj N A Zub (seen here closest to the camera), on the Southern Front in March 1942. The titling on the Il-2's fuselage reads *Smert Fashistskim Okkupantam* ('Death to Fascist Invaders'). (*Oleg Rastrenin and Andrey Yurgenson*)

- Pavel Fedorovich Zhigarev was the forgotten man of Soviet wartime air power. He was brought in immediately before the German invasion and the arrest of all three of his predecessors and held the VVS together. He was sent to Siberia in April 1942 in a dispute over aircraft deliveries, being given command of an air army in the Far East. (*Der Adler*)

- Aleksandr Aleksandrovich Novikov would lead the VVS with distinction from April 1942, but the strain made him an alcoholic. After the war he and Aviation Industry Minister Andrei Shakhurin were jailed for ignoring defects in Soviet aircraft production following accusations by Stalin and aircraft designer Yakovlev. (*Der Adler*)

- A line-up of 8th GvBAP personnel during the regiment's investiture with the Guards Banner in March 1942. The unit was commanded by Lt Col F P Kotlyar from October 1938 to February 1942, when he was replaced by Maj G S Kucherkov, who accepted the banner at the investiture. (*Dmitriy Khazanov and Aleksander Medved*)

- A shot that illustrates the Luftwaffe's continuing supremacy 12 months into the air war on the Russian Front – the tail of an Il-2 shot down by future semi-centurion Oberfeldwebel Otto Wessling of 9./JG 3 on 11 June 1942. (*via John Weal*)

- Cap askew, personal victory stick well in evidence, Feldwebel Rudolf Müller is congratulated on achieving II./JG 5's 500th collective kill. This photograph was taken at Petsamo in June 1942. (*via John Weal*)

- Standing by the tailplane of his 'Yellow 10' at Petsamo on 30 June 1942, just four months into his operational career, Unteroffizier Hans Döbrich of II./JG 5 seems to be wondering how many more kills – over and above the 18 already booked on the rudder of the Bf 109F seen here – will be required to finish carving his still more than half-empty victory stick. (*via John Weal*)

- Aircraft of the *Gruppenstab* StG 2 in the summer of 1942. The nearest machine's fuselage code, 'T6+BC', and the numeral '2' on the wheelspat, points to it being the mount of either the unit's adjutant or operations officer. The likeliest candidate for pilot of both machines is Leutnant Günther Schmid, who is known to have served as Hauptmann Dr Kupfer's *Gruppenadjutant* before taking over as *Staffelkapitän* of 5./StG 2 in late 1942. (*via John Weal*)

- The commander of the pre-war Austrian Air Force, Generaloberst Alexander Löhr changed sides during the Anschluss of 1938 and was given *Luftflotte* 4, which he led until the summer of 1942 when he became a military commander in the Balkans. (*Der Adler*)

- Summer 1942 in the Crimea, and the pilot of 8./KG 51's '9K+GS' runs up his engines and starts to roll. In this excellent close-up shot of the business end of a Ju 88, the additional 20mm MG FF cannon (painted white) projecting from the ventral gondola is clearly visible. (*via John Weal*)

- During the summer of 1942 pilots and groundcrews of attack aircraft regiments converted single-seat Il-2s into two-seat aircraft and armed them with 12.7mm UBT or 7.62mm ShKAS machine guns for rear defence against German fighters. About 1,200 single-seaters were modified in such a way. In this photograph, Il-2 air gunner Sgt Baklar Saakyan is strapped in behind a makeshift ShKAS defensive machine gun mounting, which appears to have come from a Tupolev SB-2 medium bomber. (*Oleg Rastrenin and Andrey Yurgenson*)

- Novikov's recognition of the abilities of Fedor Iakovlevich Falaleev saved him when the latter was made the scapegoat for VVS failures during the Kharkov Offensive in 1942. He became VVS Deputy Commander-in-Chief and Chief-of-Staff and was appointed Marshal in August 1944. (*Der Adler*)

- A celebration of 5./KG 3's Oberfeldwebel Friedrich Kralemann's 200th mission. Kralemann (centre) flew his 260th, and last, mission on 10 September 1942 when, despite severe injuries that were to cost him his left eye, he managed to bring his crippled machine (minus cabin roof canopy and ventral gondola) back to base. Over a year later, on 29 October 1943, Kralemann was awarded the Knight's Cross, before finally succumbing to his wounds on 1 December 1943. (*via John Weal*)

- Clutching a bunch of flowers, Major Dr Ernst Kupfer, *Gruppenkommandeur* of II./StG 2, shares his cockpit with a lucky piglet upon returning to Oblivskaya after completing his 400th operational mission in August 1942. Visible in the background, right, is one of the unit's Gotha Go 242 transport gliders. (*via John Weal*)

- Pilots run to La-5 fighters, which made their debut in the autumn of 1942.

Although initially proving inferior to the enemy, the Lavochkin – particularly in La-5FN and La-7 forms – later became highly regarded. (*Courtesy of the Central Museum of the Armed Forces, Moscow via Stavka*)

- Maintaining one of the two 37mm Flak 18s under a Ju 87G anti-tank aircraft similar to that in which Rudel was credited with 519 victories. The value of heavy cannon against tanks was demonstrated by the Hs 129, although some sceptical pilots removed them in 1942. (*Der Adler*)

- A petrol bowser is used during the refuelling of a VVS Boston. The Douglas 'bombing twin' equipped VVS-Frontal Aviation bomber regiments and ADD intruder regiments, and with the Mitchell made up almost half the medium bombers received by the Soviet Union between 1942 and 1944. (*EN Archive*)

- A smashed He 111 transport at Stalingrad is surrounded by the bodies of its crew and probably those who wished to be passengers. The loss of Ju 52/3ms in the Stalingrad airlift disrupted Luftwaffe training because many aircraft, instructors and advanced students were lost. (*Der Adler*)

- Richthofen benefited from having access to a purpose-built command train, which played a key part in supporting Manstein's counter-offensive in March 1943. Communications security was maintained by plugging the train into landlines or using couriers in Storchs like the one seen here flying overhead. (*Der Adler*)

- Major Reinhard Seiler, *Gruppenkommandeur* of III./JG 54 (a post he held from October 1941 until mid-April 1943), is greeted by his dog soon after returning from a mission. Assuming command of I. *Gruppe* in the spring of 1943, Seiler was severely wounded on the second day of Operation *Zitadelle*. Retired from operations, he ended the war as *Kommodore* of training *Geschwader* JG 104. (*via John Weal*)

- German bombs strike a Russian railway marshalling yard, but this picture could easily show the reverse. When *Fliegerkorps* IV staged the 'strategic' *Unternehmen Zaunkönig* most of its targets were actually marshalling yards and railway junctions. (*Der Adler*)

- The bomb aimer/front gunner of a He 111 waits as the pilot runs up the engines before take-off. Bomber missions in the East grew shorter and shorter, and by 1943 could last as little as ten minutes. (*Der Adler*)

- Three types of bombs are seen under the wing of this Pe-2 of 261st SBAP during the summer of 1943. The armourer to the right is resting his foot on a captured German SC 250, while the nearest bomb is a FAB-100 with a welded body. Behind it are FAB-100s with cast-iron bodies. (*Dmitriy Khazanov and Aleksander Medved*)

- A group of Il-2s have their engines run up prior to flying yet another combat sortie in the Kursk sector in the summer of 1943. (*Oleg Rastrenin and Andrey*

Yurgenson)

- One of the ten Heinkel *Kampfgruppen* taking part in *Zitadelle* was III./KG 55. This photograph, taken in the summer of 1943, shows Hauptmann Oskar Dettke (the *Kapitän* of 9. *Staffel*) upon the completion of his 300th combat mission. Note the *Staffel*'s 'Snorting bull' emblem above the celebratory garland on the machine's tail. (*via John Weal*)

- A petrol bowser has drawn up to refuel a Ju 87D of Oberstleutnant Gustav Pressler's 7./StG 1. The spats, which are synonymous with the Ju 87, have been removed because they could sometimes collect mud and cause take-off or landing accidents. (*Der Adler*)

- Although transformed from *Stukageschwader* into *Schlachtgeschwader* in October 1943, it was still business as usual for most Ju 87 units for many months to come. The first light dusting of winter snow has already fallen as this unidentified Ju 87D-5 prepares for take-off with a full weapon load. Note the hefty *Dinortstab* on the 250kg (550lb) underwing bomb. (*via John Weal*)

- A formation of Pe-2 'Peshka' (Pike) long range dive-bombers. The aeroplane's short range meant that by 1944 bomber divisions equipped with the Pe-2 usually had a Boston regiment attached to extend their reach. (*Courtesy of the Central Museum of the Armed Forces, Moscow via Stavka*)

- A squadron of Yak-9D fighters of 6th GvIAP-ChF escorts naval Bostons of 36th MTAP-ChF during an operation in the summer of 1944. The Yakovlev fighters were among the most successful in Soviet aviation history, although they were not without faults. (*Courtesy of the Central Museum of the Armed Forces, Moscow via Stavka*)

- A Pe-2 of the second squadron, 12th GvBAP, in winter camouflage. This is a late-series bomber with the antennae mast relocated to the windscreen frame and individual engine exhaust stubs. Note that this aircraft has its tactical number painted on the fuselage, which was a feature unique to naval regiments. VVS RKKA Pe-2 units usually applied this number to the vertical tails of their aircraft. (*Dmitriy Khazanov and Aleksander Medved*)

- The only Heinkel bombers remaining in the East during the winter of 1944–45 were those of KG 4. These late war He 111H-20s, which were fitted with a turret in place of the earlier variants' dorsal gun positions, are believed to be aircraft of II./KG 4, with the *Gruppenstab*'s 'DC' in the foreground. (*via John Weal*)

- In the harsh conditions of the Soviet north, reindeers were used to transport bombs to Pe-2s of 114th GvBAP. This regiment became famous through its participation in countless combat operations against German and Finnish forces in this theatre, and it ended the war with the title of Kirkenes Red-Banner and Kutuzov Order regiment, commanded by Maj A N Volodin. (*Dmitriy Khazanov and Aleksander Medved*)

- Maior Grigoriy Rechkalov and his P-39Q Airacobra of 16th GvIAP. Rechkalov was very much an individualist in a collective society, and he had 56 individual and six shared victories, most in the aircraft the Russians called the Kobra. (*EN Archive*)

- *General der Flieger* Karl Koller was the Luftwaffe's last chief-of-staff and final de facto commander. He had earlier worked with *General der Flieger* Günther Korten to develop *Fliegerkorps* IV into a strategic bombing force. (*Der Adler*)

- Generalfeldmarschall Robert Ritter von Greim, was the last Commander-in-Chief of the Luftwaffe. He was flown into besieged Berlin by his mistress to receive the appointment personally from Hitler. For most of his time in the East he commanded *Luftflotte* 6. (*Der Adler*)

- The Luftwaffe's largest transport was the Me 323 Gigant, an example of which is seen here ready to evacuate a load of wounded men with its forward clamshell doors open. It could carry loads of 20 tonnes (including 120 troops or 60 casualty stretchers), compared with 2–2.5 tonnes in the Ju 52/3m. (*Der Adler*)

BIBLIOGRAPHY

BOOKS

Anushchenkov, P. S. and Shurunov, V. E. *Tretyeya Vozdushnaya* (Third Air Army). Voenizdat, Moscow, 1984

Bergström, Christer, *Bagration to Berlin – The Final Air Battles in the East: 1944–1945*. Ian Allan Publishing, Hersham, 2008

Bergström, Christer, *Barbarossa – The Air Battle: July–December 1941*. Ian Allan Publishing, Hersham, 2007

Bergström, Christer, *Kursk – The Air Battle: July 1943*. Ian Allan Publishing, Hersham, 2007

Bergström, Christer, *Stalingrad – The Air Battle: 1942 through January 1943*. Ian Allan Publishing, Hersham, 2007

Bochkarev, P. P. and N. I. Parygin, *Gody v Ognennom Nebe: Aviatsiya Dalyeiego Deistviya v Velikoii Otechestvennoii 1941–1945 gg* (Years in the Fiery Sky: Long Range Aviation in the Great Patriotic War of 1941–1945). Voenizdat, Moscow, 1991

Brookes, Andrew, *Air War Over Russia*. Ian Allan Publishing, Hersham, 2003

Conversino, Mark J., *Fighting with the Soviets: The Failure of Operation Frantic 1944–1945*. University Press of Kansas, Lawrence, KS, 1997

Corum, James S. *Wolfram von Richthofen: Master of the German Air War*. University Press of Kansas, Lawrence, KS, 2008

Davtyan, S., *Pyataya Vozdushnaya* (Fifth Air Army). Voenizdat, Moscow, 1990

Dvoryanskii, E. and A. V. Yaroshenko, *V Ognennom Kolyetse* (In the Ring of Fire). Eesti Raamat, Tallin, 1977

Erickson, John, *The Road to Stalingrad: Stalin's War with Germany Volume 1*. Weidenfeld & Nicolson, London, 1983

Erickson, John, *The Road to Berlin: Stalin's War with Germany Volume 2*. Weidenfeld & Nicolson, London, 1983

Fedorov, A. G., *Aviatsiya v Bitve pod Moskva* (Aviation in the Battle for Moscow). Nauka, Moscow, 1975

Forczyk, Robert, Campaign 245, *Demyansk 1942–1943: The Frozen Fortress*. Osprey Publishing, Oxford, 2012

Forczyk, Robert, Raid 30, *Red Christmas: The Tatsinskaya Airfield Raid 1942*. Osprey Publishing, Oxford, 2012

Foreman, John, Johannes Matthews and Simon Parry, *Luftwaffe Night Fighter Combat Claims 1939–1945*. Red Kite, Walton-on-Thames, 2004

Frieser, Karl-Heinz (ed.), *Das Deutsche Reich und der Zweite Weltkrieg Band 4: Der Angriff auf der Sowjetunion*. Deutsches Verlag Anstalt, Stuttgart, 1983

Frieser, Karl-Heinz (ed.), *Das Deutsche Reich und der Zweite Weltkrieg Band 6: Der Globale Krieg*. Deutsches Verlag Anstalt, Stuttgart, 1990

Frieser, Karl-Heinz (ed.), *Das Deutsche Reich und der Zweite Weltkrieg Band 7: Das Deutsche Reich in der Defensive*. Deutsches Verlag Anstalt, Stuttgart, 2001

Frieser, Karl-Heinz (ed.), *Das Deutsche Reich und der Zweite Weltkrieg Band 8: Die Ostfront 1943/1944*. Deutsches Verlag Anstalt, Stuttgart, 2007

Glantz, David M., *Kharkov 1942: Anatomy of a Military Disaster through Soviet Eyes*. Ian Allan Publishing, Shepperten, 1998

Glantz, David M. and Jonathan House, *When Titans Clashed: How the Red Army stopped Hitler*. University Press of Kansas, Lawrence, KS, 1995

Golovanov, Aleksandr Evgenyevich, *Dalyenyaya Bombardirovochnaya* (Long Range Bomber). Delyeta, Moscow, 2004

Gordon, Yefim, *Soviet Air Power in World War 2*. Midland Publishing, Hinckley, 2008

Green, William, *Warplanes of the Third Reich*. Galahad Books, New York, 1990

Griehl, Manfred, *Luftwaffe '45: Letzte Flüge unde Projekte*. Motorbuch Verlag, Stuttgart, 2005

Gruppa Aemorov (Group of Authors) 16th VA, *Voenno-Istoricheskii Ocherk o Boevom Puti 16i Vozdushnoi Armee (1942-1945)* (Military History Sketch of the 16th Air Army), Voenizdat, Moscow, 1973

Gruppa Aemorov 17th VA, *17ya Bozdushnaya Armiya v Boyakh ot Stalingrada do Veny* (The 17th Air Army in the Battles of Stalingrad to Vienna). Voenizdat, Moscow, 1977

Gruppa Aemorov PVO, *Voiska Protivovozdushnoi Oborony Strany* (Air Defence Troops). Voennoe Izdatelyestvo, Moscow, 1968

Gruppa Aemorov VVS, *Sovetskie Voenno-Vozdyshnye Sily v Velikoi Otechestvennoi Voine 1941–1945* (Soviet Air Force in the Great Patriotic War of 1941–1945). Voenizdat, Moscow, 1968

Gubin, B. A. and V. D. Kuselev, *Vosyemaya Vozdushnaya* (Eighth Air Army). Voenizdat, Moscow, 1980

Hardesty, Von and Ilya Grinberg, *Red Phoenix Rising: The Soviet Air Force in World War II*. University Press of Kansas, Lawrence, KS, 2012

Hayward, Joel S. A., *Stopped at Stalingrad: The Luftwaffe and Hitler's Defeat in the East 1942–1943*. University Press of Kansas, Lawrence, KS, 1998

Higham, Robin, John T. Greenwood and Von Hardesty (eds), *Russian Aviation and Air Power in the Twentieth Century*. Frank Cass, London, 1998

Khazanov, Dmitriy and Medved, Aleksandr, Osprey Aircraft of the Aces 102 – *MiG-3 Aces of World War 2*. Osprey Publishing, Oxford, 2012

Khazanov, Dmitriy B. and Vitali Gorbach, *Aviatsiya v bitve nad Orlovsko-Kurskoi Dugoi:*

Oboronitelyenyeii Period (Aviation in the Battle of the Orel–Kursk Salient: Defensive Period). Izdatelyestvo, Moscow, 2004

Khazanov, Dmitriy Borisovich, *Bitva za Nebo. 1941: Ot Dnepra do Finskogo Zaliva* (Battle for the Sky, 1941: From the Dnieper to the Gulf of Finland). Yauza, Eksmo, Moscow, 2007

Khazanov, Dmitriy B. *1941: Voina v Voedukhe-Gorbkie Uroki* (1941: The War in the Air – The Bitter Lessons). Yauea, Eksmo, 2006

Klink, Ernst, *Das Gesetz des Handelns: Die Operation 'Zitadelle' 1943*. Deutsches Verlags-Anstalt, Stuttgart, 1966

Kozhevnikov, M. N., *The Command and Staff of the Soviet Army Air Force in the Great Patriotic War 1941–1945 (Komandovanie i Shtab VVS Sovetskoi Armii v Velikoi Otechestvennoi Voine 1941–1945 gg)*. Superintendent of Documents, US Government Printing Office, Washington, DC, n.d. (Izdatelyestvo 'Nauka', Moscow, 1977)

Krasnoznamennaya, *2-ya Vozdushnaya Armiya v Boyakh za Rodinu* (2nd Air Army in the Battles for the Motherland). Monino, 1965

Mellinger, George, Osprey Aircraft of the Aces 56, *LaGG & Lavochkin Aces of World War 2*. Osprey Publishing, Oxford, 2003

Morzik, Fritz and Gerhard Hümmelchen, *Die Deutschen Transportflieger im Zweiten Weltkrieg: Die Gesichte des 'Fussvolkes der Luft'*. Bernard & Graefe Verlag für Wehrwesen, Frankfurt am Main, 1966

Muller, Richard, *The German Air War in Russia*. The Nautical and Aviation Publishing Company of America, Baltimore, MD, 1993

Murray, Williamson, *Strategy for Defeat: the Luftwaffe 1933–1945*. Air University Press, Maxwell Air Force Base, AL, 1983

Neulen, Hans Werner (trans. Alex Vanags-Baginskis), *In the Skies of Europe: Air Forces Allied to the Luftwaffe 1939–1945*. The Crowood Press, Marlborough, 2000

Newton, Steven H. (ed.), *Kursk: the German View – Eyewitness Reports of Operation Citadel by the German Commanders*. Da Capo Press, Cambridge, MA, 2002

Nokiforov, V. G. (ed.), *Sovetskaya aviatsiya v Velikoy Otechestvennoy voyne 1941-1945 gg.v. tsifrakh* (Soviet Aviation in the Great Patriotic War 1941–1945, Glavnyy Shtab VVS, GU VVS SSSR), Moscow, 1962

Novikov, A. A., *V Nebe Leningrada: Zapiski komanduyushchego aviatsiei* (In the Sky of Leningrad: Notes of an Aviation Commander). Nauka, Moscow, 1970

Parrish, Michael, *Sacrifice of the Generals: Soviet Senior Officer Losses, 1939–1953*. The Scarecrow Press Inc., Lanham, MD, 2004

Plocher, Generalleutnant Hermann, *The German Air Force versus Russia 1941 (USAF Historical Studies No. 153)*. Arno Press, New York, 1965

Plocher, Generalleutnant Hermann, *The German Air Force versus Russia 1942 (USAF Historical Studies No. 154)*. Arno Press, New York, 1966

Plocher, Generalleutnant Hermann, *The German Air Force versus Russia 1943 (USAF Historical Studies No. 155)*. Arno Press, New York, 1967

Polak, Tomas with Christopher Shores, *Stalin's Falcons: The Aces of the Red Star*. Grub Street, London, 1999

Rohwer, Jürgen and Gerhard Hümmelchen, *Chronicle of the War at Sea*. Greenhill Books, London, 1992

Rudenko, Sergei Ignatyevich, *Krylyeya Pobedy* (Wings of Victory). Meshdunarodnye Otnosheniy, Moscow, 1985

Schramm, Percy Ernst (ed.), *Kriegstagebuch des Oberkommandos der Wehrmacht: Band IV, Zweiter Halbband*. Bernard und Graefeverlag für Wehrwesen, Frankfurt am Main, 1941

Seaton, Albert, *The Russo-German War 1941–45*. Arthur Barker Limited, London, 1971

Stedman, Robert F., Warrior 122, *Jagdflieger: Luftwaffe Fighter Pilot 1939–45*. Osprey, Oxford, 2008

Stedman, Robert, Warrior 99, *Kampfflieger: Bomber Crewmen of the Luftwaffe 1939–45*. Osprey, Oxford, 2005

Svetlishin, Nikolai Andreyevich, *Voiska PVO Strany v Velikoii Otechestvennoii Voine: Voprosy Operativno-Strategicheskogo Primeneniya* (National Air Defense Forces in the Great Patriotic War: Questions of Operational and Strategic Use). Nauka, Moscow, 1979

Timokhovitch, I. B., *Sovetskaya Aviatsiya v Bitve pod Kurskom* (Soviet Aviation in the Battle of Kursk). Voenizdat, Moscow, 1959

Vershinin, K. A., *Yetvertya Vozdushnaya* (Fourth Air Army). Voenizdat, Moscow, 1975

Weal, John, Osprey Aviation Elite Units 13, *Luftwaffe Schlachtgruppen*. Osprey Publishing, Oxford, 2003

Ziemke, Earl F., *Stalingrad to Berlin: The German Defeat in the East*. Office of the Chief of Military History, United States Army, Washington, DC, 1971

Ziemke, Earl F. and Bauer, Magna E. *Moscow to Stalingrad: Decision in the East*. Military Heritage Press, New York, 1988

ARCHIVES

Bundesarchiv, Militärarchiv, Freiburg, Germany

Imperial War Museum, Duxford, England

UK National Archive, London, England

US National Archives, Maryland, USA

WEBSITES

All Aces website, sub-site Opganieatsinnaya Struktura VVS RKKA: allaces.ru – details of hundreds of Russian air units.

Axis Biographical Research: Luftwaffe (Gareth Collins and Michael Miller): http://www.geocities.ws/orion47.geo/ – the prime site for Luftwaffe general biographies.

The Generals of WWII: www.generals.dk – valuable source of biographical data.

Gyges Publishing Company: http://www.Gyges.dk/

I Remember: www.iremember.ru. – hundreds of accounts by veterans.

Istrebitelyenye Polki VVS i VMF 1941-1945 (Fighter regiments of the Red Army and Navy Air Force): http://avia-hobby.ru/publ/soviaps/soviaps.html

The Luftwaffe 1933–1945 (Michael Holm): http://www.ww2.dk/. – the prime site for Luftwaffe research.

Military Books: militera.lib.ru. – online library of Russian books.

Russian Air Force biographies (Kto Estye Kto): http://www.airforce.ru/staff/who_is_who/index.htm

Soviet Shipping losses by Andrey Nelogov: http://www.shipsnostalgia.com/guides/Soviet_Merchant_Marine_Losses_in_WW2#BALTIC-SEA-IN-DETAILand BLACK-SEA-INDETAIL – details of every merchantman lost during the war.

Soviet Aviation in the Great Patriotic War by the Numbers (Podgotovka Kadrov i Pezervov Voenno-Vozdushnymi Silami Krasnoh Armii): http://www.ilpilot.narod.ru/VVS_tsifra/index.html – sources of most statistics taken from Soviet Ministry of Defense, Navy Ministry, VVS and ADD Staffs and GVF.

INDEX

Baltic Sea Air Force (VVS–KBF) 30–31, 74, 77, 88, 111, 154, 156, 208, 222, 223, 241, 247
Baltic States 25, 29, 31, 32, 33, 57, 64, 65, 73, 76, 197, 221–22, 223
Bauer, Hptm Herbert 50
Bauer, Oberst Joachim 192, 193, 227, 228
Begeldinov, Talgat 50
Belau, Hptm Egbert 242
Beletskii, Gen-maior Yevgeniyy 123
Belorussia 29, 33, 72, 73, 194, 208, 215–18, 219
Beria, Lavrenti 25, 57, 58, 106, 237
Berlin 103–4, 158, 159, 250–55
Black Sea Air Force (VVS-ChF) 31, 226, 231
Black Sea Fleet 121, 128
Beust, Oblt Hans-Henning Freiherr von 50
Black Sea Air Force (VVS-ChF) 87, 104–5, 111, 117, 120, 121, 122, 127, 151, 162, 163, 165, 187, 192, 192, 194
Bock, GenFeldm Fedor von 33, 39, 62, 71, 72, 77, 90, 92, 93, 94, 96, 113, 124, 125
Boenicke, Gen Walther 198
Bogatsch, Gen Rudolf 35
Brockdorff-Ahlefeldt, GenLt Walter Graf von 98
Bulgaria 33, 198, 228, 230
aircraft 229, 241
Bülowius, GenMaj Alfred 123, 124, 152, 153, 171
Busch, GenFeldm Ernst 195, 196

C

Carganico, GenMaj Viktor 142
Caucasus, forces/fighting in 113–14, 124–25, 126, 128, 136, 148–51, 152, 162–64, 214, 239
Chernykh, Gen-maior Sergei 65
China 16, 19, 55, 119
Chirskov, Polk B. F. 226

Christ, Oberst Torsten 155
Civil Air Fleet (GVF) 17, 18, 35–36, 59, 78, 79, 81, 105, 106–7, 121, 134, 147, 172, 183, 191, 196, 204, 214, 215, 218, 228, 238
commissars 127–28
Conrad, GenLt Gerhard 231
Crimea, forces/fighting in 76, 85–87, 113–14, 115, 116–21, 161, 180, 184, 186, 190, 192–94
Croatian aircraft 122, 162
Czechoslovakia, forces/fighting in 233, 251, 254, 255,
aircraft 226, 241

D

Danilov, Polk Stepan 74, 76
deception operations 120, 122
Deichmann, Gen Paul 171, 173, 174, 176, 177, 179, 180, 181, 186, 187, 188, 191, 193, 194, 195, 227, 230, 231, 232
Dessloch, Gen Otto 139, 150, 151, 171, 173, 177, 180, 182, 184, 187, 188, 189, 190, 191, 194, 196, 213, 224, 225, 227, 228, 229, 230, 231, 232, 244, 253, 254
Devyataev, Starshii Lt Mikhail 42
Deyuva, Polk Georgii 120, 121
Dinort, Oberst Oskar 77
Douhet, Gen Giulio 27, 34, 237
Duboshin, Polk Aleksei 102

E

Efremov, Vasilii 50
Eremenko, Gen-polk Andrei 137
Erlykhin, Polk Evgenii 76, 156
Ermachenkov, Gen-maior Vasilii 87, 88, 117, 122, 162, 163, 192, 194

F

Fach, Hptm Ernst 186
Falaleev, Gen-polk Fedor 85, 86, 117, 118, 119, 180, 181, 210, 247
Falck, Maj Wolfgang 205
Falkenstein, GenMaj Sigismund Freiherr von 222, 223, 244, 247, 250
Fiebig, GenMaj Martin 70, 83, 92, 93, 94, 95, 115, 122, 124, 125, 126, 130, 131, 132, 138, 139, 140, 141, 142, 145, 146, 148, 161, 162, 171, 228, 244, 247, 248, 250
Filatov, Kapt Aleksandr 42–43
Filippov, Polk Ivan 67, 159
Finland 16, 43, 74, 76, 78, 205, 208, 221, 236–37
    Winter War 16, 17, 24, 26, 27, 70, 79, 112, 149
Fonaryov, Ivan 50
Förster, Gen Helmut 44, 73, 154
Förster, Oberst Hans 142
Frankenberg und Proschlitz, Maj Egbert von 48
Freitag, ObLt Bruno 43
Fröhlich, GenLt Stefan 115, 151, 228, 229, 232
Frontal Aviation Air Force (VVS-FA) 27, 66, 91, 209
Fuchs, GenMaj Robert 195, 196, 213, 218–19, 242, 248, 249
fuel consumption/production 22, 42, 89, 99, 114, 155, 172, 173–74, 213–14, 216, 219, 220, 226–27

G

Galland, GenMaj Adolf 213
GCI systems 112, 126, 130–1, 133–34, 143, 157, 176, 181

Gheorghiue, Gen Ermil 131
glider operations 76, 90, 99, 151, 153, 190, 231, 246, 253
Glinka, Maj Boris 52–53
Glinka, Maj Dmitri 52, 53
Golovanov, Aleksandr 17, 55, 69, 93, 103, 104, 105, 106, 107, 108, 109, 131, 134, 153, 158, 173, 178, 183, 190, 200, 202–3, 203–4, 210, 214, 236, 237–38, 239, 243, 247–48, 250, 251, 252, 253, 254
Gorbatsevich, Polk Leonid 55
Göring, Reichsmarschall Herman 36, 37, 38, 62, 70, 141, 144, 147, 149, 151, 160, 169, 170–1, 186, 233, 234, 235, 245, 252–53, 265
Goryunov, Gen-lt Sergei 120, 122, 126, 148, 149, 150, 151, 162, 163, 171, 180, 181, 182, 183, 184–85, 187, 188, 191, 226–27, 228, 230, 231, 232, 232–33
Greece 228, 229
Greiffenberg, GenLt Hans von 129
Greim, Gen Robert Ritter von 44, 80–1, 82, 84, 85, 86, 88, 115, 122, 145, 151, 152, 153, 154, 155, 156–57, 171, 173, 174, 175, 177, 179, 194, 195, 196, 199, 200, 204, 206, 213, 214, 215, 216, 218, 219, 220, 221, 223, 224, 225, 227, 232, 234, 242, 243, 244, 244–45, 246, 249, 250, 251, 252, 253, 254
Grizodubova, Maj Valentina 106–7, 108, 109
Gromadin, Gen-polk Mikhail 102, 206, 207, 241
Gromov, Gen-lt Mikhail 112, 152, 171, 178, 179, 194, 209
Guderian, GenOb Heinz 44, 70, 71, 72, 77, 83, 84, 92, 93
Gudymenko, Gen-lt Petr 207
Gvozdkov, Gen-lt Georgii 112

H

Hagen, GenMaj Walter 229
Halder, GenOb Franz 39, 40, 62, 73, 77,
    90, 94, 98, 100, 132
Handrich, Oberst Gotthardt 232
Helbig, Oberst Joachim 249
Hess, Deputy Fuhrer Rudolf 38
Himmler, Heinrich 38, 244, 248
Hitler, Adolf 25, 28, 32, 33, 36, 37, 38,
    40-1, 48, 59–60, 62, 72, 73, 77, 85, 95,
    96, 97, 98, 99, 100, 113, 115, 116, 118,
    124, 125, 128, 129, 141, 144, 145, 146,
    148, 149, 150, 153, 155, 164, 169, 170,
    174, 177, 180, 186, 192, 208, 213, 222,
    223, 227, 231, 233, 234, 235, 246, 252,
    253, 254
Hitschold, Maj Hubertus 43
Hoepner, GenOb Erich 73
Höfer, Maj Heinrich 50
Holle, GenLt Alexander 227, 228
Home Air Defence (PVO) 55–56, 80
    aircraft 29, 30, 69, 92, 95, 100, 111,
        122, 123, 126, 130, 132, 137, 158,
        165, 172, 187, 191, 206–7, 208,
        209, 222
    operations 24, 28, 55–56, 57, 60, 100,
        101–2, 123–24, 130, 132, 191, 200,
        206–7, 209
Hoth, GenOb Hermann 44, 125, 128,
    129, 140, 148
Hozzel, Oblt Paul 161
Hube, Genl Hans-Valentin 189, 190, 191,
    194
Hungary 43, 80, 114, 159, 191, 226, 228,
    230–31, 237, 239, 246
    aircraft 122, 124, 148, 173, 180, 184,
        187, 188, 189, 213, 224, 231,
        232, 239

I

Ionov, Gen-maior Aleksei 29, 57, 58, 73, 74
Isupov, Polk Aleksandr 42
Italian aircraft 122, 124, 126, 142, 145
Izotov, Gen-maior Vladimir 102, 163, 259

J

Jeschonnek, Gen Hans 36, 37, 39, 62,
    88–89, 98, 115, 120, 140, 141, 144,
    149, 160, 170, 171

K

Kammhuber, Gen Josef 203, 205
Kartakov, Gen-maior Vasilii 108, 109
Keller, GenOb Alfred 32, 39, 40, 44, 73,
    74, 75, 76–77, 78, 83, 98, 154, 155,
    156, 171, 196, 197
Kesselring, GenFeldm Albert 39, 44, 62,
    65, 69–70, 72, 73, 77, 83, 88, 92, 94,
    95, 100, 144
Khryukin, Gen-maior Timofei 119, 120,
    122, 123, 125, 126, 129, 130, 131, 132,
    133–34, 137, 143, 144, 148, 162, 171,
    182, 183, 184, 185, 188–89, 192, 193,
    194, 209, 217, 220, 221, 247
Khudiakov, Gen-lt Sergei 152
Kirov, Sergei 15, 56
Kirponos, Gen-polk Mikhail 80, 81, 85
Kleist, GenOb Ewald von 44, 81, 83, 84,
    86, 118, 119, 148, 184, 187, 191
Klimov, Polk Ivan 100, 101, 102
Klintzsch, Oberst Ulrich 247, 250
Kluge, GenFeldm Günther von 151, 153,
    164, 173, 174, 177, 179, 194, 195, 201
Koldunov, Kapt Aleksandr 53
Koller, GenMaj Karl 171, 186, 233, 235, 253